INSIDERS' GUIDE® TO
PALM BEACH COUNTY

D0956630

HELP US KEEP THIS GUIDE UP TO DATE

We would love to hear from you concerning your experiences with this guide and how you feel it could be improved and kept up to date. Please send your comments and suggestions to:

editorial@GlobePequot.com

Thanks for your input, and happy travels!

INSIDERS' GUIDE® SERIES

INSIDERS' GUIDE® TO
PALM BEACH COUNTY

FIRST EDITION

STEVE WINSTON

INSIDERS' GUIDE

GUILFORD, CONNECTICUT
AN IMPRINT OF GLOBE PEQUOT PRESS

All the information in this guidebook is subject to change. We recommend that you call ahead to obtain current information before traveling.

To buy books in quantity for corporate use or incentives, call **(800) 962–0973** or e-mail **premiums@GlobePequot.com.**

INSIDERS' GUIDE ®

Copyright © 2010 Morris Book Publishing, LLC

ALL RIGHTS RESERVED. No part of this book may be reproduced or transmitted in any form by any means, electronic or mechanical, including photocopying and recording, or by any information storage and retrieval system, except as may be expressly permitted in writing from the publisher. Requests for permission should be addressed to Globe Pequot Press, Attn: Rights and Permissions Department, P.O. Box 480, Guilford, CT 06437.

Insiders' Guide is a registered trademark of Morris Book Publishing, LLC.

Editor: Amy Lyons
Project Editor: Lynn Zelem
Layout Artist: Kevin Mak
Text Design: Sheryl Kober
Maps: Trailhead Graphics Inc. © Morris Book Publishing, LLC

Library of Congress Cataloging-in-Publication Data is available on file.
ISBN 978-0-7627-6039-8

Printed in the United States of America
10 9 8 7 6 5 4 3 2 1

CONTENTS

RETIRÉ DE LA COLLECTION UNIVERSELLE
Bibliothèque et Archives nationales du Québec

Directory of Maps

ABOUT THE AUTHOR

Steve Winston has written or contributed to fourteen books. He first saw Palm Beach County when he took a job as a cub reporter for the *Palm Beach Post*. And he's had "sand in his shoes" ever since. Steve is an adventurer and mountain-climber who's traveled widely all over the world, and his articles have appeared in major media in the United States and abroad. In pursuit of "the story," he's been shot at in Northern Ireland, been a cowboy in Arizona, jumped into an alligator pit in the Everglades, flown World War II fighter planes in aerial "combat," climbed glaciers in Alaska, explored ice caves in Switzerland, and trained with a rebel militia in the jungle. He can be contacted at his Web site, www.stevewinston.com.

ACKNOWLEDGMENTS

This is the fourteenth book which I have written or contributed to. And, like the other ones, I had more than a little help from my friends and my family.

I couldn't have done it without my friends. They are a group of people—some of whom don't even know each other—that has always been there for me. In many cases, for virtually my entire adult life. When tragedy has struck, they've gathered around me in a tight, protective circle, and they've helped carry me through. When things have gone well, their pride and joy in my accomplishments burst from them. They're always there for me, with encouraging words, optimistic predictions, and an undying faith in my ability to tell a story.

Then there are my daughters, Jessica and Alyssa. I don't always manage to show it (as I'm sure they'll tell you!), but they are the joys of my life. They bring me incredible pleasure and incredible wonder . . . still, more than 22 years after the eldest (Jessica) was born. My heart seems to grow larger when I'm around them—especially those all-too-rare occasions when I get them both together. They make me feel that I have a true stake in this world, a stake that goes beyond my own existence. And I'm very, very proud of them . . . of the young ladies they already are, and the adults they're becoming. In my darkest periods of life (everybody has them!), I have held onto them the tightest. Because, to me, they are life itself.

Then there's Meryl. The love of my life, the woman who has helped make me whole, the woman who has helped me feel reborn. She looks at me—still—with such incredible love in her eyes. She tells me—all the time—"don't worry, you'll get it done." She listens—still—with wide-eyed wonder at the adventures I've been privileged to have in many parts of the world. She listens—still—raptly to my stories of being shot at in Northern Ireland, or of racing my Triumph as a teenager, or of being thrown out of a reception for Queen Elizabeth (just because I attempted to crash the party without a ticket!), or of playing basketball until the wee hours—outside in the snow—in college, or of hitchhiking through Europe. She's a calming, loving, wise presence in my life. And there are so many things for which I can never repay her. Meryl, for your undying love and your undying faith in me . . . this one's for you.

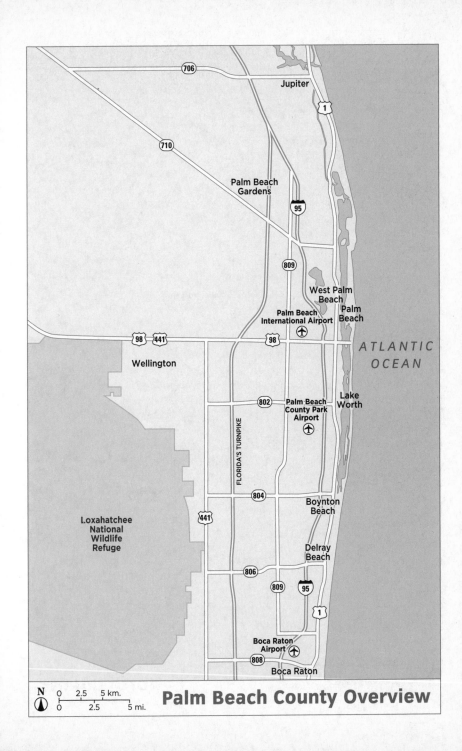

Palm Beach County Overview

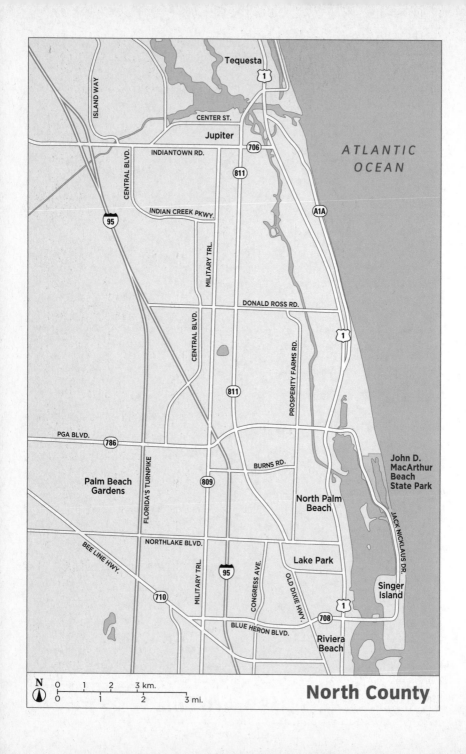

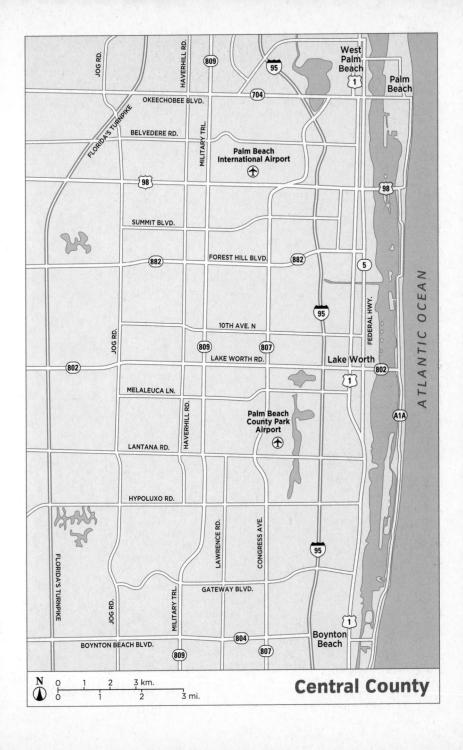

Central County

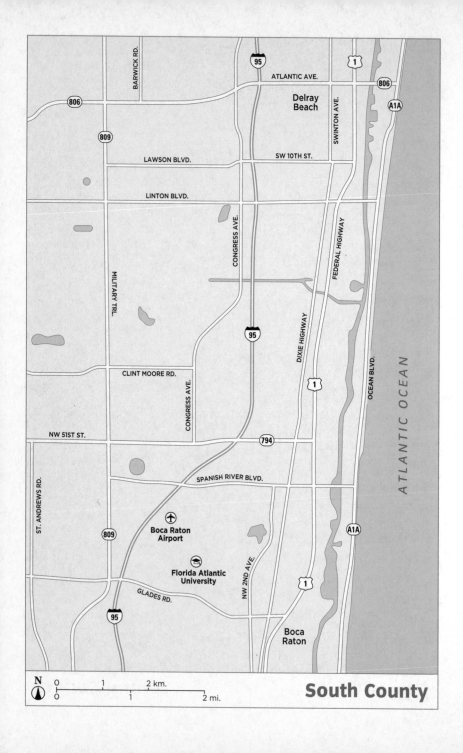

South County

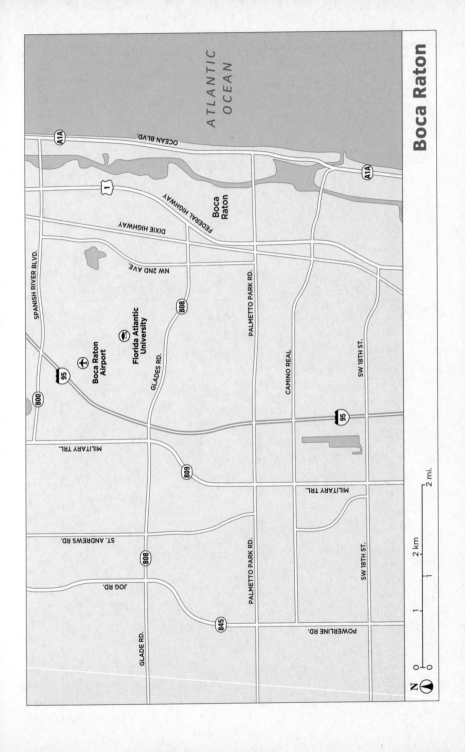

Boca Raton

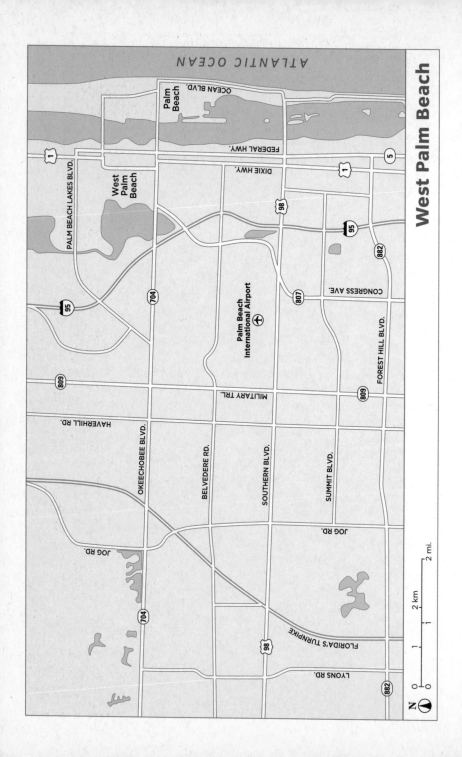

West Palm Beach

PREFACE

I'll never forget the first time I saw Palm Beach County.

It was 6 a.m. on a late-winter day. I was sitting in a darkened plane, on a pitch-black runway at Hartford/Springfield International Airport in Connecticut, looking out the window at the patches of snow I could make out through the darkness. Icy rain and sleet was pelting my window.

Three-and-a-half hours later, I walked out of the terminal at Palm Beach International Airport, into 76 degrees, gently swaying palm trees, and the bluest sky I had ever seen. And I was hooked.

In Palm Beach County, on the Southeast Florida coast about 60 miles north of Miami, not everything is as it seems.

To you, the reader, for instance, who may be sitting thousands of miles away, Palm Beach County might convey an image of just that . . . palm-fringed beaches soaked in perennial sunshine. If you've heard of the county at all, it's probably in relation to its two most well-known towns, Palm Beach and Boca Raton. And if you've heard of those two towns, it's probably with regard to the rich people ("old rich" in Palm Beach, "new" in Boca) who reside in them, cruising in their Bentleys and Rolls-Royces to those palm-lined beaches, after lunch at the club, of course.

Some of your images are true. The reputations of those two towns are well-founded (although, Boca, in particular, has a lot of people just like you and me). Yet, there are close to a million-and-a half people in Palm Beach County and most of them drive not to the beach every day, but to work. And they do it in Nissans and Chevys and Hondas, not Bentleys.

In fact, Palm Beach County is anything but homogeneous. There are high-tech corridors with large companies, and neighborhoods best avoided. There are skyscrapers (well, perhaps we should call them junior skyscrapers) and sugar-cane fields. There are urban centers and tiny hamlets. There are beaches and Everglades. There is 21st-century sprawl, and there are flat, empty hammocks and mangroves. There is every conceivable kind of restaurant here because there is every conceivable race, religion, and ethnic group represented here. There are retirement communities, and new high schools built to serve the burgeoning young population.

There's suburban tract housing, and trailer parks. There are magnificent gated communities, and temporary shacks housing migrant workers. Reborn downtowns, and suburban sprawl. Great centers of learning, and spots of great poverty.

All of which is by way of saying, really, that Palm Beach County isn't all that much different from most other places—other than the fact that it does have one of the richest towns in the world, perennial sunshine, and, yes, those beaches.

I first drove through Palm Beach County years ago, when I arrived here as a cub reporter for the *Palm Beach Post*. The county had less than a million people then. I-95—which today connects Key West to Maine—hadn't even been finished; there was a gaping hole in part of Palm Beach County where you had to veer west to catch the Florida Turnpike (to go south). And when you passed through "the big curve" in Boca Raton, you were passing through a town that was still a small, very provincial place, packed with Old Money and "snowbirds" who fled to their primary homes up north as soon as spring came.

Since then, Palm Beach County has known boom and bust, hero and scoundrel, sunshine and gloom, the high-life and the low, the glitter and the grit. And that's part of the beauty of the place . . . you never know what you'll find under the veneer.

Palm Beach County continues to change, to move, and to reveal special surprises and secrets. And the fact that it's not always what it seems makes it, in my opinion, one of the most fascinating places in a state that's still, in some ways, the last frontier. Palm Beach County has an energy—recession or not—that's palpable. There's always *something* going on here, whether it's an international film festival or a scandal in City Hall.

It's colorful, it's dynamic, it's always on the move, and always metamorphosing with the seasons. For people all over the world, it's still a great place to visit and to live. But one thing will probably never change, though. It will always have that beach—47 miles of it. It will always have water all around—on the beach, on the Intracoastal Waterway, and in the lakes and rivers and canals. And it will always have warm sunshine when the rest of the country is shivering.

HOW TO USE THIS BOOK

As noted previously, Palm Beach County residents generally break the area up into three distinct geographical entities—**South County (the most populous area), Central County, and North County.** For the purposes of this book, we'll generally put listings for such things as art festivals and attractions in the same geographical order, from South County to North.

In those three sections are some 38 municipalities, ranging from urbanized cities such as West Palm Beach (seat of county government) to the tiny hamlets ringing Lake Okeechobee, in the area called the Muck by the locals. We'll focus mainly on the bigger towns (and surrounding areas):

- **South County**—Boca Raton, Delray Beach
- **Central County**—Lake Worth, Boynton Beach, West Palm Beach, Palm Beach, Wellington
- **North County**—Palm Beach Gardens, Singer Island/Riviera Beach, North Palm Beach, Lake Park, Jupiter, Tequesta

A few things to know:
- The area code for the entire county is 561.
- Streets run from east to west.
- Avenues run from north to south.
- Places, Terraces, Courts, etc. generally run from north to south

Throughout this book, you'll find a variety of Insider Tips about the county, often provided by those who know it best—people who have lived and worked here for many years. Some of them will be prominent people in South Florida media, government, the arts, business, and literature. These may be personal vignettes, notes on local history, satirical in nature, educational, or just plain funny. But all of them will shed light on the fascinating mixture of people, cultures, and lifestyles that is Palm Beach County.

Moving to Palm Beach County or already live here? Be sure to check out the blue-tabbed pages at the back of the book, where you will find the **Living Here** appendix that offers sections on relocation, real estate, education, and media.

You may, on occasion, hear a Floridian talk about how he/she has "sand in his shoes." That's a popular expression down here and the meaning is simple. It refers to a person who comes down to Florida, either on vacation or to live here, and who is transformed by the experience. It may be when you're walking on the beach at sunrise. It might be when you're cruising along the Intracoastal at sunset. It may be when you see the colors change as they reflect on the buildings, in the vivid color-changes as the sun moves through a winter day. It may be while you're hauling in a big fish in the ocean. "Sand in your shoes" means that minute when you realize that you've really fallen in love with Florida. And that you're never "going home" again ... because this is now home.

AREA OVERVIEW

Palm Beach County has its share of special places and special moments. The ocean at sunrise, for instance, when the sun rises up suddenly from a darkened haze to sprinkle the horizon with burnt oranges and purples and fiery pinks and intense yellows, lightening the aquamarine waters as it moves. The electricity of the city of West Palm Beach (the county's true urban center) at night, when thousands move happily among the restaurants and shops and clubs of City Place and Clematis Street. The Everglades at sunset, when the harsh colors of the day are replaced by the all-consuming quiet of America's only tropical "jungle" at night. The old neighborhoods adjacent to downtown West Palm Beach, with their whimsical Spanish/Mediterranean mini-"palaces" built a century ago. Worth Avenue in Palm Beach, where you can roam the renowned shops among the wealthiest people in the world, and where it's fun to browse even though the only thing you may be able to afford is an ice-cream cone.

Gumbo Limbo Nature Center in Boca Raton, where the dense tropical vegetation brings home the realization that this area was a wilderness not all that long ago. Jupiter Lighthouse, in the northern part of the county, which served as a beacon of life for all of those shipwrecked sailors who went down with their ships in their quest for treasure of one sort or another. Cruising the Intracoastal Waterway off Jupiter, past mansions of the rich and famous, and deep-green inlets. The scores of outdoor art festivals running from Autumn to Spring, with their great art and their interesting artists and tons of happy people roaming through it all, in cool air that seems to invigorate the soul.

And Flagler Drive in downtown West Palm Beach, where the city meets the water, where you can gaze across at the mansions and legendary old hotels of Palm Beach while standing in front of a striking glass office tower.

THE LAY OF THE LAND

Palm Beach County is the northern terminus of what's called **"The Gold Coast,"** a three-county area of South Florida (with a fourth, the Keys, of Monroe County, added in for demographic purposes) with some six-million residents. This is the most populous area of the state by far.

Most cities and towns in the region are within twenty miles of the Atlantic Ocean, so you're never very far from an ocean breeze.

To the west is the Everglades and the area around Lake Okeechobee, mostly undeveloped except for a few towns populated largely by agricultural workers and small business workers. (In fact, I'm writing this right now from a "Western" town [about twenty miles from the ocean] . . . and the Everglades dikes are just two miles west of my house).

Miami, with its magnificent skyline edging Biscayne Bay, is about fifty miles south of the southernmost town in Palm Beach County (Boca Raton). Fort Lauderdale, now a striking city in its own right, is about twenty miles south. The northern tip of the Florida Keys is about two hours' drive south, and Key West about five hours. And Palm Beach County is the closest southern-U.S. area to a foreign country; the island of Bimini, in the Bahamas, is only about fifty miles away.

Palm Beach County is actually the largest of Florida's 67 counties, with 2,034 square miles. And it boasts 45 miles of beaches. Residents tend to divide the county into three parts: South County (anchored by Boca Raton and Delray Beach); Central County (anchored by the Palm Beaches, Lake Worth, Boynton Beach, Wellington); and North County (anchored by Palm Beach Gardens, Jupiter, Tequesta, Riviera Beach/ Singer Island).

Even though Palm Beach County is part of the four-county area referred to as "South Florida," it's entirely distinct from the rest of the region. In fact, its three main geographic areas are entirely distinct from each other.

South County is more corporate, more upscale developments, more swanky shops, more sophisticated, and probably more in the Fort Lauderdale "orbit" (even though Fort Lauderdale's in Broward County) than that of West Palm Beach.

Central County is more old-money (Palm Beach), more urbanized (West Palm Beach), and, at the same time, more countrified, as well (the Western Communities, the Acreage). And folks here look to West Palm for their entertainment and diversion.

North County is quieter, with smaller towns and simpler pleasures, and often seems a million miles away from the Miami-Fort Lauderdale megalopolis . . . and a million miles away from South County, as well.

Just how different is South County from North? Well, people in Boca Raton or Delray Beach think nothing of going to Miami (about an hour away) for a ballgame or a festival. And the shops and restaurants of Fort Lauderdale are a playground for many of them.

People in North County, however, hardly ever go to Fort Lauderdale or Miami. And that's just fine with them. They feel fortunate to be in a pretty, quiet area in which the only rush-hours are those you hear about over the radio (in West Palm Beach), and in which the golf and fishing are always nearby. In fact, many people have moved to Palm Beach County to get away from the congestion farther south . . . and many of them end up in North County. Folks in the north tend to be very protective of their lifestyle, and just a bit leery of the people from "the South" who've moved up the road to escape the congestion and other problems.

i Palm Beach County is much like any other urban-suburban area in America—there's some crime. Don't feel that because you're in sunny South Florida, that we have no bad guys. We do. You just have to take the same common-sense precautions that you would anywhere else. Lock your door—in your hotel room and in your car. Don't flash a lot of money. Don't flash a lot of bling (jewelry!). If you have doubts about a certain neighborhood—particularly after dark—don't go there. And always look around at your surroundings, which like other areas of our country, can change quickly. Just use common sense. Your hotel desk will be happy to advise you about any unsafe areas in town.

And you'll occasionally hear one of them say that they don't want the area to become like our Broward County neighbor to the south of us . . . "another Fort Lauderdale."

MAJOR CITIES

Palm Beach County has 38 municipalities, ranging from the urban towers of West Palm Beach to little hamlets edging the Everglades. Here are the cities that most people in the county would say are "anchors" (south to north).

Boca Raton

Sprawling, from the urban feel of downtown to the far-western suburbs that are also called Boca Raton . . . even though they're not in the city limits. There are about 90,000 people in the City of Boca Raton . . . but the total in what's considered "Boca" is closer to a quarter of a million. (Like many towns in South Florida, Boca is surrounded by unincorporated areas to the west that are outside of city limits, but have "Boca Raton" addresses.) Boca Raton has a reputation . . . and probably all of it is true. A small, clannish. Old-Money town prior to the early 80s, Boca was changed forever by the invention of the PC at its IBM facility then. It's now a sophisticated city of great shopping and restaurants, and a vibrant cultural scene. Now it's filled with rich young (and old) entrepreneurs, as well as average families who have to work hard. However, I always describe Boca as a "moveable Mercedes showroom."

Delray Beach

(Pop. 65,000) Left for dead only twenty or thirty years ago, downtown Delray Beach was a dark place with many empty storefronts, with about as many entertainment options as Sing-Sing. Thanks to some enterprising civic visionaries, however, it's become a town that's received publicity all over the country for its dramatic turnaround. Downtown is now a vibrant, throbbing magnet at night for people of all ages, who frequent interesting shops, atmospheric sidewalk cafes and bistros, and exciting dance and music clubs. And the streets that were once deserted are now lined with cobblestone sidewalks and old-time gaslight street lamps . . . and tons of traffic.

Boynton Beach

(Pop. 67,000) Like other cities in South Florida, Boynton Beach had lost momentum in the seventies and eighties. Its downtown core was not doing well, its population was aging, and many of its residents went elsewhere to shop. But things started changing with the addition of the Boynton Beach Mall in the mid-eighties. That sparked a trend to shop locally. In the past decade, the unincorporated areas of West Boynton also became a very attractive place to live, with beautiful developments springing up, and attracting young, professional families. Between 2000 and 2006, in fact, the population increased by an average of a thousand each year.

Lake Worth

(Pop. 36,000) Until the past ten years, Lake Worth was just an unsightly exit on the way to the Palm Beaches on I-95, marked by its old high school facing the highway and a factory whose smokestack was belching thick gray smoke. But, like other cities in Palm Beach County, Lake Worth has really reinvented itself in recent years. A can-do civic spirit has turned things around. And a workaholic group of entrepreneurs took what had been the city's biggest blemish—it's crumbling old buildings—and transformed it into the city's biggest asset. They re-structured, rebuilt, and re-painted those buildings, and then filled them with art galleries and artists' studios, trendy cafes, interesting performing arts companies, and fun, unique shops that blended in perfectly with the old buildings. Now, Lake Worth is definitely worth at stop at the I-95 exit, instead of racing past it.

Wellington

(Pop. 56,000) Twenty years ago, this was "horse country." And it still is. The area is filled with equestrian farms, and you can still see people on horseback as you drive around. Every winter, Wellington is filled with many of the finest polo players in the world, who play in leagues here, and who also participate in some of the sport's most prestigious tournaments—held right here. But Wellington, now is much more than just horse country. It's a bona fide town, friendly people, good shopping, plenty of small businesses, and good neighborhood restaurants. It even got its own high school a few years back. The Mall at Wellington Green is now one of South Florida's preferred destinations for shopping and entertainment. And the town has some really beautiful neighborhoods.

West Palm Beach

(Pop. 82,000) West Palm Beach is yet another story or urban redemption in Palm Beach County. Twenty years ago, it had many boarded-up storefronts, nothing doing after dark, and the only people who lived downtown were poor people. And the only people who came downtown in the daytime were the people who worked in the government offices (it's the County Seat). In

the nineties, however, everything changed. City Place, a magnificent European-style downtown mixed-use project, filled up with upscale shops, designer names and department stores, and unique galleries and bistros. People started coming from the day it opened . . . and haven't stopped. Another dramatic upswing came with the development of upscale high-rise apartments building around City Place, bringing more professionals who worked in the city to live in the city . . . and those new professionals, of course, shopped, ate, and danced at City Place. When the Kravis Center for the Performing Arts opened in 1992, it brought a world-class cultural venue to downtown West Palm—and world-class performers. That, in turn, generated tremendous crowds coming downtown for the shows, and eating or dancing or playing here before and after the shows. At the same time, Clematis Street, in the heart of downtown, underwent a startling transformation; and it, too, is now glittering at night with trendy bistros and dance clubs. West Palm Beach now actually has its own skyline of twenty and thirty-story office buildings and condos. And it sits in a beautiful setting . . . right on Lake Worth (not the town, the lake!)

Palm Beach

(Pop. 10,000 permanent; 30,000 seasonal) Get off I-95 at Lantana Road, and follow it east to A1A. Head north (left) on A1A. For about 4 or 5 miles, you'll pass one towering condominium after another, all edging the ocean on your right. Then you'll come around a big bend in the road . . . and you'll think you've landed on Shangri-La. To the right is the ocean. And to the left are—one after the other—the most palatial, most expansive, most magnificent, most whimsical, most out-of-this-world homes you'll ever see. Some of them are like Moroccan castles, with spires and towers. Some are like Medieval Spanish palaces, with red brick and barrel-tile roofs and arched windows. Some are like Greek monuments, white from top to bottom, with huge columns in front. Some are like Caribbean hideaways, with yellow window shutters and tropical design. Then, as the road veers away from the ocean, these homes are on both sides of you. Look through the trees, and you can see the Kennedy Compound on the right. Look to the left as the road veers, and you'll see Mar-A-Lago, all Mediterranean towers, built by Charles W. Post of Post Cereals fame, and later inhabited by Donald Trump. There's even one mansion that people swear looks like a funeral home. Then you'll come to Worth Avenue, considered by many the most beautiful street in the world, where if you have to ask the price . . . you can't afford it. This is Palm Beach, island of fantasy.

Palm Beach Gardens

(Pop. 49,000)—A decade or two ago, Palm Beach Gardens was a quiet town inhabited by mostly well-off people who loved to play golf at the PGA headquarters and the PGA National Resort. But then other people wanted in on the lifestyle here, and so did many companies, who began establishing regional offices here. Then came The Gardens of the Palm Beaches, an upscale regional shopping mall. And the population exploded—increasing 35 percent just from 2000 to 2006. These were not necessarily wealthy golfers, though. These were young people and professional people and young families, who began working in those corporate offices and in the mall. Now, Palm Beach Gardens is the retail, business, and

entertainment center of North County. And folks who live here will tell you that the city has still managed to maintain its friendliness, and its green spaces.

Jupiter

(Pop. 50,000)—Like everywhere else in Palm Beach County, Jupiter has experienced dramatic growth over the past couple of decades. Until the 1990s, this was a quiet little backwater town. But then—as they do with most all quiet backwater towns—people discovered it .They discovered the beach-side location, the nice lifestyle, and the easy-going way of life. And they came; many, in fact, came from the Miami and Fort Lauderdale areas. Jupiter's growth has been nicely controlled, though; and it's grown outward, rather than upward. There are cute shopping centers, and little out-of-the-way galleries and craft shops. There are nice parks, and open-air concerts. There's Spring Training for two Major League teams here; and each of those teams (Florida Marlins and St. Louis Cardinals) have minor league teams that are based here. The beach—which is one of the prime turtle-nesting areas on Earth—is beautiful. And—perhaps best of all—despite the growth, the lifestyle is still very pleasant.

FOR MORE INFORMATION

Within the 2,034 square miles of Palm Beach County are lifestyles and workstyles and residential styles and culinary styles as diverse as anywhere. If you're interested in visiting Palm Beach County, the place to start would be the **Palm Beach County Convention & Visitors Bureau** (www.palmbeachfl.com; 800-554-7256).

And if you're interested in living here there are a number of chambers of

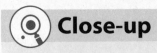 **Close-up**

The Kennedys in Palm Beach

For six decades, America's first family of politics, the Kennedys, called the island of Palm Beach "home" (at least, it was one of their homes).

It was to the family compound on Palm Beach that President-elect John F. Kennedy retreated for the holidays in 1960, after the victorious conclusion of an exhausting campaign. It was to the compound that the family came after its various and storied tragedies, to regroup on the sea and the salt air. It was to St. Edward Church on Palm Beach that the matriarch of the family, Rose, would come every Sunday she was here, often with a flock of tow-headed young Kennedys surrounding her, almost until her last days. (Many of those young Kennedys would spend wonderful afternoons at Green's Pharmacy right across the street, where they gorged on chocolate shakes and other treats.) And it was to the compound that the Kennedys came to retreat, refresh, and re-invigorate themselves through good times and bad . . . and, often, to be caught by paparazzi playing their famous games of touch-football on the beach.

The Kennedys left an indelible mark on Palm Beach. And the 2009 passing of Ted Kennedy, the sole surviving brother of America's most famous family, brought an end to an era.

The Kennedys were already famous—but not legendary—when they bought the spread on the beach in 1933. Joseph and Rose Kennedy paid $115,000 for the home and the land—then a virtual fortune. But they weren't the first well-known family to live in it; it had actually been built by Rodman Wanamaker, founder of the famous Philadelphia department store of the same name. And the home had a pedigree even before it rose out of the beach. Wanamaker's architect had been the one-and-only Addison Mizner, who was to leave an indelible mark on the county with his bright-white, red-roofed, Mediterranean-style buildings.

As the twentieth century progressed into its last third, Americans became more and more attached to this special family, who seemed to inhabit a magical world the press dubbed "Camelot"—especially after John Kennedy's presidential victory in 1960.

But, as the years unfolded, of course, the rest of us saw that the Kennedys, like any other family, had their share of tragedies, as well. And some of the younger generation had legal problems caused by incidents that occurred in Palm Beach, among them a death from a drug overdose and an internationally covered rape trial in which there was an eventual acquittal.

In 1994, three years after the rape trial, the family put the home up for sale. The reason given—at least, publicly—was that it was no longer large enough for a family with 35 grandchildren. The asking price was $7 million. But, after a year on the market, the family sold it for just under $5 million.

With the sale of the house, an era came to an end. And with the passing of Ted Kennedy, so did a legacy.

It's rare to see a Kennedy on Palm Beach these days. But, to the many island residents who knew them and loved them, the Kennedys will always be here.

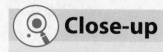

Close-up

Palm Beach County Celebrities List

Aaron, Hank—baseball Hall-of-Famer; West Palm Beach

Buffett, Jimmy—Palm Beach County must be Margaritaville! Palm Beach

Carter, Cris—football great; Boca Raton

Cavuto, Neil—FOX News; Singer Island

Clark, Jim—Netscape founder; Palm Beach

Close, Glenn—actress; Wellington

Damone, Vic—singer; Palm Beach

Dent, Bucky—former baseball player; Delray Beach

Dimucci, Dion—rock and roll singer; Boca Raton

Dobbs, Lou—former CNN anchor; West Palm Beach

Ecclestone, Llwyd and Diana—famous developer and socialite; Palm Beach

Evert, Chris—tennis great; Boca Raton

Giuliani, Rudy—America's mayor; Palm Beach

Griese, Bob—football great; Jupiter

Gumbel, Bryant—TV personality; Jupiter

Hamilton, George—actor; West Palm Beach

Hanna, Jack—TV personality; Jupiter

Havlicek, John—basketball great; West Palm Beach

Jones, Tommy Lee—actor; Wellington

Jordan, Michael—basketball great; Jupiter

Kluge, John—TV mogul; Palm Beach

Koch, Bill—mining mogul; Palm Beach

Kraft, Bob—owner of New England Patriots football team; Palm Beach

Kravis, Henry—financier (eg: The Kravis Center for the Performing Arts); West Palm Beach

Lemieux, Mario—hockey great; Ocean Ridge

Limbaugh, Rush—conservative commentator; West Palm Beach

Lipton Farris, Celia—actress, socialite; Palm Beach

Mahoney, Tim—former U.S. Congressman; Palm Beach Gardens

---

commerce in the major cities that can help. Here are a few of the larger ones:

South County

Boca Raton Chamber of Commerce—www.bocaratonchamber.com; (561) 395-4433.
Greater Delray Beach Chamber of Commerce—www.delraybeach.com; (561) 278-0424.

Central County

Chamber of Commerce of the Palm Beaches (serving the West Palm/Palm Beach area)—www.palmbeaches.org; (561) 833-3711.
Palm Beach Chamber of Commerce—www.palmbeachchamber.com; (561) 655-3282.

Marshall, Leonard—football great; Boca Raton

Moss, Randy—football great; Boca Raton

Mottola, Tommy—music mogul; Palm Beach

Musburger, Brent—TV sportscaster; Jupiter

Namath, Joe—football great; Tequesta

Nicklaus, Jack—golf great; North Palm Beach

Norman, Greg—golf great; Boca Raton

Newton-John, Olivia—singer, actress; Jupiter Inlet Colony

Orr, Bobby—hockey great; Jupiter

Palmer, Jim—baseball great (and undies pitchman); Palm Beach

Parcells, Bill—football coach, executive; Jupiter

Patterson, James—writer; Palm Beach

Peltz, Nelson—entrepreneur, Wendy's/Arby's Group, Snapple; Palm Beach

Reynolds, Burt—actor; Jupiter

Roddick, Andy—tennis star; Boca Raton

Ross, Stephen—entrepreneur, owner of Miami Dolphins; Palm Beach

Schar, Dwight—owner of Washington Redskins, Finance Director of Republican National Committee; Palm Beach

Schmidt, Mike—baseball great; Jupiter

Seymour, Stephanie—supermodel; Palm Beach

Shula, Don—former Miami Dolphins coach; Palm Beach Gardens

Springsteen, Bruce—The Boss; Wellington

Stapp, Scott—singer for Creed; Boca Raton

Stewart, Rod—singer; Palm Beach

Torres, Tico—drummer for Bon Jovi; Jupiter

Trucks, Butch—drummer for Allman Brothers Band; Palm Beach

Trump, Donald (aka "The Donald")—Palm Beach

Trump, Ivana—socialite, jet-setter; Palm Beach

Vanilla Ice—singer; Wellington

Williams, Venus & Serena—tennis stars; Palm Beach Gardens

Wilson, Ralph—owner of Buffalo Bills football team; Lantana

Greater Lake Worth Chamber of Commerce—www.lwchamber.com; (561) 582-4401.

The Greater Boynton Beach Chamber of Commerce—www.boyntonbeach.org; (561) 732-9501.

The Wellington Chamber of Commerce—www.wellingtonchamber.com; (561) 792-6525.

North County

Northern Palm Beaches Chamber of Commerce (serving the areas around Palm Beach Gardens, Jupiter, Tequesta, Riviera Beach, Lake Park, North Palm Beach)—www.npbchamber.com; (561) 746-7111.

WEATHER

Everybody Talks About the Weather . . . and in Palm Beach County, most of the time it's beautiful. Summers are hot and steamy, generally with thunderstorms during the late-afternoon. Winters are generally beautiful. But there's an occasional cold snap that may even leave your teeth chattering. On rare occasions I've seen it actually go down into the thirties. And when that happens— although even temps in the fifties are considered a "cold snap" here—it can sometimes stay that way for four or five days. Moral of the story? If you're coming in winter, sure, bring your bathing suit; the weather will probably be great. But, just in case, don't forget to also pack a sweater and a light jacket.

Then there's the H-word. And it wouldn't be fair to you if we didn't discuss it. **Hurricanes.** (And we're not talking the University of Miami Hurricanes here, folks.) Some years—such as the fall of 2009—we get a free pass, and atmospheric conditions play out in such a way that we're never really threatened. Other times—such as in '04 and '05—fuggedaboutit. We were hit hard in '04 by Frances and then, only a few weeks later, by Jeanne. And these were no ladies. Then, a year later, we were hit head-on by Wilma. After those two seasons, our previous complacency about hurricanes disappeared forever.

Hurricane season, according to the books, lasts from June 1 until Dec 1. But there are never hurricanes (out there in the ocean) in June, and almost never in July. Activity doesn't really start picking up until late August, and continues into mid October. If you haven't been hit by then, you're generally home-free. So there's really less than a two-month period in which we have to fret about the weather forecasts.

Bottom line? Just use common sense. If you're planning a trip here in late summer or early fall, just keep tabs on our local weather, and on what your own weather person says is doing "out in the tropics." Do keep in mind, though, that hurricane hits—especially in a limited space like Palm Beach County—are relatively rare. And hurricanes that hit in other parts of the state generally don't affect our weather much, other than an increased possibility of rain.

High-Season, Low-Season

One of the most important things to know about South Florida is that, in contrast to much of the rest of the country, there are really only two seasons. And they're not summer and winter! Actually, they're "High" and "Low." **High Season** starts around the first of November, and last until May. **Low Season** takes over in May, and lasts through October.

In High Season, the weather is generally magnificent . . . cool, clear nights generally in the sixties, and sunny days in the seventies and eighties. This is the time of year—in contrast to the rest of America—when Palm Beach County comes alive. There's opera, there's dance, there's song. There are art festivals and food festivals and music festivals and antique festivals (and even a festival devoted to the "stinking rose"—garlic) every weekend. Downtowns are alive with people-parades often lasting into the wee hours. There's a spirit in the air as vibrant as the air itself. Hurricane season is over. The night skies have too many stars to count. The sea breezes are almost luxurious. The colors of the buildings and the flora are more vivid. And Palm Beach Countians—who sometimes tend to hibernate during the hot summer months—are out enjoying it all.

The only problem with all of this (according to some Palm Beach Countians) is that everybody else—meaning visitors and "snowbirds" is out enjoying it all, too. That means the roads are more crowded in High Season . . . as are the restaurants, the movies, and the shopping centers. And, as far as visitors are concerned, you'll have to pay more for the privilege of wonderful weather and the joys of the season . . . sometimes, a lot more.

During High Season, hotels can book up quickly (especially if there's a lousy winter up north); this not only impacts availability, of course, but also price. If you're visiting (and even if you live here), you'll end up doing some standing in line, wherever you go. And—particularly during the Holiday Season—you may not be able to get a rental car unless you've reserved early. And you'll pay more for the car you do get.

Low Season is a different story. There's no getting around it—South Florida's hot in the summer; mid-seventies to low eighties at night, and generally in the high-eighties to low-nineties in the daytime. But the humidity—often in the eighties or nineties—makes it feel even hotter. The sun is very direct, and very intense. There are plenty of bugs. Late-afternoon thunderstorms rolling east from the Everglades (they generally clear up by evening, though). Hurricanes whose "projected paths" have to be watched very carefully in the fall. And, certainly, much less going on in the way of entertainment and diversion.

However, this is also the time when hotel rooms can be half the price (or less) they are during the winter. This is the time when restaurants run more specials (and you won't have to wait on line). This is the time when the shops offer sales (and when you can ramble through the malls much easier). This is the time when you can get pretty much whatever rental car you desire . . . at a much more reasonable price. And this is the time when you can get a tee-time pretty much whenever you want it.

GETTING HERE, GETTING AROUND

Palm Beach County doesn't have a major city in it. But it does have rush-hour traffic, especially during the Season. Try to avoid I-95 between the hours of 7 and 9 a.m., and also between 4:15 and 6:15 p.m. If you get trapped behind an accident there, you could spend a couple of hours just sitting in traffic. Also, listen for local radio reports about the Florida Turnpike, especially around West Palm Beach; this area can be congested, as well. Also, if you can, avoid using one of the major east-west roads in Boca Raton during rush-hour, including Palmetto Park Road, Glades Road, and Yamato Road.

BY AIR

The gateway to Palm Beach County—from just about anywhere in the world, with connections—is **Palm Beach International Airport (PBIA)** (561-471-7420).

The airport is served by 15 airlines, including most of the majors—American, Continental, Delta, JetBlue, Northwest, Southwest, U.S. Airways. Growing national carriers such as Spirit and AirTran also fly here. International service is provided by BahamasAir and Air Canada. And several regional airlines also service PBIA.

Upwards of 400 flights a day take off or land here, and nearly 7 million passengers a year pass through. And you can get here from more than 40 cities across the United States, Canada, and the Bahamas. The airport is modern, easy to navigate, and user-friendly, with plenty of parking and an attractive terminal and shops.

Palm Beach International is convenient, as well. It's located pretty much in the geographic center of the county, only 2.5 miles from downtown West Palm Beach, and just

off I-95, the main north-south highway in South Florida. And it's also convenient to the Florida Turnpike, the other main north-south road.

BY BUS OR TRAIN

If you prefer the train to flying, **Amtrak** offers long- and short-distance rail transportation throughout the United States (800-872-7245; www.amtrak.com).

And if you prefer to "leave the driving to (them)," **Greyhound** has a terminal in West Palm Beach (800-231-2222; www.greyhound.com).

CAR RENTAL

The following car rental companies are found at Palm Beach International Airport. Most of these companies also have rentals at various locations around the county. Call ahead for information (especially during winter's High Season!).

- **Alamo Rent-a-Car**—(800) 327-9633; www.alamo.com
- **Avis Rent-a-Car**—(800) 331-1212; www.avis.com
- **Car Rentals from Budget**—(800) 527-0700; www.budget.com
- **Dollar Rent-a-Car**—(800) 800-4000; www.dollar.com
- **Enterprise**—(800) 325-8007; www.enterprise.com
- **Hertz Rent-a-Car**—(800) 654-3131; www.hertz.com
- **National**—(800) 227-7368; www.nationalcar.com
- **Thrifty**—(877) 283-0898; www.thrifty.com

i South Florida is vulnerable to occasional electrical blackouts especially in the summer, when air-conditioning usage surges. It doesn't happen too often. And when it does, it's generally restricted to a compact area. But if it happens when you're in your car, you need to know the rules of the road—because traffic lights won't be working. Actually, the rules are very simple. Just treat every traffic light as if it's a four-way stop sign. Make sure you yield the right-of-way, rather than being a road-hog. Be sure to drive defensively . . . we have our share of road crazies here, too. And don't panic. Police usually arrive fairly quickly to direct traffic.

GROUND TRANSPORTATION

Hotel shuttles are provided by many local hotels. Contact a hotel directly at the Hotel Transportation Automated Reservation Center, terminal Level One, or through a public pay phone.

My Palm Beach County

"Palm Beach Country truly has the best of everything—the most beautiful beaches, the most challenging golf courses, an incredible array of cultural institutions and environmental treasures, along with fabulous restaurants, hotels and shopping centers. And don't forget the weather, which is heaven-on-earth at least half of the year and sizzling summer fun the other half.

And the people—what an amazing variety of people from all over the world, combining a New York attitude with the spicy flavor of the Caribbean and South America, mixing common-sense Midwestern values with Ol' South chivalry. Of course, the crazy drivers on the streets and thoroughfares are something else entirely—but no place is perfect!"

—Gary Schweikart,
President, PR-BS

IMPERIAL TRANSPORTATION PBC, INC.
(561) 689-3663 or (888) 369-9852

Transportation Services

Taxis are easily found just outside the main PBIA terminal. And there are numerous taxi companies throughout the county. Taxi fares average around $12 from the airport to downtown West Palm Beach, and approximately $75 to $80 from the airport to Boca Raton, about 25 miles south.

PALM BEACH TRANSPORTATION
(561) 684-9900
Taxi and limousine service is available at the transportation desk at each end of the terminal building, Level One.

YELLOW EXPRESS SHUTTLE
(561) 242-6444
Provides a share-a-ride, door-to-door transportation service to and from Palm Beach International Airport. This is a 24-hour service and no reservations are needed for arriving passengers.

PUBLIC TRANSPORTATION

PALM TRAN
(561) 841-4200
www.co.palm-beach.fl.us/palmtran/
Palm Beach County's public bus transportation offers regular services throughout the county. Regular fare is $1.50, children under eight free.

TRI-RAIL
(800) 874-7245
www.tri-rail.com
This rail service provides transportation between West Palm Beach and Miami (approx. 60 miles south), with numerous stops in-between. Depending on which station you get off; from West Palm Beach to Boca Raton costs $8.45.

HISTORY

Who would have known—who *could* have known—all those centuries ago, that this once-mosquito-infested backwater would become one of America's premier tropical playgrounds? And who could have known that this isolated outpost of civilization would one day be home to one of the world's most splendid areas of good taste and the good life? It would have seemed impossible that, one day, when the world's most exclusive hideaways were discussed, one of them would be this place in Florida where almost no one lived a little more than a century ago. No one could have imagined that this relatively recent no-man's-land would now be populated by nearly a million-and-a-half people, from all parts of the world and all walks of life, simply trying to carve out lives for themselves in this blessed piece of sub-tropical paradise.

HOW IT ALL STARTED

Palm Beach County has been touched by a number of civilizations.

The first residents of the area arrived quietly, and didn't leave much behind. They were the **Calusa** and the **Tequesta Indians,** who arrived here about 15,000 years ago . . . most likely in search of food, fresh water, and game. The wetlands that characterize the western part of the county today were not here then. Instead, the Indians found an arid, desert-like landscape that was not very supportive of plant life, nor of the animal life for which they were searching. (Climate changes 5,000 to 6,000 years ago apparently caused Lake Okeechobee to overflow its banks . . . which, in turn, helped create the Everglades.)

These early arrivals were hunter-gatherers, and they developed a unique culture based on the watery environment that surrounded them, living on fish and shellfish taken from the ocean, rivers, and lakes, along with berries, roots, nuts, and fruits from the Earth.

They didn't have a written language, and so we have no written record of their existence—or their disappearance. But Mother Earth has left a sort of historical record . . . in the burial sites, pottery shards, camping grounds, and "midden mounds" (containing tools and artifacts of daily Native American life) that suddenly come up to the surface every time an Everglades restoration project starts digging. Many of the sites housed villages of the people the Spanish later called "Tequesta," as well as the Calusa. There are also sites from the **Seminole** and **Miccosukee,** who had apparently followed the Tequesta to South Florida.

Shards of pottery—some with decoration—and human remains (including teeth) have been found, dating back to as early as 2,000 B.C. The earliest written descriptions of these people actually came from the Spanish explorers who conquered them and then tried to convert them to Christianity. It was apparently easier for the Spanish to write about these people than to do the conquering and converting. But after two centuries of war, and European diseases to which the Indians had never before been exposed (and therefore had no immunity to), the Tequesta were not very much of a cohesive tribal unit any more. The Spanish rounded up many of the remaining tribal members, stuffed them into crowded quarters at the bottom of ships, and sent them to the then-Spanish port of Havana. Isolated bands of survivors apparently then joined up with the Creek tribe, and that union eventually became the **Seminole Nation.** Today there are still six Seminole reservations in Florida ... but none in Palm Beach County.

The first of the Spanish to arrive here was **Ponce de Leon,** in 1513, on his ill-fated search for the Fountain of Youth (which, had he found it, might conceivably have saved him from an early death by Indian poison-arrow???). He sailed his ship into what we now call the Jupiter Inlet. And he named the inlet **Rio de la Cruz** (River of the Cross). He apparently didn't stay long, however, and left with nary a trace.

After Ponce de Leon, we can sort of skip ahead a few hundred years ... because, really, not all that much of note happened in South Florida during that time, as opposed to the constant struggle for influence among a number of flags and nations up the coast in northern Florida. Much of South Florida was a mosquito-infested swamp, with searing temperatures, the constant threat of disease, and all types of wild critters (and wild characters).

In 1838, another explorer, a Spanish sea captain whose name, unfortunately floated into history alongside him, sailed into the Boca Raton Inlet and decided to give it a name based on its appearance.

Unfortunately, the shape that most came to mind (his mind, anyway) was that of a rat—the mouth of a rat, to be precise. But the rest of the story has sometimes been misinterpreted.

The Spanish word "boca" (or mouth) was often used, as well, to describe an inlet, while "raton" (literally, "mouse") was used as a term for a cowardly thief. And, no doubt, the good captain was applying the "inlet" meaning. The "Thieves Inlet," Boca Ratones, began appearing on 18th-century maps ... unfortunately, however, on 18th-century maps of the Biscayne Bay area of Miami. By the beginning of the 19th-century, the term was mistakenly being applied to the Boca Raton Inlet. The "s" and the "e" were eventually dropped from this title by the 1920s (but the correct pronunciation remains Rah-tone). And so the area that eventually came to become one of Florida's most-upscale (and most well-known) communities was named for (take your pick) A: a cowardly thief; or B: the mouth of a rat.

Other sea captains weren't quite as lucky as the one who sailed into the Boca Inlet, however; they didn't have the luxury of time to name much of anything. Many ran into disaster in the seas off South Florida and had to abandon their sinking ships—which were often sinking as much from the weight of the gold and treasure aboard (much of it apparently looted from the ships of other sea captains!) as from damage from the sea.

So many ships went down here, in fact, that in Martin County, just to the north, the locals built a **"House of Refuge"** for those shipwrecked sailors who were lucky enough to make it to shore. (And it's still there, beautifully preserved.)

And—though some folks opine that South Florida's called "The Gold Coast" because of its relative wealth and its lifestyle—others say it's because of the ships that went down here, and all the gold still left in them.

VISIONARIES AND DREAMERS

Also in 1838, the U.S. Army established a foothold in the area, building a fort in the northern part of the county, in what is now Jupiter. This was the first permanent non-Indian settlement in the area. The soldiers were soon followed by civilian residents who felt the area was now safe enough for settlement. And by 1860 the locals were caring for the **Jupiter Lighthouse** that the Army had been built a year earlier (it's still a local landmark).

In the 1890s, the man who turned Palm Beach County into Palm Beach County came here—and Palm Beach County would never be the same again. **Henry Flagler,** who had made a fortune in Standard Oil, had moved to northern Florida in the hope that the climate would help his ailing wife. Unfortunately, it didn't, and she died two years later. But around the time, an enterprising South Florida woman named **Julia Tuttle** sent Flagler an orange blossom—in winter—in the hope that he would develop South Florida. Flagler was delighted to see this orange blossom in the middle of winter . . . and his mind, apparently, began racing. He began to see the potential of the southern part of the state being transformed into a resort and business center. So he began buying up a bunch of small railroads along the east coast of the state, and amalgamated them into the **Florida East Coast Railroad.** In so doing, he opened up Palm Beach County to the world . . . although, at that point, the area now known as Palm Beach County was actually still part of Dade County, which stretched all

the way to the Keys. In order to house the wealthy business magnates he was attracting to take a look at the area, Flagler later built what is still one of the two most famous hotels in Palm Beach County, **The Breakers** (originally the Palm Beach Inn).

The Breakers wasn't his first hotel here, however. That would have been the Royal Poinciana, which he opened in 1894. His railroad stopped in the tiny hamlet of West Palm Beach, which made it easy for visitors to then cross Lake Worth to get to the island of Palm Beach . . . and his hotel. Money, of course, was no object to Flagler, one of America's wealthiest men. And he kept adding on to his hotel until it became the largest in the world, with 1,100 rooms.

In 1896 he opened the Palm Beach Inn, right on the ocean. Because Henry Flagler was Henry Flagler, and his connections were legion, his two hotels soon began attracting other extremely wealthy people. They came from all over the country . . . the oil drillers, the land developers, and titans of business. And, soon, they began coming from all over the world.

Surprisingly, though, instead of requesting rooms at the huge, and elegant, Royal Poinciana, many people began asking for rooms "by the breakers," at the smaller Palm Beach Inn. And that's why, in 1901, Flagler renamed the inn "The Breakers."

In 1897, Flagler opened the first golf course in America, adjacent to the inn. He made it only nine holes, though—he apparently thought this strange new game was just a passing fad.

Tragedy eventually struck. On June 9, 1903—as Flagler was enlarging the wooden inn for the fourth time—it caught fire and burned to the ground. Two weeks later, Flagler, now 73, announced that the inn would be rebuilt, better than ever. And, furthermore, it would be open by the winter "Season." Many people snickered. But not the ones who knew Henry Flagler.

On Feb. 1, 1904, true to Flagler's boast, The Breakers did re-open, only eight months later. And his boast wasn't an idle one; it really was bigger and better than before. Rooms—including three "squares" a day—started at the princely sum of four dollars, beyond the range of most folks at that time. But it sure wasn't beyond the range of the Rockefellers, Vanderbilts, Astors, Carnegies, J.P. Morgans, Hearsts, Penneys (J.C.), and Posts (C.W., of Post Cereals) who flocked here to mingle in a rarefied atmosphere with their own kind. They were joined by a bevy of presidents, kings, and princes.

Bad luck struck twice at The Breakers, however. Amazingly, it burnt down again in 1925, by which time Flagler was gone. But his heirs were Flaglers, too, of course. And they made the same boast he did—that it would reopen, bigger and better, and before the start of The Season the following year. And they, too, made good on their boast. The Breakers—now built in the style of a luxurious Italian Renaissance palace—reopened on Dec. 29, 1926. Again, the hoi polloi began flocking here. And they haven't stopped since (although the hotel also now has prices meant to appeal to guests of somewhat more modest means, as well).

Not everyone who came to Palm Beach County in those days was a Henry Flagler, though. Many folks arrived here with barely the shirts on their backs, looking for a new life.

In 1905, a Japanese emigrant named **Joseph Sakai** bought some land in the southern part of the county, in what is now Boca Raton. Sakai planned to build an agricultural enterprise. He foresaw a "colony" of other Japanese to help him work it, and to establish new lives in this new land. And he named his colony **"Yamato,"** after a province from which the ancient emperors of Japan once ruled.

Sakai began offering farmland to other Japanese emigrants, and then advertised in Japan for more workers. But getting workers, apparently, was not the problem. The real problem was that these workers weren't going to stay for long without women whom they could court, and hopefully, marry. So Sakai also began advertising in Japan for women to come over and marry into his colony. And some, also looking for a new life in a new country, actually did.

The life at Yamato was a very hard one. The settlers had to constantly battle the heat, disease, the mosquitoes, and the very long distance to market. Eventually, the colony began to successfully grow pineapples, and to market them around the region. But the group could never sustain a successful long-term business, and many ended up giving up their dreams and returning to Japan. (Today, however, the settlement is still memorialized by the name of one of Boca Raton's main thoroughfares—**Yamato Road.**)

A few of those emigrants, however, were determined to make their visions come through, and they stayed. One of them was a young man named **George Morikami.** He built a successful life here for himself and his family. In the mid-1970s, Morikami donated his home and part of his land (which is today in Delray Beach) to Palm Beach County, in order to create a museum and park that would memorialize the early Japanese settlers, and that would be a place where people could learn about Japanese culture and tradition. Today his museum and park are one of South Florida's true cultural treasures, called the Morikami Museum and Japanese Gardens (see Attractions).

COLORFUL CHARACTERS AND LIVING LEGENDS

This area became Palm Beach County in 1909, when it was carved out of Dade County (now Miami-Dade County), becoming Florida's 47th county (today there are 67). At that time, it also comprised Broward (Greater Fort Lauderdale) to the south, Martin (to the north), and Okeechobee (to the west) counties. And only about 5,300 people lived in an area that exceeded 6,000 square miles. However, one by one, the other counties gained their own governance . . . and Palm Beach County became the Palm Beach County we know today in 1925.

As word about Florida—and the Palm Beach area—spread, the region began developing a somewhat unwelcome reputation—as a get-rich-quick place. And as a result, it began attracting get-rich-quick schemers and dreamers of all stripes. People began flooding in, lured by the promise of great fortune and perennial sunshine . . . businessmen, construction workers, carpetbaggers, con-artists, woodsmen, teachers, politicians (corrupt and not), land barons, scoundrels, slicksters, hucksters, growers, farmers, snake-oil salesmen (and women), real estate developers, traders, trappers, entrepreneurs, shippers, scalawags, speculators, fishermen, cattle barons, laborers, pioneers, preachers, pimps, homesteaders, and just about every other type of person—moral and not-so-moral—that you can imagine.

Many of them still live on in legend. One of the biggest legends—and one of the biggest people, was **Trapper Nelson,** a backwoodsman who didn't have much use for other people or modern civilization. He lived like a hermit in the murky swamps and mangroves of the northern Everglades. And he truly was a mountain of a man, the stuff of legends. He stood 6'4" and weighed 240 pounds, and was called "The Tarzan of the Loxahatchee River." His home was a log cabin that he built himself. He ate only what he could kill—and he never went hungry. He hunted, he fished, he trolled the marshy hammocks (little islands) of **"The River of Grass."** And he apparently had very little fear of the alligators, water moccasins, rattlesnakes, and panthers who also trolled the River of Grass.

Trapper Nelson caught so many wild creatures that he eventually built a small zoo to house them. Blessed with a bit of an entrepreneurial streak despite his wilderness ways, he arranged for tourist boats to bring visitors up the Loxahatchee to visit his zoo. And when they arrived, he provided additional entertainment by wrestling with some of the animals. Despite his isolation, however, he had an eye for the ladies, many of whom were apparently charmed by his macho ways. And he apparently had an eye for real estate, as well—because he eventually ended up with 800 acres.

After some years, however, life in the jungle began robbing Nelson of his judgment. He eventually became paranoid that people were trying to steal the land he had bought over the years. As he grew older, he began complaining of stomach pains, among other ailments. He wasn't the type to go to a hospital, however. So he did what any self-respecting jungle-hermit would do. He diagnosed himself—with cancer.

What happened next, we'll never know for sure, though there are a hundred

The Ghost of Trapper Nelson

Trapper Nelson lived in the wilderness along the Loxahatchee River, deep in the interior of the area that is now Jonathan Dickinson State Park. He was entirely self-sufficient. He cut wood to build his own cabin and whatever conveniences he had inside it. He ate only what he could kill. He wrestled alligators. He was a towering man, and, according to legend, no slouch with the ladies. He began to get somewhat paranoid in his later years, claiming that people were trying to steal his land and the little zoo and riverside tourist stop he had built. He also believed he was dying of cancer. A friend found him in 1968 at his cabin, with a huge shotgun hole in his stomach. No one has ever fully explained how he died. But many county residents believe his spirit is still there, in that old cabin, creaking in the ceiling, or watching them over their shoulder as they look around. There was one famous case, in the mid-nineties, in which a female park ranger claimed to have had a conversation with him—in which he was making a pass at her. We'll never know about the veracity of that conversation. But we do know that a large number of visitors to his creaky old cabin in the jungle claim to have had encounters of the paranormal kind with him. So, if you visit . . . don't go alone!

theories. But this we do know. Trapper Nelson was found dead on his property on July 24, 1968, with a shotgun nearby. The county coroner ruled it suicide, and that Trapper had done himself in because he certainly didn't want to live life in a sickly state. But, to this day, some Palm Beach Countians maintain that it was a jealous lover who "done him in," or a disgruntled landowner or trading acquaintance.

Trapper Nelson lives on to this day in Palm Beach County legend. He was certainly bigger than life, in more ways than one. But he was also just one of many colorful characters who still live on in local legend. Another one for the books was **"The Barefoot Mailman."** The "Mailman" was actually many men; these were the carriers on the first mail route (established 1885) between Palm Beach and Miami. There were no cars, then, of course, so these men had to walk the 68-mile route. But, you're no doubt thinking, there were certainly horses. True. But there was just one problem. There would be no way to find enough water for horses.

So they walked. In the searing heat of the summer, when there's almost no escape from the sun. In the dry cold snaps of the winter. Through the thunderstorms of the spring. And through the hurricanes of the fall. On dirt roads between distant towns which didn't yet have electricity. Through swarms of the appropriately named horseflies. On the beach. And on the water, as well; they generally rowed boats for 28 miles of the trip.

A round-trip took six days. The barefoot route continued until 1892, when a rock "road" (of sorts) was completed from Jupiter to Miami, and the mail contract was taken over by the Bay Biscayne Stage Line.

But the Barefoot Mailman—and his determination to brave the elements and the natural surroundings—also still lives on in legend.

Meanwhile, other enterprising sorts were discovering that you could grow fruits and vegetables here . . . a lot of fruit and vegetables. Soon orange groves (pretty much gone today) dotted the landscape. And oranges and other citrus fruits from this region—as well as green beans—eventually found their way into refrigerators all over the country.

The 1920s brought to Palm Beach County another entrepreneur who would enter the lore of Florida.

Addison Mizner was a well-known architect, but not just an architect. He was also a visionary. He brought a flamboyant, Spanish/Mediterranean style to South Florida that has remained in Palm Beach County to this day.

In May of 1925, the town of Boca Raton was incorporated. And the newly named City Council decided to bring in Mizner to create a city that could also become a true tropical resort and a playground for the wealthy. He completed the magnificent **Cloister Inn**—today still part of the renowned Boca Raton Resort & Club—in 1926. He also designed a new city hall for the new city, which was completed in 1927. Today the restored **Town Hall** is the home of the Boca Raton Historical Society and is open for tours. It still resonates with the style and elegance of that gilded age.

Mizner wasn't done, though; he had many more grand plans for Boca Raton. But the end of the land boom in 1926, and the Depression in 1929, put an end to them.

Today, though, Addison Mizner's influence is still felt all over Boca Raton, and even in the unincorporated communities to the west of town. His influence is felt in Boca's magnificently landscaped pocket parks downtown, as well as in its shops, restaurants, and office buildings, still filled with the tiled arches, fountains, plazas, Moorish windows, and the gentle curves of that time. And, truth be told, you can't go very far in Boca today—or in other parts of Palm Beach County—without seeing Addison Mizner's name. On shops. On housing developments. On restaurants. On streets.

PALM BEACH COUNTY AT WAR

After the Depression, of course, came World War II. And the immense impact of that event not only changed America, it changed Palm Beach County, too, forever.

In 1942, the Army Air Corps, looking for a place where it could conduct all-year-long training, established its only war-time radar training school in Boca Raton, at the site of what is today Florida Atlantic University (FAU) and the Boca Raton Airport. At that time, Boca had only 723 souls. But the Air Corps facility brought over 30,000 servicemen, as well as families and civilian employees, to the tiny community. And Boca would never be the same.

In fact, that was true of pretty much the entire county. In 1940, even before the war, the U.S. Army Air Corps established **Air Transport Command at Morrison Field,** west of West Palm Beach. The army added barracks and other buildings to support some 3,000 soldiers.

In all, a staggering total of more than 45,000 pilots either trained or flew out of West Palm Beach from 1940 to 1945, in addition to some 250 women from the Women's Army Corps (WACS). A thousand men worked 24/7 to make sure the aircraft in which they flew were battle-ready.

Even the posh community of Palm Beach—which wasn't even on the mainland—was not immune from the rigors of war. The U.S. Army established a Ranger camp at the northern tip of the island, which was then undeveloped. The camp accommodated about 200 men who had seen combat, and who had then been rotated home. They lived in somewhat-Spartan conditions, in canvas tents, and maintained a few tanks and gun emplacements, just in case the enemy materialized off the coast.

As the war progressed, many of Palm Beach's plushest hotels—including the Breakers and the Biltmore—were converted to military hospitals. In the spirit of the times, many Palm Beachers shucked their tuxedos and gowns and put on fatigues and nurses' uniforms, and went off to staff these hospitals, and to help out on the bases. The U.S. Navy had first established a presence in Jupiter, in the northern section of the county, in 1890, followed later by the Coast Guard. After Germany attacked Poland in 1939 to start World War II, the Navy established a communications/listening post here. It intercepted messages among German submarines—the dreaded U-boats—prowling Florida waters, and sent them along to Allied ships, as well as to Washington, D.C.

After Pearl Harbor, "Station J," as it was called, was bulked up to a hundred men, listening in on and trying to decode enemy messages.

Even the smaller towns in the interior, around Lake Okeechobee, got into the war. A German POW camp was established in the isolated town of Belle Glade, and its prisoners were sometimes used for work projects left undone by the dearth of young men at home. Some POWs worked in a nearby bean-cannery, while others helped build the dike around the huge lake, which, to this day, keeps it from flooding lakeside towns.

In 1941, with most Florida National Guardsmen already serving on active duty, the state legislature created the **Florida Defense Force.** The Palm Beach County FDF worked on communications and intelligence tasks, and on monitoring the coast for German submarines. Eventually the group expanded to include the **First Air Squadron.** The "force" was not as fearful as its name implied, however, it was basically made up of some fifteen local pilots in their own little "puddle-jumper" planes, who painted "First Air Squadron" on their craft. These pilots patrolled the local skies and seas day and night.

Like all conflicts, World War II spawned its share of stories and legends. There's one very colorful legend associated with World War II in Palm Beach County. Because of the heavy toll inflicted on American shipping by German U-boats patrolling offshore, many Navy, Coast Guard, and Merchant Marine vessels cruising along the Atlantic coast began using the Intracoastal instead of the ocean. In addition to the extra degree of protection from enemy submarines, there was sometimes a bonus in it for the sailors, many of whom had spent up to a year at sea. Occasionally a kind-hearted captain would direct the crew to anchor the boat at one of the waterside "watering holes" along the Intracoastal, and would give the sailors liberty for the night. The sailors—many of whom couldn't remember the last time they had seen a woman—used that time to good opportunity. And many of them came back aboard the next morning in much better spirits than when they had left the night before. (Although others among them came back suffering from too many spirits—of the alcoholic kind.)

Hundreds of thousands of service men and women trained in Palm Beach County, which provided an ideal base for the armed forces because you could train year-round. And many of them, recalling the eternal sunshine, came back to live here.

The war hit home here in some ironic ways. For example, German U-boats had a field day with American shipping off Palm Beach County, torpedoing ships at night so often that residents in beachside communities could actually sit outside and watch American ships burn.

POST-WAR PALM BEACH COUNTY

Palm Beach County went through the fairly quiet fifties and the turbulent sixties pretty much out of the consciousness of most Americans. Yes, Palm Beach was still a hangout for the rich-and-famous, and some well-to-do industrialists and company presidents had begun to move into the Boca Raton area. But, for the most part, this remained a small county with a low profile, which rarely made the papers except for a huge charity or social event at which the paparazzi could photograph celebrities.

That all changed in the seventies, though. And one of the reasons was a rather unlikely one—**The National Enquirer.** The paper was owned by a man named **Generoso Pope,** a New York newspaperman and publisher who had bought the *Enquirer*—then in New York—in 1952. Pope moved it to Lantana, in Palm Beach County, in 1971, and oversaw the paper's tremendous growth. Americans seemed to have an appetite for the paper's blend of Elvis sightings and conspiracy theories with exposes and, even some self-help articles on issues such as diet and health. And people who had once been somewhat embarrassed about reading the tabloid began openly buying it at newsstands and supermarkets.

They bought it even more when Elvis was on the cover . . . especially after his death in 1977.

"An Elvis cover can generate sales of 4-5 million copies in a week," one of the editors once told me.

Generoso Pope's paper had a reputation for being somewhat sensationalistic, true; but, apparently, the millions who bought it to devour the latest news about celebrities, unusual natural phenomena (or ghosts of famous people), or about how they could make their own lives better, didn't seem to care.

Pope had a bent for publicity, and for hiring the best journalists he could find. In the seventies, he found many of them in Great Britain, which, at the time, had a number of daily newspapers whose approach was somewhat similar to the Enquirer's.

For better or worse, the paper kept growing, generating notice for this highly profitable publisher in Palm Beach County, Florida. Shortly after that, a few of the celebrities about whom The Enquirer had written sued the paper for libel or printing false information, bringing even more publicity to Palm Beach County.

During that period, the county was starting to experience tremendous growth. Palm Beach was enhancing its role as a world-renowned playground for the jet-set (with some younger millionaire-entrepreneurs and executives also moving in). West Palm Beach, although it had fallen into some disrepair, was developing plans to turn into a genuine urban core for the county. Boca Raton was developing a Master Plan to create a vibrant downtown. **Florida Atlantic University (FAU),** which is now an integral part of the state-university system, first opened its doors.

Towns and cities were starting to spread westward, as well, with schools and homes and businesses being carved out of areas that had been basically wilderness just a few years before. New towns such as Wellington were being created in what had been swamp and heavy vegetation before. And they were even talking about putting in asphalt roads in The Acreage, which is still an area in which you can walk a long time before seeing a neighbor's house.

> **i** "It occurred to me very strongly that someone with sufficient means ought to provide accommodations for that class of people who are not sick, but who come here to enjoy the climate, have plenty of money, but could find no satisfactory way of spending it."—Henry Flagler, 1883

THE IBM EFFECT

Then came **IBM.**

In 1967, IBM moved a small computer facility from out-of-state to the quiet bedroom community of Boca Raton. Slowly, over the years, the facility grew, in both size and number of employees. People began talking in mysterious tones. Something big was, apparently, going on here. And an increasing number of young IBM "techies" were being transferred to Boca—or requesting transfers—to be a part of it.

These people were professionals with good incomes. They had families with young children and wives who worked. And they began changing the face of Boca Raton, transforming it from a staid, conservative community where executives went to retire, into a vigorous young town where professionals now went to create.

IBM brought them here by the thousands. Of course, these professional families needed homes in which to live, schools for their children, upscale places where they could shop, and good restaurants where they could spend their disposable income. And the housing developments, schools, shops, and restaurants followed quickly.

In addition, other tech enterprises followed IBM's lead and relocated—or started up—here.

IBM, meanwhile, was maintaining a military-like secrecy abut what was going on at its Boca facility. Here and there, though, leaks occurred. There were secret plans to develop some sort of computer that could be used by individuals, not just companies, referred to as **"Project Chess."** The code name for the new computer was **"Acorn."**

On Aug. 12, 1981, IBM released their new computer, re-named the **IBM-PC.** The "PC" stood for "personal computer." And with the introduction of that term, IBM changed our vocabulary forever.

IBM changed Palm Beach County and Boca Raton forever, as well. At its peak, in 1984, the company had 10,000 people working at its Boca campus, most of whom had now developed roots in the community. In a very real sense, IBM made Boca Raton the community it is today. And its legacy is still apparent every day. In the Mercedes and BMWs that clog Boca's streets. In the new technology start-ups. In the vibrant international corporate climate (with companies such as Siemens and Office Depot). In the magnificent developments with multi-million-dollar homes. In the new schools. In the swank shops and shopping centers. In the many elegant restaurants.

IBM is pretty much gone now. Over the years, the company began shrinking the facility, moving much of its operations to

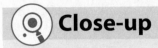

Close-up

Florida's Finnish

The area around Lake Worth and Lantana has sometimes been referred to as Little Finland. In fact, it's home to the world's second-largest Finnish expatriate community. In the 2000 census, there were 25,700 people of Finnish descent in southern Florida, most of them concentrated in southern and central Palm Beach County. In addition there were about 5,000 winter residents ("snowbirds," as we call them down here) from Finland, or of Finnish descent from other areas of the United States and Canada.

Finnish is the fourth most widely spoken minority language in the Lake Worth–Lantana area after Spanish, Creole, and Russian. Some of the Finnish immigrants came to service ships in the two largest cruise ports in the world (Miami and Fort Lauderdale), because many cruise ships are built in Finland. In recent years, a number of Finnish companies that service/renovate these ships have also set up shop here.

In Lake Worth's Finnish community, it's possible to go to the market, the hairdresser, the drug store, the cleaners, a motel, the hardware store, the newsstand—even a funeral home—without speaking a word of English. The Lake Worth–Lantana area is ideal for retirees, as the climate is favorable, there are plenty of activities, and the area is safe. And the decade of the 1990s saw a number of Finnish retirees come to this area to live.

Charlotte, NC. Now, there's just a small office with about a hundred employees on ground that once held 10,000. But other companies are using the buildings to create entrepreneurial dreams of their own. And many of IBM's people never moved. They stayed here and made lives for themselves and their families. They helped create new business ventures. They got involved in charitable and social causes. They helped develop western Boca Raton, and, later on, many of them began moving back east, invigorating the downtown area.

Boca Raton is now an international destination in its own right, with distinctive resorts for vacationers, and excellent hotels for business travelers. And it was IBM that put Boca on the map.

THE MODERN ERA

The growth of Palm Beach County hasn't stopped since.

Just as it had begun to spread westward, the county's growth also spurted in its northern sections. Palm Beach Gardens became a lovely city with greenery all around, and eventually became the home of the **Professional Golfer's Association (PGA),** the governing body of professional golf internationally. This was accompanied by the opening of the beautiful PGA National Resort, which began attracting golfers from all over the country.

Palm Beach International Airport grew exponentially, expanding its terminal and its runways, adding new hotels, and becoming a convenient, less-frazzled gateway to South Florida. The Port of Palm Beach—actually

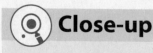 **Close-up**

How Lake Worth Got Its Name

Lake Worth shares its last name with another town. In 1841, Colonel William Jenkins Worth, an accomplished career soldier, took command of troops fighting in the Second Seminole War in Florida. The war had been raging for six years by that time, with no real conclusion in sight. So Colonel Worth came up with a unique way of ending it. He declared the war over in 1842—even though the Seminoles had not surrendered. (They remain, to this day, the only tribe that has never signed a peace treaty with the United States) Though that war may have "ended," however, Colonel Worth's fighting was far from over. He was transferred west during the Mexican War, which started in 1846. He led his unit ashore at Vera Cruz during the American invasion of Mexico, and led them victoriously into Mexico City A few months later, for his exploits, Worth was promoted to major general, and later put in charge of what was then called the "Department" of Texas. He didn't serve long, however, dying from cholera in 1849. But he left his name behind, in the cities of Lake Worth, FL, and Fort Worth, TX.

in Riviera Beach—expanded, as well, to increase the larger numbers of international freighters arriving here (along with a couple of day-cruise liners).

Cities began re-creating themselves, with dramatic new residential, business, and cultural developments that inaugurated "new" downtowns. In the early nineties, Mizner Park went up in Boca Raton. This was an urban core of upscale high-rise apartment buildings, and fancy shops and restaurants on the bottom floors, along with an amphitheater and the **Boca Raton Museum of Art.**

Also during this time, City Place was developed in downtown West Palm Beach, giving the city a true urban core, and also sparking revitalization in the neighborhoods and commercial districts around it. Then, across the street from City Place, came the **Kravis Center for the Performing Arts,** a world-class entertainment center.

Meanwhile, these trends also sparked revitalization on **Clematis Street,** the once-neglected heart of downtown, now also the site of atmospheric clubs and restaurants.

Downtown Delray Beach, in the early nineties, was a dull, derelict place filled with failing businesses and questionable characters. City officials re-developed it into a different kind of city core, with gaslight streetlamps, trendy restaurants and nightclubs, great jazz spots, and even a gas station that was converted into an outdoor bar with live musicians. Soon after came upscale apartment projects, bringing more residents—and more life—to downtown. Today Downtown Delray is one of South Florida's hottest spots, with a fascinating, never-ending people-parade, and an excitement in the air (especially on weekend nights) that's palpable.

The aging city of Lake Worth decided to use its "character" to advantage; and today it's filled with unusual bistros and shops and artists' studios.

The gilded town of Palm Beach, too, metamorphosed. Today, there's "new money" (along with more ethnic and religious diversity) that previously would have been unheard of on the island. And Worth Avenue has become one of the most magnificent shopping streets in the world, filled with Mediterranean architecture and winding alleyways and sun-splashed courtyards where you can watch artists work in their studios, and the kind of shops that don't bother to display their prices in their windows—because if you have to ask, you can't afford it.

A growing sophistication in the county's residents demanded artistic, folk, and cultural events to match. And today—especially during The Season—Palm Beach County has more events on its calendar than you could possibly attend. Then, of course, there are the "refugees" from "down south" on the coast, who fled what they considered the congestion and crime of larger cities but still demand the same amenities to which they're accustomed.

More colleges and universities sprang up, as well, such as Lynn University in Boca and Palm Beach Atlantic in West Palm.

Just how fast has the county grown? The 1980 census showed 577,000 people here. In 1990 there were 864,000. In 2,000 there 1,132,000. And projected figures for 2010 are somewhere in the 1.3 to 1.4 million range. That means that Palm Beach County's population has more than doubled in just thirty years.

There must be a reason for that. And it's the same reason that so many people come to vacation here, or to live here:

Palm Beach County, unlike so many other places, is still writing its own history.

ACCOMMODATIONS

The concept of luxury lodging arrived in Palm Beach County at the turn of the 20th century, when Henry Flagler built The Breakers in Palm Beach. It blossomed even further a few years later, when Addison Mizner built The Cloisters (now the Boca Raton Resort & Club). These are still the two *Grande Dames* of Palm Beach County hotels.

They were soon followed by The Colony in Delray Beach. Since then, every other conceivable type of lodging has broken ground here, from historic bed and breakfasts to economy, extended-stay to family places, chain hotels (both elegant and plain) to upscale resorts and comfortable roadside inns.

Price Code

The price code for listings is based on the hotel's average room price per night during high season. *NOTE:* Various local hotel taxes are not included in the price-code key.

$.................... Under $100
$$ .... $100 to $199
$$$ .... $200 to $300
$$$$ .... More than $300

Unless otherwise noted, all listed establishments accept major credit cards.

Also, a note about the listings for resorts. There are some classic definitions of what comprises a resort, as opposed to a nice hotel. For example, a resort will generally offer a wide selection of rooms and suites, along with restaurants, lounges, golf, recreational activities, fitness facilities, perhaps a few shops, a spa, and maybe child-care services.

Palm Beach County—and all of South Florida, for that matter—doesn't always go by the classic definition of resort. Yes, many of the resorts here have all or most of those amenities. But not all of them do.

Sometimes, Palm Beach Countians may call it a resort if it has a long and glorious history. Or if it happens to be located on the beach. Or on a golf course. Or even if it just happens to have the word "resort" in its name.

One thing's for sure, though: If it's called a resort in this book, you can be confident that it's a first-class—and, in some cases, world-class—facility. You can expect a lot and you'll get it.

Whatever your taste in lodging, you'll find it here. And you'll find it where you want it.

SOUTH COUNTY

Resorts

THE BOCA BEACH CLUB $$$$
900 S. Ocean Blvd.
Boca Raton
(561) 447-3000 or (800) 992-4023
www.bocabeachclub.com
The Boca Beach Club is a sister-property of the nearby Boca Raton Resort & Club and also part of the Waldorf–Astoria Collection. It's actually risen like a phoenix; it was more

or less torn down and then re-opened again in 2008. Unlike the Boca Resort, the Beach Club—as you might expect—is actually on the beach. And because they're sister properties, if you stay at either of the hotels, you're welcome to use any of the facilities at the other one. There are 212 rooms, most with a king bed, two queens, or two doubles, ranging from the 420-square-foot Standard Room to the 1,260-square-foot Ocean Vista Two-Bedroom Suite. The rooms are open, modern, and airy with imaginative "moderne/Florida" furniture and soft colors, and many have large terraces overlooking the ocean. They all come with coffeemakers, plush bathrobes, hair dryers, in-room safes, and a mini-bar. Microwaves and minifridges are available on request and for a fee.

Restaurants and lounges are luxurious and sophisticated. The Seagrille, overlooking the ocean, offers fresh fish specialties, light fare, and cocktails. Beaches Cafe & Snack Bar is a poolside restaurant. The Ocean Bar offers the smart colors, angles, and materials of contemporary styling, with seating indoors and on an outdoor terrace. And, of course, all of the restaurants and nightspots at the Boca Raton Resort & Club are just five minutes away by car, shuttle, or water taxi.

Along the half-mile of private beach, guests can kayak, wind-surf, sail, or snorkel. Boogie-boards, inner-tubes, and floats can all be rented. The Pool Oasis actually has three pools. And, if you plan on sailing your own boat here, there's a 32-slip marina at the Resort & Club.

The Beach Club also has some executive-board-size meeting rooms, as well as the Dunes ballroom for larger events. It has the bloodlines, now, of both its older-sister resort and of the Waldorf–Astoria name. No smoking.

THE BOCA RATON RESORT & CLUB $$$$
501 East Camino Real
Boca Raton
(561) 447-3000 or (888) 543-1277
www.bocaresort.com

This is the queen of South County hotels, now part of the prestigious Waldorf–Astoria Collection. And it has been a legend since Addison Mizner built it—as The Cloisters—in 1926. In designing it in a classic Mediterranean style, Mizner actually determined the architectural style of the growing town to which, today, people come from all over the world.

There are 1,047 rooms at the resort that now encompasses a 27-floor tower (which you can see from miles away), the original pink Cloisters building, and a few bungalows. There are seven restaurants and three lounges. One of the restaurants is Cielo, a wonderful continental/Italian dining experience located at the top of that tower. You can look out into what seems like forever . . . tall towers and waterways and yachts and greenery trailing into a horizon turned into a fiery kaleidoscope by the setting sun.

The Old Homestead restaurant is a chip off the old New York steak house of the same name. Try if you dare, the 42-oz. Meat Packing District Long Bone Rib Steak for two, or the 46-oz Porterhouse Steak. Morimoto is a sleek Japanese restaurant and raw bar, where the ambience is as stunning as the cuisine. Lucca is an elegant Mediterranean restaurant, overlooking the Intracoastal. And Serendipity is a whimsical candy-colored fantasyland, where you can pick up a light dish along with any number of ice-cream and candy treats.

The Palm Court, a breakfast area in the morning, turns into a plush lounge at night. Named after the resort's founder, Addison

Mizner, and paying tribute to his penchant for exotic pets, Mizner's Monkey Bar provides a sophisticated selection of cocktails, martinis, and cigars.

The lobby is reminiscent of a luxurious Spanish palace, with rich woods, magnificent chandeliers, and marble and stone all over the place.

There are two championship golf courses, a tennis complex, and the (Chris) Evert Tennis Academy. There are shops with everything you might need. There's wonderful art. The resort is just minutes from anywhere in Boca, including the beach, upscale shopping/entertainment plazas, cultural venues, and historic sites. From the time you drive through the wrought-iron gates of this magnificent resort, you'll know you're in for something special. Pets allowed only in bungalows; must be under 20 pounds.

Hotels and Motels

**BEST WESTERN
  UNIVERSITY INN** $$
2700 N. Federal Hwy.
Boca Raton
(561) 395-5225 or (800) 780-7234
www.bestwestern.com
This hotel has been a landmark on Federal Highway for 40 years. It's in downtown Boca, convenient to shops and restaurants, and just down the road from the designer shops and special restaurants of Mizner Park and Royal Palm Plaza. It's also near the beach and numerous golf courses, and there's a shuttle to the airport. Each of the 90 rooms has a coffeemaker, microwave, and a minifridge, and the hotel offers a continental breakfast. There's also a swimming pool and a whirlpool, a fitness center and a restaurant, Bentley's Seafood & Grill. For comfortable rooms and real convenience, this is a good place to stay.

**BOCA RATON BRIDGE
  HOTEL AND MARINA** $$$
999 East Camino Real
Boca Raton
(561) 368-9500 or (866) 909-2622
www.bocaratonbridgehotel.com
The Boca Raton Bridge has been setting a high standard for this area since 1976. It's only a couple of blocks from the beach, sitting right on the Intracoastal Waterway. Each of the 121 rooms and suites has a king-size bed and a queen, and each faces either the Intracoastal Waterway or the Atlantic. Each room has a coffeemaker, microwave, minifridge, and iron/ironing board. The public spaces are smart and contemporary. There is free wireless Internet, a nice pool overlooking the Intracoastal, a fitness center and sauna, and massage services. When you want to get away from it all, you can—on the water, with a ride-a-wave rental. You can enjoy a great al fresco meal or a cocktail at Watercolors Restaurant & Bar on an expansive deck practically right on top of the water. Enjoy the ongoing boat parade, from tiny sailboats to multi-million dollar waterborne palaces. The rooftop Carmen's at the Top of the Bridge has long been a popular spot with locals as well as guests, and its Sunday brunches are legendary. The hotel is convenient to downtown Boca, golf courses, and the shops and trendy dining spots of Mizner Park, Royal Palm Plaza, Town Center Mall, and Boca Center, along with several cultural venues. Pets under 40 pounds allowed; $100 fee.

**BOCA RATON MARRIOTT
  AT BOCA CENTER** $$$–$$$$
5150 Town Center Circle
Boca Raton
(561) 392-4600 or (888) 888-3780
www.marriott.com

Finding a Deal

You may have more bargaining power with hotels than you think. Florida—especially South Florida—has been one of the hardest-hit areas of the nation (if not *the* hardest hit). And when there's a recession, of course, less people travel. Many hotels in South Florida have had vacancy rates of 25 percent at times. And as a result, some are willing to bargain (even if they won't admit it!). Always check the Internet price of rooms before calling the hotel; if there's a difference in price, insist on the lower one. Always make sure you trot out whatever card in your wallet might make you eligible for a discount—AAA, AARP, your insurance company, etc. If you can't get a lower price, then inquire about an upgrade. Or ask them to throw in the last day for free. And, lastly, if you have some flexibility in your schedule, but you don't want to come during summer, try to come during "Shoulder Season"—just before or after High Season. For example, if you're thinking about coming in Mar, consider Apr instead; that's when rates start to go down. And if you're thinking about going in Nov, consider Oct instead—right before the rates go up.

What better place for a stunning Marriott than amidst a collection of Boca Raton's most fashionable shops and restaurants? Right outside your door is an array of some of the most distinctive eateries in a town known for distinctive eateries. Uncle Tai's is considered by many locals to be the finest Chinese restaurant in town. Morton's the Steakhouse . . . well, the name and the reputation say it all. Rocco's Tacos & Tequila Bar is just as quirky and just as much fun as it sounds. Big City Tavern is reminiscent of the great urban taverns of northern cities, and it's one of Boca's great gathering spots. Sample some to-die-for treats at Hoffman's Chocolates or Little Barker's Bakery.

After you're done eating, drape yourself in some fine men's clothing at Jos. A. Bank Clothier or Guy La Ferrera—Italian fashion that was voted one of the 100 Best Clothing Stores in America, or women's clothes at Boutique A La Mode. Get some gourmet foods or wines to bring home to friends and family, at Joseph's Market. Or just grab a chair and absorb the very "Boca" ambience of these unique shops and restaurants, in an expansive courtyard with fountain.

It's not necessary, by the way, to walk outside the Marriott to find distinctive eateries; the hotel has its own, as well. The Absinthe Restaurant serves American classics such as steak and seafood in a classic French ambience with a bar and an outdoor patio. Club Boca serves casual fare at the pool, along with mixed drinks and cocktails.

The hotel has 256 rooms, each with a full bed and a king, along with coffeemaker and fridge. The lobby—complete with a see-through mini-waterfall in a glass sculpture—is elegant and distinctively designed, with a touch of modern and a touch of retro. The bright-looking guest rooms have recently been renovated, with granite and walnut highlights, rainfall showers, and down comforters. You'll also find a modern business center and fitness center.

In addition, Boca Center is also the site of one of South Florida's finest art festivals every winter.

BOCA RATON PLAZA HOTEL & SUITES $$
2901 N. Federal Hwy.
Boca Raton
(561) 750-9944 or (866) 425-5130
www.bocaratonplaza.com

Each of the 95 rooms in this conveniently located hotel has either a king-size bed or two doubles. The Boca Raton Plaza opened in 2003, and boasts a tropical ambience in the middle of the action in Boca. It's close to Mizner Park and the rest of downtown Boca. The restaurant Our Place Bar & Grill on the premises is open for breakfast, lunch, and dinner. There are a heated pool, 24-hour fitness center, poolside tiki bar, and 24-hour business center. Each room has a safe, coffeemaker, microwave, minifridge, and ironing board. This hotel is centrally located for lovers of the arts; it's within a few minutes of the Boca Raton Museum of Art, The Children's Museum of Boca Raton, and the International Museum of Cartoon Art, along with several performing arts companies.

THE COLONY HOTEL & CABANA CLUB $$
525 East Atlantic Ave.
Delray Beach
(561) 276-4123 or (800) 552-2363
www.thecolonyhotel.com

When you walk into the yellow Mediterranean fantasy called The Colony, with its red-tiled roof and its twin towers with Moorish arches and windows, you almost expect to see Humphrey Bogart and Ingrid Bergman having a drink at the streetside bar, or in one of the shaded alcoves just inside the pastel-walled, wicker-filled, high ceiling-fanned lobby.

The Colony Hotel was built in the golden year of 1926, and the same family has owned it since 1935. It's a Delray Beach Historic Landmark and is on the National Trust for Historic Preservation's list of Historic Hotels. The 48 guest rooms and 22 two-bedroom suites feel almost like rooms in an elegant private home. Many still have the original walnut-wood furniture (which has aged beautifully), with hardwood floors of Dade County pine, vintage tropical accents, evocative artworks by local artists, dark wood headboards, period lamps, wicker chairs, and Venetian blinds. The walls are tropical pinks and yellows. Each unit has an ironing board; there's a paper waiting outside your door in the morning, and a free continental breakfast waiting for you downstairs. Pets accepted, $25 per day/per pet.

The Colony also has its own private beach club for guests, called the Cabana Club, five minutes away. Here, amidst seagrapes and coconut palms, is a 250-foot spread of private beach, with a salt-water pool, cabanas and umbrellas on the beach, and lunch available.

Golf? There are more than a hundred courses within a 40-minute drive of the Colony. Tennis? The renowned Delray Beach Tennis Center—with several major tournaments a year—is just seven blocks away. Shopping? The hotel has seven interesting shops, ranging from clothing to toiletries, and from gifts to jewelry. And, of course, the hotel's sitting on Atlantic Avenue, Delray's beautiful downtown boulevard of boutiques, bistros, galleries, and clubs.

COURTYARD BY MARRIOTT
BOCA RATON $$

2000 N.W. Executive Center Ct.

Boca Raton

(561) 241-7070 or (800) 450-4442

www.marriott.com

This hotel was built in 1994, and each of the 152 guest rooms here has been recently renovated. The hotel is very close to the swanky shops and restaurants of Boca Town Center, and also to I-95—which means you're no more than an hour from just about anywhere in the region.

Each of the comfortable, contemporary rooms has a coffeemaker, hair dryer, iron/ironing board. The pool area is expansive and pleasant. The Courtyard Café is open for breakfast, and there are more good restaurants in Boca Raton than you could ever hope to sample. If you've a hankerin' to hit the links, there are numerous golf courses within just a few miles. And the on-site fitness center is open 24/7.

i There are a few things you should never leave home (or hotel) without in South Florida. One of them is sunscreen. Unless you live here, you have no real idea of how strong the sun actually is—even in the winter. In fact, we South Florida locals are always warned by our dermatologists not to drive with our left arm resting on the window. And to always put sunscreen on . . . even if we're only running errands. It's advice you may come to appreciate after a few days here.

CRANE'S BEACHHOUSE
HOTEL & TIKI BAR $$$

82 Gleason St.

Delray Beach

(561) 278-1700 or (866) 372-7263

www.cranesbeachhouse.com

Crane's is one of the places where South County residents head for a great time—even if they're not staying there. The Tiki Bar—filled with tropical foliage and right next to the waterfall pool—is one of the area's hottest places to meet and greet, and you may see local celebrities, writers, artists, and politicians there. In fact, Crane's is known for its fun events, such as the Barbie and Ken Look-Alike Contest in 2009 to celebrate the iconic couple's 50th birthday.

Opened in 2001, the hotel is right by the beach and within walking distance of downtown Delray and Atlantic Avenue, where you can wander amidst all types of shops and galleries and all types of people, along brick sidewalks illuminated by gas-lit street lamps. The 27 rooms at Crane's Beachhouse each have one king-bed and one queen, and most have full kitchens. Each of them is funky and charming in its own way, with beds with carved headboards, colorful murals by local artists, distinctive wall sconces and furniture (real wood), and an ambience that's very tropical and very Key West.

There are dozens of good restaurants nearby, ranging from innovative Oriental (Lemongrass Asian Bistro) to seafood (City Oyster & Sushi Bar) to pizza (Rotelli's) to swanky American (32 East). In addition, you'll find art galleries, ice-cream shops, and chocolatiers. And you'll find, as well, a very colorful people-parade on weekend evenings, generally running into the wee hours.

When you stay at Crane's, you're ideally positioned to take advantage of downtown Delray's vibrant outdoors events ranging from Art & Jazz on the Avenue (live jazz, bluegrass, and pop music, plus plenty of food, along a three-block stretch of Atlantic Avenue that's closed to traffic) to the half-dozen or so major art festivals that take place every winter, as well as the tennis tournaments (often luring big names) at the Delray Tennis Center.

DELRAY BEACH MARRIOTT $$$$
10 N. Ocean Blvd.
Delray Beach
(561) 274-3200 or (877) 389-0169
www.marriottdelraybeach.com

This is an AAA Four-Diamond property. You can't beat the location, right on the beach and within walking distance of Delray's beautifully restored downtown. Having been built back in the 1930s, the hotel is a masterpiece of Old Mediterranean colors and architecture with earthen exterior, red roof, and rounded arches. This was previously another hotel. Marriott took possession of the property in 1999, and today the 180 guest rooms and 88 suites are stylish and luxurious, with tropical colors and Caribbean and Country-French touches in the furniture and the ambience. Each room has one king and one double bed, along with mini-bar, safe, coffeemaker, Wi-Fi, and free morning newspaper. In addition, some hotel packages offer continental breakfast.

If you're interested in doing business, there's a business center and 12 flexible meeting rooms with 14,000 square feet. If you'd prefer to work up a sweat, there's a fitness center with personal trainer available and a beautiful pool area. On the other hand, if you'd prefer to just relax and let someone pamper you, the N Spa has a hundred ways to do it, with touch therapies, body and facial treatments, and a variety of massages that will relax and rejuvenate every muscle in your body.

Later on, at The Seacrest Grill, you can surround yourself with contemporary-American ambience while sampling some of the freshest offerings from the ocean that you can see outside. If you'd rather eat in your bathing suit, you can do so at Cascade's, which offers informal poolside dining and snacks. End the evening at O'Grady's Bar in the lobby, where there's live entertainment and smooth cocktails and drinks.

EMBASSY SUITES HOTEL
BOCA RATON $$$
661 N.W. Fifty-third St.
Boca Raton
(561) 994-8200 or (800) EMBASSY
www.hilton.com

This hotel was built in 1994 and is located near I-95. Each of the 264 suites has a private bedroom and a living area. Suites are well-equipped with a microwave, refrigerator, coffeemaker, hair dryer, iron/ironing board, and either one king-size bed or two doubles. There's a nice pool area with a whirlpool, a fitness center, and high-speed wireless Internet throughout along with a business center. The rooms are comfortable and the bedding is plush. There's complimentary cooked-to-order breakfast and complimentary manager's cocktail reception. The Twin Palms Restaurant is inside a beautiful tropical atrium and features excellent steaks and seafood. And tons of other distinctive Boca Raton restaurants are nearby, along with numerous corporate offices and business campuses within a few blocks.

South County Vacation Rentals

There are not a lot of vacation rental homes available in South County. But if you'd like to look for one, these Web sites may be helpful.

- www.vacationrentals.com
- www.escaperental.com
- www.vacationrentalsbocaraton.com
- www.alwaysonvacation.com
- www.forgetaway.com
- www.cheapleaf.com
- www.vacationhomerentals.com
- www.vamoose.com

HILTON GARDEN INN BOCA RATON $$$
8201 Congress Ave.
Boca Raton
(561) 988-6110 or (800) HILTONS
www.hiltongardeninn.com

Each of the 149 rooms at the Hilton Garden Inn has one king and one double bed, and there is an extra per-person charge for more than five in a room. Built in 2002, the hotel is close to I-95, offering easy access to anywhere in South Florida; you're 10 minutes from downtown Boca, a half-hour from Fort Lauderdale and West Palm Beach, and an hour from Miami. Each room has a microwave, coffeemaker, refrigerator, and complimentary *USA Today* at your door every morning. The rooms are done with touches of both Old English and tropical. And the pool is heated in winter. There's a business center and a well-equipped fitness center. The Great American Grill serves a breakfast buffet along with lunch and dinner; The Pavilion Lounge & Patio offers a place to get away from it all with a tall, cool one; and the Pavilion Pantry offers you a 24/7 convenience-store opportunity to pick up some food to satisfy your munchies.

HOLIDAY INN EXPRESS— BOCA RATON $$
8144 West Glades Rd.
Boca Raton
(561) 482-7070 or (800) 465-4329
www.holidayinn.com

Holiday Inn is another chain at which you expect comfortable accommodations, a number of amenities, and a reasonable price. It's been hosting millions of American families and business travelers over the past several decades. This one's in West Boca Raton, right at the Florida Turnpike, about 7 miles from downtown Boca. The Holiday Inn Express has 97 rooms, each with one king or two double beds. It was built in the mid-1970s and renovated in 2004. Its turnpike location means that you can be anywhere on the Gold Coast—from Miami to the south to Jupiter to the north—within an hour. And its Glades Road location means that it's just 2 miles from tony Town Center Mall (and it's actually located in the Lakeside Shopping Center, with hundreds of shops and restaurants in the immediate area). Each room comes with coffeemaker, iron/ironing board, free morning paper, and free continental breakfast. Some come with minifridges. You can work up a sweat in the fitness room, cool off in the pool, or stay in touch with the office at the business center.

HOLIDAY INN HIGHLAND BEACH $$$
2809 S. Ocean Blvd.
Highland Beach
(561) 278-6241 or (888) 465-4329
www.highlandbeachholidayinn.com
Along a narrow strip of land on the ocean just north of Boca Raton, three- and four-story palaces of varying styles line the beachfront, generally eliciting loud gasps from anyone who drives by. Most of us can't afford to live in Highland Beach. But many of us can afford to stay there for a week or two, at this excellent Holiday Inn. Although the hotel was built in the late 1960s, it has been renovated periodically. The 109 guest rooms and six suites offer a wonderful opportunity to live—at least temporarily—in this ritzy little enclave. There are no stores in Highland Beach; in fact, other than those beachfront "palaces" and some condominiums, there's pretty much just a small fire station and city hall/post office. Nonetheless, you're just 3 miles from downtown Boca and 3 miles from downtown Delray. Rooms here have coffeemakers, minifridges, iron/ironing boards, and free morning paper, and microwaves are available on request. A full-service restaurant called Latitudes proffers breakfast, lunch, and dinner, while Cabanas Lounge has live entertainment. As is the Holiday Inn custom, kids under 12 eat free. A fitness center takes care of your exercise needs, and a business center takes care of your professional ones. It's a family-oriented place. Just make sure to keep your eyes on the road as you drive past those beachfront fantasy-homes!

RENAISSANCE BOCA
  RATON HOTEL $$$
2000 N.W. Nineteenth St.
Boca Raton
(561) 368-5252 or (800) HOTELS1
www.marriott.com

This is a boutique hotel with a distinctive atmosphere. The lobby is filled with marble and features a working fireplace (yes, it can sometimes come in handy if the winter weather is chilly or damp). Public spaces and guest rooms (184 rooms, five suites, with kings or two doubles) now exude an air of quality and comfort, with an interesting decor that combines tropical, modern, and Old English elements. Coffeemakers are in all rooms, along with iron/ironing boards and a free morning paper at your door. The deck has a heated pool and a whirlpool. There's an on-site fitness center and a complete business center. Dining options include the Umbria Restaurant, with the flavors of Italy (open for breakfast, lunch, and dinner) and the Oasis Café & Pool Bar, at poolside, open for lunch and dinner.

This hotel has a premium Boca location. The Renaissance is convenient to the Town Center Mall and Glades Plaza, with over 200 shops and 30 restaurants. Good restaurants nearby include Sushi Masa Japanese, Seasons 52 for American, and The Melting Pot for fondue. Everything else in Boca is close, as well, from the colleges and universities to the major office complexes.

SEAGATE HOTEL & SPA $$$
1000 E. Atlantic Ave.
Delray Beach
(561) 665-4800 or (877) 57-SEAGATE
www.theseagatehotel.com
At the Seagate, island ease meets urban-chic, and the ocean soothes you as the city stirs you. The Seagate is one of the newest additions to South County's list of luxury boutique properties, having opened in late 2009. If location is everything, the Seagate's in the perfect place. It's situated at the end of Atlantic Avenue, Delray Beach's chic downtown thoroughfare, which is filled with some of the hottest dining

spots and clubs in South Florida, along with a unique collection of shops and boutiques. And it's just a block from the beach.

The hotel's 162 rooms come with coffeemaker, microwave, minifridge, iron/ironing board, and continental breakfast. The decor is a mixture of chic/moderne and striking colors and textures, emphasizing dark woods and tropical touches; and the marble bathrooms feature bubble-jet bathtubs. There's high-speed wireless Internet, a private beach club with a British colonial style, oceanview restaurants, and water sports rentals. There's an award-winning chef at the Atlantic Grille, which boasts innovative contemporary cuisine, an emphasis on natural ingredients, and a variety of private nooks. The hotel has a soft-nautical theme, and the public places feature 5,000-gallon aquariums. And there's meeting and event space, both inside and out.

The Seagate Spa & Fitness Center is 8,000 square feet of first-class products, services, and equipment, along with a yoga center and several private-treatment suites. Here, the approach is holistic and natural. And you're guaranteed to walk out of the spa feeling 100 percent different than when you walked in.

THE SUNDY HOUSE $$$
106 S. Swinton Ave.
Delray Beach
(561) 272-5678 or (800) 865-4495
www.sundyhouse.com

The Sundy House has been legendary around these parts since its opening 12 years ago. It's actually an old house that's been around since the early 1900s, an expansive Victorian inn with an Old Florida ambience, a surrounding acre of tropical vegetation, legendary Sunday brunches in its airy restaurant, and a wicker and woodsy airiness. In fact, it's listed on the National Register of Historic Places.

Each of the 11 themed rooms has original artwork, natural elements native to South Florida, eclectic furniture with dark wicker and carved woods, and views of the beautiful gardens. And one of them is a private cottage with full kitchen and dining room, living room with fireplace, and master bedroom with a hot tub.

The award-winning restaurant has specialties from around the world, indoor or al fresco dining, and an extensive wine list. The Roux Bamboux Lounge is a sophisticated gathering place for before or after dinner. A continental breakfast is complimentary. And when you go to the Sunday brunch, you'll run out of appetite long before you run out of choices.

You'll find some unique touches at the Sundy House, like Florida's only freshwater swimming pond—with fish in it. A beautiful gazebo for contemplative or romantic moments. An ambience of serenity amidst the action of downtown Delray.

The beach is only a mile away (and Sundy House provides free shuttle transportation). And the shops and restaurants of Atlantic Avenue and Pineapple Grove are just a few blocks away.

WYNDHAM GARDEN HOTEL, BOCA RATON $$
1950 Glades Rd.
Boca Raton
(561) 368-5200 or (877) 999-3223
www.wyndham.com

The Wyndham Garden looks much like a beautiful Spanish hacienda with tile roofs, stucco surfaces, stone fountains, and a courtyard with colorful foliage. And this hacienda is perfectly situated for exploring the Boca Raton/Delray Beach area because it's right on I-95. You can be in the Palm Beaches in a half-hour and in North County in only 15 minutes more.

Although the hotel has been a Boca landmark since the 1970s—until recently as a Holiday Inn—it's been remodeled. And now the technological touches inside the walls are in perfect synchronicity with the relaxing ambience outside of them.

The 184 rooms have kings or two doubles, and coffeemakers, iron/ironing boards, and free morning paper come standard. Suites also have microwaves and minifridges. And all the wonders of Glades Road are right out the door. Restaurants such as the Cheesecake Factory and Brewzzi's are within walking distance, as is the beautiful Town Center Mall with anchors such as Nordstom, Saks, and Bloomingdale's, and more than 150 shops and bistros. (Town Center is the place to really see the beautiful people of Boca. And if you keep a keen eye out you'll often see a celebrity or two.) As you head west on Glades Road, you'll pass an incredible assortment of restaurants, ranging from bagels to sushi.

The Wyndham has a nice restaurant called Boca Cucina that specializes in Italian. There's also a Starbucks on the premises for those caffeine cravings, as well as the Wyndham Garden Café lounge. There's a fitness center, business center, pool, hot tub, and meeting space. Pets accepted up to 20 pounds; $75 flat fee.

CENTRAL COUNTY

Resorts

THE BREAKERS $$$$
One South County Rd.
Palm Beach
(561) 655-6611 or (800) 273-2537
www.thebreakers.com

When you get a room at The Breakers, you're not just getting a room, you're getting a piece of history. As noted earlier, this is the Queen of Palm Beach County hotels. The 540 rooms and suites range up to $6,000 per night (yes, $6,000), although—especially in low season—there are occasionally moderately priced rooms to be had.

Set amidst 140 beachfront acres on one of the most valuable pieces of real estate in the world, The Breakers has 472 guest rooms and 68 suites. The resort has spent a quarter-of-a-billion dollars over the past decade to integrate all the most modern conveniences and technologies without changing the things that have made it so special to so many people for so many years.

There are nine restaurants on-site, including French (L'Escalier), steak (The Flagler Steakhouse), spa (The Beach Club), seafood (the outdoor Ocean Grill, or the indoor Seafood Bar), Asian (Echo), Classic American (Top of the Point). There are five lounges; at the elegant Tapestry Bar, for instance, you can wine on cocktails while you dine on caviar.

If you want to be treated like a king or president, have a treatment or two at The Spa at The Breakers, which has been called one of the top 25 spas in North America. Get your golf game back in gear at the Rees Jones or the Ocean courses. Dive into one of the five oceanfront pools or slide into one of the four whirlpools.

Browse the 11 on-site boutiques, including Burberry, Guerlain, and Ralph Lauren, or just wander around the stately lobby and admire the art work and the elegant style. Walk down to the seawall and the beach just beyond. Or stretch your legs and walk to the nearby sidewalk cafes, or the shops on Worth Avenue.

You're only a few minutes away from the excitement of West Palm Beach, just across the bridge. But the nice thing about The Breakers is that you're also in a world of your own—a world of luxury, taste, and history. And a world to which you'll return, again and again.

FOUR SEASONS RESORT
PALM BEACH $$$$
2800 S. Ocean Blvd.
Palm Beach
(561) 582-2800 or (800) 819-5053
www.fourseasons.com

Four Seasons stands for world-class resorts for a discriminating clientele who expect the best in accommodations, amenities, and service. And this Four Seasons maintains the standard.

Built in 1987, the hotel sits right on the ocean. Even the tiniest of details is thought about in great detail before you even walk in the door. Each of the 197 guest rooms (which includes either one king or two doubles) and 13 suites has a balcony with table and chairs overlooking the ocean, the gardens, or the pool. All bathrooms are marble with soft, think robes and fine toiletries. Each unit has a coffeemaker, minifridge, iron/ironing board, complimentary morning paper, flat-screen TV, hair dryer, and safe. And the rooms are bright and airy with comfortable furniture and light colors.

The Spa at the Four Seasons is a beautiful hideaway with the finest natural products in the world and an atmosphere of secluded luxury. Take the Seagrass Room, for instance; it's the ideal spot for couples, with two treatment beds, a private steam room, and a lounging area. The Willow Room, on the other hand, is what the hotel calls a "private gentlemen's retreat," where a guy can get a haircut or facial while watching a ballgame on a huge TV. At the Four Seasons, you can even arrange to get a massage in your room.

Then there's the dining. The Restaurant is open for dinner only. Here you can enjoy fresh seafood and South Florida specialties such as Yellowtail Snapper Florida Keys in a contemporary setting, along with innovative specialty cocktails. There's live entertainment on weekends. The more casual Ocean Bistro is open for breakfast, lunch, and dinner, serving classic American comfort-food.

The 24-hour fitness center offers an incredible assortment of machines and equipment, an available personal trainer, and classes such as yoga, tai chi, and pilates. The pool overlooks the ocean, and attendants are available with lemon water, chilled face cloths, Evian spritz, and fresh fruit during daylight hours. Golf? Guests at the Four Seasons have privileges at the nearby Atlantis Golf Club, which offers an Old Florida ambience and superb greens. There's tennis at the hotel, with a pro shop and lessons from a pro. Every conceivable type of water sport is available on the beach, including sea-turtle watching. There's a full-service business center. And the Four Seasons has 22,000 square feet of flexible meeting space, from boardrooms to ballrooms.

OMPHOY OCEAN RESORT $$$$
2842 S. Ocean Blvd.
Palm Beach
(561) 459-2711
www.omphoy.com

You may never stay at a resort with a more interesting name—nor a more distinctive style. The Omphoy opened in 2009. It's the only oceanfront boutique hotel on the island of Palm Beach, and it was the first new hotel on the Palm Beach oceanfront in 18 years. It's only minutes from Worth Avenue, one of the most famous shopping streets in the world. The 134 rooms have either one king or two queen beds. All have porcelain floor tiles; custom-designed furniture with dark wickers and light walls, in a sort of seaside/modern motif; and views of either the Atlantic or the Intracoastal.

The hotel was designed to evoke a sense of well-bring in its guests, and of peace of mind, to be a place where the stresses of modern life seem to melt away, and the spirit seems to be re-born under the indulgence of a superb staff and an enlightened design. The design emphasizes the luminescence of moving water and is tinged with Oriental influences. The pool area is lined with palms, and there's a soft waterfall. This peaceful, natural ambience continues with the appropriately named Exhale Spa, with world-class products and services and a Meditation Garden with three teak pagodas and calming fountains.

Reigning in the kitchen at Michelle Bernstein's at The Omphoy is the celebrity chef of the same name, a 2008 James Beard award-winner who presents wonderful seafood, meats, and imaginative appetizers. You can enjoy it all with floor-to-ceiling ocean views, and a wonderful wine list, as well. And the O-Bar has quickly become one of Palm Beach's places to see-and-be-seen.

PALM BEACH MARRIOTT SINGER ISLAND BEACH RESORT & SPA $$$$
3800 N. Ocean Dr.
Palm Beach, Singer Island
(561) 340-1700 or (888) 213-0414
www.marriott.com
The 239 rooms in this Singer Island resort are all suites because this is a condominium hotel. The units are all privately owned, but managed by Marriott, which acquired the property in 2009. Both the facility and the service have already been improved by the Marriott brand. All of these one- and two-bedroom units have separate living rooms, and many have ocean or Intracoastal views. Each has stainless-steel appliances, granite countertops, and flat-screen TVs. They're inviting and airy, with comfortable modern furniture, light-colored pastel walls, and eclectic pieces of art. Each one has a coffeemaker, microwave, private bath, fully equipped kitchen, iron/ironing board, and a complimentary *USA Today* each morning.

Outside is a beautiful beach and a multi-faceted resort, and a hundred ways to enjoy them. There's a spa that will caress your senses as well as your soul, a gift shop, a complete business center, a fitness center, two swimming pools, a whirlpool, and a Kid's Club. Nearby are three golf courses, hiking and biking trails, kayaking, sailing, fishing, a nature trail, scuba diving, snorkeling, surfing, and tennis. If you're here to frolic, you've got the whole Atlantic Ocean right in front of you. And if you're here to do business, there are 12 meeting rooms of various sizes, and also the Outdoor Terrace for larger events.

The Marriott has two dining choices. Solu serves seafood, steaks, and chops, along with other American favorites. The Lagoon Grill serves up more casual dishes.

And most of Palm Beach County is within a 20-minute drive in any direction.

RITZ-CARLTON PALM BEACH $$$$
100 S. Ocean Blvd.
Manalapan
(561) 533-6000 or (800) 542-8680
www.ritzcarlton.com
Manalapan is a tiny community just south of West Palm Beach with 321 lucky residents

who live the good life. And it's the perfect spot for a Ritz-Carlton. As those who have stayed here before know, a Ritz-Carlton is, perhaps more than anything else, an *experience*.

A tan, red-roofed castle rising on the beach, this hotel was built in 1991. Its 310 rooms, most of which have either a king or two doubles, are set amidst seven tropical acres and a private beach. All rooms feature marble baths with rain showerheads and separate bathtubs, Italian custom-made mahogany furniture, wireless Internet access, and complimentary morning paper. There's a state-of-the art fitness facility for those who want to stay in shape, and the comprehensive business center is very well-equipped. The pool area is one of the most beautiful in Florida. Tennis courts are on-site, and excellent golf is just a couple of miles away. Parasailing, jet-skiing, and kayaking are among the water sports offered.

You'll never taste cookies again like the ones offered in the Club Lounge in the afternoon, and you'll enjoy at least one of the five dining options on the premises. At Temple Orange, you can eat indoors or al fresco; either way, you'll see the ocean while you enjoy Italian/Mediterranean cuisine. This restaurant is open for breakfast, lunch, or dinner. At the Stir Bar and Terrace you can enjoy cocktails and light dishes during the day and at night, bask in the glow of the outdoor fire-pit while enjoying Flames of the Fire desserts (such as crème puff tic tac toe) and international coffees. The Breeze is an ocean-front cafe offering Caribbean-inspired specialties and drinks for lunch (no charge for the view!). At the world-class Eau Spa you can sit in a swinging chair in the Garden while indulging in imaginative goodies that take the senses for a very pleasurable ride, before your treatment, after your treatment, or even without a treatment. And you can even choose an option called Oceanfront Cabana Dining in which a custom meal is prepared only for you and your party in a private cabana.

Then there's the aforementioned Eau Spa with its water-gardens and rainfalls, and its 42,000 square feet of pure indulgence and pampering. In the Self-Centered Garden you can relax on a swinging chair while swishing your feet in a pool of shallow water. Or you can relax on waterfall benches while being caressed by warm, gently falling water. Create your own beauty kit at the Scrub and Polish Bar. Or get a massage, perhaps using aromatherapy, or warm stones, or thermal hydrating of the hands and feet. There are 19 private spa villas . . . three of them for couples only.

Hotels and Motels

BEST WESTERN INN OF AMERICA $
7051 Seacrest Blvd.
Lantana
(561) 588-0456 or (877) 915-2378
www.bestwestern.com
Best Western Inn of America offers convenient lodging in the quiet little town of Lantana, just south of the Palm Beaches. Its 68 rooms have either one king-size bed or two queens. And they all come with free Internet, coffeemaker, microwave, minifridge, iron/ironing board, in-room safe, free morning paper, and continental breakfast. There's a heated pool, as well. Lantana is an interesting little town with pleasant surprises, one of them being the road to the beach, which is lined with all types of funky, one-of-a-kind shops and seafood places with fresh catches. Lantana was also the home of—until the 1990s—the *National Enquirer*

(and its 100-foot-high Christmas tree), which helped make Palm Beach County famous in the preceding decades.

BRADLEY PARK HOTEL $$$$
280 Sunset Ave.
Palm Beach
(561) 832-7050 or (800) 822-4116
www.bradleyparkhotel.com

The Bradley Park Hotel was built in 1924 by a flamboyant gambler named Cornel E. R. Bradley (and nicknamed "Mr. Lucky") to house the high-rollers who came to gamble at his Beach Club casino next-door. Today, the hotel has been designated a Historical Landmark by the Palm Beach Historical Society.

From its earth-tone colors to its arched Moorish windows and French doors, to its brown tile roof and its green awnings, the Bradley Park exudes understated Palm Beach elegance. When you walk in, you'll be stepping on a marble floor and you'll be surrounded by beautiful antique furnishings, thick Persian carpets, and detailed ceiling murals.

There are 32 guest rooms and suites, all of which have either king- or queen-size beds. Accommodations come with coffeemakers, microwaves, and iron/ironing boards, and most have full kitchens. There's a charge for more than two adults in a room, at a rate of $20 per person per night. Rooms have a definite European ambience, with dark woods, carved headboards, Tiffany lamps, fine English or Persian rugs, and traditional art on the walls.

Coco Palm Beach is the hotel's restaurant, offering innovative Pan-Asian cuisine with names such as Crouching Tiger/Lotus Blossom or Shanghai Surprise, in a sophisticated ambience. At the C'est Si Bon Gourmet Market downstairs you can pick from large selections of fine cheeses, wines, champagnes, and other items to enjoy in your room or at a picnic on the nearby beach. And if you'd like to sample some of Palm Beach's other culinary spots, the bistros and outdoor cafes of Royal Poinciana Way are just around the corner. Pets up to 45 pounds allowed for a $75 flat fee.

BRAZILIAN COURT
HOTEL & BEACH CLUB $$$$
301 Australian Ave.
Palm Beach
(561) 983-4292 or (888) 706-0395
www.thebraziliancourt.com

If you're looking for a boutique hotel with classic Palm Beach elegance—and a raft of awards to prove it—look no farther than the Brazilian Court. This hotel has won awards from major publications such as *Condé Nast Traveler* and *Travel & Leisure,* and it's been featured in *Vanity Fair* and *Architectural Digest.* It's got an AAA four-Diamond rating, and a Mobil Four-Star rating. It's won the *Wine Spectator* Best of Award for Excellence. The hotel's Café Boulud is run by two of the most famous "cooks" in America, Chef Daniel Boulud and Executive Chef Zach Bell. And this yellow building with red roof and wrought-iron and wood accents exudes atmosphere.

Surrounded by tropical courtyards, the Brazilian Court provides world-class service. The hotel opened in 1926, the Golden Age of Palm Beach. The entire facility was renovated in 2008 and now has 80 studios and suites. The colors are European, the millwork is mahogany, the cabinetry is hand-crafted, the ambience colonial, and the new technological touches include whirlpool bathtubs. Pets allowed, under 25 pounds; $100 flat fee.

Concierge service is 24/7. The pool is heated in winter, alongside a hot tub. There's a library, in-room safes, a fitness center, and private meeting, dining, and banquet facilities. There's a world-renowned Frederic Fekkai Salon & Spa, one of only five in the world. And—oh, yes—a private beach club for hotel guests a few blocks away, to which you're chauffeured by limousine and at which you can enjoy seaside dining.

The Brazilian Court is also the home of one of Palm Beach County's most celebrated restaurants. Chef Daniel Boulud instantly made it so when he opened his Café Boulud here in 2003, the first outpost of his famous New York restaurant. Café Boulud is richly appointed and bright, with huge, colorful paintings and murals. The menu features traditional French with a splash of international, and much of the produce comes from Boulud's own garden.

Just outside the doors are the best of Palm Beach—the beach, shops, galleries, and restaurants of Worth Avenue, plus dozens of championship golf courses. And just across the bridge is the best of West Palm Beach—the Kravis Center for the Performing Arts, City Place, performing arts companies, the Armory Art Center, and the Norton and Flagler Museums.

CHESTERFIELD PALM BEACH $$$$
Cocoanut Row
Palm Beach
(561) 659-5800 or (800) 243-7871
www.chesterfieldpb.com
National Geographic Traveler called The Chesterfield "a gem of a hotel." It's a boutique, Four-Star hotel, and you'll see why as soon as you pull up. Built in 1926, it's been designated a Historic Landmark. It's an imposing white-stucco building with red-and-white awnings, ornate carving around the red-tile roof, and

Moorish arched windows. On arrival, you'll be welcomed with a glass of sherry and cookies. You'll soon find that the 52 rooms and suites, each decorated differently, are done in a comfortable blend of Victorian and Palm Beach, with marble bathrooms, soft bathrobes, and French doors.

The location is prime—3 blocks from the beach, five minutes from great golf, within 15 minutes of numerous cultural venues, and 3 blocks from Worth Avenue, where names such as Chanel, Hermes, Neiman Marcus, Tiffany, and Saks Fifth Avenue are only the tip of the world-class shopping list. The Leopard Lounge restaurant serves international favorites in a luxurious Old English setting, with live entertainment every night. The adjoining Leopard Bar is one of Palm Beach's hottest nightspots. And the pool area is a wonderful hideaway, surrounded by low pink-stucco walls and vegetation.

THE COLONY PALM BEACH $$$$
155 Hammon Ave.
Palm Beach
(561) 655-5430 or (800) 521-5525
www.thecolonypalmbeach.com
This is another one of the old-time Palm Beach boutique hotels that oozes charm and sophistication. Built in 1947, The Colony—known as a gathering place for the island's rich-and-famous as well as its literati—has 83 rooms and seven villas. Its soft-yellow-and-white exterior and classic architecture and awnings suggest a first-class experience. And the hotel delivers.

It's recently been renovated, and the guest rooms and public areas are set in classic British West Indies furnishings and decor. The rooms have pale-yellow walls, draperies with tropical motifs, and imported Mahogany tables, chairs, dressers, and armoires.

43

The suites all have living rooms with sofa beds. If you're the type who needs room, lots-of-room, you can rent the Presidential Penthouse, with 1,640 square feet and spectacular views of Palm Beach and the Atlantic Ocean; the Duke of Windsor Penthouse, with 1,910 square feet with floors of polished Jerusalem Stone and panoramic veranda views; or the seven Mediterranean villas that run up to 2,700 square feet, each with its own private pool and sundeck.

The people-watching is great at the Polo Bar or the airy Palm Court. And you never know what people you might end up watching; recent guests have included Presidents Bill Clinton and George W. Bush, Prince Edward, and Princess Sofia. Earlier guests have included the Duke and Duchess of Windsor; Marjorie Merriweather Post, the daughter of C. W. Post of cereal fame (and a former Palm Beach resident); along with show-business and fashion luminaries such as Liza Minnelli, Victor Borge, Bill Blass, Liberace, George Hamilton, and Phyllis Diller.

The Colony is also known for the superb cabaret entertainment and well-known performers at the Royal Room Supper Club, many of whom come direct from Broadway or prominent Manhattan clubs. In fact, the *Palm Beach Post* has called the Royal Room "probably the best place for cabaret on the planet."

There's live music at the Polo Steakhouse, ranging from jazz to Motown, as well as some of the best steak dishes in the county, often prepared at your table and which can also be eaten al fresco on a patio. Around the corner is the storied Worth Avenue, a classic example of Addison Mizner architecture, the world's most famous shops (among them Cartier, Tiffany, Gucci, Ferragamo, Tourneau, Neiman-Marcus, and Saks Fifth Avenue),

high-end boutiques, and world-class art galleries, in addition to wonderful restaurants and hand-dipping chocolatiers.

COMFORT INN & SUITES, LANTANA $–$$
1221 Hypoluxo Rd.
Lantana
(561) 582-7878 or (877) 424-6423
www.comfortinn.com
This Comfort Inn is conveniently located in a town that's close to the center of Palm Beach County, and pretty close to anywhere. One of the things it's closest to, though, is the beach. Lantana's beach—and the roads to it—are laid-back and colorful, with every color of the rainbow represented in wooden shops and in the sailboats and wind-surfing craft in the waters.

The hotel's 60 rooms and suites come with either one king or two queens, and all have coffeemakers, microwaves, free high-speed Internet, minifridges, iron/ironing boards, and free morning paper. All come with a complimentary full breakfast. Suites also have bathtub whirlpools and sofa beds. There's a business center, newly expanded fitness room, heated outdoor pool, and laundry facility. And you're only 15 minutes from the Palm Beaches to the north, and 15 minutes from Delray Beach and Boca to the south.

COURTYARD BY MARRIOTT BOYNTON BEACH $$
1601 N. Congress Ave.
Boynton Beach
(561) 737-4600 or (888) 236-2427
www.courtyardboyntonbeach.com
The Boynton Beach area is convenient to both South and Central County—you're only about 15 minutes away from Atlantic

Avenue in Delray and the shops and restaurants of Boca Raton, and you're the same distance from the attractions of West Palm Beach. The hotel and all of its 168 rooms—with one king or two queens—have been completely renovated recently. Each room has a microwave and an ironing board. There's a nice lobby cafe, along with workareas. The pool is heated in winter, and the hotel also has meeting facilities. Rooms and public areas are pleasant and contemporary, and there's a "Go" board in the lobby that lists such things as local weather forecasts, attractions, and what's going on in the area.

CROWNE PLAZA WEST PALM BEACH $$$
1601 Belvedere Rd.
West Palm Beach
(561) 689-6400 or (888) 689-6892
www.cpwestpalmbeach.com

The Crowne Plaza is a touch of urban sophistication on the periphery of downtown West Palm Beach. It's located adjacent to Palm Beach International Airport, and only a few minutes from anywhere in town. And it's within close proximity to 140 golf courses. The interior is a sharp-looking combination of Moderne and Art Deco, earth-tones and dark woods, and nearly half of the 219 guest rooms are actually suites. The hotel has excellent meeting space—fitting for a hotel next to an airport and not far from the Palm Beach County Convention Center—and there's also a beauty salon.

The Kravis Center for the Performing Arts, the shops and restaurants of City Place, and the Flagler Drive downtown waterfront are all within minutes. The rooms and suites come fully equipped, with coffeemakers, microwaves, minifridges, iron/ironing boards, and free morning paper. The Atrium Restaurant

My Palm Beach County

"Living in Palm Beach County is like living in a postcard—picture perfect every day!"

—Jorge Pesquera, President & CEO, Palm Beach County Convention and Visitors Bureau

serves good old all-American favorites for breakfast, lunch, and dinner, and the adjacent Atrium Lounge also has a full dinner menu.

DAYS INN WEST PALM BEACH $
2300 Forty-fifth St.
West Palm Beach
(561) 689-0450 or (800) 329-7466
www.daysinn.com

Located just to the north of West Palm Beach, the Days Inn is ideally situated for exploration of both Central and Northern Palm Beach County. And, even better, it's right on I-95—so you have immediate highway access to anywhere.

The hotel won the Days Inn Chairman's Award for Excellence in 2009. It was built in the mid-1970s, and the 180 rooms come with coffeemakers, iron/ironing boards, and complimentary morning newspapers outside your door; in addition, some have microwaves and minifridges for a fee. A small business center is on-site. Pets accepted; $30 flat fee.

There's a large swimming pool, a hot tub, putting green, shuffleboard courts, and an IHOP right on the premises that is open 24/7. The nightlife and cultural amenities of the Palm Beaches are only a few minutes to the south, and the golf, baseball, and shopping of North County a few minutes to the north.

FAIRFIELD INN & SUITES
PALM BEACH $$$
2870 S. Ocean Blvd.
Palm Beach
(561) 582-2585 or (888) 236-2427
www.fairfieldinn.com

The Fairfield Inn & Suites, open since 2000, has 98 rooms and suites with a view of the water. Totally renovated in 2007, the hotel is backed by the Intracoastal Waterway, and fronted by the Atlantic, on a choice piece of Palm Beach real estate. If you drive up to the hotel via the ocean road (A1A) from the south, you'll pass magnificent mansions owned by some of the richest people in the world, in styles ranging from Classical Greek to Spanish/Mediterranean to Moorish-castle, fronting an ocean that's light on beachgoers but heavy on startlingly clear blues, greens, and aquas.

You can enjoy an Early Eats complimentary hot/cold breakfast before starting to explore this Oz-like island. Marriott knows how to treat visiting businesspeople and meetings, so each room has a comfortable desk, with wireless Internet, and there are several meeting rooms with flexible space. There's a fitness center, a business center, large pool, and even miniature golf. You'll find several good places to eat, ranging from deli to seafood, within a mile or so. Laundry facilities are onsite. And the magic of Worth Avenue and other smart shopping boulevards such as Royal Poinciana Way are just down the street.

HAMPTON INN & SUITES,
BOYNTON BEACH $$-$$$
1475 W. Gateway Blvd.
Boynton Beach
(561) 369-0018 or (800) HILTONS
www.hamptoninn.com

Midway between Boca and Palm Beach, this hotel was built in 1997, and the 164 rooms have been newly renovated. It also has an interesting extra—a complimentary trolley to the beach, the restaurant district, the Boynton Beach Mall, and the Tri-Rail station. At the nearby Boynton Beach Oceanfront Park, you can fish, swim, or picnic. Also close by are the Arthur R. Marshall Loxahatchee National Wildlife Refuge, the Mangrove Nature Park, and the Schoolhouse Children's Museum.

Rooms are equipped with all the amenities you'd expect at a Hampton Inn—coffeemaker, microwave, minifridge, iron/ironing board, free morning paper, hair dryer, free wireless Internet; there's also a free continental breakfast, heated swimming pool, business center, fitness room, and some special discounts at local attractions, golf courses, etc.

HAMPTON INN & SUITES
WELLINGTON $$$
2155 Wellington Green Dr.
Wellington
(561) 472-9696 or (800) HILTONS
www.hamptoninn.com

The town of Wellington is considered the sweet spot of the western communities, with nice neighborhoods, good schools, beautiful equestrian and polo-grounds (and competitions in both disciplines), and an incredible array of shopping and entertainment options at The Mall at Wellington Green. The 134 rooms offer either one king or two queen beds. The rooms have coffeemakers and iron/ironing boards, and the hotel also offers an airport shuttle and discounts at various area attractions and golf courses. Rooms have a somewhat-English air, with plush beds and bedding, impressive headboards, comfortable chairs, and soft colors on the walls. A hot breakfast is complimentary. There's a pool and fitness center, of course, along with a business center and quality meeting space. The surrounding area has a lot of nice family restaurants, particularly Italian, American, and barbecue.

Out here in the "West," you're close to such attractions as Lion Country Safari (where you drive through and the animals roam freely around your car) and the Loxahatchee National Wildlife Reserve. And you're just minutes from the shops of Wellington Green, where you can roam among 1.3 million square feet and some 170 specialty shops and restaurants, plus four anchor department stores: Macy's, Dillard's, JCPenney, and Nordstrom.

HAMPTON INN WEST PALM BEACH FLORIDA TURNPIKE $$$
2025 Vista Pkwy.
West Palm Beach
(561) 682-9990 or (800) HILTONS
www.hamptoninn.com
Its location at the Florida Turnpike makes this Hampton Inn convenient for quick getaways—Miami's about an hour south, and Orlando about three hours north. If you're a duffer, it's even better; the renowned Emerald Dunes Golf Course is adjacent to the hotel. The hotel was built in 2004, and its 110 rooms offer coffeemakers, microwaves, minifridges, iron/ironing boards; there's a free continental breakfast, special discounts at some area attractions and golf courses, along with a heated pool. If you've a mind to stay in touch with the business world, you can do so at the business center. Close to the hotel, you'll find several steak houses and chain restaurants, along with a few good ice-cream places. Palm Beach International Airport's only 10 minutes away, and downtown West Palm Beach, with

its nightlife and cultural attractions, just a few minutes farther.

HOLIDAY INN EXPRESS BOYNTON BEACH $-$$
480 W. Boynton Beach Blvd.
Boynton Beach
(561) 734-9100 or (800) 465-4329
www.ichotelsgroup.com
The Holiday Inn Express Boynton Beach is located right off I-95, which means you're no more than 45 minutes from anywhere in Palm Beach County. Built in the mid-1970s, the hotel offers 100 rooms with one king or two full-size beds. Accommodations are airy and comfortable, and rooms come equipped with coffeemakers, microwaves, minifridges, iron/ironing boards, and free morning paper. There's a complimentary continental breakfast, and a complimentary Managers' Reception with wine and cheese in the late-afternoon. Renovated in 2006, the hotel also offers barbecue grills, so you can cook up something for yourself. In addition, the hotel can offer special deals on nearby attractions and golf.

The hotel caters to both business travelers—with a 24-hour fully equipped business center—and leisure travelers, with its proximity to shopping, attractions, golf, and deep-sea fishing. Both types of travelers will appreciate the 24-hour fitness center. And you're only 1 mile from the beach, and 4 miles from downtown Delray Beach and fabulous Atlantic Avenue.

HOLIDAY INN WEST PALM BEACH TURNPIKE $$
7859 Lake Worth Rd.
Lake Worth
(561) 968-5000 or (800) 465-4329
www.ichotelsgroup.com

Surrounded by tall pine trees, this Mediterranean-style building has a nice courtyard with pool, along with business center, fitness center, and free Wi-Fi. Opened in the early sixties, the inn has 114 rooms, with either one king-size bed or two doubles, and each with coffeemaker, microwave, minifridge, ironing board and iron, and free morning paper. There's a Perkins Restaurant & Bakery in the hotel serving American food, and space for meetings and events. Kids eat for free at all Holiday Inns. There's even a tennis court and on-site laundry facilities.

Nearby are the South Florida Fairgrounds, the equestrian events in Wellington, The Mall at Wellington Green, golf, and the Palm Beach Skate & Ice Zone. And your location near the Florida Turnpike means you're no more than a few hours from anywhere in South or Central Florida.

HOTEL BIBA & BIBA BAR $$
320 Belvedere Rd.
West Palm Beach
(561) 832-0094
www.hotelbiba.com
Ever since it opened in 2000 in a historic structure built in 1939, this has been one of the most interesting, talked-about, funkiest, and (there's just no other way to say it) one of the all-time coolest hotels in South Florida.

The original hotel on this spot was one of the first motor-lodges built in the United States, and it was a prime example of an architectural style called Bermuda Vernacular. It's in the heart of the upscale El Cid historic district on the edge of downtown West Palm. A few years ago, the hotel was totally gutted and re-done from the inside-out. Today it's a fascinating juxtaposition of that historic architecture, modern design, and Retro (1960s) elements in the interior (such as

---

My Palm Beach County

"For the past 14 years, I've been very fortunate to live and work in Palm Beach County. I'm proud to be an executive of Office Depot, a company dedicated not only to our customers and employees, but also to the Palm Beach County community in which we work. Over the years we've hosted hundreds of entrepreneurs in our business leadership conferences in our Boca Raton Global Headquarters . . . many of them from Palm Beach County."

—Monica Luechtefeld, Executive Vice President of E-Commerce for Office Depot, Boca Raton

---

hanging beads in some of the closets!), and serene green spaces. Rooms are bright and inviting, with hand-crafted mirrors and headboards, mahogany furniture, luxurious linens with down pillows, CD players, and Aveda bath products and toiletries. It's whimsical on the inside, and relaxing on the outside.

The hotel has 40 rooms and one suite; most have a king or queen, or else two doubles. A free continental breakfast is provided, with treats such as locally baked Cuban pastries, locally grown organic citrus fruits, and Hawaiian coffee. There's also a pool. Every Wed evening is Champagne Party Night, with a DJ and a party that runs into the wee hours. And the Biba Bar is legendary around here. With eclectic, retro-furniture of a hundred brilliant colors, and an Asian-style outdoor garden with teak benches, Biba Bar is a feast for the eyes. There's live jazz and reggae on weekend nights, and a nice variety of music on the other nights. And there's an urban-hot-spot "buzz" that gets you as soon as you walk in. And you're only minutes from anything in West Palm Beach, and just across the bridge from Palm Beach.

**HYATT PLACE WEST PALM
BEACH/DOWNTOWN** **$$**
295 Lakeview Ave.
West Palm Beach
(561) 655-1454 or (800) 233-1234
www.hyatt.com
Opened in February 2009, this hotel is in the heart of downtown West Palm Beach, 1 block west of waterfront Flagler Drive; 3 blocks from the beautiful shops, restaurants, and urban plaza of City Place; and three blocks from lively Clematis Street, the original heart of West Palm, now renovated and filled with funky clubs, bistros, and boutiques.

The Hyatt gets a lot of business travelers and it doesn't hurt that it's located only a few blocks from the Palm Beach County Convention Center. Small corporate meetings, executive board meetings, and training classes can be held here, and there's free Internet throughout the facility. There's 24-hour room service, and complimentary continental breakfast. (But no pool.)

Leisure travelers, however, also love this hotel, because it's so centrally located, not only as far as being downtown but also to just about everything else in the county. The decor is contemporary and distinctive. There's a bakery cafe and a wine-and-coffee cafe. Each room has a 42" high-definition flat-panel TV. In the stylish Gallery area you can pick up soups, sandwiches, a variety of ready-to-go snacks, and lunch and dinner entrees, all day (and night) long. There's a Stay Fit Fitness Center and a whirlpool.

Right outside the door are dining options such as Morton's the Steakhouse, Nature's Way Café, Saito Japanese Steakhouse, Taverna Opa (Greek), and Rocco's Tacos and Tequila Bar, one of the new dining sensations of West Palm Beach. And as soon as you walk out that door, you'll find yourself in the middle of a revitalized, thriving urban center.

LAQUINTA INN WEST PALM BEACH **$**
5981 Okeechobee Blvd.
West Palm Beach
(561) 697-3388 or (800) 642-4271
www.laquinta.com
The 114 rooms in this hotel opened in 2000 all offer coffeemaker, hair dryer, iron/ironing board, free Internet, complimentary continental breakfast, free morning newspaper, and laundry facilities. Each room has either one king-size bed or two doubles. There's also a swimming pool. You're about 10 miles from The Mall at Wellington Green; about 9 miles from downtown West Palm Beach and from Lion Country Safari; 8 miles from the beach; and 4 miles from the Palm Beach Kennel Club. Applebee's, Chili's, and Island Jack's restaurants are immediately adjacent to the hotel, and numerous other eateries are nearby. Pets up to 25 pounds allowed.

MOTEL 6—LANTANA **$**
1310 W. Lantana Rd.
Lantana
(561) 585-5833 or (800) 466-8356
www.motel6.com
Built in 1983, this motel has 154 rooms with one queen-bed and one single. There's a small charge for more than three people in a room. It's only a mile from the beach, and it's situated right off I-95 so you're

only 15 minutes from downtown West Palm Beach and about the same from Boca Raton. Nearby attractions include the West Palm Beach Zoo and the South Florida Science Museum, which also has an excellent planetarium with interesting overhead star-shows. There's a pool, a coin laundry, and wireless Internet, along with plenty of places to eat in the surrounding area. Lantana is very much a beach community, and the road to the beach is lined with funky shops and eateries.

PALM BEACH OCEANFRONT INN $$
3550 S. Ocean Blvd.
Palm Beach
(561) 582-5631
www.palmbeachoceanfrontinn.com
Somewhat of a Palm Beach landmark, having been open since 1965, this hotel is true to its name, as it sits directly on the Atlantic. Each of the 59 rooms and suites has a coffeemaker, microwave, and iron/ironing board, and some have a minifridge and minikitchen. There's a pool and the poolside Tides Bar & Grille, where there's always music playing and always great cocktails. And there's a full-service restaurant called Tides Oceanfront Grille, which boasts of being the closest restaurant to the ocean in South Florida. You can also dine al fresco here, on a deck overlooking the ocean. At night there are a million stars overhead and the serenity of the ocean waves washing ashore in the darkness. As you might expect, seafood specialties are king here, with items such as surf and turf, lobster ravioli, and fresh mahi mahi. There's night-time entertainment here from Thurs through Sun, and also a Caribbean Party Night every Sun.

The Palm Beach Oceanfront Inn also has free wireless Internet, complimentary daily newspaper, and a business center. In addition, you can avail yourself of free DVDs from the hotel's collection. There's meeting space both indoors and outdoors.

The inn can often arrange special discounts at area attractions and golf. At the hotel, you can rent bikes or kayaks. You're convenient to downtown West Palm Beach and all of its attractions. And you can walk— any time you want—on one of the world's most famous beaches, among swaying palms and sea oats. Pets accepted under 20 pounds; $35 per night.

RED ROOF INN $
2421 Metrocentre Blvd. East
West Palm Beach
(561) 697-7710 or (800) 733-7663
www.redroof.com
At a Red Roof Inn, you get clean, comfortable accommodations for a reasonable price. This one was built in 1998 but renovated a few years ago, with contemporary furniture and new bathrooms with granite countertops. The 129 rooms have either one king or two doubles; some have microwaves and mini-fridges, and all get a complimentary newspaper in the morning. There's free wireless Internet, a pool, and a complimentary 24/7 coffee bar. From here, you can walk to the Rapids Water Park, where your kids (and you) will have the wettest, wildest time of your life. In addition, you're only 10 minutes from Palm Beach International Airport, 15 minutes from downtown, and 20 minutes from the five championship golf courses at the PGA National Resort in the northern part of the county. There are plenty of family and fast-food restaurants nearby, along with the old-time charm of a Cracker Barrel Restaurant. Pets up to 50 pounds stay for free.

RESIDENCE INN BY MARRIOTT, WEST PALM BEACH $$
2461 Metrocentre Blvd. East
West Palm Beach
(561) 687-4747 or (800) 331-3131
www.marriott.com

Built in 1999, the hotel was fully renovated in 2009. And, like any Marriott, there are a lot of extras. Each of the 78 rooms comes with queen-size beds, along with coffeemaker, microwave, iron/ironing board, a complimentary hot buffet breakfast, and a living room. And all of them also come with a fully-equipped kitchen, as well as high-speed Internet, granite countertops, and stainless-steel appliances.

The Residence Inn has a pool and hot-tub; a complimentary Evening Social from Mon through Thurs, which includes a light meal, soft drinks, and beer; and a complimentary dinner every other Mon night, provided by local restaurants who are doing their best to entice you. There are some good seafood and steak restaurants within five miles, as well as a Cheesecake Factory and the upscale Mark's at City Place, run by Mark Militello, a well-known chef and restaurant owner in South Florida. And if you'd prefer to do your own cooking, there's a barbecue grill and picnic area.

If, on the other hand, you've become a bit too sated by the local eateries, you can work it off in the hotel's exercise room or on the surrounding walking/jogging paths. And your West Palm Beach location means you're within a half-hour of just about anywhere in the county, from the chic shops and restaurants of Boca and Delray to the quiet little seaside towns of North County. Pets allowed for a $75 one-time fee.

Central County Vacation Rentals

As in the rest of Palm Beach County, vacation-rentals here are not a big slice of the visitor-accommodations pie. However, the following Web sites might be of service.

- www.casacoco.net
- www.grandview-gardens.net
- www.city-oasis.com
- www.hominginn.com

ROYAL INN HOTEL, ROYAL PALM BEACH $
675 Royal Palm Beach Blvd.
Royal Palm Beach
(561) 793-3000 or (800) 428-5389
www.royalinnhotel.com

The Royal Inn provides a nice place to stay out in the western communities, where the traffic is sparser and the pace is mellower. Built in 1966, the hotel has 165 rooms and suites, and spreads out over 8 acres and nine buildings. Rooms have one king-bed or two doubles; all have microwaves and minifridges, and some have coffeemakers. Lake Challenger is right behind the property, and many of the family units and suites have private balconies overlooking it. There's an Olympic-size swimming pool and attractive deck overlooking the lake, as well.

A Spanish/Mexican restaurant called El Toro is on the property, although not affiliated with the hotel. In addition, there are several fast-food restaurants nearby. The Royal Inn Hotel is about a half-hour west of the Palm Beaches, and very convenient to the South Florida Fairgrounds and the equestrian events in Wellington. Pets allowed in certain rooms; $12 per night/per pet.

STUDIO 6 WEST PALM BEACH $
1535 Centrepark Dr.
West Palm Beach
(561) 640-3335 or (800) 466-8356
www.motel6.com

Studio 6 is perfectly situated for exploring the Greater Palm Beaches. It sits right on I-95 at the Belvedere Road exit on the south side of West Palm Beach. It's less than a mile from Palm Beach International Airport and just minutes from the Kravis Center for the Performing Arts, City Place, the West Palm Beach Zoo, South Florida Science Museum, The Rapids waterpark, and the South Florida Fairgrounds. The hotel's I-95 access also means you're only about 20 minutes south of Jupiter's Roger Dean Stadium, home of the Jupiter Hammerheads, a minor-league affiliate of the Florida Marlins. Each room has a coffeemaker, microwave, and minifridge, along with some dishes; most are done in light colors and light woods. Pets up to 50 pounds are allowed at a charge of $10 per day.

WEST PALM BEACH
MARRIOTT $$–$$$
1001 Okeechobee Blvd.
West Palm Beach
(561) 833-1234 or (800) 376-2292
www.marriott.com

Marriott took over and upgraded this hotel in 2004—and the results are wonderful. There are 342 guest rooms and 10 suites. Each of the guest rooms has either a king or two double beds, along with coffeemaker, minifridge,

in-room safe, hair dryer, iron/ironing board, and a free morning paper. Depending on the room, there's also a possibility of a free continental breakfast. The hotel boasts a fitness center and full-service business center. You can relax in a beautiful pool or soak it all up in a hot-tub. Before or after all that swimming and soaking, you can enjoy breakfast, lunch, or dinner in the hotel's Bistro Ten Zero One, which has a reputation for good seafood and steaks, and also has a full bar. Also in the hotel is a Starbucks.

The location is ideal for exploring West Palm Beach and the surrounding areas. Within a block or two is just about every type of ethnic restaurant you can imagine, among them Italian/American (Brewzzi's), International (Cheesecake Factory), American (Kona Grill, City Cellar, Ruth's Chris Steakhouse), Greek (Taverna Opa), Asian (Wild Ginger Asian Bistro), and Italian (Il Bellagio). In fact, also within a block or two is City Place, the massive urban re-development project that transformed West Palm Beach in the mid-1990s. It's an impressive collection of designer names and unusual shops, atmospheric restaurants, and good places for chocolates or ice cream, all centered around an urban plaza on which you're quite likely to see mimes, magicians, or musicians. Many of the restaurants have outside sections, so you can enjoy all types of interesting cuisine while watching a great—and constant—people-parade.

Also nearby are Lion Country Safari (where the animals look at *you* as you drive through in the comfort of your car); the beaches; the nightlife of Clematis Street; the Cruzan Amphitheater; the Kravis Center for the Performing Arts; the wonderful Armory Art Center; and the Palm Beach Water Taxi. The West Palm Beach Marriott offers special deals at various times of the year.

Bed-and-Breakfasts

**GRANDVIEW GARDENS
BED & BREAKFAST** $$
1608 Lake Ave.
West Palm Beach
(561) 833-9023
www.grandview-gardens.com
Not only is the Grandview Gardens Bed & Breakfast located in the historic district of Grandview Heights, it's also adjacent to all the modern wonders of downtown West Palm Beach. And it's just across the street from the Armory Art Center, an old National Guard armory that's been transformed into a repository of great art from local artists, craftspeople, and photographers.

Built in 1925, this old house was re-born as a B&B in 2004. It's now an oasis of tranquility in this vibrant urban area. Owners Peter Emmerich (a graduate of the world-renowned Lausanne Hotel School in Switzerland) and Rick Rose (degree in hospitality management from Florida State) have pains-takingly nurtured this property back to its original grandeur. With tropical plants all around the exterior, the yellow house is now a masterpiece of Spanish/Mediterranean architecture, with rounded windows and arches and a brown barrel-tile roof.

Each entrance is private, and each balcony faces the pool or garden. Although the five rooms have a definite Mediterranean flair, each is individually decorated, with distinctive art and antiques. The Royal Poinciana Room has a dark-wood four-poster bed, and Old Master-type frames around the art and mirrors. The Everglades Room has light tropical colors and a wrought-iron bed. There's terra cotta earth-tone flooring throughout the inn. The living room has plush leather sofas and hand-carved furniture and chairs. And the entryway into the inn is through arched French doors, into a room of bright-red walls and blue tile accents, with rich woods and ceramics.

Grandview Gardens is pet-friendly with two rooms appropriate for pets (40-pound limit). There's a dog park right across the street, in fact. If, on the other hand, you feel like leaving Fido to his own devices for a few hours or a day, the inn has a special arrange-ment with VIP—Very Important Paws—a very nice doggie-hotel and day-care facility a few blocks away.

There's wireless Internet access, a pool, and bicycles available. There are tennis and basketball courts directly across the street in Howard Park. The breakfasts? Worth writing home about: a European continental buffet, with a variety of fresh fruit, cereals, breads, muffins, cheeses, yogurts, cakes, and hot dishes. And, of course, you're within walking distance of virtually every restaurant, every gallery, shop, museum, antiques shop, performing arts venue, and historical spot in West Palm Beach.

**HIBISCUS HOUSE BED &
BREAKFAST** $$
501 Thirtieth St.
West Palm Beach
(561) 863-5633 or (800) 203-4927
www.hibiscushouse.com
The Hibiscus House was actually the first bed and breakfast establishment in Palm Beach County, at least in modern times (1991). But its history goes back much farther than that. It was built in 1922 by David Dunkle, Mayor of West Palm Beach, in the Old Northwood section of town during one of the frequent Florida land booms. Today this area is a National Historic District. As the 20th century wore on, the once-grand home fell into disrepair. But when Colin Rayner bought it in 1991, he took great pains to restore it to its previous state.

Now there are five beautiful rooms—a few of which have minirefrigerators—and a pool. Sumptuous breakfasts are served each morning in the tropical gardens surrounding the pool, or in the formal dining room; these breakfasts might consist of coffee or tea, fresh fruit, eggs, sausage, bacon, and French toast. And the meal is served from 8 to 10 a.m., so you don't have to rush to be at breakfast the same time as everyone else.

The Hibiscus is an inviting-looking white house with blue window frames. Each room is unique, and most are named after their individual color schemes—Red Room, Green Room, Peach Room, Burgundy Suite, and the Garden Room (next to the hibiscus garden). They are all whimsical collages of Old English furnishings and furniture, with ornate wooden or wrought-iron beds, huge headboards and posts at the foot of each one, period-paintings with gilded frames, ceiling fans, Oriental rugs, Victorian-style chairs, and antiques all over the place. French doors lead out onto private terraces or balconies overlooking the pool or the gardens. And the owners host a complimentary cocktail gathering every evening at 6 p.m.

And—although you may feel like you're back in the early 20th century at the Hibiscus House—you're only a few minutes away from the 21st-century attractions and cultural amenities of downtown West Palm Beach, as well as great golf and water sports. Children/families are welcome.

MANGO INN BED AND
 BREAKFAST   **$$**
128 N. Lakeside Dr.
Lake Worth
(561) 533-6900 or (888) 626-4619
www.mangoinn.com

Mango Inn Bed and Breakfast consists of three buildings—the main house (with eight guest rooms), a former-carriage house now called The Pineapple Suite, and The Cottage. And when you walk onto the property—through a gate and along a wooded stone path—you'll know you're in for something special.

The main house dates from 1915. Built by the first mayor of Lake Worth, it's a striking yellow house with a brown roof, awnings over the first-floor windows, and Bahamian-type shutters over the ones on the second floor. The property was converted to a bed and breakfast in 1995, and the current owners bought it in 2008.

Today, the two suites have in-room whirlpools. Each of the other eight rooms has its own individual style, with beach/nautical themes, Florida-style furnishings, pastel walls of light-yellow or blue or green, and wicker furniture. Some of them have four-poster or wrought-iron beds (kings in the suites, queens in the guest rooms). All the rooms have coffeemakers, and some have minifridges. Each one is named after a Florida fruit or flower—Mango Suite, Bougainvillea Room, etc.

The living room of the main house has a floor-to-ceiling stone fireplace and hardwood floors. The rear of the area is filled with lush tropical vegetation, and stone fountains, and there's a pool. In the breakfast area, which is outside and covered by an awning, you'll find colorful stucco walls and wicker chairs. And on those tables is a spread that's as appealing to the eye as it is to the palate—cereals; homemade breads, rolls, and cakes; scones; cinnamon rolls; a selection of cheeses; hard-boiled eggs; fruit; and hot entrees such as mango strata—eggs with ham, cheese, and artichokes; and French toast stuffed with fresh blueberry compote, or with mangoes grown right on the property.

It's only two blocks to downtown Lake Worth, which has been revitalized by young entrepreneurs who created art galleries, shops, and restaurants, highlighting the original architecture and buildings, rather than destroying them. Children 14 and up are welcome.

i There's only one hostel of any note in Central County—The Tropics, 307 North M St., Lake Worth, FL 33460, www.hostelz.com.

PALM BEACH HISTORIC INN $$$$
365 South County Rd.
Palm Beach
(561) 832-4009
www.palmbeachhistoricinn.com
The Palm Beach Historic Inn fits in well on this gilded island, with its high arches and light-colored exterior and white window-trim. The building's been painstakingly restored to its old elegance, but now also has all the modern touches. The nine rooms and four suites have hardwood floors, distinctive antiques, and the patina of Palm Beach's Golden Age. But they also have private baths and refrigerators. And each day begins with a complimentary continental breakfast in those rooms. Palm Beach Historic Inn is a block from the beach, and two blocks from Worth Avenue.

SABAL PALM HOUSE BED
AND BREAKFAST $$
109 N. Golfview Rd.
Lake Worth
(561) 582-1090 or (888) 722-2572
www.sabalpalmhouse.com
The Sabal Palm House is a beautiful white home with an upstairs terrace, posts and columns, bay windows, red door, and brick-tiled walkways, and fronted by a garden blooming with vibrant colors and wrought-iron chairs.

It's been an inn since 1997, and current owners John and Colleen Rinaldi took it over in 2003. There are seven rooms, one of which is a suite. There is an artist theme throughout—each room is named for and decorated after a famous painter. You might find yourself in the Renoir Suite, the Chagall Room, the Michelangelo Room, the Norman Rockwell Room, or the Salvador Dali Room. The rooms are filled with antique and hand-crafted furniture and lamps, with four-poster beds and period pieces evocative of the artist. In the Norman Rockwell Room, for example, you might feel as though you've taken a trip back to the 1940s.

Breakfast will feature items such as eggs Benedict, fresh fruit, homemade muffins, or French toast stuffed with berries and cream cheese. There's also a guest refrigerator with complimentary wine, water, and soda.

Sabal Palm House is a romantic spot that's been written about in numerous magazines and newspapers across the country. It's convenient to the re-born center of Lake Worth, with its galleries, restaurants, and funky shops. Within a short walk of the inn are restaurants such as the wonderfully named Bizarre Avenue Café, Brogues (Irish fare), Paradiso (upscale Italian), Rotelli's (great pizza), Ouzo Blue (Greek taverna), Benny's on the Beach (American), and Safire Asian Fusion Cuisine.

Lake Worth Beach is a short walk or trolley ride across the Intracoastal bridge; it's ideal for swimming, snorkeling, jet-skiing, sailing, fishing, and diving. The Lake Worth Municipal Golf Course is directly across the street from the inn, and dozens of other courses are nearby. And a whole world of Central County attractions, cultural venues, and recreation is all around you. Children over 14 are welcome.

SOUTHERN PALM BED AND
BREAKFAST $$
15130 Southern Palm Way
Loxahatchee
(561) 790-1413
www.southernpalmbandb.com

Southern Palm is tucked away in a hidden corner of Palm Beach County—the quiet western community of Loxahatchee. This area moves to a different beat than the rest of the county, and the loudest sounds you hear may be the breeze through the palm trees or the soft echoes of the natural wonderland all around you.

Built as a bed and breakfast in 1997, this house is set amid 20 serene acres of rural Florida and surrounded by tall pines and clear lakes and ponds. Sherry Reed, who built it and still owns it, says that a lot of her visitors are equestrians competing at nearby Wellington, or rowers using the rowing center nearby. But she also caters to couples and to families with children over 12.

Here, in this quiet setting of rural Americana, is a bit of France. The eight rooms are decorated in Country French style, with wooden floors and chests, and eclectic antiques and furniture. In five of them, French doors open to private balconies. (However, there are also some modern touches, including wireless Internet and a minifridge in each room.) Breakfast—a continental combination of homemade baked goods, granola, fresh fruit, and yogurts—is served from 7:30 to 9:30 a.m. And you have the choice of having it in the dining room or in your own room overlooking a tropical lake.

The name Loxahatchee means "river of turtles" in the Seminole language, and in this area you'll see a lot more than just turtles. You're only minutes away from the lions, tigers, giraffes, elephants, zebras, ostriches, water-buffalo, and friends at drive-through Lion Country Safari. The animals here are quite used to human visitors in cars, and you'll be amazed at the way they nonchalantly gather around your car and cross the road right in front of you. You're also close to the Arthur R. Marshall Loxahatchee National Wildlife Refuge. At this 220-square-mile wilderness, you can see Florida the way it's been for a million years.

On the other hand, at the Southern Palm, you're also less than a half-hour from the lights of West Palm Beach, and the glamour of Palm Beach. Children 12 and up are welcome.

Campgrounds/RV Parks

JOHN PRINCE PARK CAMPGROUNDS—
LAKE WORTH
www.pbcgov.com/parks/camping/
johnprincepark/

KOA—LION COUNTRY SAFARI
www.koa.com/where/FL/09310
(561) 793-9797 or (800) 562-9115

KOA—PAHOKEE/LAKE OKEECHOBEE
www.koa.com/where/FL/09338
(561) 924-7832 or (800) 562-0250

VACATION INN RESORT
www.vacationinnrvpark.com
(561) 848-6170

NORTH COUNTY

Resorts

HILTON SINGER ISLAND OCEANFRONT RESORT $$$

3700 N. Ocean Dr.
Singer Island
(561) 848-3888 or (800) HILTONS
www.hilton.com

Singer Island is its own little piece of paradise. Set apart from the mainland by the Intracoastal Waterway—and the highest bridge you'll ever cross—it's a very special spot in Palm Beach County.

The 223 guest rooms and suites at this Hilton property run the gamut from one-bed island-view to upper-level ocean view. All are open and airy and light-colored, bringing the deep blues of the Florida skies and the aquamarine ocean and Intracoastal into even sharper focus. Every room has a minibar, coffeemaker, hair dryer, iron/ironing board, walk-out balcony, work desk, and minifridge, along with extra touches such as Crabtree & Evelyn toiletries. If you've got business to conduct, there are meeting rooms and a full-service business center.

You can swim at a pool overlooking the ocean, go jet-skiing or snorkeling, or work out in the fitness center, and perhaps afterward, work out the kinks in a hot tub. There's golf everywhere around you—more courses than you could play if you stayed here for months. A gift shop has snacks and sundries, and a newsstand lets you keep up with what's going on in the world (if you really want to!).

The seaside Coconuts Restaurant specializes in the bounty of the ocean, with items such as spicy rare tuna or blackened mahi mahi with lemon. And if you ever get a hankering for the bright lights and amusements of the mainland, it's just on the other side of that very-tall bridge. Pets up to 75 pounds allowed for $75 non-refundable fee.

JUPITER BEACH RESORT & SPA $$$$

5 North A1A
Jupiter
(561) 746-2511 or (866) 943-0950
www.jupiterbeachresort.com

Picture a piece of Paradise tucked alongside a thousand feet of pristine private beach in the picturesque town of Jupiter. It's all here. One of the most beautiful beaches in South Florida lies behind the Jupiter Beach Hilton, splendidly unoccupied during the day, and occupied mostly by nesting turtles at night. The hotel leads tours at night to the nesting grounds, where you can watch from a distance. There are no lights allowed on the beach at night, and the hotel urges guests to be conscious of the fact, that, when they are laying eggs, too many bright lights can drive the turtles away.

One of the nicest restaurants in the area, Sinclair's Ocean Grill, allows you to feast on fresh fish specialties from the ocean outside in an ambience of relaxed elegance. Sandbar Restaurant is a casual place for old favorites and light snacks, fronting the ocean. And you can sip a tropical tall one at Sinclair's Lounge, where the entertainment is lively and local.

The Spa at the Jupiter Beach Resort has a Waterfall Room and a Tea Bar, where you can relax either before or after treatments such as the Tropical Sugar Rub, SweThai Massage, or De-Stress Massage. There's a beauty salon in the spa. There are modern touches that integrate perfectly with the tranquil atmosphere, such as state-of-the-art music systems and upscale natural products. And there's an air of relaxed elegance that permeates the entire area, along with wonderful natural floral and forest aromas.

In addition to the beachfront, it has a heated pool, fitness center, and lighted tennis courts. The 159 rooms include 34 suites, as well as luxurious penthouse accommodations where you can practically see forever. Each of the rooms has a coffeemaker and minifridge, and some have microwaves. The ambience is Florida/Caribbean—soft colors and pastels, local artists on the walls, and comfortable, light-wood tables and chairs. Pets under 25 pounds allowed; $25 per night.

Then there's the town of Jupiter itself, symbolized by its famous lighthouse. Jupiter's first Anglo settlers were the U.S. Army, and later the Navy, in the mid-1800s. They were soon followed by civilians, who helped maintain the lighthouse first constructed in 1860, in an effort to stem the number of shipwrecks. Today the Jupiter Inlet Lighthouse & Museum—only 2 miles away—is open to the public (see the Attractions section); you can climb to the top and see what the early settlers saw, and you can peruse paraphernalia from those days. The town of Jupiter itself is filled with charming shops and restaurants. Everything in North County—as well as the Palm Beaches—is only a 20-minute drive away.

PALM BEACH MARRIOTT SINGER
 ISLAND BEACH RESORT & SPA $$$$
3800 N. Ocean Dr.
Palm Beach, Singer Island
(561) 340-1700 or (888) 213-0414
www.marriott.com
Built in 2007, this hotel really gives you room to stretch with 239 luxury one- and two-bedroom condos with full kitchens, living

rooms, and washer/dryers, along with coffeemakers, microwaves, and iron/ironing boards. The views of the Intracoastal or the Atlantic are often spectacular. And there's a real coral reef sticking out into the ocean. The Marriott has two pools and plenty of oceanfront activities. Si Spa is an elegant, quiet hideaway, where you can get pampered from head to toe. The fitness center has a nice variety of equipment and machines. There's a full-service business center. Solu is the signature restaurant here; it has great seafood, chops, and steaks and is open for breakfast, lunch, and dinner. You can enjoy casual American and island cuisine for lunch at The Lagoon Grill. There are three golf clubs nearby, and tons of water-recreation choices all along the beach. In addition, West Palm Beach is just 15 minutes away.

PGA NATIONAL RESORT & SPA $$$
400 Avenue of the Champions
Palm Beach Gardens
(561) 627-2001 or (800) 863-2819
www.pgaresort.com
This is the headquarters of the Professional Golfers Association, and there are five championship courses here. You may have heard of some of the course-designers, as well—names like Nicklaus, Palmer, and Fazio. PGA National was opened in 1981, and was renovated in 2007. The 339 guest rooms and suites have king-size beds or two doubles. If you need more room, there are also 40 two-bedroom club cottages. Accommodations all have coffeemakers, minifridges, iron/ironing boards, free morning papers, in-room safes, terrycloth robes, and complimentary continental breakfast. They're spacious and modern, with views of lakes and golf courses. Both the fitness center and the business center are very well-equipped.

Pools and whirlpools are scattered all around the resort. And there's a shuttle to and from the airport. Pets accepted, up to 75 pounds; $250 refundable deposit.

Eight different restaurants on the property can supply pretty much any type of dining experience. One of the best is provided by the Ironwood Grille, which serves up classic American favorites such as fresh seafood and steaks, in an ambience of reds and golds, teak furnishings, and soft lighting. The Wave Bar & Grill provides poolside dining and drinks. Cafe Pronto, in the lobby, serves Starbucks coffee along with a variety of treats and light snacks. Waters of the World Café offers spa cuisine in an outdoor setting.

The Spa at PGA National is one of the best. This is a 40,000 square-foot facility with 56 treatment rooms and more than a hundred treatments available. And you can soak in the wellness-restoring waters of the Dead Sea or the Pyrenees Mountains.

If you want to meet where the pros play, there's a 39,000 square foot meeting facility with 23 rooms. And if you want to play more like the pros play, you can take instruction from the best teachers in the world at the PGA Center for Golf Learning and Performance.

Hotels and Motels

**BEST WESTERN
 INTRACOASTAL INN** $–$$
810 South US 1
Jupiter
(561) 575-2936 or (800) 780-7234
www.bestwestern.com
The 52 rooms in this inn have either one king bed or two doubles, and some of the king rooms have hot tubs. Each room has a coffeemaker, hair dryer, microwave, minifridge, iron/ironing board, free morning newspaper,

and complimentary continental breakfast. If a room has more than two adults, there's a charge of $10 per person per night. And you can't beat the location—right on the Intracoastal Waterway, which runs from Florida to Maine. The pool is right on the Intracoastal, so you can watch all kinds of craft—from the ridiculous to the sublime—glide by as you do your laps or just float in the sunshine. The beach is just a couple of blocks away. In addition, there are plenty of restaurants in the area, among them seafood, Italian, Chinese, Japanese, and American.

**DOUBLETREE HOTEL & EXECUTIVE
 MEETING CENTER** $$
4431 PGA Blvd.
Palm Beach Gardens
(561) 622-2260 or (800) HILTONS
www.doubletreewestpalmbeach.com
This is a beautiful Doubletree property, with lots of amenities for both business- and pleasure travelers. It's recently been remodeled, enhancing the look and the atmosphere. Each of the 275 rooms comes equipped with a coffeemaker, minifridge, iron/ironing board, and a free morning paper. Some have microwaves. Most have balconies looking out over this growing area of North County. The hotel also features a select inventory of "Pure" guest rooms, which have undergone a process to improve the air quality in them and are allergy-friendly.

The fitness center has state-of-the-art weight-lifting and cardiovascular equipment. Shuttle service to local shops and restaurants is available. You can wander around the tropical gardens, or relax at the tiered waterfalls. You can enjoy a latte at the Starbucks in the lobby or pick up some cinnamon rolls or other treats. You can swim in the heated outdoor pool, surrounded by palm trees and colorful hibiscus flowers. Or you can sip a specialty drink at the open veranda overlooking the pool area.

Doubletree does dining, too. The Oz Restaurant has a serene, Oriental-type ambience but serves the best of Florida cuisine, with influences ranging from zesty Latin to classic Southern to seafood caught in local waters. And—talk about Florida cuisine—the key lime pie is famous here. Fusion Lounge, in the lobby, serves tropical drinks and light snacks.

You might want to keep your clubs in the car—because you can't drive more than a few minutes without seeing a beautifully manicured golf course; there are a dozen in the area. Ditto for tennis. And you're close to the fashionable shops and restaurants of the Gardens Mall.

As noted in its name, the Doubletree is a prime meeting spot in North County. There's free Internet throughout the hotel. There's a full-service business center. There is more than 10,000 square feet of flexible meeting space. The rooms are impressive spaces, with classic furniture and modern technology. The staff is experienced at handling a wide variety of meetings. And when the meetings are done, the cookies in the lobby are truly incredible! Pets under 25 pounds allowed; $25 per night.

EMBASSY SUITES PALM BEACH
GARDENS $$$
4350 PGA Blvd.
Palm Beach Gardens
(561) 622-1000 or (800) HILTONS
www.embassysuites.com

This hotel opened in 1990, and has been recently renovated. Each of the 160 units is a suite, of course, and each has either one king bed or two doubles, in addition to a pull-out sofa. There's an on-site laundry room. Each suite comes well-equipped, with a coffeemaker, microwave, minifridge, iron/ironing board, and free morning paper, and you get a free continental breakfast.

The public spaces are well-equipped, as well. The atrium is filled with tropical foliage and Oriental footbridges over little ponds with swans. There's a heated outdoor pool, a Jacuzzi, and a sauna. The Precor Fitness Center has top-flight equipment and machines. Tennis facilities are here. And you may never have to leave the premises for the usual sundries. There's a convenience store and a newsstand, along with a pantry with food-to-go and a gift shop. In addition, the meeting facilities are first-class, from conference board rooms to the 500-capacity grand ballroom.

There's a Manager's Reception every evening, where you can socialize with fellow guests while enjoying light fare and drinks. The brand-new Atrium Grill offers a good variety of food and an impressive wine list, and is open for breakfast, lunch, and dinner.

At the Concierge Desk, you can find out everything you need to know about the area. For example, Embassy Suites is only 10 minutes from Roger Dean Stadium, where you can see the St. Louis Cardinals and the hometown Florida Marlins during Spring Training in Feb and Mar, and the Marlins' minor-league affiliate, the Jupiter Hammerheads (as in shark) the rest of the season. You're also close to the championship golf at PGA National headquarters, to the shops and dining options of the Gardens Mall, and to the beach and its myriad recreational opportunities. The hotel is in the heart of bustling Palm Beach Garden, and is the only full-service all-suite hotel in town.

FAIRFIELD INN & SUITES
BY MARRIOTT $$
6748 W. Indiantown Rd.
Jupiter
(561) 748-5252 or (800) 228-2800
www.fairfieldinnsuitesjupiter.com

Even though this hotel opened in 2000, the entire property was renovated in 2009 from the ground up. There are 110 rooms and suites; the rooms have either one king or two full-size beds, and the suites each have a king and a pull-out sofa. Coffeemakers, iron/ironing boards, free morning paper, free wireless Internet, and free hot breakfast are standard here, and some rooms also have microwaves and minifridges. Pets up to 50 pounds stay free. And the location is excellent—close to both I-95 and the Florida Turnpike, and only 4 miles from the beach.

If you like the Florida Marlins—and most baseball fans in these parts do—you'll love the fitness room, which is done in a Marlins motif with silhouettes and interesting artistic touches on the walls. It was all done by a local artist, and the new look matches the new equipment. And if you really love the Marlins, or the St. Louis Cardinals, you can see their spring training games at nearby Roger Dean Stadium. Here you can watch the teams' two minor league affiliates, the Jupiter Hammerheads and the Palm Beach Cardinals, all season long. You're also near the Maltz Jupiter Theatre, the Burt Reynolds & Friends Museum, Palm Beach International Raceway, and the Jupiter Inlet Lighthouse & Museum.

The Fairfield has a nice pool area with a whirlpool. In the beautiful new lobby, there's 24-hour complimentary hot coffee and tea service. For business travelers, the inn is convenient to the offices of numerous major companies, among them Allstate Insurance, Brink's Security, Centex Construction, Florida Power & Light, Scripps Research Institute, Tyco, and Siemens Corporation.

There are a number of popular family restaurants nearby, such as Applebee's, Chili's, IHOP, Panama Hattie's, R. J. Gators, and the Crab House.

HAMPTON INN PALM
BEACH GARDENS $$
4001 RCA Blvd.
Palm Beach Gardens
(561) 625-8880 or (800) HILTONS
www.hamptoninn.com

This Hampton Inn has a long list of awards about which to boast. It was the Conrad Hilton Award winner for both 2001 and 2002, and it was rated one of the top 10 hotels in America in 2003 for the quality of its service. The 116 rooms come with either a king-bed or two doubles, and many have pullout sofas. Each one has coffeemaker, microwave, minifridge, iron/ironing board, and free morning paper. If you want to play at the Hampton Inn, there's a fitness center and a pool. If you want to work, there's a business center and meeting rooms, and complimentary high-speed Internet access everywhere. If you want to eat or drink, there's complimentary breakfast and a complimentary beverage area.

The hotel is pretty much in the middle of everything in this town called "The Golf Capital of the World." One of the things you'll notice is that there's green everywhere you look. In fact, nearly a third of the city's land is devoted to green, environmentally friendly spaces.

But there are a lot of friendly spaces, such as the posh Gardens Mall with more than 160 fine specialty shops and restaurants. Bloomingdale's, Saks Fifth Avenue,

Macy's, and Nordstrom are all here, along with all manner of clothing, electronics, accessories, art, and gift shops. When you get hungry from all this shopping, there's a food court, and, in the Downtown at the Gardens section, a Cheesecake Factory and numerous specialty places with deli, sushi, or ice cream.

The Eissey Theater for the Performing Arts is nearby, as is a world-renowned bakery from Europe called PAUL. The vibrant nightlife and cultural excitement of West Palm Beach is only 10 miles away.

HILTON GARDEN INN PALM BEACH
   GARDENS $$
3505 Kyoto Gardens Dr.
Palm Beach Gardens
(561) 694-5833 or (800) HILTONS
www.hilton.com

Opened in 2008, this hotel is in the heart of the growing Palm Beach Gardens area. It sits on downtown's Lake Victoria, with a fountain in the middle, and footbridges allowing you to walk to shopping, dining, and major office complexes. The Gardens Mall is adjacent. Many of Palm Beach County's 147 golf courses are nearby. The hotel's 175 units include 17 suites and five family suites. Each room has either a king bed or two queens. There is a charge for extra people in a room, at the rate of $10 per person per night. The rooms are comfortable and modern. Each has a coffeemaker, microwave, minifridge, iron/ironing board, free morning paper, free wireless Internet, and work desk.

In addition, there's an on-site laundry facility, news stand, convenience store, gift shop, and a 24-hour Pavilion Pantry stocked with everything you might have forgotten. There's a pool, of course, and a fitness center. The Great American Grill serves great American food, at breakfast, lunch, and dinner, overlooking the lake (which glows with romantic lights in the evening). The Pavilion Lounge is a great spot to unwind at night.

There's a 24-hour business center with everything you could possibly need in terms of printing, faxing, and copying. The hotel offers advanced audio-visual equipment for rental. There are 14 meeting/event spaces ranging from boardroom to ballroom, including a number outside.

Nearby are offices of corporations such as Florida Power & Light, General Electric, Professional Golfers Association, Scripps Research, and United Technologies. At the Hilton Garden Inn, you're 5 miles from the beaches of Singer Island, 6 miles from Major and Minor League Baseball at Roger Dean Stadium, and 6 miles from John D. MacArthur State Park.

HOLIDAY INN EXPRESS NORTH PALM
   BEACH OCEANVIEW HOTEL $$
13950 US 1
Juno Beach
(561) 622-4366 or (800) 345-8082
www.holidayinn.com

Built in 1992, the entire facility was gutted and then renovated in 2009, from top to bottom, from public areas to pool to guest rooms. So, for all practical purposes, it's a "new" hotel. The 108 rooms all come with one king- or two double-beds, and all come standard with coffeemaker, microwave, minifridge, iron/ironing board, free newspaper, and an award-winning complimentary continental breakfast. There's also a pool and fitness center, a business center, and an on-site florist. Pets allowed; $20 per night/per pet. You can see live ocean turtles next door at the Marine Life Center. The hotel is less than a block from the beach. Also less than a block are a number of good restaurants, among them The Juno Beach Fish House, The Hurricane Café, and the Thirsty Turtle. Baseball at Roger Dean Stadium is only 3 miles away, the Burt Reynolds Museum and Park is only 4 miles, Jonathan Dickinson State Park is only 5 miles (as is The Gardens Mall), and downtown West Palm Beach is only 15.

INN OF AMERICA $
4123 Northlake Blvd.
Palm Beach Gardens
(561) 626-4918 or (800) 587-6875
www.innofamerica.com

Inn of America is close to I-95, making it no more than 40 minutes away from pretty much anywhere in the county, including Boca Raton and Delray Beach. The inn is a three-story building wrapped around a courtyard pool that's heated in the winter. Each of the 95 rooms has either a king-size bed or two doubles, and all come with microwave, minifridge, iron/ironing board, free newspaper, and free continental breakfast, along with free coffee and juice from 6 a.m. to 9 p.m. There are many well-known chain restaurants nearby, such as Applebee's, Cheesecake Factory, Chili's, Olive Garden, Red Lobster, and R. J. Gators, along with neighborhood places offering Chinese, Thai, seafood, and steak. The beach is only minutes away, and you're close to downtown West Palm Beach, as well as numerous museums and attractions.

LA QUINTA INN & SUITES JUPITER $$
34 Fishermen's Wharf
Jupiter
(561) 575-7201
www.laquintainnjupiter.com

This hotel, built in 1989, joined the La Quinta Inn family in 2006. You can walk to the beach, the Burt Reynolds Museum, the Dubois Pioneer Home, and the Maltz Theatre. And you can also walk to a dozen restaurants, such as Chili's, Dairy Queen, Duffy Draft House, and the wonderfully named Too Bizarre. You're close to a half-dozen golf courses, among them Abacoa, Jupiter Dunes, Jupiter Hills, and North Palm, as well as colorful local spots like the Juno Beach Pier. All of the 101 light-colored (and light-wood furniture) rooms feature free high-speed Internet access, coffeemaker, microwave, minifridge, hair dryer, iron/ironing board, and complimentary hot-and-cold continental breakfast. And there's a pool, fitness center, and laundry facilities on-site. Pets up to 50 pounds allowed.

PALM BEACH GARDENS
MARRIOTT $$$
4000 RCA Blvd.
Palm Beach Gardens
(561) 622-8888 or (800) 678-9494
www.marriott.com

There are 273 guest rooms and six suites, and each have king-beds or two doubles. There are plasma TVs in every room, along with coffeemakers, iron/ironing board, free high-speed Internet, and complimentary morning newspaper.

There's a pool and a fitness center with both cardiovascular equipment and free weights. Within a 15-mile radius is just about every kind of outdoor recreation enjoyed in Palm Beach County—horseback riding, jet-skiing, jogging, kayaking, sailing, scuba diving, snorkeling, squash, and water-skiing among them. You can't go very far in this area without seeing a golf course; there are four excellent courses in the area, in fact: The Abacoa Golf Club, Emerald Dunes, Iron Horse, and Palm Beach Gardens Golf Club.

The nearby Lane Spa offers a variety of facial, foot, and body treatments. And there are numerous places to play tennis in the area. There are 13 meeting rooms with 10,000 square feet of space, including a ballroom, as well as exhibition space on-site.

There are numerous places to eat, drink, and party in the area, as well, especially at the nearby Gardens Mall and its trendy Downtown at the Gardens, where you can find some of the hottest restaurants and nightspots in town. Here you'll find P. F. Chang's China Bistro, which serves some of the most imaginative Chinese dishes you'll ever see, along with favorites such as California Pizza Kitchen and Ruby Tuesday's. The mall is anchored by Bloomingdale's, Saks Fifth Avenue, Macy's, and Nordstrom. And there are some 160 other stores offering everything from that dress or jewelry you absolutely must have to the wristwatch or music or gift that you just want.

The hotel offers some quality nightlife options, as well. The Blue Fire Grille, open for breakfast, lunch, and dinner, boasts American specialties like steaks and seafood, along with pasta dishes and other favorites. The Waterway Café, known for its seafood, serves up specialties such as tropical mustard glazed salmon and waterway fra diavolo for lunch and dinner. There's a Starbucks on-site. After you're done eating, if you're in the mood to "hoof it," head over to Club Safari (in the hotel), an Aztec-themed spot with state-of-the-art sound and laser equipment, 10-foot-high video screens, and a popular DJ spinning the dance-music, hip-hop, and chart-toppers. Club Safari's been one of North County's most popular dance spots for years, and a couple of polls also called it

---

North County Vacation Rentals

These Web sites may help you in your search:

- www.jupiterflrentals.com
- www.vacationhomerentals.com
- www.vamoose.com

---

one of the 100 best bars in the world.

SEASPRAY INN & BEACH RESORT $$
123 Ocean Ave.
Palm Beach Shores, Singer Island
(561) 844-0233 or (800) 330-0233
www.seasprayinnbeachresort.com

Even for Singer Island, the area in which the Seaspray Inn is located is quiet. It's on the southernmost tip of the island, mostly residential, and there's not much traffic. In business since the late-1960s, the hotel provides a great getaway. There are 50 rooms, with king-size beds in some and doubles in others. Each has coffeemaker and iron/ironing board; microwaves and minifridges are available for a fee of $5 per night. Pets up to 25 pounds allowed; $15 per night/per pet. The Top 'O Spray Rooftop Oceanview Restaurant, which has views that seem to go on forever, has American specialties such as fresh seafood and prime rib. (It's open for breakfast, lunch, and dinner.) The adjacent lounge features specialty drinks concocted by the hotel's own bartenders, called Hurricanes and Tiki drinks.

Singer Island is home to a large deep-sea fishing fleet, many of whose craft are available for charter. In addition, you can charter a boat to take you cruising along the Intracoastal, past undeveloped islands with stands of tropical mangroves and past homes of people to whom money has never been much of an object. The island also has several good golf courses, as well as tennis courts. And if you're in the mood to extend your vacation, The Port of Palm Beach, just across the bridge, is headquarters of a few ships that ply the Caribbean.

SUPER 8 NORTH PALM BEACH $
757 US 1
North Palm Beach
(561) 848-1424 or (800) 800-8000
www.super8.com
This 100-room motel has been completely re-modeled over the past few years. Each room has one king-bed or two doubles, and all come with coffeemaker, microwave, minifridge, iron/ironing board, hair dryer, and free continental breakfast. And the location can't be beat—2 miles from the beach. There's golf at the North Palm Beach Country Club, a mile away. Shopping and restaurants at the Gardens Mall, a few miles away. And you're only about 8 miles from West Palm Beach. The Super 8 has a business center and a pool. There are plenty of good family restaurants nearby—Carrabbas, IHOP, Denny's, and T.G.I. Friday's. For those nights when you just have to have a steak as big as Texas, there's a Ruth's Chris Steak House.

TRAVELODGE RIVIERA BEACH $
3651 Blue Heron Blvd.
Riviera Beach
(561) 844-2601 or (800) 578-7878
www.travelodge.com
Opened in 2007, the Travelodge's 100 rooms offer either a king bed or two doubles. And

they're very well-equipped, with coffeemakers, microwaves, minifridges, iron/ironing board, free morning paper, and free continental breakfast. There's a swimming pool and a laundry room. And attractions such as the Sun Cruz Casino Boat, the Palm Beach Kennel Club, the Singer Island beaches, and downtown Wet Palm Beach are all within a very short drive. Pets allowed for $20 flat fee.

WINDSOR GARDENS HOTEL $$
11360 US 1
North Palm Beach
(561) 844-8448 or (866) 503-8880
www.wghotel.net
Opened in 1989, the Windsor Gardens has a lot to offer, not the least of which is its location. It's 2 miles from the beaches of Juno Beach and Singer Island; 2 miles from the Intracoastal Waterway; 3 miles from the Gardens Mall, and surrounded by good golf courses.

The 90 rooms at this hotel have one king or two doubles, and there's a $10 per night charge for each extra person (in existing bedding). Each room has a coffeemaker and iron/ironing board, and some come with microwave and minifridge; all come with a complimentary continental breakfast. There's a pool and a fitness center. The hotel is smartly and interestingly designed, with touches of stone, classic American, wicker, and modern. Pets allowed; $35 flat fee.

The extra touches go far beyond the hotel's location. There's an excellent restaurant called Secrets Piano Bar & Grill, where noted chef Joseph Angelucci proffers up wonderful American cuisine tinged with a touch of Asian. His signature dishes include voodoo shrimp and what some local folks believe is the finest hummus in America. In addition, every month the *Palm Beach Post* sponsors a Best of the Best themed wine dinner here.

Another great touch is the 13,000 square feet of meeting space. Spaces run the gamut from intimate boardroom to sprawling ballroom, and even the ballroom can be divided up into three smaller spaces. If you hold a meeting here, you'll be able to utilize the first-class catering department, which can provide anything from sushi to caviar—and the services of Chef Angelucci.

This area has an abundance of dive shops and charter boats, so you can explore the brilliantly colored coral reef up-close-and-personal, as well as the numerous sunken ships in the area. Tennis and golf are nearby, as well, in addition to West Palm Beach attractions such as the Dreher Park Zoo, Lion Country Safari, and Raymond Kravis Center for the Performing Arts.

RESTAURANTS

What, exactly, is South Florida cuisine? If you ask 10 Palm Beach County residents, you may very well get 10 different answers. One thing's for sure. What was considered South Florida cuisine just 10 or 20 years ago has a much different definition today. The reason is that South Florida—and Palm Beach County—have experienced such dramatic growth in recent decades. Much of that growth came from emigrants to this country who brought with them the flavors, spices, tastes, and specialties of their native lands. Some foods, however, have always been South Florida specialties and always will.

Take **stone crabs,** for example. They're heaven on a plate to most folks in Palm Beach County. They're succulent and juicy, especially when dipped into a special sauce. And the fact that they're only available half the year—Oct 15 to May 15—makes them even more of a local delicacy. Another specialty is **key lime pie.** There are two types—green and yellow. The yellow version is the one that actually comes from limes grown in the Florida Keys. It's considered the "real" key lime pie. A thin, delicious crust—generally with big crumbs on the edges—surrounds a soft, tart center with a taste you won't soon forget.

Then there's **conch** (pronounced "konk"). These days, because of fishing limits, most of it probably comes from the nearby Bahamas. But this shellfish is ubiquitous in Palm Beach County restaurants. Once a chef extracts the meat from the shell, it takes a lot of pounding with a wooden hammer to soften it up. Try a spicy conch salad or the tamer conch fritters—conch that's fried into crispy balls, with some spices added on the surface. Crunchy, crispy, and very tasty. For another seafood treat, the **grouper** sandwich is a traditional favorite here, with spicy cole slaw and either tartar sauce or red cocktail sauce.

There's **barbecue,** of course. It's never gone out of style here. And there are a number of colorful places where you can sample some great ribs, chicken, beans, and fries.

Food gets more exotic from there. In fact, there are places in Palm Beach County where you can get something of a vicious sense of retaliation, by turning the tables of the traditional food chain. For example, there are a few places where you can have **alligator,** or **shark,** or **rattlesnake.** Other tastes of the exotic include **frog's legs,** caught in the nearby Everglades and generally fried and crispy, or **hearts of palm,** a type of vegetable taken from the inside of a palm tree and served in a salad.

In recent years, there have been a lot of additions to the local cuisine list. Palm Beach County cuisine, once distinctly Floridian and American, is now truly international. The Cuban culinary influence, pretty much confined to Miami in the late 20th century, has made it to Palm Beach County. Such specialties as ropa vieja (chipped beef in a red sauce) and arroz con pollo (chicken with rice) are no longer foreign to local folks.

Restaurants serve **Cuban, Brazilian,** and **Argentine** specialties, as well as **Caribbean** fare. There are now a few **Jamaican** places where you can enjoy spicy jerk chicken with a red strip beer. In fact, in recent years, some local chefs have been experimenting with a style of cooking dubbed **"Floribbean,"** combining the flavors of Florida and the Caribbean (see Close-up in this chapter.). Of course, there have always been good **Chinese** restaurants, and recent years have also seen an influx of **Japanese, Thai,** and, occasionally, **Middle Eastern** restaurants.

Like all the other chapters in this book, this one is arranged geographically, starting with South County, then Central County, and then North County. Within each of these three geographic sections are break-downs by specialty; listed alphabetically. Assume that all restaurants listed accept major credit cards, unless otherwise noted.

Price Code

Our price-code key is based on the average price of dinner *entrees* for two—exclusive of cocktails, wine, appetizers, desserts, taxes, and tip.

$.....................$5 to $10
$$ ....$11 to $20
$$$ ....$21 to $30
$$$$ .... More than $30

In Florida, state law prohibits smoking inside an eatery. Wheelchair-accessibility is also mandated by state law. A few restaurants may stay open later during "Season"—Nov 1 to May 1—than in the other months. With regard to full-bars, assume that the restaurants listed (with exceptions such as pizza places, etc.) have them, unless otherwise noted.

Now, sit back, relax, and enjoy Palm Beach County's wonderful restaurants, from American to vegetarian!

SOUTH COUNTY
American

BOCA DINER $
2801 N. Federal Hwy.
Boca Raton
(561) 750-6744
If you thought the days of real-live diners were gone with the drive-in movie theaters, think again. Boca Raton has a real, honest-to-goodness diner that people have been flocking to for what seems like forever. The emphasis is on American comfort food, with a bit of Greek thrown in for good measure (the spinach pie is an often-requested specialty). The soups are great; try the chicken soup. And the comfort food is—there's no other way to say this—really comforting. When you dig into the meat loaf and gravy with mashed potatoes, or the turkey with cranberry sauce and stuffing, or the brisket of beef, you'll feel very "comforted." Ditto for the hamburgers. As you might expect from a real diner, the desserts are great—apple pie and cheesecake.

BRU'S ROOM SPORTS GRILL $–$$
35 N.E. Second Ave.
Delray Beach
(561) 276-3663
www.brusroom.com
Bru does, indeed, know sports . . . because Bru is Bob Brudzinski, former linebacker for the Miami Dolphins. He's a local hero around here. And he runs one of the most popular gathering places in South Florida. His menu is an interesting combination of innovative new items and old favorites. The appetizer

list has the usual onion rings and nachos. But you'll also find items like hot peppers (jalapeño peppers stuffed with cream cheese) and the Southwest egg roll (chicken, black beans, corn, cheese, cilantro, and spinach in a deep-fried egg roll). The wings and the ribs are great, as well, as you might expect. And there's always sports on the TVs.

But many Palm Beach County folks come to Bru's Room especially for the hamburgers. If you're starving, go for the half-pound black angus burger. If you think spice is nice, go for the hot-n-bleu-burger, a Cajun-spiced burger with bleu cheese and hot mayonnaise sauce. Bru's barbecue burger is another half-pounder, cooked in Bru's own barbecue sauce, and topped with melted cheese, bacon, and Tabasco fried onions. And the patty melt is smothered in melted cheese and sautéed onions, and served on rye bread.

Bru's being Bru's, there are always special events here, such as the Flutie Brothers Band, featuring former NFL quarterback Doug Flutie; Knockin' Knoggins Trivia Contests; and annual events such as the White Trash Bash. And many of Bob Brudzinski's old pals from the Miami Dolphins often stop by, such as Kim Bokamper, a former Dolphins lineman who's now a local sportscaster.

THE FALCON HOUSE $$$
116 N.E. Sixth Ave.
Delray Beach
(561) 243-9499
www.thefalconhouse.com
The Falcon House is a contemporary American restaurant and bar in downtown Delray Beach, featuring small plates, big drinks, and good times. There's an innovative menu, decor that's casually elegant, and a steady stream of people coming in to see what all

the fuss is about. There's a big bar inside, a seating area outside, hundreds of glasses hanging from the ceiling, and—surprise!—pictures of falcons all over the walls.

Tapas, of course, are a concept that originated in Spain long ago—small samplings of various foods, in small plates continuously brought to your table. The Falcon House has transformed this concept to include samplings of American treats and nouvelle cuisine, as well. Chef Joshua Hedquist has a way with filet mignon; Hawaiian tuna poke, which comes to your table with crushed honey-toasted macadamia nuts, sesame seeds, crispy taro chips, and chili-scallion soy; and with Thai peanut chicken satay, marinated and grilled chicken skewers, with vegetable fried rice. His desserts are perfect compliments to his meals. The Mississippi mud pie with chocolate fudge sauce will make you wish you were down on the bayou. And the warm apple cobbler with vanilla ice cream and caramel is just as good.

The Falcon House mixes a mean cocktail, as well. The Ultimate Margarita is a mix of Milagro Silver tequila, agave nectar, lemons, and limes. The Falcon lemonade is Van Gogh Acai Blueberry Vodka, muddled lemons, and sugar.

HENRY'S $$$
16850 Jog Rd.
Delray Beach
(561) 638-1949
www.henrysofbocaraton.com
Henry's serves good, old-fashioned comfort food. But the atmosphere is hardly down-home; it's a warm, smart-looking place that won *Boca Raton* magazine's Reader's Choice Award for Best American Cuisine. It's an expansive place with a large bar and al fresco dining outside. Chef John Belleme was

named a Chef to Keep Your Eye On by *Esquire* magazine. At Henry's, he's come up with appetizers such as beef franks in a blanket with honey-mustard dipping sauce, and rice cracker-crusted yellowfin tuna, seared rare with a light glaze. There are daily classics, as well. You might try southern fried chicken with mashed potatoes and gravy, or spaghetti and chicken meatballs, or roast rib of beef with creamed spinach. The desserts are every bit as much comfort food as the entrees. How about frozen tiramisu, with layers of espresso ice cream, sponge cake, Myer's Dark Rum syrup, and chocolate shavings. Or Kit Kat—layers of chocolate and crunchy peanut butter mousse, with hazelnut caramel.

SEASONS 52 $$$
2300 N.W. Executive Center Dr.
(on Glades Road)
Boca Raton
(561) 998-9952
www.seasons52.com

This restaurant is popular with businesspeople at lunchtime, and with a sophisticated Boca crowd at night. It's a grill and wine bar with an ambience to match and an adult crowd. Culinary director Clifford Pleau and master sommelier George Miliotes keep this crowd in the know, with a monthly newsletter informing them of the latest trends in cooking and wine. Pleau emphases purity in his cooking, and the freshest ingredients—and nothing on the menu is more than 475 calories. Miliotes has a wine-by-the-glass program that allows patrons to mix and match wines with each course, and he makes annual trips to South Africa to blend Indaba Chardonnay for Seasons 52. He's won a raft-full of awards, among them *Wine Spectator*'s Award for Excellence. The restaurant has won awards, as well. *Porthole* magazine awarded Seasons 52 its Editor in Chief Award for 2010 for Best Restaurant.

Appetizers include spicy tandoori chicken skewers with mango chutney. Entrees boast dishes such as caramelized sea scallops with roasted asparagus and sun-dried tomato pearl pasta; and grilled tack of New Zealand lamb with potatoes, asparagus, and balsamic red onions. You can end with pecan pie with vanilla mousse or mango cheesecake.

32 EAST $$$$
32 East Atlantic Ave.
Delray Beach
(561) 276-7868
www.32east.com

Even on Delray's fabulous Atlantic Avenue, this smart, sophisticated eatery will catch your eye for its smart, sophisticated crowd eating outside, and for the innovative two-level design inside. This restaurant was established in 1996, on the site of an old auction house. It's a true American bistro, with the street-side terrace allowing you unlimited access to the great people-parade. The interior's a testament to contemporary American style, with upper- and lower-level dining areas, and hardwood floors on the upper level, a full-service bar, a grand piano, and different wines pictured on the walls.

The food matches the ambience. Executive chef/partner Nick Morfogen was named one of America's top new chefs in 1996, by *Food & Wine* magazine. Try his pan roasted Mississippi quail appetizer, stuffed with chorizo, corn, and manchego, on mashed potatoes with sherry wine pan sauce. For your entree, you might try the brine cured prairie grove pork chop with pancetta braised escarole, along with cinnamon spiced mashed yams with autumn fruits brown butter. And if you still have room for dessert after this, go for the crème brûlée or the cacao berry chocolate truffle cake.

Asian

LEMONGRASS   **$$**
420 East Atlantic Ave.
Delray Beach
(561) 278-5050
www.lemongrassasianbistro.com
This is a popular restaurant with a decor that can best be described as minimalist Oriental. The chairs are bright white, the lighting is very-funky track- and hanging-lighting, and there are several golden statues of an Oriental goddess. The food is very colorful and very fresh, with an emphasis on natural elements. There's also outdoor dining, right on the Atlantic Avenue sidewalk.

The lemongrass roll is a good way to start dinner here; it's pork, mushrooms, and water chestnuts that are deep-fried and then wrapped in rice paper. Also try the curry puff, a fried pastry stuffed with ground chicken, onion, yellow curry, and sweet potatoes, and served with cucumber relish. For entrees the Hawaiian Dancer combines scallops, chicken, pineapple, carrots, snow peas, bell peppers, and cashew nuts in tamarind sauce. The KC Rainbow is a sushi roll of tuna, salmon, yellowtail, imitation crab, asparagus, masago, and scallions, wrapped in cucumber and sesame seeds. And don't bypass Sex on the Moon—with shrimp tempura, avocado, asparagus, scallions, eel masago, and tuna, with tempura flakes on the top.

STIR CRAZY   **$$**
Boca Raton Town Center
6000 Glades Rd.
Boca Raton
(561) 338-7500
www.stircrazy.com

At Stir Crazy, you don't have to wait for food to come from the kitchen; you go to the kitchen to get the food. In this case, the kitchen's right in front of you along the wall of one side of the restaurant. You go up to make your selections from the Thai, Chinese, Japanese, and Vietnamese offerings and watch the chefs working right in front of you—cutting, chopping, slicing, dicing, and firing up the woks. Stir Crazy has a truly unique concept..

Set at the entrance to the swanky Boca Town Center Mall, this restaurant is a modern place filled with Asian touches such as hanging lanterns and paper scrolls. The food is innovative and colorful, and the atmosphere is lively and fun. If you're ordering off the menu, start with the crab cake hand rolls or the Thai sticky wings (in a sweet chili sauce); the pot stickers are great, as well. The hot and sour soup has bamboo shoots, tofu, and shiitake mushrooms. Or, you might opt for the mango salmon salad. The entrees are just as interesting. Coconut curry vegetables tossed with carrots, curry, onions, green beans, red peppers, and basil. Pad Thai is available with chicken, shrimp, or beef. The newest dessert sensation at Stir Crazy is the triple happiness chocolate cake.

i Palm Beach County leads the nation in the production of sugar and fresh sweet corn. The county produces roughly 18 percent of all sugar in the United States. It's the largest sugar-producing county in the nation, and it devotes some 400,000 acres to sugar cane—about a third of its land. Palm Beach County also leads all Florida counties in the production of rice, bell peppers, lettuce, radishes, Chinese vegetables, specialty leaf, and celery.

Bakery

OLD SCHOOL BAKERY & CAFÉ $
814 East Atlantic Ave.
Delray Beach
(561) 243-8059
It's hard to pass this bakery without going in. They specialize in multigrain breads, along with wonderful pastries and muffins. And there's even a Caribbean touch, as well, with banana bread that'll keep you coming back for more.

Barbecue

SMOKEY BONES BAR & FIRE GRILL $$
21733 State Rd. 7
Boca Raton
(561) 852-7870
www.smokeybones.com
Smokey Bones is located on State Road 7 (also called 441), west of Boca Raton. But it's truly worth a trip from anywhere. In fact, folks do come from all over South County, for a rib-stickin' taste of genuine American comfort-food that satisfies the soul as much as it does the hunger. And, as a result, the restaurant has won several awards.

There are a couple of appetizers that are really popular. The crowd pleaser is a sampler of what the restaurant calls Fire-starter Favorites—fire sticks, flippin' fingers, and smoke rings, with a nice variety of dippin' sauces. The mini mixer is three each of mini-porkies, mini-beefies, and mini-hotties (wings). The baby back ribs are excellent, as is the garlic-glazed sirloin. And you can top the meats off with stuff like steak house butter, bleu cheese crumbles, or button mushroom wine sauce.

Brazilian

GOL! THE TASTE OF BRAZIL $$$$
411 East Atlantic Ave.
Delray Beach
(561) 272-6565
www.golthetasteofbrazil.com
Brazilian is one of the up-and-coming cuisines in Palm Beach County—especially for its succulent grilled meats. And Gol! The Taste of Brazil highlights this cuisine in a very unique way. When you sit down at your table, you'll notice a disk with red on one side and green on the other. While you sample the 40-plus items at the salad bar—including Brazilian cheese-bread, crispy yucca root, and Portuguese potatoes—you keep the disk on the red side. Then, when you're ready to sample the meats and fish, you'll turn it over to green. And an ongoing parade of gaucho-garbed servers will then approach your table every few minutes, with an assortment of meats (15 different cuts), chicken, salmon, and shrimp, each grilled and spiced to perfection. A partial list: house special (picanha), top sirloin, flank steak, prime rib, pork loins, pork ribs, Brazilian sausage, chicken legs, chicken breast wrapped in bacon, lamb chops, grilled salmon, and grilled shrimp, and grilled pineapple.

It won't take you long to see why the local *New Times* newspaper gave this restaurant its award for Best Rodizio (this type of priced-fixe service) in Palm Beach County. The goodies will keep coming as long as your disk is turned to green. Then you can top your dinner off with Brazilian flan or crème of papaya. Owner Franklin Reider developed the wine list himself, and he designed the glassed-in wine cellar in the center of the restaurant from which the wines are taken.

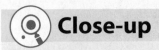 **Close-up**

Floribbean Cuisine

"Floribbean" is a word that first came into Palm Beach County lexicon in the mid-eighties and describes a type of cooking that's reflective of the area's divergent ethnic and cultural influences. And now—though you won't hear this word used that often—it's nonetheless become a staple in a number of restaurants around the area. Floribbean is a fusion of native Florida favorites with the goods, colors, and cooking styles of the counties of the Caribbean . . . most of whom are relatively close to South Florida. The Caribbean influences come mostly from Haiti, the Bahamas, Jamaica, and Trinidad and Tobago—with a dash, believe it or not, from the American South.

Floribbean tastes are nothing if not distinctive and sharp . . . and this is partly because of the heavy use of spices such as red curry, lemongrass, ginger, and scallions. The foods themselves are not necessarily all that different—there's an emphasis on poultry and seafood—but the preparations are. This type of cooking places a great emphasis on fresh ingredients, and there is a natural presentation rather than one that is ostentatious or glamorous. And the spices are almost always softened by bits of fruit, such as mango or papaya, or fruit juices. Over the years, "Floribbean" has grown to include infusions of other influences, such as Latino, and even Asian (an example of the Latino-Floribbean style would be *arroz con pollo* (chicken with rice) or white rice with black beans. Rice is a staple of this type of cooking, as is a banana-like fruit popular in South Florida called the plantain, along with onions, garlic, and peppers. And while you won't find many purely "Floribbean" restaurants in Palm Beach County, you'll find plenty of restaurants with Floribbean-influenced dishes.

Caribbean/Floridian/Latino

OLD CALYPSO $$$$
900 East Atlantic Ave.
Delray Beach
(561) 279-2300
www.oldcalypso.com

Old Calypso feels more like a redoubt of the old British Empire than it does a waterside restaurant in Delray Beach. The architecture is definitely British colonial. But the furniture and decor is actually evocative of Ernest Hemingway's wonderful house down in Key West, with its tile ceilings, floors of Brazilian walnut, and chairs with intricate tapestries.

This is a three-star restaurant, serving traditional tropical cuisine in an upscale atmosphere. To start your dinner off, try some bimini bread, sweet and fresh from the oven. Then move on to the oysters on the half shell or the crawfish and spinach dip. The Stilton bleu cheese salad is excellent. If you love good soup, don't miss the roasted corn and crabmeat chowder. The crispy fried lobster tails are stuffed with crabmeat and fried with a tempura batter, then served with butter, mustard sauce, and soy ginger sauce. The seafood paella has lobster, shrimp, scallops, mussels, andouille sausage, fish, and spinach, and it's blended with calypso rice. The Best Damn Chicken is exactly that, roasted French-style and served over a bed of potatoes, carrots, and tomatoes. There are some excellent champagnes and Chardonnays here. On weekends there's live Caribbean music to get you in that Island mood, mon. Open 365 days a year.

SOL KITCHEN $$$
4 East Atlantic Ave.
Delray Beach
(561) 921-0201
www.solkitchenrestaurant.com
Sol Kitchen is rather an interesting restaurant. Across the street from historic Old School Square, it's a colorful restaurant with a lively atmosphere, seating both indoors and out, and a very cool bar. Chef Ryan Brown is a South Florida native, which means he grew up with Caribbean and Latin specialties, as well. Emphasizing local and seasonal ingredients, he creates innovative dishes. The pan-roasted Rhode Island mussel with melted habanero-lime butter will start your evening off with a definite kick. Patrons also love his So-Cal fish taco with shredded cabbage, tomato, and lime as a starter. Popular entrees include crispy pork milanese with heirloom tomatoes, romaine hearts, and pineapple mojo; and grilled local dolphin with yucca fries, avocado, and cilantro.

Chinese

FENG LIN $
1561 South Congress Ave.
Delray Beach
(561) 278-6225
www.risingdragonusa.net
Feng Lin offers good, colorful Chinese food in a casual atmosphere. You can start off with Chinese sugar donuts (bet you can't eat just one), or a sesame ball, and then move

on to entrees like Thai curry coconut shrimp, or happy family—a combination of chicken, beef, roast pork, and jumbo shrimp with vegetables in a brown sauce. Feng Lin serves beer and wine.

RED LANTERN $$
8221 Glades Rd.
Boca Raton
(561) 482-8817
This place is a bit hard to find, tucked away in an inside corner of a busy Boca strip mall, right next to a Dunkin' Donuts, and a bit hard to see from Glades Road. But it's well worth the extra minute or two it might take you to find it. The combination plates are very popular. The hot and sour soup is very, well, hot and sour. The spare-rib appetizer is a must. And the sesame chicken and orange beef are superb. Red lantern serves beer and wine.

UNCLE TAI'S $$$
The Shops at Boca Center
5250 Town Center Circle
Boca Raton
(561) 368-8806
www.uncle-tais.com
Uncle Tai's is an elegant Chinese restaurant, where people go to enjoy an evening, not just a meal. The interior is intimate and woodsy, with clean Oriental accents. The cooking is in the style of Hunan Province. In this province, bright colors and sharp flavors are emphasized, and items such as black beans, garlic, and oranges provide both depth and seasoning to the dishes. Appetizers include the diced chicken lettuce wrap and sharkfin/crabmeat soup. The entrees are different than you'd find in most Chinese restaurants—seafood delight over noodles, Hunan-style; or sliced venison with

garlic sauce. For dessert, try the sesame fried banana and ice cream or lychee.

There really is an Uncle Tai, by the way. Wan Dah "Uncle Tai" apprenticed in a restaurant at the age of 13, in Shanghai. After living in New York and Houston for a while, he moved to Boca in 1987—and his restaurant has been one of the best in its genre ever since. Uncle Tai's has a boatload of awards, such as the Five Star Diamond Award from the American Academy of Restaurant and Hospitality Services, and *South Florida* magazine named it Best Chinese Restaurant in Palm Beach County.

Continental

CIELO $$$$
Boca Raton Resort & Club
501 East Camino Real
Boca Raton
(561) 447-3640
www.bocaresort.com/dining/cielo_by_
angela_hartnett.cfm
When you walk out of the elevator on the 27th floor of the Tower building at the Boca Raton Resort & Club, you're walking into perhaps the most extraordinary panorama you've ever seen. And you're also walking into one of the most extraordinary restaurants. South County spreads out before you, flowing into a soft horizon of earth, Intracoastal, and Atlantic. The restaurant was created by Michelin-Star Chef Angela Hartnett, and it won the 2010 AAA Four Diamond Award. This is the type of place that's an evening's entertainment unto itself.

You might start with seared Hudson Valley foie gras, with fig chutney, candied walnuts, and ginger snap tuile (a lightweight, dry cookie). Or prosecco risotto, which is baby octopus, Key West prawn, and scallops. For entrees, the butter-poached Maine

lobster has a crispy pork belly, butternut squash gnocchi, and mushroom and wine fume. Then there's the prosciutto-wrapped veal chop, with sweetbread saltimbocca, fingerling potato, and seasonal mushrooms. For dessert, you've got to try the Bailey's crème brûlée, with mocha foam and coffee beignets. *NOTE:* Cielo is open only to guests at the Boca Raton Resort & Club, or club members.

Cuban/Spanish

PADRINO'S $$
20455 State Rd. 7, Suite AA-1
Boca Raton
(561) 451-1070
www.padrinos.com/home.htm
Padrino's actually started back in Cuba in the 1930s, as a food market and winery. With the rise of Castro, Diosdado Padrino sent his wife Rosa and their two children to the United States, and he followed a few years later. They opened their first restaurant outside Miami in 1976, using the same recipes Rosa cooked in Cuba. They passed their traditions on to their son Mario and his wife Nayade, who oversees recipe development and quality-control. And the two of them have opened restaurants all over South Florida.

For an appetizer try canelones de pollo, morsels of chicken wrapped in mozzarella cheese and ham, lightly breaded and served with a light red sauce. One of Padrino's specialties is paella, a combination of chicken, scallops, shrimp, mussels, fish, and langostinos cooked with yellow rice. If you're a meat-lover, try the currasco steak, a skirt-steak char-grilled with chimichurri sauce. Cuban desserts are great, as well. One of the house specialties is Tres Leches, a homemade semi-sponge cake saturated in a sweet mixture of three milks. And at Padrino's you've got to try the flan made with cream cheese and topped with caramelized sugar sauce. Padrino's serves beer and wine. *Gold Coast* magazine voted Pardrino's Best Cuban Food in South Florida in 2007.

Deli

BAGELS WITH CAFÉ & DELI $
1732 S. Federal Hwy.
Delray Beach
(561) 279-4799
www.bagelswith.com

Bagels With is sort of a local legend around these parts . . . so much so that readers of the *South Florida Sun-Sentinel* voted it the best bagel place in Delray. It's spot with a fiercely loyal clientele, some of whom have been gathering here for years. All the old deli favorites are here: bagels, melts (tuna and otherwise), egg sandwiches, salads, soups, specialty sandwiches piled high with your favorite meats, and desserts such as rugalach and black-and-white cookies. And there are some rather unorthodox touches, as well. For example, you can create your own salad—called the fancy schmancy chopped salad. Customers here swear by the bagel dogs. And the turkey pesto sandwich has always been a big seller, with grilled honey-cured turkey, roasted red peppers, romaine lettuce, tomato, melted provolone, and pesto aioli on a grilled kaiser roll. No liquor, beer, or wine.

PASTRAMI QUEEN $$
132 Beracasa Way
Boca Raton
(561) 391-8989
www.pastramiqueenofboca.com

Owners Denise and Gary Zinger sold a bagel restaurant a few years ago to open a new deli in Boca. The decor is a bit different than the usual deli. There are chandeliers, and one wall is plastered with old black-and-white photographs of late 19th-century Eastern European life. And the background music always includes lots of Sinatra. The old specialties reminiscent of New York are very much in evidence here. Appetizers include fried kreplach with fried onions, and the Oy Vey-Royal Platter, with derma, stuffed cabbage, two potato latkes, and noodle kugel. For an entree, try the wonderfully named Dare You!—it's a full pound of any meat of your choice (tongue is extra) piled high on rye bread. The roast fresh brisket of beef will leave you feeling satisfied all afternoon. The Queen serves beer and wine.

TOOJAY'S $$
In the Polo Shops
5030 Champion Blvd.
Boca Raton
(561) 241-5903
www.toojays.com/index.html

Toojay's started as a New York Style delicatessen on the very un-New Yorkish island of Palm Beach, in 1981. And the names of the founders explain the name of the restaurant—Jay Brown and Mark Jay Katzenberg. At the time, starting a New York deli was something of a risk. But it must have paid off—because now there are 26 Toojay's restaurants, and three in Boca. Toojay's won *Boca Raton* magazine's Reader's Choice Award for Best Deli four times in recent years. And the prestigious Zagat Survey gave it the Award of Excellence three consecutive years.

This restaurant is a loud, homey place, where locals run into friends all the time, and the hostesses and servers often know their guests by first-name. Appetizers, as you might expect from a deli with such a reputation, are very . . . appetizing. The loaded latkes are crispy potato-pancake bites topped with melted cheddar, bacon, tomatoes, sour cream, and scallions. And, naturally, if it's a New York deli, you've got to try the matzo ball soup. A lot of the regulars here enjoy the grilled London broil served with mashed potatoes, mushroom gravy, and vegetable. Another favorite is the vegetable lasagna, which features roasted peppers, zucchini, yellow squash, mushrooms, and eggplant. Toss on some provolone, and served it with garlic bread, and you've got a feast. Toojays serves beer and wine. The other two Boca locations are in the Regency Court at 3013 Yamato Rd. (561-997-9911) and in Glades Plaza at 2200 West Glades Rd. (561-392-4181).

Dessert

KILWIN'S CHOCOLATES &
ICE CREAM $
402 East Atlantic Ave.
Delray Beach
(561) 278-0808
www.kilwins.com
Swarms of people line up at Kilwin's before or after eating on Atlantic Avenue, especially on weekend evenings. In truth, it's really difficult to pass this colorful shop without going in, especially when you get a whiff of what's going on inside. The place is redolent with the aroma of chocolate being mixed right in the front window, of a dozen different types of fudge being cooked and then cooled, and of apples being dipped in caramel. And the ice cream! Incredible colors and flavors and textures. Bubble gum ice cream, pralines and cream, Mackinac fudge, Kilwin's tracks (a mixture of vanilla and fudge-swirls and nuts), cherry with huge chunks, and chocolate chip. And sherbet in various brilliant candy colors. There's a real choo-choo train running around the top of the wall. And every conceivable ice cream (and chocolate) treat below it.

THE SUNDY HOUSE
106 South Swinton Ave.
Delray Beach
(561) 272-5678
www.sundyhouse.com
Ambience is everything at the Sundy House. It's a majestic old Florida house, in the Victorian style, with 11 guest rooms, lush gardens, and a freshwater, fish-filled pool in which you can actually swim. It's also one of South County's best places to eat. The chefs whip up sensory sensations that are treats for the eyes as well as the palate, such as Marsala poached pears with cranberry goat cheese, candied walnuts, and truffled honey. Or vanilla bean crème brûlée, with chantilly cream and fresh berries. Or the pumpkin trio—pumpkin flan, spiced shortbread cookie, and pumpkin ice cream with dulce de leche sauce. Need we say more?

Fondue

THE MELTING POT $$$
5455 North Federal Hwy., Suite A
Boca Raton
(561) 997-7472
www.meltingpot.com
The Melting Pot is one of the best places around to enjoy an intimate dinner with a friend or spouse. There are private, curtained booths available, and each table has burners built right into it. All cooking is done right in front of you. The experts seem to like this approach. Zagat gave the restaurant an award, and *Wine Spectator* magazine gave it an Award of Excellence for 1999–2009.

The Melting Pot is all about fondue . . . thick, spicy, hot, swirling, dipping fondue, generally made of a variety of melted cheeses. The fondue comes with fresh breads, vegetables, meats, chicken, shrimp, and apples for dipping. You just take a long fork, stick it into whichever of the above you'd like, and dip it into the boiling pot. A minute or two later, you've got a very singular taste treat. The restaurant offers some specialties—the spinach artichoke cheese fondue consists of fontina and butterkäse cheeses, spinach, artichoke hearts and garlic. And the Signature Selection is filet mignon, white shrimp, teriyaki-marinated sirloin, breast of chicken, and cedar plank salmon. Dessert here is special, as well. Try the Original, which is milk chocolate with a swirl of crunchy peanut butter. Or, you can get bananas, pineapple, and marshmallows, along with some chocolate for dipping, and have a tableside splurge.

French

LA CIGALE, A TASTE OF
  THE MEDITERRANEAN $$$
253 S.E. Fifth Ave.
Delray Beach
(561) 265-0600
www.lacigaledelray.com

Think of the French Riviera, with a splash of Greek, Italian, and Moroccan, and you'll have an idea of the cuisine at La Cigale. The owner, Francis Touboul, is a native of Marseille. And your meal can be a wonderful combination of all the nearby influences to his hometown. For example, you can start your meal with an arugula Salad, topped by sliced prosciutto, shaved Parmesan, and champagne vinaigrette. The jumbo shrimp provençal entree is served with sautéed spinach, roasted plum tomatoes, white wine garlic sauce, and a touch of Pernod liqueur. The seafood crepes are filled with scallops and shrimp, and garnished with sautéed spinach and a lobster sauce. Also excellent is the wild salmon en papillote, cooked in parchment paper and surrounded by julienne vegetables, asparagus, truffle butter, and rice pilaf. You must try the beef bourguignon cooked in red wine, with pearl onions, bacon, mushrooms, and mashed potatoes. And, with French/Mediterranean cuisine, you have to leave room, of course, for the dessert.

The decor at La Cigale is stunning. It's a collection of the abstract brightest wall art you've ever seen, running along the entire length of the walls and painted on them, rather than hanging on them. Large round lights hang from the ceiling. The bright-orange cloth napkins and dark-wood chairs stand out against the gleaming white tablecloths.

Greek

MYKONOS GREEK RESTAURANT
6897 S.W. Eighteenth St.
Boca Raton
(561) 338-3229

This restaurant is blessed with a stunning location—right on the lake, in the woodsy Wharfside Shops. The Greek salad here is excellent, crunchy and tasty and almost a meal in itself. So are the gyros, filled with chips of lamb or beef and a wonderful sauce. The eggplant dishes are very good. The moussaka is special; it's a combination of ground meat and layered vegetables. You have to wash it all down, of course, with some very strong, licorice-and-anise-tinged ouzo. But not before you also have some baklava for dessert, the sweet, sticky, flaky pastry.

Health Food

NATURE'S WAY CAFÉ $
20 West Atlantic Ave.
Delray Beach
(561) 272-6200
www.natureswaycafe.com

Nature's Way Café has been a Florida tradition since 1978. The ingredients are the freshest and obtained from local sources whenever possible. The soups and salads are homemade, the shakes and smoothies are delicious, and everything's made to order. The restaurant positions itself as a healthy alternative to fast food. Some of the favorites are the chicken walnut raisin salad sandwich, and the Mexi-melt wrap—marinated grilled chicken breast wrapped with romaine, tomato, avocado, salsa, and melted jack cheese. All of the shakes are blended with fat-free vanilla frozen yogurt and either milk or juice. The Mutty Buddy has peanut butter, banana, and honey. One of the most popular smoothies here is the Sambazon Acai. The acai, as you may know from all the publicity it's received, is a potent Amazon fruit containing guarana, vitamin E, dietary fiber, and antioxidants. In this drink, it's blended with strawberries, banana, apple juice, and crushed ice.

SWEET TOMATOES $

7110 Beracasa Way
Boca Raton
(561) 750-3303
www.souplantation.com

If a place is always crowded at dinnertime, that tells you something. And if the place is always crowded even though it's a niche restaurant, that tells you even more. Sweet Tomatoes is for salad-lovers. It's got the longest salad-buffet you've ever seen, with over 50 ingredients, some of which you've never seen before in a salad bar. And the restaurant prides itself on the freshness of its food. Within 24 hours of being in the ground, produce is on a refrigerated truck on the way to the restaurant. The food's made from scratch

daily. And if you'd like to spice up the salad experience, there's also a hot buffet with pastas, original soups such as big chunk chicken noodle and Irish potato leek, homemade muffins, and focaccia breads. And the deep kettle house chili is definitely worth going back to the bar for. No alcoholic beverages.

Indian

PUNJAB INDIAN RESTAURANT $$

1801 North Federal Hwy.
Boca Raton
(561) 392-8000
www.punjabindiancuisine.com

Punjab is a family-friendly restaurant with style, another one of those places hidden in very modest surroundings that proves to be a delightful surprise. Candles and Indian music help make the atmosphere very unusual and very warm. And there are plenty of South County folks who claim this is the best Indian food in the region.

Appetizers are as delicious as they are exotic-sounding. Try the onion bhaji, vegetable fritters with onion, cauliflower, potatoes, and spinach, with those punchy Indian spices along for the ride. The cheese pakora is homemade cheese with chickpea flour. For entrees, one of the more popular dishes is chicken vindaloo, cooked in a spicy curry. The bhuna gosht is lamb or beef cooked with onion, green pepper, garlic, and spices. And the seikh kabob is minced lamb meat on a skewer, with herbs and spices. This being an Indian restaurant, there are plenty of good vegetarian dishes from which to choose. Eggplant bharta is whole eggplants baked over an open flame, mashed and seasoned with herbs and sautéed with onion. And the alu chole is another good dish, potatoes and chickpeas with a spicy curry sauce.

Italian

ARTURO'S RISTORANTE　　　$$$$
6750 North Federal Hwy.
Boca Raton
(561) 997-7373
www.arturosrestaurant.com

This white-stucco, red-tile-roofed Tuscan villa is a longtime landmark on Federal Highway, packed for both lunch and dinner with Boca Raton residents. You'll see all sorts of well-known local residents here, from actors to writers, dancers to politicians. Arturo's has won the Award of Excellence from Distinguished Restaurants of America, *Florida Trend* magazine's Golden Spoon Award, and Best Italian Restaurant from the readers of the *South Florida Sun-Sentinel*. And the superb wine collection has earned the restaurant *Wine Spectator* magazine's Award of Excellence—every year since 1993.

The dining room is bathed in light colors on the walls, and dark woods on the furniture and the piano, huge Italian arched windows allowing in plenty of natural light, elegant chandeliers, and works of art. And you can see into the bakery as the staff concocts wonderful dessert creations and breads.

The antipasti di pesce (seafood salad) is a notable appetizer, along with the carpaccio di manzo (beef carpaccio with rugola, shaved Parmesan, oil and lemon). Seafood entrees are highlighted by sogliola con salsa allo Champagne, a whole Dover sole in a Champagne sauce, deboned tableside. Also consider the costolette d'agnello al rosmarino, lamb chops sautéed with garlic, rosemary, and wine. If you're in the mood for pasta, go for the spaghetti pescatore, a beautiful plate of shrimp, scallops, calamari, clams, and mussels in a light tomato sauce. Your server will be able to help you choose an award-winning wine to go with the food you pick. If you've taken a minute to watch the activity inside the bakery, you'll know that desserts at Arturo's are wonderful. You'll find a variety of fresh concoctions in the Dolci Arturo's (rolling cart). And the zabaglione for two is *molto buono*—hot marsala custard served on vanilla ice cream and strawberries.

MAGGIANO'S LITTLE ITALY　　　$$$
21090 St. Andrews Blvd.
Boca Raton
(561) 361-8244
www.maggianos.com

Maggiano's Little Italy is an interesting juxtaposition of sophisticated Italian dining in a large place, with a friendly, fun atmosphere. Its dark wood tables and chairs flow with servers and diners moving back and forth. There's family-style dining, as well as individual service. The restaurant packs them in, all day long and all night long. And the reason is simple—the food is great. And the experience is fun.

The bruschetta appetizer is one that you might want to order again, it's toasted Italian garlic bread with a tomato bruschetta relish made of diced tomatoes, balsamic vinegar, and roasted garlic. But if you're really going to have two appetizers, make the second one the mushroom ravioli al forno—ravioli stuffed with mushrooms, onions, Marsala wine, and Parmesan cheese, and then baked with alfredo sauce. Entrees? The garlic shrimp linguine is everything you'd imagine a wonderful Italian seafood dish to be. The veal chop contadina is a 19-oz. veal chop served with Italian sausage, vesuvio potatoes, roasted peppers, onions, and tomatoes. For a flavor of a different kind, try the gnocchi in tomato vodka sauce, a type of Italian dumpling. It's ricotta pasta with pomodoro cream, vodka, and roasted garlic. The desserts include crème brûlée, New York-style cheesecake, and Maggiano's own homemade spumoni ice cream, a blend of pistachio, chocolate, and cherry. The signature wine here is a special blend of five varietals from Robert Mondavi's Reserve (very special vintages!).

TABLE 42 ITALIAN KITCHEN & WINE BAR $$
Royal Palm Place
399 S.E. Mizner Blvd.
Boca Raton
(561) 826-2625
www.grrestaurant.com

Table 42 is situated in Royal Palm Place, one of South County's most beautiful shopping areas. The interior of Table 42 is smart and sleek, with contemporary shapes, angles, and vivid colors; yet, it's also got some of the trappings of an Italian country manor, with high archways, plush carpets, and ornate carvings on columns.

You can dine inside or out. Chef Matthew Danaher emphasizes classic Italian cuisine with a contemporary twist. Pizzas are baked in an authentic coal oven. Wine is served in authentic flasks from Italy. The sauces are all homemade, using San Marzano tomatoes. The meat comes exclusively from a western ranch at which enlightened methods are used. And the salad bowls come with a build-your-own option.

The starters give you a taste of what you're in for. The GIANT MEATBALL (in capital letters on the menu) is drenched with San Marzano sauce and ricotta cheese. The roasted artichoke comes with crispy caper aioli and oil verde. Chicken parmigiana is the signature entree at Table 42; it's encrusted in herb crumbs and mozzarella. The salmon,

with basil pesto and oil verde, is also excellent. And if you've never had pizza from a coal oven, you don't know what you're missing. It has a slightly smokey, denser, sharper flavor, and the sensation on your tongue is really nice. There are all kinds of specialty pies here, among them red onion, goat cheese, and spicy pesto. You can compliment your meal with a sweet Italian dessert such as a cannoli with chocolate shavings or tiramisu with dark-chocolate curls. Since the second half of Table 42's title is "Wine Bar," you get a good selection of award-winning wines.

VIC & ANGELO'S GRAND ITALIAN COAL OVEN ENOTECA $$$$
290 East Atlantic Ave.
Delray Beach
(561) 278-9570
www.vicandangelos.com

David Manero brought his Sunday-family-dinner tradition to America, with his restaurant named after his two cousins. The restaurant's motto is "From the Garden to the Plate" . . . and all the ingredients are imported from Italy (except for the water used to make the pizza, which comes from New York, because it makes the best crust). It's a homey place, with brick walls, high leather bench-seating in the booths, and unusual lighting fixtures hanging from the ceiling.

A before-dinner selection of Italian meats, like prosciutto di parm and finocchiona dry (cured fennel salami) are served on wooden boards. There's a variety of wonderful antipastos—hot and cold—ranging from ahi tuna crudo to grilled calamari. The larger dishes? The linguini alla fruti di mare comes with shrimp, clams, calamari, lobster, and spicy San Marzano. The tortellini comes with butternut squash, thyme, and tomato.

And the veal Angelo comes with creamy San Marzano, buffala, mozzarella, eggplant, and pasta.

But many people come to Vic and Angelo's just for the pizza. It comes out of that oven steaming-hot, and with a slightly charred crust, after being cooked at 900 degrees. It comes with a taste easily distinguishable from "regular" pizza such iterations as Don Vito, with smoked mozzarella, provolone, sausage, and roasted onions; or Mulberry Street, with eggplant, mozzarella, reggiano, and crushed red pepper. And it can come with any one of some 20 toppings.

Japanese

MASA $$
1648 South Federal Hwy.
Delray Beach
(561) 243-9116
www.sushimasa.cc

At Sushi Masa, the food looks like a work of art on your plate; it's a kaleidoscope of colors and textures that looks too good to eat. All the great Japanese dishes you've come to associate with sushi bars are here—sushi, tempura, teriyaki, udon, and sushi rolls. And all the great flavors of Thailand are here, as well—green and red curries, peanut sauces, larb (a type of meat salad, accompanied by string beans, cabbage, water spinach, and basil), along with the seafood and noodle dishes for which Thai cuisine is so famous.

Start off with the tuna tataki, perhaps; it's seared outside, rare inside, served cold with ponzu sauce, masago, and scallion. Or go Thai, with a Thai wrap of glass noodles, chicken, and mushroom rolled in rice paper and served with a sauce for dipping. Deciding on an entree can sometimes be difficult when you havetwo tasty national cuisines from which to choose. You can't go wrong,

though, with the Boca roll, which is fish, cream cheese, scallions, cilantro, and masago that is battered and fried with a spicy sauce. Or the (Japanese) yakiniku, which is slices of beef sautéed with onion, ginger, mushroom, and teriyaki sauce. Or try the Thai dish called volcano shrimp; the crustacean treats are battered and fried with chili sauce, and served on steamed vegetables.

MORIMOTO'S SUSHI BAR $$$
Boca Raton Resort and Club
501 East Camino Real
Boca Raton
(561) 447-3000
www.bocaresort.com/dining/morimoto
.cfm

Morimoto's may be the most strikingly elegant modern-design restaurant you've ever seen. A long granite sushi bar is backed by red panels with abstract blue fish, and fronted by deep-blue futuristic (but very comfortable) chairs; and, of course, there's a sushi chef working busily behind the bar. This exquisite restaurant is the first Southeastern outpost of Chef Masaharu Morimoto of *Iron Chef* fame. It fuses his Hiroshima upbringing and New York training.

Chef Morimoto's appetizers are as delicious as they are innovative. Try the tuna pizza, a crispy tortilla with tuna sashimi, jalapeño, tomato, red onion, and anchovy sauce. The carpaccio appetizer entails the chef's choice of fish, thinly sliced with hot oil and ginger. The soft shell crab maki is deep-fried, comes with asparagus, tobiko, and avocado, and is dressed in a spicy sauce. If you're in the mood to try something different, try the aji, the name for an interesting type of fish called carangidae–(horse mackerel).

The specialty cocktails and drinks are very creative, reflecting this fusion of Oriental tradition and modern decor. The Morimotini, for example, has Belvedere vodka, junmai sake, and a cucumber slice. The Hydrangea-Ajisai is infused with Absolut mandarin, St. Elderflower liqueur, lychee puree, and cranberry juice. Closed for lunch on Wed.

Mediterranean

WILD OLIVES   **$$$**
The Shops at Boca Center
5050 Town Center Circle
Boca Raton
(561) 544-8000
www.wildolives.com

Celebrity Chef Todd English owns this restaurant, so you know it's good. In 2001, English was named Restaurateur of the Year by *Bon Appetit*. He has his own cooking and travel series, *Food Trip with Todd English,* on PBS, for which he won an Emmy nomination. And he's the official chef of the airline you might take to get to South Florida—Delta.)

There's definitely a Continental touch to Wild Olives. The cocoa-colored walls sport oversized rectangular mirrors, along with colorful modern art. And there's a patio area with brown wicker chairs and ceiling fans. The cooking is as you might expect—imaginative. You can start off with appetizers such as Carpet Bagger Oysters, wrapped in beef carpaccio; or fig and prosciutto flatbread, with crispy rosemary crust, jam, and gorgonzola cheese. Then you can go on to brown sugar cured bone in rib eye, with Parmesan whipped potatoes and roasted root vegetables. And you'll want to save at least a bit of room for desserts such as cookies and cream or Todd's ricotta cheese cake, with pecan crumbles, cranberry compote, and whipped cream.

Mexican/Southwestern

BAJA CAFÉ UNO   **$$**
201 N.W. First Ave.
Boca Raton
(561) 394-5449
www.bajacafe.com

It's a bit hard to see, at first, hidden on the side of the railroad tracks in downtown Boca. But then you can't miss it; this building is a colorful collage of Southwestern colors and angles and red-tile rooflines. Tables of bright yellow and red are scattered amidst pink and yellow or lime wooden fences, wall hangings, sombreros, bright Mexican tiles, and wall art.

The culinary mix includes a bit of Baja California with Southwestern and Mexican. You must start with one of the 12 different types of margaritas, ranging from the Trillion $$$ to the Kick-Ass. Apertivios (appetizers) include macho nachoes (with too many ingredients to list!), and frijoles diablo (the devil's beans), with smashed pinto beans, spicy cheese, and pico de gallo. Or, speaking of the devil you may be interested in trying the Hellfire and Damnation Enchiladas, two corn tortillas stuffed with pulled chicken and salsa verde and topped with homemade green salsa and cheese. For entrees, try the chile verde steak (Mexican stew in a roasted tomato ranchero sauce) or the shrimp asada (white shrimp sautéed in wine, olive oil, Baja salsa, peppers, onions, and spices, and then stuffed into a flour tortilla and backed with cheese). There's plenty of good Mexican beer, of course (Corona and Dos Equis), and at last count 43 brands of tequila.

MOQUILA RESTAURANT &
** TEQUILA BAR**   **$$$**
99 S.E. Mizner Blvd.
Boca Raton
(561) 394-9990
www.moquila.com

The readers of *Boca Raton* magazine voted this one the best Mexican place in town. And that's high praise. When MoQuila opened in 2007, it was heralded as a new kind of Mexican cuisine and Mexican experience. MoQuila is a swank, cosmopolitan place with rich-looking woods, back-lit walls, wall sconces, and hanging silver lamps, augmented by authentic Mexican furnishings. The cuisine is defined by the fresh ingredients and recipes of the Mexican mountains . . . as well as 200 types of tequila. One of the most popular starters is camarones borrachos, which is "drunken" shrimp, Don Julio Silver Tequila, roasted peppers, onions, and chili butter sauce. But you can't go wrong, either, if you opt for the tartare de atún, which is yellowfin tuna tartar, grilled pineapple, guacamole pico, and pumpkin seed crackers. The sopa de tortilla (chicken tortilla soup) is also a favorite. For the *platos grandes,* the carne asada is an excellent choice; it's grilled skirt steak with roasted mushrooms, cilantro rice, crispy plantains, and chimichuri sauce. Also notable is the pescado con miel de agave—grouper glazed with agave nectar, and garnished with green beans, roasted hearts of palm, and pineapple-jicama salsa. For dessert, try the wonderful churros, fried fritters coated with sugar and cinnamon.

UNCLE JULIO'S   **$–$$**
449 Plaza Real
Boca Raton
(561) 300-3530
www.unclejulios.com
Border-style Mexican is the cuisine served in this family-friendly, colorful restaurant, with its large wall murals of Mexican life, Mexican wall sconces, deep-pinks and bright oranges, old hanging mirrors with ornate wooden frames, and woven wall hangings.

In addition to the old favorites like tacos, enchiladas, and tamales, Uncle Julio's specializes in marinated and mesquite-grilled beef and chicken fajitas, ribs, quail, frog legs, and jumbo shrimp. And Uncle Julio's is also known for a drink called The Swirl, which is a frozen concoction of layered margarita and homemade sangria.

Appetizers include chile con queso, a spicy blend of chili and cheeses (you can add sausage), and spinach quesadillas. The Mexican corn chowder is thick and tasty, as is the poblano beef fajita soup. For your entree, consider the quail a la parilla, mesquite-grilled and then basted with a chipotle barbecue sauce; or the Juarez, pork ribs smoked over a mesquite fire, with a choice of chicken, beef, or combination fajitas, and chipotle barbecue sauce. When it comes time for dessert, it's hard to resist the sopapillas, which are Mexican pastries sprinkled with cinnamon and powdered sugar, and served with warm honey for dipping. But if you do find yourself resisting the sopapillas, you might want to head for the cajeta—vanilla ice cream with toasted coconut and pecans, with the restaurant's own caramel sauce and whipped cream on top. Then there are the margaritas, which, beside the aforementioned Swirl, include specialties like the Chambord Margarita (frozen, made with Chambord liqueur) and Baja Gold (a frozen margarita mixed with Corona Beer).

Middle Eastern

SABRA MEDITERRANEAN GRILL   **$$**
9874 Yamato Rd.
Boca Raton
(561) 451-8100
www.sabragrillbocaraton.com
Sabra Mediterranean Grill is in a brand-new shopping center in West Boca Raton. It's

decorated in earth-tone walls and Middle Eastern accents, with a large mural of Jerusalem (painted by owner Jayne Rosen) on the wall. It's a lively, family-friendly place, and it's become a real gathering place for lovers of authentic Israeli and Middle Eastern cooking.

All the traditional dishes are here— grilled chicken, beef, kafta (balls of minced or ground meat), lamb kabobs, Israeli salad, baba ghanoush, hummus, stuffed grape leaves, and falafel pita sandwiches, filled to the brim. For those who like it hot, there's S'hug, made from hot green chili peppers. And the grilled meats are great. The Kafta Kebob Platter includes two skewers of ground beef mixed with parsley, onions, and seasoning. The Shawarma Platter is turkey and lamb grilled on a traditional vertical rotisserie. There's also a Vegetarian Platter with hummus and different salads. For dessert, there's sticky, wonderfully crunchy-and-sweet baklava, along with sweet pita chips, Sabra's own concoction of sugar-and-cinnamon pita chips.

Pizza

MAMA'S PIZZA & PASTA $
19785 Hampton Dr. #6
Boca Raton
(561) 483-5454
You'll have to look around a bit for Mama's; it's somewhat hidden in a tiny strip mall back from the street. But the search is well worth it. This little place has been around for nearly 30 years, still run by the same family. And it's a delightful Boca secret. There's a full menu, and it's all good. But you come to Mama's for the pizza; it's legendary among Boca folks. It's known particularly for the crust, crispy and delicious. The atmosphere is like that of the old-time pizza places you remember, with photos of places to which the owners have traveled. Everyone's treated like family here, and many of the regulars have been coming since the place opened. Try the sausage and pepper or the sausage and pepperoni pizzas. And if you're looking for consistently great pizza take the trouble to fine Mama's Pizza & Pasta. Serves beer and wine. Cash only; no credit cards.

ROTELLI'S $–$$
501 East Atlantic Ave.
Delray Beach
(561) 272-7270
www.rotellipizzapasta.com
Rotelli's has the greatest location—right in the heart of Atlantic Avenue, the popular dining, clubbing, see-and-be-seen spot. Despite its glitzy surroundings, this is a "regular" place with great Italian food and consistently good pizza. Joe Bilotti, a former airline pilot, opened the restaurant because of what he considered an unmet need in South Florida. Here you can see the real chefs making it in the cooking area. The calzone and the stromboli are cheesy and crusty and bursting with good stuff. The veal parmigiana is great. The pasta dishes are good. And the hot and cold sandwiches are a big favorite. But people from all over South County come here for the pizza.

You can get cheese pizzas with a long list of toppings, including artichoke hearts or grilled chicken. But the real stars here may be the gourmet pizzas, which you can get in personal-size as well as standard-size. The chicken Marsala pizza comes in a base of mushrooms and marsala wine, topped with grilled chicken, mushrooms, and two cheeses. The Napoletana comes with sausage, pepperoni, onions, mushrooms, green peppers, and pecorino and mozzarella cheeses. And the baba ghanoush brings a little bit of the Middle East to Italy, with a base of eggplant, tahini, olive oil, and garlic, and topped with spinach, tomato, mozzarella, gorgonzola, and pignoli nuts.

Seafood

BOSTON'S ON THE BEACH $$$
40 South Ocean Blvd. (A1A)
Delray Beach
(561) 278-3364
www.bostonsonthebeach.com
Boston's has been serving wonderful food and spectacular views for nearly 30 years. It's right across the street from the ocean. And it has a fun, casual atmosphere typical of oceanside places. There's casual dining, live music, and sports-viewing on the first floor, an area called The Beach by the restaurant. Upstairs, though, in The Upper Deck, it's a different story. The atmosphere is a bit more formal, and the food is more upscale. Management also recently added the Back Bay Tiki Bar, a smoker-friendly environment where you can enjoy cocktails and music on the outdoor stage.

One of the big attractions at Boston's On the Beach is Monday Reggae Nights. And the food's a pretty compelling attraction, as well. Consider starting off with the seared jumbo sea scallops—on top of grilled tomatoes with greens, and smoked bacon beurre blanc. In addition, the Ipswich steamers (clams) are incredible; swish them in the broth before you dip 'em in the butter!

As far as entrees go, many people come here for the coconut and macadamia encrusted grouper, which comes with mint-cucumber relish, mango papaya salsa, island rice, and vegetables. The steak tyrolienne is an aged New York strip, with fried onions, artichoke hearts, the restaurant's signature steak sauce, UpperDeck potatoes, and

vegetables. Among all of the great desserts here, two stand out in particular. The chocolate bomb is a dark, dense cake filled with bittersweet chocolate and chocolate morsels. And the strawberry shortcake comes with strawberries piled on top of biscuit, and smothered with chantilly cream.

CITY FISH MARKET $$$
7940 Glades Rd.
Boca Raton
(561) 487-1600
www.buckheadrestaurants.com
City Fish Market's an attractive white building with a whimsical red-tile roof, piercing the blue Florida skies in a variety of shapes and angles reminiscent of the great resorts of a century ago. And it's set amidst a lake and tall trees in West Boca. Chef Anthony Hoff spent his boyhood in the Philippines, and emigrated to Maryland with his family when he was 12. He then earned a degree from Johnson and Wales University, a well-known cooking school in Miami. As a result, his style has been forged by a number of different culinary influences. He offers one of the largest selections of fresh seafood in South Florida . . . so fresh, in fact, that the menu actually changes twice daily.

If you come with a few people, you've got to try the fresh market iced tower (for two, four, or six); it's a platter brimming with Maine lobster, jumbo gulf shrimp, Alaskan king crab, and Maine oysters on the half shell. The creamy New England clam and cod chowder is warming and delicious, and the New Orleans seafood gumbo and jasmine rice will make you feel like you're in the French quarter. The surf special is lobster & frites, a cold water lobster tail that's flash-fried, and served with a honey-mustard sauce, drawn butter, and french fries. The restaurant's signature dish is stuffed Flounder with shrimp, crab, sea scallops, and mushrooms, in a white wine sauce. And repeat-customers at City Fish Market will tell you to try the lemon sole francese, sautéed in lemon butter and capers, with vegetables and potato. There's also a lively lounge area, offering small plates of appetizers, a good wine selection, and plenty of company if you like watching football with friends.

CITY OYSTER $$$
213 East Atlantic Ave.
Delray Beach
(561) 272-0220
www.bigtimerestaurants.com

Imagine an exciting, lively restaurant with the feel of an elegant Old-Time tavern, with brick walls, high tin ceilings, and bright paintings, and a grand bar that runs the entire length of the place. Imagine that restaurant sitting smack in the middle of one of the liveliest urban streets in South Florida. Then imagine that the seafood on your plate was most likely in the ocean or a river only a day before. You'd be imagining City Oyster, one of the most popular places on Atlantic Avenue, where people gather to eat, drink, and have a grand old time.

Because this place has oyster in its name, there's a chalkboard in the dining room which alerts guests to the daily oyster selection. To get your evening started, Chef Dennis Teixeira serves up appetizers like oysters Rockefeller or mussels in white wine and shallots. Then you'll move on to the entrees—lobster risotto with mussels, perhaps, or the surf & turf, with petite filet, Maine lobster tail, red bliss potatoes, and vegetable.

When it's time for dessert, Teixeira doesn't make the picking process any easier.

After seeing another diner with the caramel nut cookie basket with raspberry sorbet, you might want that. But then, after seeing someone else with the tiramisu, with espresso, mascarpone, white Chocolate, you may change your mind.

Steak

THE CAPITAL GRILLE $$$$
Boca Raton Town Center
6000 Glades Rd.
Boca Raton
(561) 368-1077
www.thecapitalgrille.com

The Capital Grille is known for an elegant ambience and for steaks and seafood that are world-class. Mahogany paneling, art deco chandeliers, and brass accents set the tone for a special evening. You can order a glass of wine—from the award-winning list of more than 5,000 bottles. American Culinary Federation recently bestowed its Achievement of Excellence Award on the restaurant.

You'll start with an appetizer like pan fried calamari with hot cherry peppers (the calamari is sautéed in garlic butter until crisp, then tossed with peppers and scallions for a finish with a kick!). If your dining companion, by any chance, starts off with the prosciutto wrapped mozzarella with vine ripe tomatoes (mozzarella wrapped in prosciutto and lightly sautéed, and served with crostini, fresh basil and a balsamic glaze), make sure you swap a few bites.

Capital Grille features excellent entrees from both the turf and the surf. The bone-in kona crusted dry aged sirloin with caramelized shallot butter is a sharp treat for the tongue, with caramelized shallots, seasonings and coffee rub. Many guests, in fact, claim it as their favorite. The broiled fresh lobster is also wonderful, the flavor enhanced by the caramelized natural sugars. The quality of the desserts is in line with the rest of the meal. The fresh strawberries Capital Grille combines strawberries, handmade vanilla ice cream, and the restaurant's own ruby port- and-Grand Marnier sauce; after one bite, you'll know why it's the signature dessert here. The chocolate hazelnut cake is a chocolate-lovers nirvana—layered with dark-chocolate mousse and coated with a hazelnut chocolate ganache.

MORTON'S THE STEAKHOUSE $$$$
5050 Town Center Circle
Boca Raton
(561) 392-7724
www.mortons.com

When it comes to great steaks, Morton's is the ultimate. This restaurant has a reputation as one of the best steak houses in the country—if not the world. And that reputation is well-earned. From the quality of the aged prime meats to the mahogany-accented decor, and from the white-glove service to the superb collection of wines to accompany your dinner, an evening here is an experience to savor. Even *Consumer Reports* (July 2009) chipped in on the chorus of praise for the restaurant, when it gave Morton's New York Strip Steak its Excellent rating. *Wine Spectator* gave the restaurant its Award of Excellence.

Two of the best appetizers here come from the sea, rather than the pasture—the tuna tartare, and the broiled sea scallops wrapped in bacon. Then there's the meat; it's all Midwestern grain-fed beef, direct from Chicago—the filet mignon, double cut, the filet Oskar. And even Morton's prime burger will tickle your taste buds. The desserts are just as tempting as the appetizers and entrees, particularly the legendary hot chocolate cake and the upside-down apple pie.

OLD HOMESTEAD $$$$
Boca Raton Resort and Club
501 East Camino Real
Boca Raton
(561) 447-3682
www.theoldhomesteadsteakhouse.com

The Old Homestead Steakhouse has a distinguished heritage; the original in New York has roots in pre-revolutionary times. However, this one has a somewhat more contemporary edge to its motto, boasting that it specializes in the four major food groups: Beef. Beef. Beef. And beef.

From the moment you walk in, you'll be enveloped in an atmosphere of mahogany walls, cherry-red leather booths lining the walls, mirrors, and old bookshelves—an atmosphere that shouts, "classic American steak house." And the Old Homestead doesn't disappoint; *Wine Spectator* magazine gave it an Award for Excellence in 2008, partially because of the breath and quality of the wines it can offer. The only steaks they sell are prime, dry-aged steaks—porterhouse, filet mignon, and New York sirloin. Their Kobe beef is not only domestically-raised, but also hand-massaged. And they take great pride in offering what is probably the world's most expensive—and perhaps its best—hamburger.

Executive Chef Oskar Martinez is considered one of the best in the business. And the appetizers and entrees that are trotted out from his kitchen are works of art on a plate, the perfect amount of slight-pink on the inside, the perfect amount of grilled on the outside.

One of the best appetizers is the filet mignon carpaccio, with truffle oil and shaved Parmesan. Also good is the Bang Bang Shrimp; it's battered in tempura, and served with ginger chipotle and ancho chili. The restaurant's signature entree is the filet mignon (16 ounces of it) on the bone. As for that most expensive hamburger in the world, it's a 20-oz. American Kobe burger, with small fried potatoes, chipotle ketchup, and stone-ground mustard. Those for whom price is no object might be interested in the Japanese Kobe steak or the filet mignon on the bone with colossal lobster tail.

RUTH'S CHRIS STEAK HOUSE $$$$
225 N.E. Mizner Blvd., Suite 100
Boca Raton
(561) 392-6746
www.ruthschris.com

Ruth's Chris Steak House is one of the best steak houses in America, having won more awards than we could possibly list here (the readers of *Florida Monthly*, for example, voted it Best Steak House in the state. The appetizers are as good as the steaks. The seared ahi tuna is complemented by a sauce with hints of ginger, mustard, and beer. The veal osso buco ravioli is saffron-infused pasta filled with veal osso buco and fresh mozzarella cheese, and served with sautéed baby spinach and a white wine demi-glacé. And the entrees? The classic prime cuts of steaks are all here—filet, petite filet, rib eye, cowboy rib eye, New York strip, porterhouse, and T-bone—are all here, grilled and spiced and accompanied to perfection. If you'd like to try something besides steak, consider the stuffed chicken breast; it's a roasted free-range double chicken breast stuffed with garlic herb cheese and served with lemon butter. Ruth's Chris doesn't skimp on the desserts, either. The caramelized banana cream pie is a creamy white-chocolate banana custard in a flaky crust, topped with caramelized bananas. And the chocolate sin cake is a very-chocolatey cake soaked in espresso.

CENTRAL COUNTY
American

BANANA BOAT $$
739 East Ocean Ave.
Boynton Beach
(561) 732-9400
www.bananaboatboynton.com

When you think of casual Palm Beach County dining, you think of the Banana Boat—and local people have been thinking of it for more than 30 years. The Banana Boat's still one of the best places to be in Boynton Beach, a great casual spot overlooking the Intracoastal, with good old American comfort food, good live music, and a lively, happy atmosphere in which to enjoy it all. It's a rambling white, nautically themed place. For an appetizer, patrons love the Pu Pu Platter, a plate filled with wings, spring rolls, ribs, and popcorn shrimp. The char-grilled Chicken nachos are great, too. The salads are colorful and very good; take the pecan crusted chicken, for instance, lightly fried and honey-basted over baby greens and berries. The Bermuda triangle (chicken, crabmeat, and tuna salads) is also good. For an entree, the fish is always fresh-caught here. And also try the crab cakes bubbaloo, sautéed crabmeat with garlic and herbs.

**CAFÉ 1451 AT THE
  NORTON MUSEUM** $$
1451 South Olive Ave.
West Palm Beach
(561) 832-5196
www.norton.org

After browsing among classic pieces of art from some of the world's most famous artists, sculptors, and craftspeople, browse among the American classics at Café 1451. The menu here is always changing according to the big exhibit on display. And—fitting for a notable art museum—creative cuisine is always on exhibit here. For example, the menu is often divided into The Classics (such as shrimp cocktail or an omelet); The Contemporaries (such as smoked corn chowder with braised bacon, or the apricot and goat cheese tart); On Broadway (wild crimson Snapper); or The Avant Garde (lunch specials named after classic movies). Desserts? One recent special was a series of delicious pastries entitled Off the Wall: The Human Form in Sculpture. Starbuck's Coffee available, along with cocktails, wine, and beer.

FIVE GUYS FAMOUS BURGERS
AND FRIES $
871 Village Blvd.
West Palm Beach
(561) 625-3888
www.fiveguys.com

When you walk into Five Guys Famous Burgers and Fries, you're walking through a time-machine back to the 1950s. You're surrounded by a checkerboard of reds and whites and retro designs. You almost expect Richie Cunningham and Potsie and the Fonz to walk through the door. And—whether you were around in the 50s or not—if you love a great burger, you'll remember this place. The specialties of the house are plain and simple. Cheeseburgers, thick and juicy; bacon burgers; and fries, Five Guys-style and Cajun. You can even get a kosher-style hot dog, a cheese or bacon dog, a cheese-and-bacon dog, or a veggie or grilled-cheese sandwich. Five Guys points out that their

beef is fresh, never frozen, that they use only peanut oil, and that their menu is trans-fat free. However, if you're like most folks who come in here, you're not here for health food. You're here for an incredible hamburger.

SOUTH SHORES TAVERN &
PATIO BAR $–$$
502 Lucerne Ave.
Lake Worth
(561) 547-7656
www.southshorestavern.com

This is a cool, casual, funky place where any type is welcome—including bikers—and where anything goes, as far as dress and attitude. It's a convivial gathering spot where folks are friendly, and it's won local awards for Best Live Music. Plain and simple, South Shores Tavern & Patio Bar is just a fun place with satisfying American food and plenty of activity going on. And you can enjoy it all from inside the tavern or outside on the tropical patio or sidewalk cafe.

The menu's filled with wings, soups, great burgers, and specialty sandwiches, along with some entrees like shrimp scampi (jumbo shrimp tossed with garlic, white wine, lemon and butter, and served over linguini) and sesame seared tuna (tuna steak covered with sesame seeds, pan-seared to order, and served with fork-smashed potatoes, vegetables, and a tropical fruit salsa). There are generally specials on beer, along with special nights for bikers, ladies, etc. And the motto of South Shores Tavern says it all: "Kick back. Relax. And enjoy." Serves wine and beer.

STONEWOOD GRILL & TAVERN $$
The Mall at Wellington Green
10120 Forest Hill Blvd., Suite 110
Wellington
(561) 784-9796
www.stonewoodgrill.com

Stonewood has a warm, inviting atmosphere that you feel the moment you walk in. Dark-shaded walls, stone columns, and interesting artworks made for a comfortable dining experience. And the aroma—of hand-cut steaks or seafood cooking over an oak-burning grill—only enhances the impression. Chef Mike likes to create some dishes with a bit of a bite. And when you try his blackened chicken pasta with fresh baby spinach, asparagus, and sun-dried tomatoes in a chardonnay cream, you'll be glad he does. Also distinctive is the oak grilled tenderloin skewer, with portobello mushrooms, zucchini wedges, red and yellow bell peppers, and Bermuda onions. There's now a new gluten-free menu, and the restaurant has a well-stocked wine selection. If you're a chocoholic, your cravings will definitely be satisfied here. The chocolate bread pudding is heavenly . . . and the seven-layer chocolate cake drizzled with chocolate fudge is even better!

Bakery

THE TULIPAN BAKERY
740 Belvedere Rd.
West Palm Beach
(561) 832-6107
www.tulipanbakery.com

At the Tulipan Bakery, smelling is everything . . . but seeing is even better. The list of local favorites is endless; and people drive here from miles around to get their own. There are a number of Cuban-influenced favorites, as well. There's an apricot mocha Cake, a yellow cake layered with apricot and mocha filling, and topped with mocha frosting; a strawberry shortcake, yellow cake layered with strawberry filling and whipped cream, and topped with whip cream frosting, pineapple slices, and peanut pieces; and chaja, a yellow cake layered with peaches, whipped cream, and dulce de leche filling.

Chinese

FON SHAN CHINESE RESTAURANT $
4735 North Congress Ave.
Boynton Beach
(561) 641-0500

This is an unheralded Chinese restaurant that nonetheless draws rave reviews. In fact, it often draws what, for a Florida Chinese restaurant, is the highest praise—it's often compared with the great New York Chinese restaurants. The barbecued ribs are great, as is the finger-lickin' sauce they come with. The garlic chicken with eggplant comes in a spicy brown sauce. Keep an eye out for the lobster specials, too; you get your choice of four different styles of lobster. You can even enjoy diet dishes, which come with no MSG, sugar, salt, or corn starch, and they're surprisingly good. Try the steamed mixed vegetables delight, or the steamed shrimp and chicken delight. Serves wine and beer.

WAH HOUSE CHINESE RESTAURANT $
1300 N. Military Trail
West Palm Beach
(561) 682-1689

Sometimes, the seemingly out-of-the-way places in little strip malls provide the best dining experiences. When you ask local people about Wah House, for instance, they'll tell you the portions are huge, and the food is delicious. Make no bones about it, this place has a way with chicken. The honey chicken is really good . . . and it's actually *chicken*, instead of mostly breading. And the General Tso's chicken is also excellent, nicely spiced and very satisfying. Serves wine and beer.

RESTAURANTS

Continental

RENATO'S $$$$
87 Via Mizner
Palm Beach
(561) 655-9752
www.renatospalmbeach.com

Palm Beach residents are discriminating in their culinary tastes. So, when a restaurant on this island has been open for 24 years it's worth taking notice. Renato's is certainly a Palm Beach dining experience, nestled just off Worth Avenue past a covered wooden archway and filled with an elegant ambience of soft lighting and continental accents. The menu—described as "continental cuisine with an Italian flair"—is just as impressive.

One of the best appetizers is the carpaccio di manzo, thinly sliced filet mignon with arugula olive oil and shaved Parmesan. If you're in the mood to start off with fish rather than meat, choose the salmone affumicato, Norwegian smoked salmon with garnish and toast points. And it only gets better from here. The gazpacho soup is memorable. And the only problem with the entrees is that you'll have a hard time choosing. The cernia alla tirreno is sautéed black grouper, with polenta, spinach, fennel, black olives, and a pernod/tomato broth. The scaloppini alla gorgonzola is sautéed veal scaloppini, gorgonzola, and shiitake mushroom cream sauce. And the bistecca di manzo? One of the best-tasting filet mignons you'll ever have, in a Barolo wine sauce. Before you run out of steam after feasting on the appetizers and entrees, however, keep in mind that the chef at Renato's whips up some of the best pastries in Palm Beach.

BICE RISTORANTE $$$$
313 Worth Ave.
Palm Beach
(561) 835-1600
www.palmbeach.bicegroup.com

Bice is understated elegance, with light-brown woods, beautiful wall sconces, French Doors, light walls, outdoor dining on the shaded tropical patio, and the kind of white-glove Northern Italian/Continental service you can get only in a place like Palm Beach. It's one of a very select group of restaurants, known not only throughout Palm Beach County, but also throughout South Florida. And it's a longtime favorite of the International Set that frequents Palm Beach during The Season, as well.

The carpaccio (raw meat or fish, sliced thin and nicely seasoned and sauced) is considered one of the best appetizers here. In addition, there are a half-dozen different types of antipasto, among them sliced beef tenderloin with arugula and shaved parmesan cheese, and baked eggplant with fresh mozzarella and marinara sauce. As for entrees, if you've got a yen for something exotic, the squid-ink ravioli filled with minced fish and seafood is superb. One of the old favorites here is the air-dried beef with black olives. Others include the veal scallopine with lemon and capers sauce; the grilled Atlantic salmon with sauteed vegetables; the pan-seared sesame tuna with vegetables and olive salad; and the beef tenderloin filet with mushroom sauce and vegetables ratatouille.

The wine cellar is one of the best in Palm Beach . . . and that's saying something. And the desserts are scrumptious and distinctive, sometimes created on a whim by a very creative staff that's often in the mood to experiment.

Cuban

DON RAMON   **$$**
7101 S. Dixie Hwy.
West Palm Beach
(561) 547-8704
www.donramonrestaurant.com

Since 1990, Don Ramon restaurant has proclaimed that "Mi casa es su casa." And it's true to Palm Beach County residents who love Cuban food, this place has felt like home for 20 years. It has the ambience of a real Havana restaurant. And it has the cuisine, as well. For an authentic taste of Old Cuba, you can start off with the appetizer called chicharrones de pollo, chicken chunks with sautéed onions; or the yucca rellena (stuffed yucca). Follow that with the sopa de frijoles negros (black bean soup). And there are many very good entrees here. One of them is the bistec delmonico, a flavorful rib eye steak marinated and served the with sautéed onions. Another one is the milanesa de pollo, which is boneless breast of chicken breaded, deep-fried, and then topped with Spanish Creole sauce, ham, and melted mozzarella cheese.

Cuban desserts have just the sweet touch needed to follow up the main courses. Don't leave without trying the tres leches, three-milk wet cake topped with meringue. Don Ramon also offers coupons on its Web site, along with five-peso "notes" from the "Banco Central de Cuba" for discounts.

HAVANA   **$$**
6801 S. Dixie Hwy.
West Palm Beach
(561) 547-9799
www.havanacubanfood.com

Havana calls its cuisine "the best Cuban food in town." And an awful lot of Palm Beach County residents will agree. This place has the feeling of a street in Old Havana, with

its stucco earth-tones, its tropical plants, its brown-tile floor, the old photos on the walls, and its overhanging balcony, complete with wrought-iron railings. Owner Roberto Reyes (a native of Cuba) and his family owned a successful ice cream shop in Miami until 1992's Hurricane Andrew basically blew it away. The family left Miami for West Palm Beach. But once there, they missed the wonderful Cuban food that had been so readily available in Miami. So they did the natural thing—started up their own restaurant. Since 1993, they've been serving dishes such as chicharrones de pollo (deep-fried chicken chunks topped with sautéed onions), bistec especial (grilled skirt steak), and enchilado de camarones (shrimp in a wine Creole sauce). Also try a side dish of tostones con mojo (green plantains with mojo). The food here is spiced to perfection—although many long-time patrons like it hot! You can wash it all down with a café Cubano, and some flan, a wonderful caramel custard. If you're the type that gets hunger pangs late at night, and *only* Cuban food will do, don't worry; Havana has a 24-hour walk-up window.

HAVANA HIDEOUT   **$**
509 Lake Worth Ave.
Lake Worth
(561) 585-8444
www.havanahideout.com

This is a special place. A place decorated in whimsical—Latin and otherwise—accents, with a friendly staff, and a collection of upcoming events that never seems to stop. And, oh, yes, the food's great, too, with a collection of Cuban specials that are as tasty as they are reasonably priced. Motorcycles at the door are a pretty standard sight. There's live music, dancing, and even a hot tub in the back, where you can make new friends while listening to the music.

My Palm Beach County

"I live in the south end of West Palm Beach, which over the years has become Spanish restaurant heaven. Not too far, at Dixie and Forest Hill, is Havana, which really serves the best Cuban food in town. A window is open all night, so you can get snacks and a cafe con leche at 3 a.m. if you want it—although that seems counterproductive if you actually hope to sleep. But music plays all night at the corner, and it's just a very happy place."

—Carol Carnevale, Editor,
the *Palm Beach Daily News*
("The Shiny Sheet")

Havana Hideout has Taco Tuesdays, Bike Night Thursdays, and open mic nights. And the casual Cuban food is great. The two-hand tacos come with pork, chicken, fish, or beef. The Cuban pressed sandwich has ham, garlic pork, mozzarella cheese, pickles, and mustard. The ceviche and chips comes with fresh fish, avocado, capers, salsa, citrus juice, garlic, and onions. And the pionono is sort of a tropical shepherd's pie—seasoned ground beef layered between sautéed plantains.

The sangria's very good, and there are all kinds of beers and ales, from a local brew called Native Lager to a Colorado brew called Hazed and Confused. For dessert, try one of the house specialties—a pineapple tamale, or chocolate chili pepper ice cream.

Dessert

SLOAN'S ICE CREAM
City Place
700 South Rosemary Ave.
West Palm Beach

Sloan's' slogan is "Where the elite meet to stuff themselves." You may or may not consider yourself "elite," but when you walk inside this adult (and juvenile) fantasyland, you'll definitely consider stuffing yourself. Sloan's is like being a kid again. It's mint-green on the outside, pink on the inside, and filled with feather boas, unusual toys, and a choo-choo train that's actually running. The colors, the smells, and the tastes will make a marshmallow out of the strongest dieter. So it's best not to resist, and to immerse yourself.

The flavors are always changing, and they're always eye-catching. You might try some apple-pie ice cream, for example, or some Circus (cotton-candy flavor with gummy bears). Others that may be in the case are peppermint pattie, Snicker's frozen yogurt, and Sloan's white. Or, if you'd rather sample the candies than the ice cream, there's plenty from which to choose, ranging from old-fashioned candy apples to incredible chocolate that almost seems to caress your mouth. A second West Palm Beach location is at 112 Clematis St. (561-833-4303).

French

CAFÉ BOULUD $$$$
Brazilian Court Hotel & Beach Club
301 Australian Ave.
Palm Beach
(561) 655-6060
www.cafeboulud.com
Daniel Boulud made himself a name as one of the world's great chefs with his namesake restaurant in New York. He chose the Brazilian Court for the very first outpost of that restaurant. And when he opened Café Boulud in 2003, he transformed the dining scene on the island of Palm Beach. Café Boulud is a treat for the eye as well as the palate, with bright colors and imaginative artworks and

murals. The menu features traditional French with a garnish of international and American. Zach Bell, a James Beard Foundation nominee for Best Chef in the South, now presides over the kitchen on a day-to-day basis, adding his own personal touches to Boulud's cuisine. And—as Boulud is known for his emphasis on natural ingredients—much of the produce comes from his own garden.

When you come to Café Boulud, start off at the beautiful lounge to enjoy a drink before dinner. If you have a group, inquire about reserving the terrace or one of the private dining rooms, where you can entertain in true style. Choose either from the menu or from one of the price-fixed dinners. If you're in the mood for something from the sea, the Casco Bay cod comes with celery victor and brandade galette, in a fennel-lemon powder lobster sauce. If you're in the mood for meat, Daniel's duo of beef is a combination of short ribs braised in red wine and steak creamy polenta, with porcini ragout and roasted carrots. And if you're in the mood for dessert, go for the carrot cake, with cream cheese, poached pineapple, and ras el hanout sorbet. Or the key lime pie, with toasted meringue and buttermilk sorbet. Or the chocolate-lemon gâteau, with hazelnut coulis and lemon-praline sorbet.

CAFÉ L'EUROPE $$$$
331 South County Rd.
Palm Beach
(561) 655-4020
www.cafeleurope.com
From the day it opened in 1980, this restaurant has been drawing not only the cream of Palm Beach Society, but also an unending procession of entertainment and fashion celebrities, titans of industry and government, famous artists, writers, and royalty.

And it's easy to see why. High arched windows with mahogany French doors, a polished wood bar, beautiful wall sconces, and tasteful chandeliers.

Owners Norbert (the chef) and Lidia (she runs the place) Goldner bring an international perspective to the restaurant. He's of European heritage and received training at some of the finest cooking schools in Europe. She's from Brazil and traveled the world for many years with the late, great Pan American Airways.

Dining at L'Europe is truly an epicurean experience to be savored slowly and enjoyed for hours. You might want to start the night off with a little Iranian caviar—$230 an ounce, or some of the Russian, at $172, or the American, at $38. After that, you may want to move on to what the restaurant refers to as its classics, for example, perhaps an entree like grilled beef tenderloin, with Belgian dndive meunière, pearl onions, pommes puree (pureed potatoes), and Pinot Noir reduction. Another good bet is the cappelacci trasteverina, pasta "envelopes" filled with spinach and ricotta Cheese with a tomato basil sauce. For dessert, the appropriately called chocolate goddess sake is layered with chocolate sabayon, chocolate truffle cream, caramel, and dark chocolate mousse quenelle with a little macadamia nut brittle ice cream thrown in for good measure. Closed Mon.

L'ESCALIER $$$$
The Breakers Hotel
One South County Rd.
Palm Beach
(561) 659-8480
www.thebreakers.com/restaurants_lounges/l_escalier
Dining at this restaurant (one of the most renowned in South Florida) is truly a

gastronomic tour de force. L'Escalier means "the staircase" in French, and with each course you'll feel as if you're ascending even higher. The restaurant has received the coveted Five Diamond Award from AAA. Since its opening in 1981, it's been awarded *Wine Spectator's* highest honor—the Grand Award—every single year.

The room is filled with mahogany and soft candlelight, and that certain ambience that only the really great restaurants have. A server will help you make selections from the cart of fine cheeses that will be brought around, and afterward from the champagne or wine carts (with 1,600 choices) created by Master Sommelier Virginia Philip—one of only 142 people in the world with that title.

At L'Escalier, you can take your choice of two price-fixed menus (three or five courses), or simply order a la carte off the main menu. And there's no such thing as a bad choice. The Colorado lamb loin comes with barigoule artichokes, tomato compote, pine nuts, Nicoise olives, eggplant ravioli, lamb sausage, and Piquillo lamb jus. The poussin au vin is young chicken, which comes garnished with globe carrots, salsify, chanterelles, pickled pearl onions, roasted sweet potato, and pinot noir sauce. Dessert at L'Escalier may qualify as the best you've ever had. Particularly if you choose the chocolate coulant, a wonderful swirl of hibiscus gelee, pistachio espuma, and malted chocolate ice cream. Closed Sun and Mon.

PISTACHE $$
101 North Clematis St.
West Palm Beach
(561) 833-5090
www.pistachewpb.com
Pistache is a bit of France in downtown West Palm Beach, sitting right on the waterfront

on Clematis Street. It's a true Parisienne bistro, with an Art Nouveau interior reminiscent of between-the-wars Paris, and dining both inside and out. Red leather benches, large antique mirrors with gilded frames, round turn-of-the-century lamps hanging from the ceiling, and French paintings give this restaurant a comfortable ambience. You can dine outside on the patio, overlooking Centennial Park, the fountains, and the Intracoastal Waterway.

One of the favorite dishes at Pastiche is the sweet potato & coconut mahi-mahi, a delicate, tasty fish that's served with baby greens, heirloom tomatoes, green beans, pine nuts and coconut ginger dressing. The veal scaloppini has also earned a good reputation; it's served with mashed potatoes, haricots verts (French green beans, longer and thinner than most American varieties), morels, and a mushroom-Madeira sauce. And Pastiche, with its Clematis Street location, is perfectly positioned for after-dinner entertainment options.

Greek

SKORPIOS II $$
6685-B Lake Worth Rd.
Lake Worth
(561) 432-9910
www.skorpiosii.com
Skorpios II is another one of those sweet neighborhood surprises hidden in a nondescript strip mall. Owners Nick and Louse Goussis serve authentic specialties in an atmosphere bathed in the blue and white of the Greek flag, and painted with wall murals of the Greek countryside. If the weather's nice, you can sit and eat outside—under blue and white umbrellas. As you might expect, the Greek salad is excellent here, and the distinct flavors of all the various

ingredients mesh together very well. The lemon chicken and lentil soups are also good. The most popular dish here is Nick's Special, a platter filled with items like spinach pie, moussaka (layered vegetables and ground meat), pastitsio (baked pasta with meat sauce), stuffed grape leaves, rice pilaf, and vegetables. But patrons also love the lamb chops, with five chops marinated in olive oil, rosemary, lemon juice, and garlic, all of which results in a smoky, delicious flavor. For dessert there's the sweet pastry called baklava, of course, as well as sugared almond cookies called kourabiethes, and homemade rice pudding with cinnamon on top. Skorpios serves beer and wine.

Indian

INDIA PALACE   **$$**
4778 Okeechobee Blvd.
West Palm Beach
(561) 478-5606
www.theindiapalace.com
The India Palace is always busy, which gives you some idea of its popularity in central Palm Beach County. It's another neighborhood place that generates a real loyalty among its customers. And the food is authentic and nicely prepared. Many guests start off with one of the distinctive Indian breads; among the popular ones are chapati (a thin bread baked on the griddle), tandoori roti (whole-wheat flour baked in a tandoori oven), and onion kulcha naan (unleavened bread stuffed with onions and baked in a tandoori oven). If you love chicken, try the chicken palak, boneless and cooked in creamy spinach. Try the lamb curry, spiced with a hint of fire. If you're a vegetarian, you've come to the right place; the aloo chhole is a North Indian dish of onions and chickpeas with potatoes. Top it all off with

the sweetness of gulab jamun, a dumpling that's made out of cottage cheese and dried milk, then deep-fried and dipped in sugar syrup. India Palace also has a popular lunchtime all-you-can-eat buffet. Serves beer and wine.

International

LEOPARD LOUNGE &
** RESTAURANT**   **$$$$**
The Chesterfield Hotel
363 Cocoanut Row
Palm Beach
(561) 659-5800
www.chesterfieldpb.com
In this wonderful old hotel, every room and hallway oozes class. And the same is true of the Leopard Lounge & Restaurant. Chef Gerard Coughlin cooks up a collage of international dishes, emphasizing English and American classics and even throwing in some Asian influences. He uses local and seasonal ingredients whenever possible. His own personal favorites include Angus beef; Australian rack of lamb with ratatouille and yukon gold potatoes; and beef tenderloin with wild mushrooms, asparagus, manchego potato galette, and glacé du vin. He also whips up a molten chocolate cake with vanilla ice cream for dessert, which you can enjoy with a variety of specialty coffees. In the adjoining Leopard Bar, you can enjoy innovative drinks and cocktails, and the restaurant's own home-made flavored vodkas.

Italian

PARADISO   **$$$$**
625 Lucerne Ave.
Lake Worth
(561) 547-2500
www.paradisolakeworth.com

In the heart of revitalized downtown Lake Worth, Paradiso is an inviting-looking white building with rich woods on the front doors, over which hangs a blue awning. Inside, the atmosphere is one of Mediterranean elegance, with magnificent wall-size murals of Italy, a large wine cellar, and private dining rooms for groups. Chef/Owner Angelo Romano's cooking has been winning accolades for years. He hones his trade at fancy resorts along the Italian Riviera and Bermuda, and, finally, brought his wonderful act to Palm Beach County in 1997. In addition to his fine cooking, he often hosts wine-tastings in the private dining area in the wine cellar.

You'll definitely want to try his vitello prosciutto e scamorza, prosciutto-wrapped veal tenderloin and smoked mozzarella in a Marsala wine sauce. People also frequently choose his filett con fegato grasso e barola, which is pan-seared filet mignon and goose foie gras, in a wonderful Barolo wine sauce. At certain times of the year truffles are available in the restaurant; these are the finest mushrooms in the world and highly prized. Market prices can be as high as $1,000 per pound. But if you've ever considered blowing a bunch of money on one true delicacy, you should perhaps make this the one.

Jamaican

DUTCH POT JAMAICAN
RESTAURANT $
431 Old Dixie Hwy.
Riviera Beach
(561) 845-2606
This is a down-home-Jamaican, family restaurant in a working-class section of town, where the atmosphere is friendly and the food is interesting and very good. You can eat inside or do take out. All the "hot" Jamaican specialties are done very well here, such as

jerk chicken, a highly spiced and very tasty dish that's probably the most well-known Caribbean dish in America. Curries (hot spices ground into a powder) are an integral part of cooking in Jamaica, and local residents really like the curried chicken and curried goat at the Dutch Pot. One of the house specialties is Brown Stew Fish, a snapperlike fish which is fried and very crispy. (And if you've ever had a hankerin' for a good piece of oxtail, you can find that here, as well.) There are 16 flavors of ice cream available for dessert. No liquor license.

Japanese

ECHO $$$
230A Sunrise Ave.
Palm Beach
(561) 802-4222
www.echopalmbeach.com
Echo is a smart, sophisticated place with imaginative modern design tinged by a touch of Oriental. Everywhere you look, there's a striking clock, table, wall motif, or lighting. You'll find contemporary touches of bamboo and silver backdropped by vivid turquoise, orange, and green. The service is first-class. And the Chinese, Thai, Vietnamese, and Japanese cuisine are just as imaginative and just as colorful as the decor.

Many people say this is the best Japanese food in Palm Beach County. The miso soup—with scallops, tofu, enoki mushrooms, and wakame (a sea vegetable)—is a perfect starter If it's sushi or sashimi you're here for, you can watch the chefs as they work to prepare specialties that are as colorful as they are good. One of their best is the spicy yellowtail sashimi, which comes with jalapeño, shiso emulsion, and garlic soy. The bluefin toro is a favorite, as is the salmon roe. All the traditional sushi favorites are here, as well, such as the California roll, tuna roll, salmon, and hamachi roll. Try the Hurricane roll, with tempura shrimp, Alaskan king crab, and asparagus, and red tobiko caviar and avocado on top. The entrees are just as beautiful and just as good. The salmon teriyaki comes with stir-fried vegetables, cilantro, and ginger; and the miso sea bass is garnished with white asparagus and bonito flakes. For a most unusual dessert, top your meal off with a tempura banana sundae, a battered and fried banana swimming in homemade ice cream, five-spiced whipped cream, dried pineapple, candied nuts, chocolate, and tapioca sauce.

Mexican/Spanish

AMIGOS MEXICAN AND SPANISH RESTAURANT $$
4720 Okeechobee Blvd.
West Palm Beach
(561) 687-2112
www.amigosmexspanish.com
Amigos is a friendly place where the atmosphere is casual and the cooking is authentic. It's a true Mexican cantina with a touch of Spain thrown in for good measure. And it's been a local favorite for years. Appetizers include favorites such as crab nachos, quesadilla spinach, and Mexican pizza. The homemade chili con carne and black bean soups are terrific. Fajitas, of course, are an old Mexican favorite, and you can get them with beef, chicken, pork, shrimp, or several combinations thereof. For an entree, try the bistec a la Mexicana, a wonderfully spiced and cooked piece of steak. And, of course, there's the usual assortment of enchiladas, burritos, tacos, and tortillas, as well as Spanish favorites such as ropa vieja, chipped beef. Top it all off with a dessert of flan (Spanish custard), or Mexican fried ice cream.

ROCCO'S TACOS & TEQUILA BAR $$
224 Clematis St.
West Palm Beach
(561) 650-1001
www.roccostacos.com
No doubt, you've eaten Mexican before. But you've never eaten Mexican like this. From the glowing multi-colored neon sign on the outside, to the elegant, slightly old-fashioned long bar inside, owner Rocco Mangel has put together the funkiest, tastiest, most innovative, liveliest Mexican restaurant you've ever seen.

True to the restaurant's name, you can sample from among 225 different types of tequila. The Margarita mix can be found nowhere else—because it's made here. The corn tortillas are made by hand, and cooked fresh in a special Mexican oven called a comal. The late-night menu, along with its location near so many nightspots, ensures that Rocco's Tacos & Tequila Bar is buzzing until the wee hours.

Start off with one of the antejitos (soups or small plates), such as tortilla soup or jalapeño rellenos (stuffed fried jalapeño peppers, with cotija—a hard cow's milk cheese—lime crema, and avocado ranch). For an entree, if you're interest is piqued by the idea of a hamburger, Mexican-style, go for the hamburguesa Mexicano, with jalapeños, Chihauhau cheese, salsa, guacamole, and fries. The chile rellenos (charred poblano chiles, Chihuahua and goat cheese, salsa rojo, crema, cotija cheese, red rice, black beans) is excellent. There are six combination platters, each giving you a good sampler of authentic Mexican cooking. And, of course, at a place named Rocco's Tacos, you've got to try Rocco's Tacos, such as cochinitas achiote (slow-roasted pork) or camarones (shrimp). The restaurant also has a fun kid's menu. And you should be here for the biggest party of the year, on Cinco de Mayo, Mexican Independence Day!

Middle Eastern

LEILA $$$
120 South Dixie Hwy.
West Palm Beach
www.leilawpb.com

Leila describes itself as a cosmopolitan Middle East grille. There's indoor and outdoor dining in an authentic atmosphere representative of Middle Eastern culture. There are artifacts of that culture all over the place, Oriental draperies and ornaments, subtle-purple seats, and soft lighting from wall sconces.

There's belly-dancing (originally meant as a form of celebration among women only, often in preparation for childbirth), called Rah-iss Sharqi in the region of its birth. There are three types of thick Turkish coffee, served in tiny demitasse cups. There are a variety of calming and interesting teas. You can also sample a hookah, that pipe you've seen in a hundred old movies. A hookah uses a special type of tobacco, different than cigarette-tobacco; it's infused with molasses, and it's mixed with different fruits—such as apricots, apples, or cherries—and other aromatic elements to produce a very unusual sensation.

The cuisine is interesting and reflective of faraway lands and cultures. All the old familiar Middle Eastern standbys are here— hummus, falafel, t'china, pita, and tabouleh salad. Try the Na'anak appetizer; lamb, beef, and pork sausages infused with port wine, pine nuts, sherry, cinnamon, clove, and allspice. One of the most popular entrees is the Leila Grill (for two), single skewers of shish tawook (chicken chunks marinated in yogurt, lemon juice, and spices), shish kabob (steak, pepper, onions, and tomatoes), lamb kabob, and kraidis (shrimp). And the Land and Sea Platter is a delicious combination of samak mishwi (flame-grilled mahi-mahi), kraidis, and shish tawook. Middle Eastern desserts are thick and sweet and filled with distinctive flavors. The baklava here, wonderfully sweet and sticky, is excellent. So is the knaffe, a traditional cake served with sweet cheeses, pistachios, and orange-blossom syrup. The signature dessert here is sokseh, a sweet chocolate biscuit with very fine powdered sugar.

Pizza

ANTHONY'S GOURMET PIZZA
& ITALIAN RESTAURANT $$
13889 Wellington Trace
Wellington
(561) 795-1686

The western communities have a much greater diversity and quality of restaurants than they did even a few years ago. And folks now make the drive from communities to the east, just to have dinner here. A good example is Anthony's Gourmet Pizza & Italian Restaurant. People come from miles around for the calzone, which is excellent, as well as the pizza. The pies are done to perfection. The tastes are sharp and distinct. The dough and crust are perfect. The toppings are great. The food comes out quickly and it comes out hot. But the locals will tell you one more thing about Anthony's, as well. The staff is superb, and they take a true personal interest in their customers. After your first visit here, they'll remember your face. After your second, they'll remember your name. And after your third, they'll remember your favorite dish. It's a charming place where you'll feel very much at home.

ROMEO'S RESTAURANT & PIZZA $–$$

4917 Southern Blvd.
West Palm Beach
www.romeospizzawestpalm.com
(561) 471-9695

People in Central County have been coming to Romeo's for years, for its great daily specials, and for the consistency and quality of its food. The sauce is home-made, and the atmosphere is inviting and comfortable. Daily specials vary—one day it might be a pizza-and-wings, another day it might be a two spaghetti dinner special, and on yet another day, the special might be 15 percent off your tab.

All the tried-and-true Italian favorites are here—spaghetti and meatballs, linguine with clam sauce, chicken francese, and fettuccine Alfredo, to name a few. But it's the pizza that really helped establish this restaurant's reputation. Romeo's has a way of perfecting crust, golden-colored and really crisp. There's a white pizza with mozzarella and ricotta cheese. There's a meat lover's pizza, with sausage, ham, meatballs, pepperoni, and ground beef. There's a vegetarian, with mushrooms, onions, green peppers, black olives, spinach, and broccoli. But the king of the mountain is Romeo's House Special, with extra cheese, pepperoni, sausage, mushrooms, green peppers, and onions. For the true pizza-lover, this is a must. And each of these pizzas comes in two different styles . . . thin-round or thick-square Sicilian. Top it off with some zeppole or a cannoli, and you'll be a very happy camper.

Seafood

BREEZE $$

The Ritz-Carlton, Manalapan
100 South Ocean Blvd.
Manalapan
www.ritzcarlton.com

Imagine an outdoor deck overlooking the Atlantic, with the sounds of the waves rushing in and the sea-breezes caressing your face. Then imagine yourself sitting there and enjoying fresh, delicious food and drink. If your imagination is vivid enough, you'll find yourself sitting at Breeze, surrounded by the luxurious trappings of the Ritz-Carlton.

Breeze has a fun way of classifying the dishes on its menu. You might want to start off, for instance, with something from the Cast Off section—blue crab taquitos, perhaps, or chicken nachos. There's the Trim Sails category, with items such as the Key West cobb salad or the tropical fruit plate. The Main Sail section has dishes like the grilled Florida grouper sandwich and the tuna melt. You can top everything off with a Breezy Treat—the key lime pie with tropical chutney and citrus Chantilly, perhaps, or the fudge brownie, with caramel mousse and raspberry. And you can't go to Breeze without trying one of their mojitos, the house specialty. These are a variety of great tropical drinks involving rums, schnapps, champagne, or liquers—among other items—in a variety of mixes and combinations. You may want to just take in that breeze and that aqua-green for a few hours, and try a couple of them.

HURRICANE ALLEY RAW BAR & RESTAURANT $

529 East Ocean Ave.
Boynton Beach
(561) 364-4008
www.myhurricanealley.com

This is a great place to kick back, relax, and enjoy the Florida-funky atmosphere, the varied clientele, and great food. Surfboards and signs, stuffed fish and nautical artifacts, a long-boat . . . pretty much anything sea-related

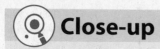

Close-up

Key Lime Pie

Key lime pie is the quintessential Palm Beach County dessert, described in fables, sung about in songs, and generally adored by generations of South Floridians. However, most Palm Beach County residents—even natives—might be surprised to learn that the key lime is not itself native to South Florida. And, actually, not even native to the Keys. It was actually imported into Florida from Malaysia (where it *is* native) in the 1500s by Spanish explorers.

Nobody really knows who first decided to use key limes in a pie. But most stories center on a cook named "Aunt Sally," who worked for Florida's first millionaire, a fellow named Charles Curry, in the late 1800s. Apparently, Aunt Sally took an informal recipe used by some local fishermen and perfected it . . . according to legend, anyway. (And there's no evidence that Aunt Sally, or anyone else, actually wrote down a recipe until the 1930s.)

Key limes are actually a sort of hybrid between lemons and limes; they're generally smaller than each, with a skin that has elements of both yellow and green. They grew in profusion around South Florida until 1926, when the worst hurricane in Florida history (they didn't have names then) destroyed most of the key lime trees. As a result, local growers began importing limes from Iran, Mexico, and other countries—meaning that, today, except for the Keys and some isolated groves in the Miami area, the "real" key lime is almost extinct.

No matter. Key lime pie—whether with a pastry crust or a graham-cracker crust— tastes like nothing you've ever eaten before, with a rich, tangy, smooth flavor that seems to caress your mouth. For the record, although it comes in broth green and yellow—and both taste fine—the "real" key lime pie is actually the yellow one.

---

that can be hung or displayed is hanging or displaying here. Owner Kim Garnsey has filled the place with things from new friends, old friends, and long-lost friends.

The food is a treat. Hurricane Alley's famous for its seafood bisque, which started with a lot of experimenting and finished as a local legend, with bay shrimp, crab, and clams. (You can also get it in The Volcano, and oversized bread bowl.) The oysters Rockefeller's a great appetizer. The tropical wave is a thinly sliced tuna steak, seared with sesame seeds, tossed over a bed of greens with an Oriental dressing. The Asian calamari salad also has an infusion of sesame seeds

and a Pan-Asian dressing. Don't forget to try a basket of conch fritters, fried to a crispy brown with a semihot seasoning, fries, and cole slaw. There's stuffed sole, several kinds of sushi, and clams, oysters, and shrimp. For dessert, most folks go with the key lime pie or some ice cream.

**MICHELLE BERNSTEIN'S AT THE
    OMPHOY** $$$
The Omphoy Ocean Resort
2842 South Ocean Blvd.
Palm Beach
(561) 540-6440
www.omphoy.com

Michelle Bernstein grew up in Miami, surrounded by the bounty of the sea and the multi-cultural and ethnic influences on the local cuisine. In 2008 she won the James Beard Award as Best Chef in the Southern United States. She's also won the Iron Chef Award, beating celebrity chef Bobby Flay in the process. And she's appeared on the *Today* show displaying some of her South Florida regional specialties. She opened Michelle Bernstein at the Omphoy, one of Florida's finest restaurants in one of its finest new hotels, in 2009.

One of her best starters is her shrimp tiradito, with aji amarillo (a spicy South American chile), soy, and cilantro. Her tuna carpaccio is bathed in a foie gras torchon "snow" (marinated in Armagnac) with apples is superb. The lobster bisque is filled with leeks, wild mushrooms, and sherry. And the cuttlefish a la plancha is enveloped in scamp-style risotto and garlic.

As for entrees, the seared wild king salmon comes in a saffron broth, surrounded by beans, rice, and baby vegetables. The Malaysian curried snapper brings you a touch of spice from the Orient, with mango, heart of palm cole slaw, and rice. And the dashi scented black cod is enhanced by the mushroom dashi broth, bok choy, and radish salad. The wine list is enormous, from countries all over the world, and states all over America. The restaurant denotes which wines go best with which dinners.

SAILFISH MARINA RESTAURANT　　$$
Sailfish Marina, Singer Island
98 Lake Dr.
Palm Beach Shores
(561) 842-8449
www.sailfishmarina.com

When you talk about fresh seafood, it's hard to get fresher than the seafood you'll have at the Sailfish Marina Restaurant. Whenever possible, it comes right off the fishing boats harbored all around. This restaurant is well-known in Palm Beach County, and perennially popular, for the quality of the seafood and the atmosphere in which it's enjoyed.

Specialties include Abaco grouper, dolphin, Florida spiny lobster, and stone crabs (when in season, mid-Oct to mid-May). Indoors, you're enveloped in a woodsy ambience filled with hanging nets and nautical paraphernalia. And outdoors, you're sitting waterside while everything from million-dollar yachts to simple rowboats passes in front of you.

Southwestern

MOE'S SOUTHWEST GRILL　　$
851 Village Blvd., Suite 502
West Palm Beach
(561) 478-8388
www.moes.com

Moe's Southwest Grill is a small neighborhood place that offers traditional Southwestern, with a lot of interesting touches. It's fast-food, Southwestern-style. This place bills itself as "Beyond the Burrito" and it is. For example, if you're a "dead ringer for a dead rocker," you may soon find a photo of yourself on Moe's wall. (Moe's has a special place in its heart for dead musicians; all the music you hear, in fact, is being performed by them.) If it's your birthday, you'll get a free Birthday Burrito.

At Moe's, freshness is important; there are no freezers, no microwaves, no animal fat, no lard, and no MSG. There's plenty of free chips and salsa with every meal. The meals taste very good; and you won't forget their names. The Homewrecker Burrito is overflowing with your choice of meat, beans, rice, shredded cheese, pico de gallo, lettuce, sour cream and guacamole. The Funkmeister Taco is filled with your choice of meat, along with beans, shredded cheese, pico de gallo and lettuce. And the Alfredo Garcia fajitas arrive sizzling at your table, with your choice of meat and garnishings such as three flour tortillas, peppers & onions, shredded cheese, pico de gallo and lettuce. In addition, there are vegetarian choices on the menu, as well. No liquor license

Steak Houses

MORTON'S THE STEAKHOUSE $$$$
777 South Flagler Dr.
West Palm Beach
(561) 835-9664
www.mortons.com
When you say Morton's, you really don't have to say much more. Everyone knows it's one of the great places for steak in America. Dark mahogany, white linens, and superb service blend with great steaks and seafood for a great dining experience. Here, even the simple hamburger is elevated to a higher place on the gastronomic pecking order. At Morton's, the oversized steaks are tender, juicy, and tasty. If you're really hungry, make a run at the filet mignon double-cut porterhouse steak, or the Chicago style bone-in rib eye steak. You can also choose from among Morton's "Slightly Smaller Steaks," such as the New York strip steak or filet oskar. And if you're in the mood for something besides steak, Morton's can place a beautiful cut of lamb chops or broiled salmon fillet, among other choices, in front of you. The side dishes offer a choice of vegetables such as garlic green beans, steamed jumbo asparagus, and sautéed fresh spinach and mushrooms. Desserts include the best New York cheesecake

you've ever had outside of New York, crème brûlée, and Morton's legendary hot chocolate cake.

POLO STEAKHOUSE $$$$
The Colony Hotel
155 Hammon Ave.
Palm Beach
(561) 655-5430
www.thecolonypalmbeach.com
If you thought that elegance, class, and sophistication were gone forever, step into the Colony Hotel. Here, in this Hammon Avenue hideaway that's still frequented by some of the most discriminating patrons in the world, a quiet luxury and a rapt attention to detail still reign. The Polo is one of the finest steak houses in Florida.

Chef Steve Darling uses only cuts from the 3 percent of meats stamped by the FDA as "prime." The steaks are then aged in special dry-air refrigeration for a minimum of 28 days; this tenderizes the steak, and also imparts a wonderful flavor. Your server will gladly show you the cut he's chosen for you. Often, your steak will be cooked right in front of you at your table. And there's al fresco dining if you'd like to eat outside.

The filet mignon, the New York strip steak, the rib eye steak, and the prime rib all come in two sizes. Each is cut, seasoned, and prepared to your liking. Although the steaks are the headliners here, there are a number of other dishes which also receive star-treatment. The lobster bisque is memorable. So are the seared sea scallops, and the sake-miso marinated baked sea bass. The potato-crusted yellowtail snapper—with baby spinach, sun-dried tomato, and feta cheese—also comes highly recommended. And if you're here for lunch, the dish most recommended by frequent guests is the

Maine lobster salad, a longtime staple here. Desserts are fit for a king. The bar area is a smart place to meet for a before-dinner cocktail or an after-dinner liqueur.

Tapas

BIZAARE AVENUE CAFÉ $$–$$$
921 Lake Ave.
Lake Worth
(561) 588-4488
www.bizaareavecafe.com

Bizaare Avenue Café is a tapas wine bar. And—like the rest of re-born Lake Worth—is now a trendy, hip gathering place for people who appreciate innovative food (and the chance to try a lot of different types of it) and interesting wines.

Tapas, of course, are little mini-portions of Spanish food, served in small dishes. In this restaurant, there are plenty of Spanish favorites but also some new dishes created here. The cafe has been highly rated by Zagat. In addition, it won Best Place for Intimate Conversation in a 2007 poll by the local weekly, *New Times*. It's housed in a 1926 building, and the eclectic decor is sort of a cross between English Country house and Nantucket eatery. And the food isn't the only thing for sale here. The chair you're sitting on is for sale, as well; so is the plate on which you're eating, and the cool art work on the wall. Jjust make them an offer! Their name, in fact, is a play between "bazaar," which is a place you buy something, and "bizarre," in which you expect to come upon unusual and strange surprises.

The restaurant also has its own wine label, with a variety of reds and whites, along with an extensive list of other wines and champagnes. And the tapas are excellent. You'll want to start off with the lobster bisque, which sets the tone for some wonderful surprises to come. There's fried pumpkin ravioli, goat cheese marinara dip, baked brie, spanakopitas (Greek spinach pie), scallop and calamari ceviche, and carmelized onion and bleu cheese "fun-do." There's also a variety of salads, crepes, pastas, and wraps, along with individual "pizaares." The entrees here—such as portobello stuffed filet, braised lamb shank, and seared salmon—are also worthy of mention.

Tex-Mex

ALEYDA'S TEX-MEX RESTAURANT $$
1890 Okeechobee Blvd.
West Palm Beach
(561) 688-9033
www.aleydas.com

In a city filled with beautiful old buildings, Aleyda's Restaurant still stands out. The exterior is earth-tone with a thick green border running around the bottom, and painted green frames around the windows. The interior is truly striking. It resembles a Mexican street, with stucco walls, stained-glass windows on the "buildings," hanging lanterns, and banners strung overhead. There really is an Aleyda, by the way—Aleyda Cardona. She's in the restaurant every day, personally attending to her guests' needs. She came to America from Colombia and began making a culinary name for herself. Eventually, she saved enough money to open this 150-seat restaurant.

For starters, there are dishes like quesadilla (Mexican-style pizza); chili fundito (a mixture of spices, cheeses, tomatoes, and chiles, in a flour tortilla); and perhaps the best chili con queso (cheeses, spices, beans, tomatoes, and chilis) in town. Fajitas are one of Aleyda's specialties of the house; they're presented sizzling at your table, and you can get them in vegetarian, steak, chicken, shrimp . . . or any combination thereof. Some of the popular entrees are chile mellizos (two ground beef tortillas, topped with chili beans and melted cheddar); the burritos platters; and the south of the border steak (really good!). Dessert? Try the deep-fried ice cream or the tres leches (soft milk cake).

Thai

PEPPERMINT THAI & SUSHI BAR   **$$**
11328 Okeechobee Blvd.
Royal Palm Beach
(561) 333-8005

Royal Palm Beach, in the western communities, is a bit out of the way. But that doesn't mean it doesn't have quality restaurants. Peppermint Thai & Sushi Bar is one of them. The atmosphere is laid-back and friendly. Local folks enjoy appetizers such as chicken or beef on a stick, with peanut sauce for dipping, are always good. They also come for the panang curry and the volcano chicken (spicy!), as well as the sushi, which is varied, colorful, and good. The Pad Thai dishes—with pork, chicken, or shrimp, and delicious Thai thick noodles and rice—are also highlights among the entrees. Located in a little strip mall, Peppermint Thai &Sushi Bar is a trip worth taking if you're staying out west.

Vegetarian

DARBSTER   **$-$$**
8020 South Dixie Hwy.
West Palm Beach
(561) 586-2622
www.darbster.com

Darbster calls itself a vegetarian bistro that caters to both the vegetarian and the mainstream diner. It has a waterside deck overlooking the West Palm Beach Canal, and some very creative vegetarian and organic

cooking. And it may very well be the first restaurant you've ever eaten in that was named after a dog—it's named after Darby, the owners' poodle. Actually, Darbster is vegan—which means no animal products at all. The "chik'n" and "cheez" dishes on the menu are actually made with soy (but taste like the real thing). The ice cream comes from coconut milk rather than cow's milk. And—considering the restaurant's name—it's no surprise that pooches are welcome.

For an appetizer, try the vegetable tempura. The palm cakes entree is made with hearts of palm rather than crab cakes, but they taste just as good. And the enchiladas (made, of course, with soy) may awaken taste buds you never knew you had! That doesn't mean that Darbster's totally ignores good old-fashioned comfort food, however, as you'll find out if you order the excellent french fries. And there's one other great feature you won't find at many other restaurants—the chef will actually prepare any concoction you come up with. Serves beer and wine. Closed Mon and Tues.

NORTH COUNTY

American

THE CAPITAL GRILLE   **$$$$**
11365 Legacy Ave.
Palm Beach Gardens
(561) 630-4994
www.thecapitalgrille.com

Palm Beach Gardens has become a real sweet spot, with pretty neighborhoods, great dining and shopping, corporate offices, and, of course, world-class golf. And The Capital Grille epitomizes the good life here. Within a few minutes after walking out of the chic Gardens Mall, you can be eating Kobe beef carpaccio or fresh lobster, and following them up with Stoli Doli martinis. It's a first-class culinary experience, in the menu, in the atmosphere, and in the service. The steaks are dry-aged on the premises, and you may be hard-pressed to pick the right wine to accompany them because there are more than 350 choices, including a Captain's List of very special wines. There's also a variety of seafood flown in fresh from both shores, and daily specials created with fresh, local, artisanal ingredients. Even the ice cream is homemade here.

One of the house specialties is the seared tenderloin with butter poached lobster, a wonderful taste combination. Bone in Kona crusted dry aged sirloin with caramelized shallot butter is just as good as it sounds, and it's one of local residents' favorites. If you prefer the surf to the turf, try the sushi-grade sesame smeared tuna with ginger rice. Try and leave some room for dessert for treats like the double chocolate mint ice cream cookie sandwich, or the cheesecake with fresh berries, nestled in a vanilla wafer crust and garnished with sweet berries and a strawberry sauce.

CORNER CAFÉ AND BREWERY $$–$$$
289 North US 1
Tequesta
(561) 743-7619
www.cornercafeandbrewery.com

Lisa Hill, owner of the Corner Café and Brewery, has 25 years of experience as a dietitian, specializing in diabetes. So you won't find any processed foods or trans fats on her menu. And Jim Hill, her husband and co-owner, has been in the restaurant business since he was a boy; he can often be found in the kitchen or serving customers. This is a warm, attractive little place with creative cooking, excellent wine, and hand-crafted beers.

There are close to 20 different appetizers, among them baked brie, fried ravioli, and lobster cigars (lobster, goat cheese, and toasted pine nuts baked in phyllo dough and drizzled in a raspberry merlot sauce). For entrees the potato encrusted grouper comes with a dijon butter sauce. The seafood newberg has shrimp, lobster, scallops, clams, and mussels, tossed with pasta in a Newberg sauce. The country platter has clams, shrimp, and sausages in a Cajun cream sauce, with cheese grits and collard greens. And the desserts are all homemade.

Then, of course, there's the brewery. Matt Webster crafts his unique beer recipes on his own custom-designed 1.5 barrel system. In 2008, his home-brewed Kolsch won bronze in the National Home Brew Competition, and his Dunkel won 5th place in the Samuel Adams Long Shot Competition. One of his staples on tap, Gnarly Barley, won Gold in the 2009 Best Florida Beer Championship.

HURRICANE GRILL & WINGS $$
7100 Fairway Dr.
Palm Beach Gardens
(561) 775-2522
www.hurricanewings.com

Hurricane Grill & Wings makes no pretenses about being anything but what it is—a consistently great place for classic comfort food, with a lively crowd and a funky atmosphere. There's a long list of appetite-pleasers. Take the Obscenely Loaded Fries appetizer topped with chopped bacon, aged cheddar and American cheeses, jalapeños, and buttermilk ranch dressing. The wings are perfectly cooked and seasoned, and the homemade kettle chips are outrageous. There's a 100 percent Angus steak burger with cheese; the Hurricane Sandwiches, like grilled mahi mahi; and Philly sandwiches served on a toasted roll with grilled onions and peppers, American cheese, and fries or slaw. From the ocean, Caribbean conch fritters, spicy and crunchy and oh-so-satisfying. The sesame seared ahi tuna salad, mixed greens topped with tuna in a spicy soy glaze, with crispy noodles, sesame seeds, and wasabi dressing. Desserts include key lime pie or mango passion cheesecake.

IRONWOOD GRILLE $$$$
400 Avenue of the Champions
Palm Beach Gardens
(561) 627-4852
www.ironwoodgrille.com
Ever since it opened, in the PGA National Resort and Spa, this restaurant has been making headlines and friends. It's a contemporary American grill, with stone walls and elegant lighting, modern art, and an intimate atmosphere. There's a huge wine list. The restaurant has been wonderfully reviewed by all the local media. And the fine seafood and certified-Angus beef are designed around organic ingredients purchased from local purveyors.

Among the favorite appetizers here are the she-crab soup, topped with a touch of sherry; and the coconut shrimp stack, with wasabi aioli and pineapple. Steaks include two sizes of filet mignon, a New York strip, and a bone-in rib eye. The seafood specialties include prosciutto-wrapped crab and shrimp, and wild Alaska salmon. Some of the other favorites are steak fritte, with Belgium frittes, tempura onion, and vanilla gastrique; panko parmesan crusted chicken roulade; and cippolini onion-sage polenta and roma tomato salsa. They're all as good as they sound. Desserts like chocolate blackout cake and fresh berries in coconut sabayonne are big hits.

Bakery

LORENE'S LOVING OVEN $
905 US 1, Unit K
Lake Park
(561) 881-9006
www.loreneslovingoven.com
Walk into this small shop, and you'll think you've gone to aroma heaven surrounded by cakes, cookies, and pies just out of the oven. Owner Lorene Hughey and her mother, head baker Altamese Kerr, create all those wonderful smells and tastes, everything from sweet potato pie to German chocolate cake, pineapple upside down cake, egg custard pie, fruit truffle, red velvet cake, and cobblers—peach, peach/apple, and blueberry and mango in season. They make 25 kinds of pie, 16 kinds of custom cakes, 13 types of pound cake, 11 types of cheesecake, and 10 types of special gourmet desserts. Closed Sun and Mon.

Cajun/Creole

THE BAYOU $$
235 South US 1
Tequesta
561-746-6636
www.bayoutequesta.com
This is a classic Cajun/Creole bar and New Orleans-inspired restaurant. The atmosphere is definitely kick-back-and-relax, with recessed lighting, period-furniture, and a French Quarter feel. The food is excellent. And it's got one of Palm Beach County's great culinary characters. Chef Joe Ronan cut his culinary chops under the legendary Paul Prudhomme in New Orleans. He can keep you listening raptly all night with his stories. Don't miss out on his shrimp étouffée, grits and lemon zest shrimp, smoked chicken pot pie, or his fantastic finger food,

like Creole-style wings with mango sauce, or fried oysters. And for a really unusual drink, you've gotta try the Guinness hot chocolate. Have it with a beignet, the wonderful fried dough covered with powdered sugar that melts in your mouth.

Caribbean

LITTLE MOIR'S FOOD SHACK $$$
103 South US 1
Jupiter
(561) 741-3626
www.littlemoirsfoodshack.com

Little Moir's is not your average restaurant. Concealed in the back of an unprepossessing strip mall along US 1 in Jupiter, it looks something like a Key West bar that's somehow been uprooted and trucked up north. It serves creative Caribbean cuisine (with a pinch of Asian for good measure), emphasizing the bounty of the local seas. Founder Mike Moir uses fresh local ingredients whenever possible and created a family-friendly place where you could also eat on an outdoors patio.

The dining area is long and narrow, with a bamboo-canopied dining bar. Along the wall are fewer than a dozen colorfully hand-painted tables. The entire place is decorated with surfboards, life preservers, fishing tackle, tropical-themed paintings, photos of customers, and even children's drawings. The cuisine includes at least 15 varieties of fresh fish. The restaurant is best known for its signature dish, sweet potato crusted fish, along with its tuna-basil roll, its panko fried oysters, and its barbecued chicken sandwich. Yet, there are plenty of customers who'll tell you to order the scallops, or the Leftovers Café Plate sampler. Spices, sauces, and fruits from the Caribbean are used liberally in the cooking. And you can wash it all down with more than 25 types of beer, many from Caribbean countries. For dessert, you've gotta go with the Whozit, a white cake with a pinkish custard on top, and whipped cream and berries on top of that.

SOLU RESTAURANT $$$$
3800 North Ocean Dr. (Singer Island)
West Palm Beach
(561) 340-1795

Asian and Caribbean seems like a pretty unlikely cuisine combination, but the Solu Restaurant—situated in the Marriott Resort & Spa at Singer Island—pulls it off. Solu refers to itself as an Asian-infused Caribbean grill. So if it feels like you're eating the food on your plate for the first time in your life, you're probably right.

Solu comes from the Latin "sol" for "sun." True to its name, this is a warm, contemporary restaurant, open and airy with a spectacular view of the ocean. But the real star here is the food. They have a seasonal menu with an emphasis on seafood and natural ingredients. You can see your dinner being cooked in the kitchen. Or you can sit outside on a covered patio. One dish with several taste experiences is the Trio of Chef's Ceviches, a combination of yellowtail snapper, turks and Caicos Island princess conch, and sea scallop tiradito. The chef personally selects the daily seafood special, which is always served with a choice of sauces. If you're not up for seafood, try the cumin dusted kurobuta pork loin, with boniato puree and ancho-guava sauce. Additionally, the prime rib generally gets rave reviews, as do the lamb chops. There's live entertainment on weekend nights, wither inside in the lunge or outside on the terrace.

Chinese

P. F. CHANG'S CHINA BISTRO $$
3101 PGA Blvd., Suite F142
Palm Beach Gardens
(561) 691-1610
www.pfchangs.com
P. F. Chang's is a national chain and is unlike any Chinese restaurant you've ever experienced. It's a place to share the food and good times with friends or family or someone special, to sample many different tastes, textures, and colors. This is, basically, *nouvelle* Chinese cuisine.

Starters include one of P. F. Chang's fanfavorites, the chicken lettuce wraps, along with items like crab won tons and salt and pepper calamari. The hot and sour soup is great, as is the Asian shrimp salad. Try the honey chicken or VIP duck, glazed with a plum sauce and garnished with flatbread, scallions, and cucumbers. Or check out the Asian marinated New York strip, or the lemongrass prawns with garlic noodles. The beef, pork, lamb, and vegetarian dishes are all distinctive. P. F. Chang's also has special Dinners for Two, with soup, starter, entree, and dessert. The latter includes the Great Wall of Chocolate (six layers of chocolate cake frosted with chocolate chips and lathered in raspberry sauce).

Dessert

GELATO GROTTO $
Legacy Place
11300 Legacy Ave., Suite 100
Palm Beach Gardens
(561) 882-7100
www.gelatogrotto.com
Gelato Grotto is named for the picturesque Grotto Azzurra (blue grotto) on the Isle of Capri. And the shop probably has as many vivid colors as that fabled isle. Gelato is made with pretty much the same ingredients as ice cream, except that it has a third of the fat-content. The shop's motto is "Waves of Flavor, Fewer Calories." The gelato is infused with a wide variety of fruits, such as cherries, pineapple, and kiwi. It's very fresh-tasting, and very creamy. It's so good, in fact, that many area restaurants use Gelato Grotto's ice cream. The flavors include favorites like cookies 'n cream, chocolate cheesecake, coconut, and roasted almond, along with standards such as vanilla and chocolate. In addition to gelato, they make gelato cakes, paninis (Italian-style sandwiches), and salads, and also serve a variety of coffees and teas.

MARBLE SLAB CREAMERY $
The Gardens
4781 PGA Blvd.
Palm Beach Gardens
(561) 799-9777
www.pgaicecream.com
The ice cream is all hand-made. The wafflecones are all baked in the store, and then hand-rolled. The fruits are fresh, the nuts are top-grade, and the candy and cookie toppings include all those wonderful flavors you remember so well from your youth. Choose from sweet cream, chocolate swiss, strawberry, cheesecake, chocolate amaretto, or butter pecan. Then a big chunk of the ice cream you've chosen is rolled onto the marble slab and mixed as you watch, with all the goodies you've chosen. Then it's all stuffed into an aromatic waffle cone. Sit back and enjoy some great ice cream!

MONDO'S AMERICAN BISTRO $$–$$$
713 US 1
North Palm Beach
(561) 844-3396
www.mondosnpb.com

Mondo's is a place with a lot to recommend it—especially an interesting and eclectic menu, and innovative preparation of these dishes. But the one thing it's famous for is its signature dessert—oatmeal pie. People come from all over North County to try the oatmeal pie. Afterwards, they keep coming back for more. But it's not just oatmeal pie. It's oatmeal pie with the perfect complementary taste—cinnamon ice cream. If you're eating dinner here, your server will probably recommend it. And, as far as recommendations go, the dining critic from the *Palm Beach Post* said it all. He said that this dessert "tastes as though it could come out of a mid-century Midwestern kitchen." And, he added, "the sweet simplicity of the dish belies its true greatness."

Fondue

THE MELTING POT   **$$$**
11811 US 1
Palm Beach Gardens
(561) 624-0020
www.meltingpot.com
This is a sister site of The Melting Pot listed under the South County section, see page 77. Try the spinach artichoke cheese fondue consisting of fontina and butterkäse cheeses, spinach, artichoke hearts and garlic or the restaurant's signature selection of filet mignon, white shrimp, teriyaki-marinated sirloin, breast of chicken, and cedar plank salmon.

Greek

OUZO BLUE   **$$-$$$**
PGA Commons
5090 PGA Blvd.
Palm Beach Gardens
(561) 776-3188
www.ouzoblue.com
Ouzo Blue is a traditional Greek Taverna and bar with a contemporary atmosphere

and innovative new takes on the old Greek favorites. It's bright and new—opened in 2009—and it approaches traditional Greek cooking with a fresh new philosophy.

You'll start off with the meze—appetizers like tirokafteri, which is feta cheese blended with olive oil and hot peppers; or spanakopita, spinach, onions, leeks, and feta cheese baked in a phyllo crust. You'll also want to sample the kalamaria, baby squid fried or charbroiled, and then seasoned with lemon. Of course, you can't be in this restaurant without trying the horiatiki (Greek salad), fresh and colorful and dripping with interesting flavors. The kebabs—lamb, beef, or chicken—are marinated in olive oil, lemon, garlic, and oregano, skewered with vegetables, and then served over rice. The lamb chops, charbroiled and seasoned with garlic, lemon, and oregano, will definitely leave you wanting more. The most popular dessert at Ouzo Blue is the traditional baklava, the classic Greek pastry made with phyllo, chopped walnuts, and almonds, and then drizzled in a honey syrup.

The restaurant also has traditional Greek dancing and belly-dancing shows nightly, and a sleek, modern bar from which a very hip crowd watches them. You can dine outdoors on the patio, or inside in the stone-walled dining room with strings of lights hanging from the ceiling and recessed, subtle lighting. You're welcome to get up and join the belly-dancers in your own version of the traditional ouzo dance.

Health Food

PYRO GRILL   **$**
Abacoa Plaza
5440 Military Trail
Jupiter
(561) 630-8990
www.pyrogrill.com

Pyro Grill has a fast-food concept with a difference. Here, the fast-food is healthy. There's not a freezer or a microwave in sight—because everything they serve is fresh and made from scratch. The restaurant specializes in grain, green, or protein-mix entrees with beef, chicken, pork, or vegetarian, served with yellow or brown rice and accompanied by tons of veggies. And that mixture is accompanied by any of the 12 sauces you choose from.

The atmosphere is modern and casual, with bright reds and yellows, high ceilings, and cool decor. You'll probably smell the aroma of spices when you walk in. You'll hear the music, and the animated conversation. Starters include el guapo—black beans, sour cream, cheddar, lettuce, yellow rice, and roasted tomato salsa; or tatonka—bleu cheese cole slaw, yellow rice, and buffalo sauce. And then you build on that, adding chicken, steak, pork, or vegetables. Then you decide where to put them—burrito, bowl, wrap, etc. Finally, what sauces would you like on top of them. Your final choice is deciding which of the freshly baked cookies you'd like to top everything off with. Serves beer only.

Italian

BRIO TUSCAN GRILLE $$
The Gardens Mall
3101 PGA Blvd.
Palm Beach Gardens
(561) 622-0491
www.brioitalian.com
At Brio Tuscan Grill, the bounty of Tuscany is brought to Palm Beach County and presented beautifully. You feel as if you're dining in a Tuscan villa when you can eat inside or out on the terrace. The menu is very large, and filled with so many interesting dishes that it's hard to choose. Start with

Brio crab and shrimp cakes with horseradish and arugula; roasted garlic, spinach, and artichoke dip with warm flatbread; or spicy shrimp with eggplant. There's also sausage florentine bruscetta with creamy spinach and provolone, and lobster bisque soup. The entrees, choose from the braised beef fettuccine, with cremini mushrooms, garlic, and fire-roasted tomatoes; roasted lamb chops in a red-wine veal sauce with potatoes and asparagus; or the seared scallops and orzo primavera. There are a number of good wines from Tuscany and around the world, along with French champagnes. You might want to enjoy them with desserts such as crème brûlée, Brio's famous cheesecake, or the amazing dolchino sampler—peachberry crostada, mocha, crème brûlée, cheesecake with raspberry sauce, applebread pudding, milk chocolate caramel cake, and tiramisu.

EVO AUTHENTIC
ITALIAN CUISINE $$-$$$
626 US 1
Tequesta
(561) 745-2444
www.evoitalian.com
Evo sees itself as "a walk back in time" to when the smell of Italian cooking filled your home, and all your relatives gathered in the kitchen to watch the goings-on. This restaurant's a popular, family-friendly place with a touch of elegance, and it's newly expanded. The new Wine Lounge has become a popular evening gathering spot, with candles and vases making for an intimate atmosphere. Evo is short for "evolution," and long on evoking the classic music and movies of an earlier period.

The appetizers get your meal off to a good start at Evo. Definitely try the calamari arrabiata, with calamari fried in flour, tossed in an Italian cherry-pepper-plum tomato sauce, and served on toasted crostini. Also good is the caprese di bufala, buffalo mozzarella with tomatoes, basil, and baby arugula, topped off with olive oil and a balsamic glaze. Pastas, as you might expect, are tender and tasty. Try the spaghettini alle vongole, pasta with little neck clams sautéed in garlic and olive oil, or the spaghettini carbonara, with caramelized onion, pancetta, and sweet peas, sprinkled with romano and cream. For an entree, consider the pollo saltimbocca, pan-seared chicken topped with prosciutto and buffalo mozzarella, served over baby spinach and topped with a marsala wine mushroom sauce. Or, consider the braciole di vitello, veal filled with prosciutto, raisins, pine nuts, parmiggiano, and herbs, then pan-seared and braised in San Marzano tomatoes, roasted garlic, and onion. There's an extensive wine collection.

Mexican

CANTINA LAREDO   **$$**
4635 PGA Blvd.
Palm Beach Gardens
(561) 622-1223
www.cantinalaredo.com
At Cantina Laredo, you really feel as if you're "south of the border, down Mexico way." With a difference, though. This isn't your standard Mexican fare; this is gourmet Mexican food, in a sophisticated atmosphere. There are daily fresh-fish specials, and grilled chicken and steak garnished by signature sauces such as chipotle-wine with portobello mushrooms or sautéed artichoke hearts and roasted red peppers. The ambience is upscale. And the margaritas and tequila are top-quality. The fish are caught daily, the beef is certified Angus, and every enchilada is hand-rolled.

The Top Shelf Guacamole appetizer is made fresh at your table. The chili con queso (chili with cheese) bowl appetizer brings home the flavors of Mexico. If you're sharing appetizers, go for the Botanas platter—tacos, chicken fajita quesadillas, chili con queso, stuffed jalapeños, and beef, shrimp, and vegetable skewers. Two of the most popular entrees are the enchiladas de camarones (shrimp, Monterey jack cheese, and roasted peppers in an enchilada on a bed of greens), and the tampico (grilled chicken breast with sautéed artichoke hearts, mushrooms, spinach, red peppers, and sour cream poblano sauce). For dessert, flan is always delicious, as is the Mexican brownie served hot on a skillet with Mexican brandy butter, along with vanilla or cinnamon ice cream.

Pizza

ANTHONY'S COAL FIRED PIZZA   **$$**
2680 PGA Blvd.
Palm Beach Gardens
(561) 804-7777
www.anthonyscoalfiredpizza.com
Plain and simple, it's the coal fired oven that does it. Creates a very unique type of pizza, crispy with a slightly charred crust, and it helps bring out a denser taste from the cheese, sauce, and toppings. This is a family-friendly place, with people all around you having fun. People love the cheese, tomato sauce, Italian salad, coal-oven roasted chicken wings, and the New York–style cheesecake. Anthony Bruno, a longtime South Florida restaurateur with family roots in Brooklyn, opened the first Anthony's Coal Fired Pizza in 2002 in Fort Lauderdale. He now owns half-a-dozen restaurants in the region. He purposely concentrates on only a few types of food—the pizza, chicken wings, a couple of salads, and a few side dishes.

And he does all of them well. Serves beer and wine.

BIG APPLE PIZZA & PASTA $
11249 US 1
North Palm Beach
(561) 627-5001
www.bigapplepizza.com

Remember New York pizza? This restaurant is proof that you don't have to go to New York to have New York pizza. At Big Apple Pizza & Pasta, the dough and the sauce are handmade, and the pizza tastes exactly like real pizza from the Big Apple.

Try the Big Apple Sampler, a platterful of the restaurant's popular garlic knots (hand-knotted dough seasoned with garlic, spices, and Parmesan cheese), chicken wings, and mozzarella sticks. Move on to the Italian wedding soup, chicken broth with pastina, meatballs, and spinach. There are a bunch of salads to choose from here, but many people opt for the antipasto salad—artichokes, olives, roasted peppers, salami, ham, capicola, tomatoes, and red onion on a bed of greens. As for the pizza, you've got to try the Big Apple's The Works 8-Toppings Pizza with everything. There's also stromboli, calzone, hot and cold subs, etc. Serves beer and wine.

Seafood

BONEFISH GRILL $$
11658 US 1
North Palm Beach
(561) 799-2965
www.bonefishgrill.com

Bonefish Grill has developed a solid reputation as a place where the seafood is consistently excellent, the ambience is friendly and lively, and you always leave happy. It resembles, in some respects, a big-city tavern but it's right here in the neighborhood. It's got a wood-burning grill that endows its fish and seafood with a full, rich quality.

You can start with bang bang shrimp fried in a spicy sauce, try the increasingly popular edamame soybeans steamed and spiced. The mussels Josephine are shipped in from Prince Edward Island then sautéed with tomatoes, garlic, basil, and lemon wine sauce. The grilled fish specialties, in fact, resemble a United Nations of the sea; there's wild gulf grouper, Alaskan halibut, Chilean sea bass, Snake River rainbow trout from Idaho, and Norwegian salmon. The sauces used to dress them are all homemade—warm mango salsa, chimichurri sauce, lemon butter, and pan Asian. They give the fish a wonderful depth and flavor. You must try the pecan Parmesan crusted rainbow trout, accompanied by artichoke hearts, basil, and lemon butter. Cocktails like the pomegranate martini and the winter white sosmopolitan get very high marks from the patrons.

KE'E GRILL $$
4020 US 1
Juno Beach
(561) 776-1167

People who love good seafood love Ke'e. The seafood here is always fresh, always cooked just right, and always looks good on your plate. There's a South Seas element to the decor, with bamboo accents, a thatched-hut ambience, and tiki torches outside. Appetizers include excellent clams, and many folks go for the Cajun spring rolls. The restaurant's known for its Chilean sea bass, grouper, and seared ahi tuna. But the most popular entree may well be the encrusted fish with pineapple mango salsa on top and creamed spinach on the side. There's a good wine selection with reasonable prices. For dessert, there's only one choice—go for the key lime pie.

PEP'S ISLAND GRILL $$
1556 North US 1
Tequesta
(561) 575-5977

Pep's features great seafood with a Caribbean touch. It's a kid-friendly place, with a laid-back tiki bar outside for those who like fresh air and good drinks with their food. Appetizers include coconut shrimp, mussels, "drunken" shrimp, and margarita flatbread. The grouper quesadillas are highly recommended. The filet mignon is juicy and very tasty, laid atop coconut rice, island slaw, and garlic mashed potatoes. The soft shell crabs get kudos from guests, as does the chicken jerk flatbread. The sauces and garnishes add a special flavor—and, sometimes, a special kick—to the dishes. The food comes with a lot of extras—mango salsa, black bean dip, flatbread, and Bimini salad.

SINCLAIR'S OCEAN GRILL $$$
The Jupiter Beach Resort
5 North A1A Hwy.
Jupiter
(561) 746-2511
www.jupiterbeachresort.com

At Sinclair's Ocean Grill, you can sit in the handsome, Caribbean-accented dining room and gaze out at the ocean where your dinner may have been caught just a few hours earlier. Sinclair's has been a popular North County spot for years. The atmosphere is intimate and romantic in the evening. Not surprisingly, seafood is the specialty here. Start off with the lobster bisque, which comes with a lobster crab fritter garnish; or the grilled portobello. When it comes to salads, the baby arugula and shaved fennel, citrus salad comes with pan-fried goat

cheese, macadamia nut brittle, and black pepper vinaigrette. Then you can get into some serious seafood. The lobster and crab stuffed grouper is a standout, with stuffed medallions, tarragon and sherry sauce, and vegetables. The grilled mahi mahi is juicy and succulent, sitting atop brown rice and vegetables. The oven roasted salmon comes with lump crab orzo, sautéed asparagus, and an herb citrus sauce. The beef tenderloin's delicious, as well, as is the tri-colored linguini. There's a good selection of wines, and excellent desserts.

Steak Houses

RUTH'S CHRIS STEAK HOUSE $$$$
661 US 1
North Palm Beach
(561) 863-0660
www.ruthschris.com

A sister site to the Ruth's Chris Steak House listed in the South County section, see page 89. At Ruth's Chris the filet, rib eye, New York strip, Porterhouse, and T-bone are cut thick to enhance the juiciness. They're seared at 1,800 degrees and then topped with a dollop of butter. Accompany them with a selection from the extensive wine list.

III FORKS PRIME STEAKHOUSE $$$
4645 PGA Blvd.
Palm Beach Gardens
(561) 630-3660
www.iiiforks.com

The hallmarks of III Forks are USDA prime beef (only the top 2 percent of all beef), a warm and inviting atmosphere, excellent service, and food that's consistently excellent. Nothing is pre-cooked here, and there are no warmers. Everything is made fresh, and made to order. The "Beef Market" side of the menu offers filet mignon, bone-in rib eye, New York strip, and the souble cut pork chop. You may want to precede these specialties, however, with one (or more) of the notable appetizers, like the seafood medley (shrimp cocktail, crab cake St. Francis, and bacon wrapped scallops), or the beef croustades. For dessert, go for the Texas pecan cake or the bread pudding. This restaurant also has a notable wine cellar. There are some 3,000 bottles of fine wine from around the world; reds are stored at 58 degrees, and whites at 45.

NIGHTLIFE

This is Palm Beach County in South Florida. Which means, for many people, the real fun doesn't start until the sun goes down. And when that sun goes down, Palm Beach County dresses up and goes out, to a variety of nightspots in a variety of areas. Each of those areas is fun in its own way. And each one offers something different. And although there's something to do at night—no matter where you are, large town or small town—there are few areas that are really night-time magnets.

In Boca Raton, there's **Mizner Park,** the heart of downtown, where some of the finest restaurants in South Florida disgorge people who then head for the smart martini bars or fancy Irish pubs. In Delray, most people head straight for **Atlantic Avenue,** with its Victorian boulevard-feel, and its clubs, restaurants, and dance spots that don't really get going until 10 or 11 p.m. on weekend nights, and keep going until . . . A bit north is the restored downtown area of Lake Worth, which converted two of its greatest assets— its old buildings and the drive of its young entrepreneurs—into clubs, galleries, independent movie houses showing independent films, and colorful bars and restaurants.

Ten miles north, **downtown West Palm Beach** is a true urban nightlife-magnet, with the shops and restaurants and open plaza of **City Place** and the nearby **Clematis Street,** empty and derelict only a few years ago, and now filled with trendy bistros, cafes, and bars. Across the Intracoastal on the island of Palm Beach, the nightlife may not be quite as frenzied. But it's just as busy, especially on **Worth Avenue.** And in North County, the area around the **Gardens Mall** in Palm Beach Gardens comes alive after the sun goes down, with excellent restaurants and great

places to dance. In fact, there are so many great nightspots in Palm Beach County that many people aren't satisfied with just one in an evening. They'll go around to two or three to enjoy several different types of experiences.

The types of nightlife? **You've got it all.** Dance clubs, bars both new-and-trendy and old-and-funky, swanky nightclubs like the ones you've seen in the movies, late-night movies, places with a tropical feel overlooking the water, and places on top of a building overlooking the city. There's jazz, modern, classical, reggae, country, ethnic, blues, Dixieland, hip-hop, rap, oldies, calypso, swing, forties, Latin, Florida "cracker" rock (think Tom Petty in his early days or Lynyrd Skynyrd from Jacksonville), southern rock, and top 40.

And if your idea of nightlife is being in places where the people-watching is fascinating, you're perfectly positioned for that, as any night-time visit to Atlantic Avenue or Mizner Park will prove.

Note: Smoking is prohibited in any restaurant or bar in Florida; the only place you can do it is if there's an outdoor patio or terrace, or if there's seating outside on the sidewalk. The police will strongly prosecute anyone who gets caught drinking and driving. Cover charges are a mixed bag; some places charge them and some don't. We'll try to let you know when there's a charge. Also, in 2009–10, Florida has been severely hit by the recession, and it's still in recession. So things can change very quickly as far as the nightlife scene.

Now, go out and enjoy. Palm Beach County awaits you!

SOUTH COUNTY

THE BLUE ANCHOR PUB
804 East Atlantic Ave.
Delray Beach
(561) 272-7272
www.theblueanchor.com
Welcome to the Blue Anchor Pub, mate, where the colors (colours!) of Great Britain are displayed proudly, you can still get a shandy (warm beer and lemonade), and it wouldn't hurt to know the latest "football" score between Manchester United and Tottenham Hotspur. This place is unabashedly and delightfully British (and it wouldn't hurt if you knew what the "chips" are in "fish 'n chips").

It's a true 19th-century British pub, located right on the Intracoastal on hoppin' Atlantic Avenue. It was Zagat-rated four years in a row (2004–07). There's a full lunch and dinner menu seven days a week. It probably has more draught beers from the British Isles than anyone else west of Piccadilly, among them Guinness, Harp, Bass, Boddingtons, Smithwick's, and Newcastle Brown Ale, as well as three different Fuller's hand-drawn ales. You walk in through 8-foot-high English Oak front doors. Inside, you're back in the 19th century with authentic Tudor architecture featuring bay windows

with wrought-iron grilling dividing them up into small sections, dark woods, V-shaped paneling running across the white walls, old-fashioned little wall lamps, British flags, soccer emblems, dark-wood beams on the ceilings, and wooden columns with coats-of-arms carved into them. Dishes include toad-in-the-hole (Yorkshire pudding), scotch egg (hard-boiled egg wrapped in a sausage), the ploughman's salad, bangers and mash (sausages, potatoes, and British beaked beans), and, of course, fish 'n' chips.

The Blue Anchor Pub is a homage to a pub of the same name erected in London in 1864, a time when Jack the Ripper prowled the London streets in search of his next victim, and when Queen Victoria ruled half the world. In fact, it actually *is* the original Blue Anchor Pub. The entire exterior of the pub, including those huge oak doors, was actually part of the original pub, and was shipped here in 1996. Many famous people walked through those doors, among them Winston Churchill; and, according to legend, a couple of Jack the Ripper's female victims spent their last nights carousing here before meeting a bloody end on the streets outside. If you happen to hear footsteps from the attic while you're here, they're probably those of Bertha Starkey, who was killed here in the early 1900s when her jealous husband found her in the arms of another man. Bertha's ghost has received plenty of coverage in the media. And some folks maintain that she's the only ghost who ever survived a trans-Atlantic crossing!

BLUE MARTINI LOUNGE
6000 Glades Rd.
Town Center Mall, Suite C-1380
Boca Raton
(561) 910-BLUE

If you're a martini maven, head for Blue Martini Lounge, which has 25 different kinds, in stunningly bright colors and in creative mixtures. And you'll have plenty of time to sample them; it's open until 3 a.m. from Sun through Thurs, and until 4 a.m. on Fri and Sat. This is one of Boca's sweet spots for nightlife. There's live music. And tapas for a light bite. The design of the place is stunning—there's no other word—with a bright-red ceiling, recessed lighting, walls and ceilings back-lit in blue (what else), posh red-leather sofas, and stylish hanging lights. You can party outside at the patio bar, inside in the stage room, or in style in the VIP Room.

The specialty martinis are as wonderful to taste as they are to look at. There's the caramel swirl, for instance, with Van Gogh Dutch Caramel Vodka, Irish Crème Liqueur, and cream in a caramel-swirled glass. Bubblicious features Three Olives Bubble Vodka with a splash of cranberry and 7. Then there's the Skinny Bitch with Van Gogh Blue Vodka, pomegranate juice, Truvia, and blueberry puree, with a lemon wedge and orchid garnish. And, of course, the Blue Martini, with Van Gogh Blue Vodka, Citronge, Blue Curacao, sour mix, and orange juice, served over ice with a glow-stick. In addition to the martinis, there's an excellent wine list here.

If you're looking for a real Boca place, this is certainly one of them.

BOCA MUSE
7136 Beracasa Way
Boca Raton
(561) 367-1133
www.bocamusecafe.com
Boca Muse is a comfortable period-place with a Roaring Twenties-type of elegance, Tiffany-paneled windows, faux fireplace, interesting wall sconces, and ornate hanging lanterns. It's the type of place where friends who meet just for lunch can end up spending most of the afternoon in happy conversation. It's a place where old friends run into each other all the time, as well. You can relax with a cup of coffee, a cocktail or wine, beers such as Flying Dog's Doggy Style Pale Ale, or with one of the excellent dishes, such as tapas, salads, cheese plates, or meatloaf. There are all kinds of special events always happening here. Live entertainment on Sat nights. Open Mic Night on Wed nights. And Trivia Night on Thurs. So relax, grab one of the funky beers, and enjoy some great times.

BOSTON'S ON THE BEACH
40 South Ocean Blvd. (A1A)
Delray Beach
(561) 278-3364
www.bostonsonthebeach.com
Boston's, of course, is one of South County's great places for seafood. But it's also one of South County's places for a rollickin' good time at its outdoors Back Bay Tiki Bar. Here (in a smoker-friendly atmosphere with plenty of good food) you can listen to all sorts of live music. More than two decades ago the restaurant started Reggae Night on Mon nights with a turntable and a DJ. Now, Reggae Night is a certified tradition here with live music, and people come from all over the county to be a part of it. You're likely to hear just about any other type of music on the other nights, including jazz, island, acoustic, ska, jam, surf, blues, Parrothead (Jimmy Buffett-style), country, and rock—often by very talented bands who are traveling around the country to perform at larger venues, as well as talented local bands. The music plays on seven nights a week. So sit back, pour yourself a tall beer or tropical drink, and let the sea-breeze wash over you.

BREWZZI
Glades Plaza
2222 Glades Rd.
Boca Raton
(561) 392-BREW
www.brewzzi.com

This has been a very popular Boca meeting place since the day it opened. It's filled with a loud, happy vibe, and a lot of (mostly) young people having fun. Here, you can watch your food being made in the open kitchen. And you can watch lagers being brewed in the glass-walled, on-site brewery. Brewzzi knows beer; it's won both gold and silver medals in the Great American Beer Fest. The Brewmaster's Special is a brand-new beer every month. The City Fest is a smooth, mellow beer with a nutty taste, and it was designed specifically for Boca Raton. Black Duke Dark is a German-type beer with a golden hue and hints of chocolate and coffee.

The Gorgonzola chips are a popular appetizer. The marinated skirt steak salad is also good. The burgers are thick and juicy, and the meatloaf ... if it's comfort food you're looking for, you'll be very comfort-able with this choice. Brewzzi's got good food, good beer, and a good vibe.

BULL BAR
2 East Atlantic Ave.
Delray Beach
(561) 274-8001

This place has become sort of a landmark, a true bar that's become famous as a colorful local hangout on The Avenue. The name pays homage to the bull dolphin; and the interior pays homage to the maritime culture of long ago, when oars were still made of wood and when men went down to the sea in boats (and went down to the local watering hole as soon as they got off their boats). There's plenty of wood here, along with all manner of nautical artifacts. This is a casual bar during the daytime, and early evening hours. As the night progresses, the South County trendies find their way in, and the dress becomes more "night-time on The Avenue"–style.

There's live music most nights, including a lively trio on weekends with electric violin, guitar, and drums. The most popular drink is the Bloody Bull, the house version of the Bloody Mary but with a twist. Also frequently requested are the bar's Screwdrivers (made with real Florida orange juice). It's a crowded place, with great people-watching. And you're right next to everything else on Atlantic.

CHOW BOCA
Royal Palm Place
400 S.E. Federal Hwy.
Boca Raton
(561) 392-3499
www.chowboca.com

Imagine a combination of traditional Oriental accents and ambience with ultra-modern chic and you've got Chow Boca. It's a supper club from 5 to 10 p.m., and then turns into a lounge from 10 p.m. until 2 a.m. It's bathed in golds and soft reds and dark woods, with a shiny dance floor and a statue of Buddha sitting prominently. The dining area is intimate and cozy, the bar is stunningly modern, and lanterns giving off a reddish glow hang from the ceilings, along with Oriental fans. The patrons are casually dressed and mostly in their twenties and thirties.

Chow Boca has become one of the smart-set's places to see and be seen (and to meet-and-be-met), to eat and drink and dance. The menu highlights sashimi dishes, such as hamachi yellowtail and diver sea scallops. The wines are fine, but Chow is known most for its selection of imaginative martinis. Try the wasabi citrullus martini, with wasabi vodka blended with sake, then infused with watermelon, cucumber, and basil. The filthy gorgeous dirty martini is a big hit with the people here, as well; it's a mix of Ketel One Vodka, olive juice, and olives. Others swear by the chocolate razzberry martini, with Skyy Razz and Godiva chocolate.

CLUB BOCA
7000 W. Palmetto Park Rd.
Boca Raton
(561) 392-3747
www.nightcure.com

At Club Boca, there's a night for everyone, including teens. This is a swank, modern, plush nightclub, with pulsating lights, music, and ambience. There are bikini contests on Thurs nights, which is also Wipe Me Down night, when ladies drink free. Sat night is Champagne Night (for older-teenagers and younger adults) when hip-hop music reigns supreme. On Mercury Friday, a DJ spins hip-hop, reggae, and Top 40 in the main room, while another DJ spins Latin, house, and Reggaeton in the Martini Room. There are "all ages" parties, and many theme nights when you'll see all the patrons dressed in a certain style, such as all in white. The dress is generally to the nines; come in something stylish, and something in which you love to dance. And be prepared to boogie—the music will get you on your feet before too long. Cover charge.

DADA
52 North Swinton Ave.
Delray Beach
(561) 330-DADA
www.dada.closermagazine.com

If Dada sounds to you like the type of unusual place where you can have a really great time—you're right. It's a 1924 two-story house turned restaurant/pub, open every day until 2 a.m. It attracts an eclectic crowd of artists, musicians, poets, writers, colorful Bohemian characters, and other creative types—as well as people interested in rubbing shoulders with these types. Local folks love the atmosphere and the special events always taking place here.

The interior is dark, intimate, and romantic, with lace window curtains, vintage clocks and drawings on the walls, and period light-fixtures. There's also outdoor seating. The events? Open mic nights, poetry slams, fashion shows, popscene Saturdays, reggae nights, Latin nights, magic nights, great bands—both local and out-of-town, even indie films. And you can take it all in while sitting on a couch in the living room and munching on fondue. The wine selection is as eclectic as the clientele., and the mojitos are great. Two of the most popular choices are the mango with mango rum, fresh mint, lime, Dada's own homemade syrup, and a splash of soda; and the pama, with pomegranate liqueur, a premium rum, lime, the homemade syrup, and a splash of soda. The left ear is a shaken martini (with a drop of grenadine at the bottom) that serves homage to Vincent van Gogh. But if you're in the mood for something smoother, try nuts and berries, a mix of Chambord, Frangelico, and cream.

In an old house like this, there are always legends. And Dada is no different. The original owner is said to still be hanging out—in ghostly form, of course—in the upstairs staff room.

DELUX NIGHTCLUB
16 East Atlantic Ave.
Delray Beach
(561) 279-4792

The food is excellent, the dancing is emphatic, and the pulsating rhythms of this club spill out onto Atlantic Avenue with a definite vibe. Guest DJ's keep the house moving with a variety of house and hip-hop. The sound system is state-of-the-art; there are no "But I don't dance" excuses here! And you can take in the whole exciting scene while relaxing on a real bed on the VIP patio. And the decor is sleek. The bar area is woodsy and modern, the lighting is down-low, and the crowd is young and hip. There are lock and key parties for singles to loosen up the atmosphere. You'll want to dress up a bit because this is truly a "night on the town." Cover charge.

GATSBY'S
5970 S.W. Eighteenth St.
Boca Raton
(561) 393-3900
www.gatsbys.net

If you're looking for a place in which to "get your game on," consider Gatsby's. This place has been hauling 'em in from all over and South County for many years. It's casual in the atmosphere, food, and drink. There are TVs all over the place showing not only South Florida's major league teams—the Marlins (baseball), Dolphins (football), Heat, (basketball), and Panthers (Hockey)—but pro and college games from all over the country. The happy hours are great here, and they're filled with happy people. And there are all kinds of drink specials: Martini Monday, Two for Tuesdays, Thirsty Thursdays, Ultimat (a brand of Vodka) Fridays, etc. If getting your game on means doing something

more vigorous than just watching, test your skill at one of the pool tables. This is a great spot for a late-night dinner, snack, or drink. And you can always catch the games on TV from Western cities!

HURRICANE PUB & LOUNGE
640-7 E. Atlantic Ave.
Delray Beach
(561) 278-0282
www.hurricanelounge.com

The Hurricane Bar & Lounge is a great place to party with friends and to listen to good live music. On Mon nights there's a Free Texas Hold 'Em party. On Wed, Thurs, and weekend nights there's live music, with an interesting assortment of bands. The place caters to a young crowd, some of whom are suits and ties and others of whom are in T-shirts and tank tops. The decor is casual, with a long wooden bar, a stage in the corner, and tables and chairs scattered about. There's also an outdoor patio. The Hurricane Bar has a good selection of wines and beers. It's a leave-your-cares-behind-and-just-have-fun type of place.

KEVRO'S ART BAR
166 S.E. Second Ave.
Delray Beach, FL
(561) ART-WORK (278-9675)

Is it a bar? Or is it an art gallery? It's both. First, you take a vacant old space along the Florida East Coast railroad tracks. Then you turn it into a chic urban-industrial space with an imaginative layout and whimsical decor. And then you fill it up with great art, much of it from local artists. The facility itself was created by artists, such as Kevin (Kevro) Rouse, a Delray resident who became the driving force behind this unique concept. Now it's a complete compound with a bar, art gallery, outdoor painting patio, and photography video studio. And the bar area features some great work by local artists and photographers, along with an eclectic collection of beers and wines. Kevro's Art Bar is filled with a wonderful collection of furniture and furnishings, both modern and retro, and in a dazzling assortment of colors. In fact the furniture, in its own way, is truly a work of contemporary design, with an exciting assortment of textures, colors, angles, and shapes. The artworks on the walls resonate with different styles, ranging from modern to abstract. A visit to Kevro's will certainly get your artistic juices flowing. And it's also a darn good time.

LION & EAGLE ENGLISH PUB
2401 N. Federal Hwy.
Boca Raton
(561) 447-7707
The Lion & Eagle English Pub has become something of a landmark on Federal Highway. When you're inside this place, it seems closer to Newcastle-on-Thames than it does the Gold Coast of Florida. The atmosphere's authentic, the red-white-and-blue of the British flag is everywhere, and here, the Queen is still the queen. This is an older place; but it's been cleaned up and spiffed up and it's now a bright—and veddy British—place to have a great time. Soccer ("football," to the British and everyone else in the world but Americans) is always on the telly, so be prepared to cheer for Man-U or Liverpool or Chelsea or West Ham, and to exchange good-natured conversation with fans of the other team. Even the international matches shown on the TVs here, which usually attract fans of both competing countries, are good-natured affairs in which everyone's very friendly.

The food has a British accent, as well, with specialties such as fry-ups (a dish made up of a variety of fried foods), Sunday roast, and shepherd's pie (layers of ground meat and vegetables topped with mashed potatoes). And there're plenty of good British and Irish beers with which to wash it down. If you're looking for a friendly place where the atmosphere is more Piccadilly Circus or Covent Garden than Boca Raton, try the Lion & Eagle.

MICHELANGELO PIANO
BAR GALLERY CAFE
25 N.E. Second Ave.
Delray Beach
(561) 272-8009
For a neighborhood piano bar with a mixture of both classical and contemporary music, Michelangelo is an excellent choice. It's a bit lower-key than the surrounding Atlantic Avenue frenzy, and its patrons wouldn't have it any other way. You can enjoy the atmosphere—which also features karaoke on Fri and Sat nights—while being surrounded by fascinating works by local artists. The ambience is smart and the guests are well-dressed, with an appreciation for good piano and good art. Two-drink minimum per person.

NAKAVA
140 N.W. Twentieth St.
Boca Raton
(561) 395-9888
www.nakava.com
This is truly one of the most unique nighttime experiences in Palm Beach County. It's a hookah lounge and kava bar. For one thing, you won't find any alcoholic drinks here. Kava is the traditional drink of a remote South Pacific island nation called Vanuatu

derived from the kava root. (Nakava claims to be the first kava bar in North America.) Kava purports to be a healthier alternative to alcohol, with calming, relaxing effects. Nakava imports its roots directly from farmers on the island, and grinds them up on the premises. The results are very different types of tea and juice, including one (Yerba Mate Tea) that is actually somewhat known here in America.

At Nakava you can also smoke the hookah, the fruit-flavored water-pipe that originated in the Middle East. The effect is a relaxing one. But that doesn't mean that you can't find plenty of good, old fashioned music and events at Nakava. The Sunset Toast honors the traditions of the people of Vanuatu, and takes place every evening. Sunday is college night, Tues is ladies' night, Thurs is poetry and acoustic music night (and after your performance, there's a good chance the club will post it on YouTube). There's live reggae and South Pacific tribal music, Halloween parties, and performances by talented local acoustic musicians.

The media—both local and national— have taken notice of Nakava. *City Link* magazine, a South Florida entertainment publication, gave it a Best Award for 2007. The readers of local alternative weekly *New Times* voted it Best Place to Mellow Out. The (late) *Boca Raton News* called it one of the top ten bars in Boca Raton. And it's also received coverage in *Boca Raton* magazine, the *Palm Beach Post,* the *South Florida Sun-Sentinel,* the *Miami Herald, USA Today,* and *Geraldo at Large.*

NEW YORK COMEDY CLUB
8221 Glades Rd.
Boca Raton
(561) 470-6887
www.nyccboca.com

At the New York Comedy Club, it's not only the professionals who vie for your laughs. Throughout the year, there are Funniest Amateur Comedian contests. And there's not just straight comedy all the time, either. There are illusionists, magicians, musical-comedians, dancers (in a manner of speaking!), ventriloquists—and people who do all of the above. And there are a number of performers whose names you may recognize.

If you're old enough to remember the 1970s TV show *Good Times,* you'll no doubt remember Jimmy Walker (the human-string bean older brother, "J. J."). He's been all over the small screen and the large in the 30 years since the show ended, with appearances in films such as *Airplane* and TV shows like *The Love Boat, Fantasy Island, The Drew Carey Show,* and *The George Lopez Show.* And he's a frequent act at the New York Comedy Club. Keith Barany has been a comedy writer for *Politically Incorrect, Seinfeld,* and *The Jimmy Kimmel Show.* You can often catch him here, as well. There's also Michael Mack, who combines outrageous impersonations and stand-up comedy with musical comedy.

The menu offers salads, sandwiches, and desserts, as well as beer, wine, and mixed drinks. However, if you're an aspiring comic, or if you think you may have some talent (even if no one else thinks so), come to the club on the last Thurs evening of each month for the open mic night. Who knows, the next time you come here after that, it may be as the star of the show! Cover charge; some shows have a minimum (drinks or food).

PAVILION GRILLE
301 Yamato Rd.
Boca Raton
(561) 912-0000
www.paviliongrille.com

The Pavilion Grille is one of Boca's places to have a great all-around evening—with dinner, drinks, and dancing. It's in the atrium area of an office building, with a huge skylight allowing in natural light, a bar-in-the-round (with room for a lot of people), strings of festive lights strewn around, palm trees even though it's indoors, and a 2,000 square foot dance floor. If you like to trip the light fandango (dance!), there are live bands as well as DJs here. And the music doesn't stop until very late.

At this place, the special events just keep coming. There's a Motown Revue every Tues night. On Wed night there's ballroom and Latin dancing. There are acts like The Shindigs, a 1960s-type band (complete with costumes) that will make you feel like boogying in your bell bottoms. There are romantic-jazz duos; Latin bands; swing, salsa, and hustle nights; and special events on occasions like Valentine's Day.

The lump crab cakes are a highly recommended appetizer, while frequent guests recommend the char-grilled Atlantic mahi mahi and the chicken Marsala for dinner. And there's a nice selection of wines (particularly Chardonnays) and champagnes. Occasional cover charge, depending on the act that night.

32 EAST
32 East Atlantic Ave.
Delray Beach
(561) 276-7868
www.32east.com

This is a wonderful place from which to view the nocturnal activity on Atlantic Avenue. It's a restaurant, however the bar has always attracted a well-dressed, sophisticated crowd. Built on the site of an old auction house in 1996, the place is chic-modern in its decor, with striking design elements all over, like checkered terrazzo floors, soft lighting from wall sconces, and eclectic art on the walls. There are comfortable couches on which to enjoy your drink. And the drinks are excellent. Some of the favorites are the espresso martini, the pomegranate martini, and the champagne cocktail. And 32 East is known for the variety and the quality of its wine list.

CENTRAL COUNTY

B. B. KING'S RESTAURANT & BLUES CLUB
550 South Rosemary Ave., Suite 236
West Palm Beach
(561) 420-8600
www.bbkingclubs.com

"The thrill is gone," according to B. B. King's classic blues hit of the same name. But if it's gone, they haven't yet told the folks at B. B. King's Restaurant & Blues Club—because they sure look like they're having the time of their lives. There's live music every night of the week, with accomplished blues, jazz, and soul musicians such as the B. B. King All Stars, The Pure Blues Band, and Derek Mack. There are great special events like Super Bowl Sunday or Valentine's Day. And it all happens right in the middle of City Place, the beautiful urban core of downtown West Palm Beach, where the dining, dancing, cocktailing, music, movies, clubbing, ice-creaming, plaza-strolling, and the people-watching go on well into the wee hours.

The ambience here is certainly blues-ey, with checkerboard floors, soft lighting, tables close to the stage, the ambience of a real blues club in New Orleans or Nashville. And the music? Soft, soulful, sweet, lyrical, evocative, melancholy, joyful, Mississippi Delta, bayou country, N'Orleans, of long-lost (but still-mourned) lovers, lost (and still-mourned) life opportunities, friends who went astray and down the wrong path, redemption, of the down-and-out times, survival, of resurrection from the depths, of the Deep South, and of the life-experiences of every one of us, no matter whether we come from the bayous of "Loosiana" or the canyons of Manhattan.

Enjoy a drink while you listen to music that will transport you to a different place, perhaps even a different time, music that will undoubtedly unlock distant memories of your own life and times. At B. B. King's, you'll see that there's a little bit of the blues in each of us. Cover charge.

BLUE MARTINI
550 South Rosemary Ave., #244
West Palm Beach
(561) 835-8601
www.bluemartinilounge.com
In West Palm Beach, where else would you put a Blue Martini but in City Place? This smart, swank lounge bathed in blue lighting fits in perfectly here in the center of nightlife in Palm Beach County. There are 25 different kinds of martinis here, in every conceivable brilliant color, among them the espresso martini (Russian Standard Platinum Vodka, Borghetti Espresso Liqueur, Irish Cream); sex in the city (Van Gogh Vodka, peach schnapps, cranberry and pineapple juice); and the 007 (Bacardi "O" Rum, orange juice, 7Up). But there's more here than just (very fashionable!) martinis. The champagnes are notable, as well, with names like Perrier Jouet, Louis Roederer, and Dom Perignon. And the tapas are great here.

You can dance to live music here or schmooze on the outdoor patio bar. The weekly schedules here are filled with special nights. Tues there's live jazz. Wed is Three

Olives Ladies Night, with each lady receiving a free Three Olive cocktail. Thurs are Azul (Blue) Thursdays, with Latin music.

BOONIE'S RESTAURANT & LOUNGE
14555 Southern Blvd.
Loxahatchee
(561) 753-9991
www.booniesonline.com
There's not a more aptly named restaurant/lounge in Palm Beach County, because "the boonies" is exactly where this one's located. It's way out west in horse country in the town of Loxahatchee. Here, cowboy boots and hats aren't for show; they're for everyday wear. "Country folks" still look you in the eye when they speak with you, and still say please and thank you. At Boonie's, folks still know how to have a rip-roaring good ole time. (And if you're old enough to remember the Marlboro Man, he hasn't gone away, he's merely gone out West to sit at the bar at Boonie's.)

There's Country Western pretty much every night, ranging from sad love ballads and romantic wishes to foot-stompin', toe-tappin', two-steppin', blastin' guitars and fiddles and pianos. There's poker for people who want to try their luck, karaoke for people who want to try their skill, and line-dancing for people who want to try out their coordination. Pool tables, of course. There's an outdoor patio (with a lot of smokers). The food's good, too; the Porterhouse, prime rib, and filet mignon are certified Black Angus beef, and the wings are great. The drinks not only taste good, but sound very cool: the cherry bomb is black cherry rum and Red Bull; the Washington apple is Crown Royal, a sour-apple mix called Apple Pucker, and cranberry juice.

CONNOLLY'S SPORTS BAR & GRILL
10045 Belvedere Rd.
Royal Palm Beach
(561) 795-0403
www.connollysbar.com

Connolly's, in the western community of Royal Palm Beach, is a genuine neighborhood bar, where everybody knows your name . . . and even if they don't know your name, they're always glad you came. It's one of the few places in Palm Beach County that allows smoking ("grandfathered" in after the laws changed). The standard bar-food favorites are all here, they're all good, and there are always great specials: $1 hot dogs on Sun, 35-cent wings on Mon, $1 tacos on Tues, and 35-cent little neck steamers on Fri.

There are free pool nights, tabletop games, dart boards, lingerie shows, video games, and 17 TVs scattered about, including three 107" projection TVs. From Wed through Sat there are notable local bands such as Knuckle Busters and Rug Burn, playing rock 'n' roll, classic rock, alternative, and blues. At the Wed Night Live Jam, you're welcome to jump on stage, pick up an instrument or a microphone, and do your thing. Readers of the *New Times*, a South Florida alternative weekly paper, voted Connolly's Best Sports Bar in 2008.

DR. FEELGOODS ROCK BAR
219 Clematis St.
West Palm Beach
(561) 833-6500
www.feelgoodswestpalm.com

Even if you have no intention of going to Dr. Feelgoods, at least go to the Web site. Like the place itself, it's creative, funky, and fun, a sort-of motorcycle video game. The place doesn't try to be anything but exactly what

it is—a great place to hear rock music in a funky atmosphere in the heart of downtown West Palm. There's a strict dress code here, mostly directed at sloppy or urban dress. Tues is Ladies' Night, and there are special events such as the White Trash Bash. Drinks made with Bacardi Rum are the specialty of the house. And the DJs are great. Cover charge. Closed Sun, Mon, Wed.

E. R. BRADLEY'S SALOON
104 South Clematis St.
West Palm Beach
(561) 833-3520
www.erbradleys.com

Opened in 1984, E. R. Bradley's has become more or less a nightlife institution in West Palm Beach, and hundreds of clubs that opened up after Bradley's are no longer here. Its location doesn't hurt, of course, it's downtown set in a garden-line setting right on the Intracoastal Waterway and convenient to the excitement of City Place and of Clematis Street. And if you're craving a late bite, this is a good place to satisfy that craving; they're open until 4 a.m.

Bradley's is named for a character who became the embodiment of the American dream, Edward Riley Bradley. He was born in 1859 into abject poverty and worked his way up as a steel-mill laborer, miner, businessman, and philanthropist. He became the top owner and breeder of racehorses in the South during the early part of the 20th century and actually owned Kentucky Derby winners. The saloon named after him caters to all types and all ages, from college kids in Florida Gators T-shirts to businesspeople in office attire to bikinis-n-boots. There are special events such as Monday Funday, Happy Hump Day, and Late-Night Barbecue.

LEOPARD LOUNGE & RESTAURANT
The Chesterfield Hotel
363 Cocoanut Row
Palm Beach
(561) 659-5800
www.chesterfieldpb.com

The Leopard Lounge bespeaks class and elegance, which makes sense because it's in one of the classiest, most elegant hotels in Palm Beach County. Colonial-style draperies, light woods, brass, painted ceilings, and wicker combine to create a relaxing feeling. The more-than-a-hint of African motif adds an element of light-heartedness and fun. For example, the lounge gets its name from the leopard-skin tablecloths and leopard-spot carpeting (and the leopard-patterned vests of some of the staff). Along with brass elephant-head bar rails and other African accents, they lend an air of edginess to this classic Palm Beach watering hole. Here, you'll find the cream of Palm Beach society, young and old.

But this place is far from stuffy. There's a dance floor, which gets pretty active as the evening progresses, and entertainment every night, ranging from classical guitarists to show-tune vocalists. The acts include people like Bill Coleman, a guitarist/singer who can range from swing to jazz and Top 40; Keiko Chokai, who can create a very romantic mood with her piano; and a versatile singer/musician duo named Pam and Dave. The bar is well-stocked with quality cognacs, grappas, bourbons, whiskeys, and cocktails. And the bartenders will create any combination you come up with. Happy hour is every day during the season. And if, by some chance, you're not feeling quite up to the dancing scene, stroll into Churchill's Cigar Room, where you can puff on select stogies and sip on smooth cognacs while

discussing the events of the day, or watching them on TV. *Palm Beacher* magazine named the Leopard Lounge Best Bar in a Hotel.

THE LIQUID ROOM
313 Clematis St.
West Palm Beach
(561) 655-2332

The Liquid Room is ultra-hip and ultra-chic, and it's a great place to boogie in downtown West Palm. The mode of attire is dress-to-impress. But it's nonetheless a friendly crowd that's here to mingle and dance. The dance floor can get crowded but be sure to take a look at the people with whom you're rubbing elbows. It could be someone like Madonna or Rod Stewart, two of the many celebrities who stop by when they're in town. (Stewart is actually something of a local; he has a home in Palm Beach County.) The music varies from house and pop to techno and hip hop. If you're in the mood to splurge (or if you happen to be one of those celebrities), there's an incredible VIP room. Cover charge.

THE LOBBY NIGHTCLUB
700 South Rosemary Ave.
City Place
West Palm Beach
(561) 651-1110
www.lobbynightclub.com

This club has always been popular. But, thanks in part to a recent top-to-bottom renovation, it's even more so. There's a new look and feel to the place, with new decor and state-of-the-art sound and lighting systems. With plush sofas and long tables, purplish walls filled with eye-catching pop art, plenty of room to dance, private nooks and crannies, another room in which the furniture and walls are bathed in orange, and a beautiful VIP area, you'll feel the vibe the moment you walk in. There's even a touch of Oriental here or there—a Buddha here, lanterns there, as seems to be the rage these days.

Owner Tommy Finneran tried to achieve a South Beach-hotel type of look, one in which there would be "no sneakers." And even a quick look around the club and the patrons will tell you that he's succeeded handsomely. This place, too, is a celebrity-magnet, and people such as RuPaul, actress Lorraine Bracco, popular band Danity Kane, and celebrity DJ Irie have all partied here.

Special events are always happening. One of them is HIP Wednesdays, where you've got to be dressed to kill or outside-you'll-be-waiting-still. (This is one of the best nights for celebrity-watching.) Ladies Night is every Thurs. There's also a monthly Burlesque Party with dancers and body painting. And if it's your birthday, you and your guests will receive complimentary admission and a complimentary bottle of wine with which to celebrate. Cover charge.

THE MONKEY CLUB
219 Clematis St.
West Palm Beach
(561) 833-65001

The Monkey Club has the largest dance floor in downtown West Palm—7,500 square feet. And it's generally filled with a young crowd that dances enthusiastically on that big floor. This is a Caribbean-style place that holds very popular Ladies Nights and special dance parties. On Sat nights, popular local radio station 95.5 broadcasts live from the club. There's a pool room in the back if you'd prefer a cue to dancing. Cover charge.

O'SHEA'S IRISH PUB
531 Clematis St.
West Palm Beach
(561) 833-3865
www.osheaspub.com

The orange, white, and green flies proudly in front of O'Shea's. The interior is just as Irish. And now they've opened up a courtyard area, complete with accents and benches from the Auld Sod. It's a wonderful place to take in the stars at night, while also taking in some live music. This pub boasts of having the biggest free St. Patrick's Day celebration in South Florida, complete with beer tents and trucks on the street, and plenty of Irish dancers, and bagpipers. There are also Trivia Pub Quizzes, free Texas Hold 'Em poker tournaments, Car Bomb Thurs with live music, and free happy hour barbecues on Fri. All the great Irish beers are here—Guinness, Harp, Smithwick's, and Murphy's, along with, of course, Jameson Irish Whiskey. There's a long list of Ireland's favorite dishes, as well: potato soup, Irish sausage roll, the classic cork BLT, the Clifden ham and cheese sandwich (traditional Irish pub fare), traditional sausage sandwich, shepherd's pie, fish 'n chips, Guinness beef pie, bangers 'n mash, and, of course, corned beef and cabbage. And you can top it all off with Bailey's ice cream dessert.

PALM BEACH IMPROV
City Place
550 South Rosemary Ave.
West Palm Beach
(561) 833-1812
www.palmbeachimprov.com

At the Improv—yes, it's one of *those* Improvs—the stars come out every night: Damon Wayans, Jeff Garlin (*Curb Your Enthusiasm, Daddy Day Care*), Paul Rodriguez (TV and movies), Brad Garrett (*Everybody Loves*

Raymond), D. L. Hughley. The Improv is a comedy club/dinner theater. Not only can you see today's stars, but you can also see up-and-coming young comics who will be the stars of tomorrow. And the laughs usually don't stop until the curtain goes down. If you're here to have dinner with your comedy, try the Argentine steak, the penne Alfredo, or the seafood platter. There's a good selection of Chardonnays with which to enjoy your dinner. The humor? It's raucous, raunchy, side-splitting, informal, audience-participation, and hilarious. (And there are no network censors!) The Improv has been making people laugh since the 1960s. Come be prepared to put aside all your worries and burdens 'cause you'll be laughing like you haven't laughed in years. Cover charge; two-drink minimum if not eating dinner.

PROPAGANDA
6 South J St.
Lake Worth
(561) 547-7273
www.propagandalw.com
Propaganda describes itself as an "Indie Rock Dive Bar and Lounge," and its mission as "music for the masses." There's a fascinating vibe here, a sort of culture-clash between the early-20th-century decor of Chinese and Russian propaganda posters and funky modern art, and the 21st-century progressive music that fills it up at night. There's really no way to describe the atmosphere at Propaganda, you've really got to see it for yourself. It's certainly the only place you'll ever see Mao Tze Tung, Uncle Sam, Lenin, and Fidel Castro sharing space with Sweet Knuckle, Dick Bronco, and The Pretty Faces. Sunday is hip hop nite, with different drink specials. Wed is Lady's Night. Thurs is reggae/ska/dub night. And the club is open until 2 a.m. every night. Local publication *City Link* called Propaganda the Best Rock Bar of 2009. *New Times* called it South Florida's Best New Venue. It's sort of a music and art warehouse for people who like new music and who like to follow the popular local DJs. This place—there's no other way to say it—is a "trip." Cover charge.

RENEGADES COUNTRY NIGHT CLUB
4833 Okeechobee Blvd.
West Palm Beach
(561) 683-9555
www.renegadeswpb.com
Renegades is country—and proud of it. This nightspot has been pulling 'em in for years. They come in their jeans and their cowboy hats, and they come prepared to party. The place is Tucson—or Laredo, or Amarillo, or Dodge City—in Palm Beach County, with a decor and an attitude that says this is definitely Cowboy Country. There's a 2,000 square foot dance floor and four antique bars. There are pool tables and video games, huge TV screens (on which to watch your favorite teams), and state-of-the-art light and sound systems. And, yes, there is a mechanical bull that'll really test your mettle (as well as every muscle in your body).

There are dance classes, from line dancing to Texas Two-Step to square dancing, to the music of country stars such as Brad Paisley, Marlee Scott, and Josh Turner. It's a young crowd that likes to party-hearty, so if wet T-shirt contests aren't your thing, beware! There are top-notch country bands to entertain them, and drink specials most nights. This is a rip-roarin', country hoe-down.

RESPECTABLE STREET
518 Clematis St.
West Palm Beach
(561) 832-9999
www.respectablestreet.com
Respectable Street proudly celebrated "24 Years of Oblivion" in 2010. A lot of words can be used to describe this place but "oblivion" isn't one of them. It's become a West Palm Beach landmark for its creative bands and its singular focus on progressive music. Among these types of music are indie, electro, punk, and alternative. Events here are just as unique as the music. For example, there's the Anti-Folk Freakout, the Annual Cheesy 80s Prom, anniversary parties for the club. The colorful crowd here floods the place for the events, and for the dancing.

ROYAL ROOM CABARET
The Colony Hotel
155 Hammon Ave.
Palm Beach
(561) 655-5430
www.thecolonypalmbeach.com
The Royal Room is one of those places—and one of those experiences—that you never forget. It's a genuine "Supper Club," steeped in the aura and the elegance of another age but filled with the best cabaret performers of this age. If they ever tried to keep a scrapbook of their press clippings, it would probably be heavier than the *Encyclopedia Britannica*. And just as impressive. (The *Palm Beach Post* hailed the Royal Room as "probably the best place for cabaret on the planet."

As soon as you walk in, you'll know you're in for a special evening. The room is bathed in light walls, red curtains, yellow tablecloths and chairs, and 1940s-nightclub-style table lamps. The silver and the crystal absolutely gleam. And the service is like something from a Humphrey Bogart movie—white glove and first-class.

You can come for dinner and a show. The steaks are excellent here, as is the salmon steak; also highly recommended are the veal chops and the sea bass. If you don't want dinner, you can still come just for the show. The Royal room features entertainers such as Johnny Rodgers, who recently finished up a run with Liza Minnelli in *Liza's at the Palace;* Lainie Kazan, one of the few performers who actually fits that old-time description of "star of stage, screen, and television"; John Davidson, who's been a Broadway and TV headliner since the 1960s; Marilyn Maye, the wonderful singer who holds the singer's record for appearances on *The Tonight Show with Johnny Carson;* and Steve Tyrell, the well-known New York nightclub crooner who's been called "a welcome addition to the list of Sinatra heirs."

RUMBASS NIGHTCLUB
106 North Military Trail
West Palm Beach
(561) 640-0678
www.rumbass.com
This is an extraordinarily beautiful nightclub, filled with striking furnishings and vivid colors and a genuine sense that you're in for an exciting night here. There are so many interior design styles that it almost makes the place hard to describe. Luxurious see-through white drapes, set behind plush settees and love seats. A stylish bar, back-lit in red, large dance floors, with different colors beamed up from the floor, imaginative lights and fixtures, decorative etched glass, glowing red candles inside little nooks in the walls. There are elements of Victorian and Oriental mixed in among the mostly modern decor. But it all works.

There are actually two dance areas at Rumbass. The Pure Lounge has hip-hop, old school, and others. And the Main Room has salsa, merengue, bachata, and Latin rock. Most of the music is played by DJs. Occasionally, though, they bring in Latin stars such as Fernando Villalona. Liquor brands include everything from Johnnie Walker to Hennessy to Jose Cuervo, and, of course, Budweiser. The crowd is young and dressed for clubbing. Cover charge.

STIR BAR AND TERRACE
The Ritz-Carlton
100 South Ocean Blvd.
Palm Beach
www.ritzcarlton.com

The Stir Bar has a sort of dual personality. By day, it's a relaxing place to just sit and watch the activity going on all around you at the Ritz-Carlton, and to enjoy a snack or drink while doing it. At night, though, the bar and terrace undergo a metamorphosis. It becomes an intimate, romantic place, bathed in candlelight and well-dressed people and brilliantly hued cocktails. You can enjoy Asian food and sake while sitting on the terrace and looking out at the ocean. It's hard to think of a more relaxing sound than the rhythmic washing of the waves onto shore. Tiny lights from distant boats bob up and down, and the stars have never seemed so clear. For an extra dose of intimacy, you can sit with your significant other on one of the incredibly plush seats around the circular firepit, where the night-time fire seems to warm your soul as well as your body.

You can nibble on jumbo shrimp or oysters, Mediterranean mezzah (toasted pita), or an artisanal cheese plate with honeycomb, figspread, and nuts. Or, you can just mellow out with a mango mojito, a mocha martini, or a hidden pleasure (Grey Goose l'orange, Chambord, cranberry, and pineapple champagne).

SUSHI GROOVE WEST PALM (GAY/ LESBIAN)
2730 South Dixie Hwy.
West Palm Beach
(561) 837-8588
www.jumponmarkslist.com

This is a place where the gay/lesbian community comes to dance on Fri nights. There are go-go dancers, two-for-one well drinks, free valet parking, and a house DJ who knows how to get people off their seats and on to the floor. The decor is Oriental-minimalist. They mix a nice drink, and the sushi's pretty good. Cover charge. Open Fri nights only.

TA-BOO
221 Worth Ave.
Palm Beach
(561) 835-3500
www.taboorestaurant.com

When Ta-Boo opened, Frank Sinatra was just starting to climb the charts. No one had ever heard of bobby-sox or hula hoops. Elvis was a skinny kid in a Mississippi elementary school, the Beatles hadn't been born yet, and Kate Smith had a hit with *God Bless America*. Pearl Harbor hadn't even been attacked yet. In fact, Ta-Boo opened up earlier that same year—1941. And it's been making Palm Beach nights special ever since.

In Florida, "hot" restaurants come and go, often to be replaced by the next "hot" restaurant. But Ta-Boo's been looking up and down Worth Avenue uninterrupted all this time. And that, in itself, says something about the food, the atmosphere, and the service. This is not just a restaurant, though; it's also a great late-night spot for a drink and romantic conversation. You'll undoubtedly see the cream of Palm Beach society here, as well as the up-and-comers who aspire to be the cream of Palm Beach society one day. Ta-Boo has secrets in every corner; among the people who've held "private" conversations here have been President John F. Kennedy, Frank Sinatra, and the Duke and Duchess of Windsor. And the legends are legion, among them that a German submarine commander during the war took a boat to shore and came in for a few drinks; and that Joe Kennedy, the scion of the clan, locked himself in the ladies room with Gloria Swanson one night.

There are more than 50 wines and champagnes to choose from, if you come in for a late-night drink, or to have a "private" conversation. And the most beautiful shopping street in the world is just out the door.

10@2 SALOON & PIANO BAR
309 Clematis St.
West Palm Beach
(561) 296-7699
www.309clematis.com

At the 10@2 (the meaning is too hard to describe here!), the theme is western, and the music is wild. You probably won't find many cowboy duels on the floor, and any six-shooters you see won't be real. But there is one kind of duel you'll definitely find here on Sat nights—dueling pianos. It's the only dueling-piano bar in West Palm Beach. And it'll be the most fun you've had in a while, pardner.

When the pianos aren't dueling, a live band is blasting rock 'n' roll with occasional country thrown in. When the bands aren't playing and signing, the patrons are; there's some serious karaoke here, too. The 2009 winner of the annual karaoke contest won $10,000. And there's $25,000 in the pot for

the 2010 winner! At the 10@2, it's country in the city. Open Thurs, Fri, and Sat nights. Cover charge (no charge for ladies on Thurs nights).

WET WILLIE'S
550 South Rosemary Ave., Suite 250
West Pam Beach
(561) 832-3017
www.wetwillies.com

First of all, we have to say it—Wet Willie's has just about the coolest Web site of any restaurant in the country (there's even a penguin bowling game you can play). And the experience inside the restaurant is just as cool. The walls are filled with huge murals incorporating all kinds of faces and shapes and artistic styles and angles. Wet Willie's specializes in frozen daiquiris—an amazing assortment of them. And the creative minds at work here are always testing and tasting new mixtures. Take the Attitude Improvement, for example, a Wet Willie's original with an orange taste that will definitely improve your attitude—with high-proof grain alcohol and Bacardi Light and Dark rums. If you've got a sweet tooth, you may want to spend some quality time with a Bahama Mama, a mixture of banana, coconut, raspberry and Bacardi Light and Dark rum. Or, you can try the ferociously popular Absinthe—illegal in most forms in the United States for over 100 years now, this drink was first made famous in some of Ernest Hemingway's writing, particularly *The Sun Also Rises*. The frozen version at Wet Willie's is made with plenty of the strong absinthe called Mythe, made in the traditional European method.

All the classic American bar foods are available here, like wings, nachos (American?), burgers, and sandwiches. Wet Willie's is a colorful collage of people, eclectic decor, and great drinks. Come, and enjoy.

NORTH COUNTY

AVERAGE JOE'S PUB
711 West Indiantown Rd.
Jupiter
(561) 747-0032
www.averagejoespubjupiter.com

Average Joe's is a real neighborhood bar, which means it's a great place to have fun. It's also one of the few restaurants or bars in Palm Beach County that allows smoking (it was "grandfathered in"). There are pool tables, video games, and flat-screen TVs all over the place. And there's something going on every single night—live music on weekends; games of Pub Trivia on Mon; karaoke Tues; Texas Hold 'Em on Wed; even occasional pajama parties. This is a place where a young, casual crowd enjoys themselves.

CLUB SAFARI
Palm Beach Gardens Marriott
4000 RCA Blvd.
Palm Beach Gardens
(561) 622-8888
www.clubsafaripbg.com

If you're young, like to dress to impress, and love to dance and mingle, this is the place for you. Located inside the handsome Marriott, this is a stunning nightclub, decorated in an ancient Aztec motif mixed with technological touches like laser light systems, video remixing, and a state-of-the-art sound system. Dance music and hip-hop are the sounds of the night here, mixed by popular DJ Captain Ron. There's a 20-foot-high tiki statue, and four bars, one of them with an airplane hanging over it. And because of all this, Club Safari has become one of the hottest places to dance in Palm Beach County. Thurs is Retro Rewind, with dance classics from the 80s and 90s. Fri is Next Generation music. Sat is Ladies' Night. The food and drinks are fine, and the dance floor is a trip in itself. Cover charge.

88 KEYS PIANO & TIKI BAR
9920 Alternate A1A
Palm Beach Gardens
(561) 627-1305
www.88keyspianobar.com

When the weekend comes, the pianos start dueling at 88 Keys. There won't be any classical music here; instead, you'll hear a wacky, wicked mixture of just about anything-but. It's loud, it's raucous, and it's funny as heck, with Elton John look-alikes and fire-blowers. You can bet your sides will be splitting. It's part improve comedy, part variety show, and part audience-participation. And you may very well find yourself singing along or dancing along. During the week there's a DJ spinning his own favorite sounds, hip-hop, Top 40, and dance among them. Special nights include Weird and Wild Wednesday and Get Rocked Thursday.

I-BAR
400 Avenue of the Champions
Palm Beach Gardens
(561) 627-4852
www.pgaibar.com

Located in the PGA National Resort & Spa, i-Bar reflects the quality of its surroundings. It's sexy, savvy, smart, and sophisticated, as is the crowd that it draws. It's become a late-night gathering spot for North County's movers and shakers. You can relax in an elegant atmosphere with a pool view while sipping your drink or watching the large-screen TVs.

There are several crowd-pleasing signature cocktails here. Some people prefer the

Blue Hawaiian—Bacardi silver blue Curacao with a splash of pineapple. Others favor the Dark and Stormy, which is Grey Goose Vodka and orange juice with a splash of Galliano. But this is a discriminating crowd that knows its wines and liquors. So there are others who will tell you about their own personal favorite, the PGA cosmo martini, with Grey Goose l'orange, Cointreau, cranberry, and a squeeze of fresh lime. You'll find a few New Age twists here. They have antioxidant-loaded sangrias; organic champagnes; and a drink called the Ecotini, made with eco-friendly 360 Vodka.

The wine collection boasts good choices from New Zealand to Spain. And there are always special events at i-Bar. One of the most popular is i-Thursdays, a weekly Thurs night party featuring two-for-one drink specials for ladies, along with giveaways and live entertainment. This is a good place to take that special someone or those special friends when you know the conversation will be great and the feelings warm.

NOCHE
2401 PGA Blvd., Suite 160
Palm Beach Gardens
(561) 472-7900

Noche turns into Noche! at 10 p.m. That's when this sophisticated supper club clears out the tables in the middle of the room, turns it into a dance floor, and becomes one of the hottest late-night spots in North Palm Beach County. Noche is the haute-spot for a well-dressed, urbane crowd that takes to the dance floor like a duck to water, turning a quiet international restaurant into a hot club with an emphasis on Latin (although the decor is an interesting mixture of Latin, South Beach, and European influences).

Overlooking a quiet marina, this club has nothing quiet about it at all once people take to the dance floor. The club reverberates with a vibrant Latin beat, and the dancing is non-stop. If you're in the hospitality business, head here on Tues nights; drinks are half-price. Popular local DJs, with names like Supreme and Dragonfly, spin Top 40, classics, and great dance music. There's live salsa on Thurs. If you get hungry from all that dancing, there's a late-night buffet—complimentary with your admission fee—most nights. And there are plenty of special evenings, Motown Nights and Latin Nights among them. Cover charge. Closed Sun.

PADDY MAC'S
10971 North Military Trail
Palm Beach Gardens
(561) 691-4366
www.paddymacspub.com

If you're looking for authentic Irish food and atmosphere, look no farther, mates and lasses. Because Paddy Mac's is a bit of the Auld Sod, with Irish memorabilia everywhere, the appropriate rustic look of a country pub, bare wood tables, and a gigantic bar. Paddy's is famous for its Bushmills Irish Coffee, a concoction of hot coffee, whiskey, and a wee bit of brown sugar. The finishing touch is cream that's been lightly whipped, then floated on top. If all goes according to form, you'll be sternly warned not to mix the cream into the drink. The idea is to sip the coffee *through* the cream, so that the spiked hot java is tempered by it instead of being overwhelmed by it. And just in case you don't pay heed, Paddy Mac's servers won't be offering you a stirrer. Or, you could just stick with the beers of Ireland; there' Smithwick's Brown Ale, Harp, and, of course, the classic Guinness Stout, the strong black brew that's still unique among beers.

But the drinks are only part of the story. *Zagat* heaped praise on the authentic Irish cooking, for dishes like the Irish cottage pie, the shepherd's pie, and the Paddy's house steak and chips. The stage resonates with the sounds of the old country on weekends, played by traditional Irish bands, as well as acoustic acts. Combined with the genuine atmosphere of the bar, the music will take you back to the Emerald Isle—even if you've never been there. The songs harken back to County Kildare, the Wicklow Mountains, the River Liffey, the Ring of Kerry, and the Cliffs of Moher. And, though you may never have been closer to Ireland than Palm Beach Gardens, you'll find yourself tapping your feet and clapping your hands.

PANAMA HATTIES
11511 Ellison Wilson Rd.
North Palm Beach
(561) 627-1545
www.panama-hatties.com
Waterfront dining, rum bar, Tiki torches, big-screen TVs. It doesn't get any better than this. Every Thurs night at sundown, there's a drum circle at Panama Hattie's, and drummers and belly dancers gather around the fire pits. Drummers beat their drums with the intent of becoming one community, and becoming more heart-, body-, and mind-centered. It's really fun!

Legend has it that during World War II, transport ships would ferry servicemen along the Eastern seaboard via the Intracoastal, to avoid enemy ships at sea. At that time, it took weeks for a ship to get from Maine to Florida. The seamen often had raging "cabin-fever" after being holed up with a few hundred of their malodorous shipmates in the bottom of a boat. The story goes that every now and then the captain of a certain

ship would allow for a night of reckless abandon, and would pull over at local watering holes. Thus, according to the legend, the birth of South Florida's Tiki Bars. Panama Hattie's has been around for a while. And locals consider it one of the best tiki bars.

The hit-drink here is the Voodoo, five different rums in a bucket big enough for two. There's a long wine list. Mon night is poker night, and happy hour is every night from Mon through Fri.

ROONEY'S PUBLIC HOUSE
1153 Town Center Dr.
Jupiter
(561) 694-6610
www.rooneyspublichouse.com
If you love the Pittsburgh Steelers, this is your home away from home during the football season. It's not coincidence that the owner of this pub has the same last name as the family that founded the Steelers in 1932, and has owned them since. So if you come here on any Sunday during football season, or any Monday night when the Steelers are on *Monday Night Football,* be prepared to be part of Steeler Nation and to scream loudly and often for the old black and gold. And be prepared to be wearing the colors proudly, because pretty much everyone else around you will be.

There's outdoor seating, however . . . so, if you feel the need, you can get away from the hubbub inside and relax out here. As you might have guessed, Rooney's is flowing with sports memorabilia. However, this is still very much a real Irish bar, and you'll see plenty of Irish memorabilia, as well, like road signs (in Gaelic and English) pointing the way to Galway or Ballyvaughan. The pub, in fact, was actually designed and crafted in Ireland. Along with the many items brought over from Ireland, you'll notice memorabilia from the Rooney family, which has a tradition of being pub operators dating back to the early 20th century.

When it comes to draft beers, you'll find a definite Irish flavor to the collection here, which includes Guinness, Harp, Smithwick's, and Rooney's Red Ale. You can enjoy them with Irish specialties such as Rooney's leek soup, shepherd's pie, or corned beef and cabbage, along with other favorites such as Rooney's burger, salads, and sandwiches. There's live music from Tues through Sat.

SQUARE GROUPER TIKI BAR
Castaways Marina
1111 Love St.
Jupiter
(561) 575-0252
www.squaregrouper.net
Remember the video for Alan Jackson's, *Its' Five O'clock Somewhere,* sung with Jimmy Buffet? Well, it was filmed right here. The bar is just as you remember it from the video—a little bit tiki, a little bit Key West-tacky, a little bit lively, and a whole lotta fun. You can listen to live music six nights a week, from good local bands as well as some well-known artists. And as you listen, you can enjoy this little piece of paradise, with panoramic views of the Jupiter Inlet and the famous lighthouse that's been its landmark for the past 150 years.

Jim Burg is the owner of the bar and adjacent marina. After spending most of his life building high-end custom homes, he bought this property that once housed a bait-and-tackle shop. He transformed it into the Square Grouper Tiki Bar and the Castaways Marina. The property has a colorful history dating back to the 1890s. Near the original roadbed of the Jupiter and Lake Worth Railroad, better known as The Celestial Railroad, a two-story hotel and saloon overlooked the waterway. At that time, well-heeled tourists were venturing south on the Indian River by steamer, or aboard their own yachts. Some spent the night at the hotel near the Jupiter dock, while others—President Grover Cleveland among them—stopped by the saloon for dinner and then went on. But hard times came, and the hotel was eventually abandoned.

In 1906, the property was purchased for $2,500. This riverfront swampland, then known as Suni Sands, was later filled in. During Prohibition, the site was used by

My Palm Beach County

"It might sound trite, but living in West Palm Beach really does offer the best of everything! Our historic neighborhood of Flamingo Park offers the kind of old-fashioned hometown neighborliness that some people think has all but disappeared. We actually know—and like—our neighbors. And we have monthly parties, an annual block party, home and garden tours, and more. Within a five minute drive (or a 15-minute bike ride!) of our hundred-year-old home we can access fabulous dining, shopping, and entertainment in Downtown West Palm Beach and Palm Beach, the ocean with its free public beach, along with world-class productions from opera to top entertainers at The Kravis Center."

—Margie Yansura, Public Relations consultant, West Palm Beach rum-runners for night-time deliveries into this sleepy fishing village. Years later, a different type of illegal activity would occur here, helping to give Jim Burg's business its name. "Square Groupers" was Coast Guard slang for bales of marijuana tossed overboard or out of airplanes and later found in the Jupiter Inlet.

Today a wide variety of specialty drinks, including Captain Morgan Rum Punch Joes, Cuervo Tequila margaritas, mojitos, and frozen drinks, are poured here. And at the Square Grouper—no need to worry—it's always five o'clock!

SWAMPGRASS WILLY'S
9910 Alternate A1A #711
Palm Beach Gardens
(561) 625-1555
www.swampgrasswillys.net

Swampgrass Willy's has one of the coolest logos of any restaurant in Palm Beach County, with a friendly-looking alligator in overalls and floppy sun-hat scarfing down a beer and a burger. The logo bursts with incredible color. And so does this place.

Readers of the *Palm Beach Post* have voted it both Best Wings and Best Live Music Venue in the area. There's live music by talented local bands, a real jukebox, poker league, pool tables, air hockey, Wii games, the popular *Guitar Hero* video game, and plenty of TVs. There's karaoke every Sun night. And if you're brave enough to step onto that stage and wring out your vocal cords in public, you can have your performance recorded and take it home on a CD that night. You can enjoy all of it with a selection of over 75 bottled beers—probably one of the largest in the county—with names such as Hazed and Confused, Dogfish Chicory Stout, and Arrogant Bastard.

There's a great party atmosphere, with dim lights, live music, cozy booths, and dark wood tables. The cuisine is American with a wide selection of appetizers, salads, sandwiches, burgers, and side dishes, along with steak, chicken, and seafood. They have a full bar with domestic and imported liqueurs, liquors, wines, and beers.

Tues night is Open Jam Night, with musicians and vocalists. And the Swamp Poker League runs on Sat, Mon, Wed, and Thurs. Swampgrass Willy's is open every night until 3 a.m. Cover charge for special bands.

UNCLE MICK'S BAR & GRILL
6671 Indiantown Rd.
Jupiter
(561) 743-8330
www.unclemicks.com

Uncle Mick's is a real country/Western place. It's got a woodsy atmosphere with Western relics all about, and a pool room. There's a dance floor where you can learn the Texas Two-Step or Western line-dancing, to live country music every weekend. There are Texas Hold-Em tournaments, and also karaoke nights. And the preferred mode of dress is jeans, Western or casual shirts, cowboy boots if you own them, and ditto for cowboy hats.

You'll find more then 20 TVs on which you can keep up with your favorite team from back home. You can watch while scarfing down some garbage fries—chili, cheese, onion, black olives, and jalapeños. The jumbo chicken wings are served plain, mild, medium, or hot. The burgers are thick and juicy. Perhaps the biggest favorite at Uncle Mick's though, is the ribs, slathered with barbecue sauce and accompanied by french fries, cole slaw, and baked beans. And there's a great selection of domestic and foreign beers with which to enjoy the food.

WATERWAY CAFÉ
2300 PGA Blvd.
Palm Beach Gardens
(561) 694-1700
www.waterwaycafe.com

It doesn't get much better than this—a romantic tropical-waterfront setting, a famous floating bar, indoor and outdoor seating, a nautical theme, great drinks, a casual atmosphere, and a great time. The Waterway Café was built in 1966 by real estate developer Jefferson Vander Wolk on the site of the former Waterway Marina. If you're coming by boat, there's more than 300 feet of dock space, available on a first-come, first-serve basis, and you can radio in your food order from your boat and pick it up when you arrive.

There's always something happening at the Waterway Café. Sunday evening, for instance, is reggae time, with the sounds of Palm Beach County's own Sweet Justice. Every night is Sunset Night because you can sit outside and nurse a tall, cool tropical drink while watching the yellow sun turn into a flaming orange as it sets to the west. This is a big gathering place during happy hour. If you're lucky, you might be nursing a specialty drink called the Broken Bridge, named for the adjacent PGA Boulevard drawbridge. There's a very good wine selection. And if you're in the mood for dinner, you're in luck; popular choices include grilled dolphin, blackened tuna, porterhouse steak, custom pizzas, and a variety of good pasta dishes.

ATTRACTIONS

Start with a place blessed with eternal sunshine and surrounded by water, a place where you can enjoy the attractions pretty much every day of the year. Add on a long and colorful history, complete with Native Americans and pirates and buried treasure and all manner of drifters, grifters, speculators, citizens, soldiers, and Everglades on one side and the ocean on the other. Throw in the fact that Palm Beach County residents come from every corner of the globe and have brought their customs, cuisines, and national histories with them. Then top it off with a layer of innovation and a spirit that has manifested itself—for better or worse—in pushing boundaries and in experiments grand and small. And you have the recipe for a place that's filled with all types of attractions.

Palm Beach County's attractions range from the vibrant to the serene, from the historical to the futuristic, and from the man-made to the natural. But one thing's for sure: You'll run out of time long before your run out of things to do!

SOUTH COUNTY

AMERICAN ORCHID SOCIETY
16700 AOS Lane
Delray Beach
(561) 404-2000
www.aos.org

On April 7, 1921, a group of 36 people in Massachusetts met to form the American Orchid Society. Ninety years later the society is still around and we're lucky enough to have it in Palm Beach County. The society views its mission as promoting and supporting the passion for orchids through education, conservation, and research. At this quiet, out-of-the-way corner of Delray Beach—adjacent to another quiet spot, the Morikami Museum and Japanese Gardens—you can discover the beautiful, exotic, and complex world of orchids. Here you'll find rare orchids growing as they do in the wild. You can wander through lush gardens woven throughout 3.5 acres, and see exquisite orchids in a 4,000 square foot greenhouse. The array of colors, shapes, sizes, and fragrances is stunning. After touring the gardens, you can stop into the Orchid Emporium Gift Shop or enjoy orchid art exhibits in the lobby.

My Palm Beach County

"One of the places that I think is really special is the Orchid Greenhouse at the American Orchid Society, on the grounds of the Morikami Museum in Delray. I went to a wine tasting there last year, and it was really . . . beautiful."

—Valerie Szymaniak, President, Three-in-One, Inc., Boca Raton

---

DELRAY YACHT CRUISES
801 East Atlantic Ave.
Delray Beach
(561) 243-0686
www.delraybeachcruises.com

This company calls it a "day-cation," and it really is. You'll glide over the calm waters of the Intracoastal Waterway on the *Lady Atlantic*, a snack in one hand and a drink in the other. It's a two-hour narrated tour past some of the area's most beautiful mansions, and a variety of marine life in its natural habitat. Most cruises head south from Veterans Park, on East Atlantic Avenue, to Boca Raton, and then back again. If you're the romantic type, however, and you've got a special person in mind, there are few things more intimate than the Sunset Cruises.

The *Lady Atlantic* is a brand-new, 105-foot boat with three decks. If you head for the top one, you can sit outside and be caressed by the soft breezes and the warm sunshine. Throughout the year, the *Lady Atlantic* offers specialty cruises in addition to the regular sightseeing tours. The Sunday Brunch Cruise, for example, is a two-hour jaunt that heads north towards Manalapan Island, one of the wealthiest communities in the United States. In addition, there are Wine Tasting Cruises; Links & Drinks cruises, complete with a putting green and a golf pro; and Friday Dinner Cruises, with an Italian buffet. During the holiday season, there is the Holiday Lights cruise, on which you sail past beautifully lit-up Intracoastal homes.

GUMBO LIMBO NATURE CENTER
1801 North Ocean Blvd.
Boca Raton
(561) 338-1473
www.gumbolimbo.org

The Gumbo Limbo Nature Center is a slice of Palm Beach County before the trappings of

---

Let's see . . . hat, sunscreen, water . . .

There must be something else we wanted to tell you to carry with you. Oh, yes . . . umbrella. If you're here in season (Oct through Apr), you probably don't have to worry about it. But if you're here from May through Sept—our rainy season—you'd better learn to carry one in the car. It rains most afternoons in May and June, when the storms rise up in the Everglades and then head east. And July and Aug can kick up some thunderstorms, as well. The rains often don't last too long, and they can clear out as quickly as they come. But they can be heavy.

---

modern life arrived. Its mission is to increase awareness of coastal and marine ecosystems through research, education, preservation, and conservation. Its primary method is to let visitors ramble through the incredible vegetation and greenery all through the site. You (and the kids) can stroll through the butterfly garden, surrounded by the brilliantly colored butterflies. You can climb the observation tower, or walk along the elevated boardwalk that winds through the coastal hammocks. You can sit in—and feel the confines of—a Chiki hut, which was home to Florida's Native Americans. You'll want to stop and spend some time at the saltwater tanks, brimming with marine life, including sea turtles, fish, sharks, and rays.

Gumbo Limbo is also a vital research center. From Mar 1 to Oct 31, the Boca

Raton Sea Turtle Conservation and Research Program conducts nesting research on a 5-mile stretch of beach. During that time, three sea turtle species (loggerheads, greens, leatherbacks) nest here and leave behind a treasure-trove of knowledge for researchers.

MORIKAMI MUSEUM AND JAPANESE GARDENS
4000 Morikami Park Rd.
Delray Beach
(561) 495-0233
www.morikami.org

In 1905, a Japanese emigrant named Joseph Sakai bought some land in the southern part of the county, on which he planned to build an agricultural enterprise. Sakai advertised in Japan for workers to come over and work in the fields, but life was hard and many eventually returned to Japan. But a few stayed. A young man named George Morikami built a successful life here for himself and his family. In the mid-1970s, Morikami donated his home and part of his land to Palm Beach County, with the request that the county create a museum and park about Japanese culture.

The Morikami Museum and Japanese Gardens is a place of quiet serenity, with 200 acres of red wooden footbridges crossing ponds stocked with koi, beautifully manicured bonsai plants, rock gardens, winding paths through the woods, and small waterfalls. The original building is a replica of a Japanese villa, with blue-roofed rooms surrounding a central courtyard, and sliding screens instead of wooden doors (visitors are requested to remove their shoes before entering). The museum building houses historical exhibitions, some 5,000 Japanese art objects and artifacts, a 225-seat theater, an authentic tea house, library, museum store with beautiful crafts from Japan, a cafe with

---

My Palm Beach County

"Warm weather, warm hospitality, and great explorations make up a large part of living in Palm Beach County in general—and Delray Beach in particular. Of course, stay-cations have become a natural fit for locals to get away but still stay close to home. As locals, we find an amazing variety of activities and attractions right here in Delray Beach—from our beaches to an abundance of gourmet restaurants, from the tranquil Morikami Museum and Japanese Gardens to concerts under the sky and art exhibitions at Old School Square, from challenging golf courses and great tennis to the nightlife along Atlantic Avenue. For me, Delray is a place to refresh your senses and revive your spirit. And it's great living and working here."

—Cathy Balestriere,
General Manager, Crane's
BeachHouse Hotel & Tiki Bar,
Delray Beach

---

excellent sushi and teriyaki, and a lakeside terrace and Japanese courtyard garden. The museum hosts several Japanese festivals throughout the year.

OLD SCHOOL SQUARE CULTURAL ARTS CENTER
51 North Swinton Ave.
Delray Beach
(561) 243-7922
www.oldschool.org

Old School Square is a National Historic Site that has won wide recognition around the country for its ongoing preservation efforts. The original early-20th-century buildings have been totally renovated, and they now house the Cornell Museum of Art and American Culture, the Crest Theatre, the Vintage Gymnasium, and restored classrooms that host world-class performances, lectures, and classes.

Old School Square Cultural Arts Center actually was one of the first efforts in the development of Delray Beach's new downtown. A group of local citizens in the 1980s raised over $7 million to renovate and adapt old school buildings set for demolition for use as a museum and a theater. The Cornell Museum is an airy place in which the floors are polished woods, and the art is displayed very attractively. It features regional, national, and international exhibits of fine art, craft, and American culture that change every six to eight weeks to keep the exhibits fresh. The Crest Theatre is now a magnificent place to watch theater, musical, and vocal performances. There's a Main Stage Series of musical and theatrical performances; the Broadway Cabaret Series; and a Lecture Series with provocative topics.

SPORTS IMMORTALS MUSEUM
6830 N. Federal Hwy.
Boca Raton
(561) 997-2575
www.sportsimmortals.com

In 1943, as an illness kept four-year-old Joel Platt in bed for a year, his parents brought him baseball cards to pass the time. Today, Platt has perhaps the largest private collection of sports memorabilia in America, if not the world. He keeps much of it in this museum, which he opened in Boca Raton in the 1990s. He can't keep it all there—because he has one million pieces! Michael Heffner, President of Leland's Auction House,

has called this collection "the largest and most valuable collection of diverse and important sports artifacts ever assembled."

If you enjoy sports, you'll wander through this museum like a small child in a world of wonder. You can see helmets worn by race drivers such as A. J. Foyt, Richard Petty, and Mario Andretti. There's an autographed photo from Don Budge, one of the early tennis greats, along with autographed racquets from Pete Sampras and a racquet used by Chris Evert. You'll see an autographed photo of baseball Hall-of-Famer Christy Mathewson, game jerseys worn by Shaquille O'Neal and old-time great George Mikan, the boxing gloves worn by Jack Dempsey when he knocked out Georges Carpentier in 1921, a putter from Gary Player, and several of Maurice Richard's Montreal Canadiens hockey jerseys. Some of the wonderful sports memorabilia is for sale, or pick up a copy of Platt's book, *Sports Immortals, Stories of Inspiration and Achievement.*

CENTRAL COUNTY

DIVA DUCK AMPHIBIOUS TOURS
The Duck Stop, City Place
510 Hibiscus St.
West Palm Beach
(561) 844-4188
www.divaduck.com

Diva Duck, a bargelike vehicle with wheels, is at home both on land and on the water. Somehow, this "duck out of water" traverses the picturesque, Spanish-castle neighborhoods of old West Palm Beach on land, and then slides into the water for a floating tour past the mansions of the millionaires. It's a 75-minute narrated tour with music. You'll start off at City Place in downtown West Palm Beach, pass those neighborhoods and the modern Palm Beach County Convention Center, then cross the bridge over the Intracoastal Waterway to the island of Palm Beach. You'll pass the Breakers Hotel, the Flagler Museum, and the Biltmore Estate. Then you'll splash into the Intracoastal and take a leisurely cruise past the mansions and the John F. Kennedy Bomb Shelter on Peanut Island. Then the *Diva Duck* hops onto land again, passing the great shops and bistros of Clematis Street before ending up back at City Place. Get ready to enjoy the most unique ride you'll probably ever take!

DREAM DOLLS GALLERY & MORE
2155 Indian Rd.
West Palm Beach
(561) 640-9575
www.dreamdollsgallery.com
Dream Dolls calls itself "the largest retail doll store in the south." Here, you can find over a hundred makes of dolls (among them Steiff) dressed in hand-sewn outfits, and created with tremendous attention to detail as far as their faces, hairstyles, etc. Many are in porcelain, while others are in wood, fiber, ceramics, or other natural materials. You'll also find a notable collection of stuffed animals and unusual wood and glass cabinets in which to put your collection, many of them hand-carved. There's also a museum with a fascinating historical look at dolls. Judene Hansen, owner of the shop, has assembled a complete collection of vintage Barbies from 1959 to today. There are one-of-a-kind dolls of queens and movie stars, draped in elegant materials. There's a chess set in which all the pieces are mini-dolls, in period dress—one side is *Alice in Wonderland,* and the opponent is *Thru the Looking Glass.* You'll find vintage Shirley Temple dolls, and Raggedy Anns from the 1930s. Dream Dolls also hosts special exhibitions, and many of the contributing craftspeople come by to sign their works.

FAMILY GOLF CENTER AT WEST PALM BEACH
5850 Belvedere Rd.
West Palm Beach
(561) 683-4544
www.thegolfcourses.net
This is not a place for "competitive" golfers or 9-handicappers. Instead, it's a place where the whole family can have fun. You'll be outside all morning in the fresh air, and the atmosphere is relaxed and casual. It's a pitch-and-putt course, with no sand traps and only a few water hazards to negotiate. It's a par-54 course, rather than the usual par-72, and every hole is a par-3. The greens are small, and no hole is longer than 140 yards—you can actually see the hole when you tee off.

HENRY MORRISON FLAGLER MUSEUM
One Whitehall Way
Palm Beach
(561) 655-2833
www.flaglermuseum.us
Henry Morrison Flagler truly had the Midas Touch. He was a very successful entrepreneur and industrialist from the age of 20. But his biggest strike was when John D. Rockefeller approached him about entering a partnership in a new company, which became known as Standard Oil, and it made Henry Flagler nationally known. In 1883, Flagler and his second wife visited St. Augustine in northern Florida. They immediately noticed two things: The climate was wonderful, and there were not enough hotels there. The rest is history.

By the time Flagler was through, he had built a railroad through the entire state of Florida, all the way down to Key West. He had built hotels in St. Augustine. He had developed the town of Palm Beach. He had built The Breakers Hotel in that new town. He had brought his rich and influential friends down to Florida, and they had spread the word about this magical new place. He also had helped build the city of Miami. In reality, he had opened up the entire state of Florida to new development, new business ventures, and to subsequent generations of visitors from all over the world.

In 1902, he decided to build himself a little something—a house on Palm Beach with 60,000 square feet and 55 rooms. He called it Whitehall. In 1913 he fell down the stairs and soon after died of his injuries. But Whitehall remains as a testament to a titan of American industry, and Florida history.

Whitehall looks like a palace in white, with huge columns and wrought-iron-railing balconies. Its wide hallways are lined with works of art, with impressive crystal chandeliers hanging from the ceiling, and grand staircases winding from one floor to the other. Today, Whitehall is a museum dedicated, in its temporary exhibitions, to Florida history and to the time in which Flagler became famous—the Gilded Age. There are also permanent exhibits on the history of Henry Flagler's life and career, and a truly exquisite lace collection. The Flagler Kenan Pavilion, designed in the style of a 19th-century Beaux Arts railway palace, houses Flagler's luxurious private railcar, No. 91. The Café des Beaux-Arts serves a fixed-menu, fixed-price Gilded-Age style lunch.

HOFFMAN'S CHOCOLATE FACTORY
5190 Lake Worth Rd.
Greenacres
(561) 967-2213
www.hoffmans.com

Thirty years ago, Paul Hoffman Sr. purchased a small candy shop. An accomplished cook, he began experimenting with chocolate, and, lo and behold, his Lake Worth/Greenacres neighbors really liked his creations. Soon Hoffman's Chocolates became sort of a local legend, and thanks to coverage in national news media such as the *Wall Street Journal* and *Bon Appetit*, they were no longer just local. Today, there are four Hoffman's stores in Palm Beach County, and one in neighboring Martin County, just to the north. The recipes are still guarded closely by the family. Each piece is still hand-made, and people are still coming to watch. This isn't a factory in the strictest sense; it's actually the original store. But you can watch the chocolate being made through the observation windows.

INTERNATIONAL POLO CLUB OF PALM BEACH
3667 120th Ave. S.
Wellington
(561) 753-0966
www.internationalpoloclub.com

The game of polo is evocative of a gentler when families gathered together on weekends to enjoy fresh air, a sport with royal connotations, and the lifestyle with which it's always been associated. Appropriate for that lifestyle is the venue at which the game is played. This venue, in the heart of Palm Beach County's horse country, is on a par with any in the world. And despite the "royal" connotations, anyone can come to enjoy the action and hear the thundering of the horses' hooves and the crack of the ball as it's hit by the wooden mallet.

The club is located in a beautiful setting, with rolling hills, lush tropical landscaping, and some of the most carefully manicured polo fields in the world. You can watch the action from private boxes, viewing stands, field-side tailgate spots, or special hospitality tents. Thousands of fans come each Sunday during the Season (winter). The club features a series of six renowned polo tournaments, and is home to the only high-goal season in the United States. Many of the world's best polo players compete here each year.

LAWRENCE E. WILL MUSEUM
Palm Beach County Library
530 South Main St.
Belle Glade
(561) 996-3453
www.pbclibrary.org/lew.htm

In the Lawrence Will Museum, the colorful history of the towns around Lake Okeechobee comes alive. Located in the Belle Glade branch of the Palm Beach County Public Library system, the museum is a treasure-trove of lore and legend about an area not really understood by the rest of South Florida. It was built during the bicentennial year of 1976, and funded largely though local sources. Mr. Will's father, Dr. Thomas E. Will, was an early pioneer in this region.

The permanent exhibits here tell the story of the isolated communities in this area, and their ties—physically and emotionally—with the lake. There are photographs—some going back to the 1930s—showing archaeological digs in the Indian mound in the area known as Chosen. There's a history of the 1928 hurricane, the biggest natural disaster to ever hit this area. You'll also find a lifelike diorama of a Seminole village in the Everglades, as well as one depicting town sites in the early 1900s. There's a mural showing the presentation of a Seminole tunic to Mr. Will by Chief Billy Bowlegs II. In addition, you'll see notes and charts written by Mr. Will; local newspapers from the 1920s to the 1960s;

an antique telephone switchboard from the Belle Glade exchange; and furnishings from the old Fear's Hotel (gotta love that name!).

LOXAHATCHEE EVERGLADES TOURS
15490 Loxahatchee Rd.
Parkland
(561) 482-6107
www.evergladesairboattours.com

The Loxahatchee Everglades Tours will take you into the heart of the Everglades, and into a world you won't see anywhere else. You'll be heading into the River of Grass, as Floridians call it, and it actually is a moving, water-based ecosystem, filled with swamps, marshes, tropical hammocks, and mangroves found nowhere else. And the wildlife? Alligators, of course, plus red-shouldered hawks, blue herons, egrets, ibises, purple gallinules (a bird), otters, armadillos, bullfrogs the size of . . . bulls, rattlesnakes, water moccasins, Burmese pythons (an unfortunate import), eagles, osprey, deer, an occasional Florida Panther, and a hundred other species found only in the Everglades. When the captain decides to turn off the engine for a few minutes, you'll marvel at the power of the beautiful silence here. Airboats were developed specifically to fly over this river of grass, and are propelled by a huge fan in the rear. Be advised that airboats are very loud and you'll be given earplugs to use if you want to. Also note that weather in the Everglades is unpredictable, so you might want to give them a call before getting in the car.

MANGROVE NATURE PARK
700 Northeast Fourth Ave.
Boynton Beach
(561) 734 4800

You can take a peak at South Florida's ecological system without driving all the way

ATTRACTIONS

west. Mangrove Park is at the dead end of Northeast Fourth Street in Boynton Beach. It's a great place for families to learn about nature together. You can take a relaxing stroll along a boardwalk, right over a natural mangrove preserve. The native trees and animals are on full display here, as are the enormous spider webs everywhere you look. You can see the Intracoastal Waterway from the end of the boardwalk. And if you come during high tide, you have an excellent chance to see manatees, Florida's lovable "sea cows." Even though it's in the middle of Palm Beach County surrounded by development, Mangrove Nature Park is a little piece of South Florida the way it once was.

MOUNTS BOTANICAL GARDEN
559 North Military Trail
West Palm Beach
(561) 233-1749
www.mounts.org

Perhaps the first thing you notice when you walk into Mounts Botanical Garden are the colors—dense greens, vivid purples, yellows, lavenders, and oranges. This place has a huge collection of tropical and subtropical plants, plants native to Florida, exotic trees, tropical fruit, herbs, citrus, and palms. Plants from six continents grace the 14 acres—and prove just how conducive Palm Beach County's climate is to growing just about anything from anywhere. Here, you'll find trees from North America's Temperate Zone, plants from arid or desert climates, and plants that can't live without frequent drinks of water. If you're a plant lover, no matter what your area of devotion, you'll find it here. Mounts stages frequent special events, among them plant sales, family festivals, and auctions. More than 60 vendors set up shop at the two plant sales each year.

PALM BEACH KENNEL CLUB
1111 North Congress Ave.
West Palm Beach
(561) 683-2222
www.pbkennelclub.com

How long has it been since you've felt the spine-tingling excitement of rooting a winner home at the dog track? Here the greyhounds race all year long, and there's now a 60-table Poker Room at the track, where you can really test your skills at the table. You can eat lunch or dinner here, as well. The Terrace is an excellent place to have lunch before the afternoon matinees. And the Paddock is a fine-dining restaurant where you can relax before the evening races.

The Palm Beach Kennel Club has a long dates back to 1932. Since then, more than 32 million people have come through the track's turnstiles. Although the track has had a number of owners over the past eight decades, the current owners are probably the most well-known—the Rooney family, longtime owners of the Pittsburgh Steelers of the National Football League. Over the years, the Palm Beach Kennel Club has featured some of the finest champions in the history of the sport.

PALM BEACH MARITIME MUSEUM/ JOHN F. KENNEDY BUNKER
Riviera Beach Marina
200 East Thirteenth St.
Riviera Beach
(561) 683-TAXI (water taxi reservations)
(561) 848-2960 (museum)
(561) 832-7428 Currie Park office of the Museum, ferry to Peanut Island
www.pbmm.org

The Palm Beach Maritime Museum on Peanut Island opened in 1999, with a poignant exhibition on artifacts from the battleship U.S.S.

147

Maine, which was blown up in Havana Harbor a century before, an event that precipitated the Spanish–American War. The great exhibitions haven't stopped since then. Today the museum and Peanut Island are fascinating mixtures of pirate legend and Cold War reality. The museum also conducts vital research into how best to protect and preserve Palm Beach County's waters and reefs.

One of the permanent exhibits on Peanut Island is President John F. Kennedy's Bunker, constructed by Navy SeaBees under the direction of the Secret Service. As tensions with Russia mounted in 1962, and fears of nuclear war mounted with them, the decision was made to build the bunker for the President, his family, and his advisors. During the Cuban Missile Crisis, the bunker was a contingency facility in case the unthinkable happened. Today, it stands as a stark reminder of the Cold War at its peak. Nearby is another reminder of our military heritage, an abandoned U.S. Coast Guard station that is open for tours and still has some of the furniture and artifacts left in it when the Coast Guard left. The Coast Guard station includes barracks, weather station and monitoring/surveillance equipment, and boathouse.

PALM BEACH PHOTOGRAPHIC CENTRE
415 Clematis St.
West Palm Beach
(561) 253-2600
www.workshop.org
The Palm Beach Photographic Centre has been around since the mid-1980s. But in November 2009, it moved into a new home in the heart of downtown, a 33,000 square foot state-of-the-art facility that has enabled it to host larger exhibitions and to expand the scope of its services to the community. As a direct result, the center has been able to expand its schedule of classes and workshops for local photography and digital-imaging enthusiasts.

The visiting exhibitions here are stunning, such as Empathy, by Ann Curry of the Today Show. Her travels around the world—and her first-hand witnessing of genocide, war, and ignorance—have turned her into a crusader for the poor and the forgotten of the earth. And she captures them magnificently in her lens. Capturing the Light, by Louis Kemper who has spent years chronicling the natural wonders of the world from Alaska to Hawaii to Iceland, from the mountains to the sea to the desert. The center also has special events, lectures, networking sessions with world-famous photographers, and a full-service Pro Shop, where you can find pretty much anything you need for your camera.

PALM BEACH SKATEZONE ICE & INLINE CENTER
8125 Lake Worth Rd.
Lake Worth
(561) 963-5900
www.pbskatezone.com
There are two rinks and your choice of ice or inline skates. Both rinks have spectator seating, and special warm zones where you can sit and watch the action. You'll also find a full-service snack bar, 42" TVs, total Wi-Fi, and a Pro Shop. You can take lessons from experienced teachers in both types of skating. You can even join an adult hockey league, roller or ice. (The same goes for kids.) There's open public skating every day.

PALM BEACH WATER TAXI
Sailfish Marina Resort
98 Lake Dr.
West Palm Beach
(561) 683-TAXI
www.sailfishmarina.com

The Palm Beach Water Taxi claims it's the best way to "sea" the Palm Beaches—and they're right. Their fleet of modern covered vessels (which hold 20 people) or catamarans (49 people) can take you to a variety of destinations, or on a narrated sightseeing cruise or a charter. One of the most popular cruises is the Palm Beach "Now and Then" Cruise. You'll glide past the mega-mansions and mega-yachts of the rich and famous. You'll cruise past the newly renovated Peanut Island, and be able to see into the back yards of these magnificent homes. The Water Taxi can also shuttle you to Peanut Island, where you can swim, snorkel, picnic, camp, or explore the John F. Kennedy Bunker, the old Coast Guard Station, and the Palm Beach Maritime Museum. Or, if you'd like to experience "Clematis By Night" (every Thurs night), you can take the Water Taxi to downtown, make your rounds of the clubs, restaurants, and galleries, and then head back to the taxi.

RAGTOPS MOTORCARS
2119 South Dixie Hwy.
West Palm Beach
(561) 655-2836
www.ragtopsmotorcars.com
A 1936 Chrysler Airstream Convertible Sedan, a 1940 Ford Hot Rod Woody Station Wagon, 1946 Chevy Pick-Up Truck/Hot Rod. If you ever think back to that dream-car you wanted to buy when you were young, but didn't, this is the place for you. This original three-story building was designed as a Cadillac and La Salle (which died in 1940) dealership. Now, however, there are three buildings on two city blocks, filled with classic cars valued at over $2 million. There's memorabilia, a soda bar, mini-drive-in theater, Tropical Art Deco showroom where you can buy the cars, Club La Salle for special events, and The

Station, which is filled with old station wagons. There's also a gift boutique where you can find really cool clothes (with really cool logos), small automotive accessories (such as fuzzy dice), and original car art. They've also recently opened Café Carbucks.

VISIT PALM BEACH
Riviera Beach Marina
200 East Thirteenth St.
Riviera Beach
(561) 881-9757
www.visitpalmbeach.com
Visit Palm Beach is one of the top providers of recreational activities, excursions, and events in South Florida. They can teach you to kayak and take you kayaking, in the calm waters of Lake Wyman, to small mangrove islands that are inaccessible to power boats, or to Dr. Munyon's Island, an unspoiled 45 acres. They can take you parasailing—you'll glide 800 feet over the Atlantic Ocean, attached to a towing boat, with only the birds for company, and schools of dolphins and manatees below you. They'll teach you how to snorkel in the clear aquamarine waters off the Palm Beaches. And they can set up fishing trips and charters for you, or a day on a catamaran.

NORTH COUNTY

BLOWING ROCKS NATURE PRESERVE
Jupiter Island
574 South Beach Rd.
Hobe Sound
(561) 744-6668
www.nature.org
Blowing Rocks Preserve is a magnificent barrier island nature sanctuary, located on Jupiter Island, between the Atlantic Ocean and the Indian River Lagoon. The Preserve protects a variety of natural habitats, including

beach dune, coastal strand, mangrove wetlands, tropical hammock, and oak hammock.

Its rocky Anastasia limestone shoreline is the largest on the Atlantic coast. During extreme high tides and after winter storms, the rough seas crash into the rocks with a ferocious intensity and roar. The results are plumes of saltwater that shoot up as high as 50 feet. It's an impressive sight for which the preserve was named. Visitors can explore a boardwalk with interpretive signs along the Indian River Lagoon. This body of water stretches for 156 miles up the coast of Florida, and is the most diverse estuary in North America—with 50 species of endangered plants and animals. They'll also see a butterfly garden with native plants, and a beachside nature trail. The Hawley Education Center contains rotating educational and art exhibits, and a series of programs and workshops is given in the on-site classroom.

Each of the seasons is different here. In winter, osprey are plentiful. In spring, beach sunflowers and butterflies bloom. And in summer, turtles come ashore to lay their eggs; their tracks are often visible in the sand.

JUPITER INLET LIGHTHOUSE & MUSEUM
500 Captain Armour's Way
Jupiter
(561) 747-8380
www.jupiterlighthouse.org
The Jupiter Lighthouse has been guarding this coast since 1860, when it was built by the U.S. Cavalry. In an area that's a virtual graveyard of sunken ships, the lighthouse has been a beacon of light in more ways than one.

The complex includes the lighthouse that you can climb, a museum in a newly restored Coast Guard building offering exhibits on Florida history and a gift shop, and the DuBois Pioneer House, which is currently closed for renovation. The Jupiter Lighthouse, with its dramatic tower of red brick, is the oldest structure in Palm Beach County. There are 105 steps to the top, very winding, very narrow steps. It's worth the trek, though, because the view from the top is memorable, of the mighty Atlantic, the Intracoastal, and the green lands of Florida. It doesn't stand on a rocky cliff by the edge of the sea, as do the northern ladies of the Atlantic coast. But this lighthouse does stand on a natural hill of shell and marine sand, at an elevation of 41 feet—which is Everest-like in Florida. As more and more ships foundered and then went down on submerged reefs and sandbars here in the mid-1800s, Congress in 1853 finally appropriated $35,000 to erect "a first-order lighthouse" to mark the reef lying off the Jupiter Inlet and act as an aide to navigation. Although construction began in 1855, a series of delays—Indian attacks and "Jupiter Fever," from mosquitoes and sand flies ran up the cost during the Third Seminole War, and the final price tag was over $60,000.

LOXAHATCHEE RIVER CENTER
805 North US 1
Jupiter
(561) 743-7123
www.loxahatcheeriver.org/ environmental_center.php
The Loxahatchee River Environmental Center "River Center" traces the flow of the Loxahatchee River from its headwaters in Palm Beach County, through the cypress floodplain, into the central embayment, and finally out through Jupiter Inlet into the Atlantic Ocean and the Gulf Stream. At the

River Center, you can explore the history of the watershed, its extraordinary environmental value, the dangers of ever-increasing growth in the area, and programs now underway to help preserve this complex and valuable eco-system.

Here, there are interesting displays, interactive exhibits, and live tanks that trace the river system from a freshwater cypress swamp to seagrass-dominated estuary to marine ecosystems. The Loxahatchee is Florida's first Federally designated Wild and Scenic River; and this center is the best chance to learn about it. The River Center hosts diverse traveling exhibits. Regular exhibits include Our Changing Watershed; an aquarium with fish and plants from the three different zones of the Wild and Scenic River; a "Critters" area with spiders, frogs, snakes, and fossils; other aquariums with seahorses and oysters; and a touch tank where you can, of course, touch some of the plant and animal life.

MAJESTIC PRINCESS CRUISES
Lake Park Harbor Marina
105 Lake Shore Dr.
Lake Park
(561) 254-0424
www.majesticprincesscruises.com
There are few better ways to spend an afternoon or evening than gliding along the Intracoastal Waterway on a luxurious modern yacht. Majestic Princess offers lunch, dinner, and Sunday brunch cruises. And each one is a dream voyage past wetlands, uninhabited hammock islands, nesting birds such as eagles and ospreys, and estates.

The cruises are narrated, so you'll know exactly what you're seeing (or whose house you're seeing). And there's a good lunch buffet. On the dinner cruise, you'll slip silently past beautiful homes with glowing lights. And the Sunday Brunch cruise features a buffet table groaning with good stuff. The Intracoastal is protected water, so your ride will be like a glide. You have the option of sitting outside on the upper deck, warmed by the sun and caressed by the breeze. And if you're lucky, you'll get to see dolphins.

PALM BEACH INTERNATIONAL RACEWAY
17047 Beeline Hwy.
Jupiter
(561) 622-1400
www.morosomotorsportspark.com
This 2.034-mile racing course, with 11 turns, features some of the fastest and most challenging corners, elevation changes, and straightaways offered by any track in North America. It's actually an Indy Car testing facility. This racing park actually first gained fame as a drag strip that is still here. This is the proving ground for hardcore hot-rodders— Drag Racing. Here, you go fast or go home. This 1/4-mile strip hosts many local, regional, and national events. Then there's go-karting, which is a true pulse-pounding thrill. This is an 11-turn, 7/10 mile road course, offering the versatility and flexibility needed for pros and amateurs alike. The cars here are souped-up, jacked-up, and painted-up. The crowds really get into it. It's loud, fast, and frenetic fun.

KIDSTUFF

Think all the fun in Palm Beach County's just for adults? You couldn't be more off-base. This is a great place for kids. There are all kinds of special places and special attractions just for them—from one end of the county to the other. There are places to play. Places to learn. Places to see. Places to discover. Places to act or sing or dance. Places to watch other people act or sing or dance. Places of majestic natural beauty, where they can commune not only with nature, but with the animals who inhabit it. Places with great food, and great fun. In Palm Beach County, kids are so special that they have their own complete set of attractions. That's one of the reasons that families tend to visit here again once they've been here the first time—because kids have as much fun as their parents! And you'll enjoy sharing it all with them!

SOUTH COUNTY

BOCA RATON CHILDREN'S MUSEUM
498 Crawford Blvd.
Boca Raton
(561) 368-6875
www.cmboca.com
The Boca Raton Children's Museum is a colorful, interactive place where kids can explore the past, the present, and the future. The museum itself is a historical marker; it's in an old house called Singing Pines built a hundred years ago.

The museum believes that the most important thing inside its doors is a child's imagination. Every one of its exhibits and programs is geared to fostering that imagination. So the concept of play is encouraged, be it interactive or imaginary. Sixty-thousand children pass through these doors each year—and nearly every one of them insists on staying longer when their parents say it's time to go. In FACES Multicultural Room, a child can feel the echoes of history by dressing up in a traditional costume from Ireland or Africa, or by hearing the musical instruments, looking at the books, or touching the crafts from countries all over the world. They can dig for fossils, play-act at being a bank executive in a scale-model bank with a real safe, or do the weekly shopping in the kid-size aisles of Rickett's Corner Store, a replica of Boca Raton's first grocery. These are just some of the Activity Centers scattered all about the museum that help bring alive science, decision-making, exploration, and history to children.

Children can touch the animals at Audubon & Friends, with a bunch of little critters ranging from rodents to seaside crabs and pretty much everything in between. On Dr. Digg's Back Porch, kids can learn how to identify fossils and old artifacts. In Lillian's Kitchen they can see the housewares and utensils used by Lillian Williams, the home's original owner, a century ago. The Children of the Wilderness exhibit shows the history of Singing Pines—the handsome old wooden home in which they're standing—and all the people who lived here.

**BOOMERS FAMILY
RECREATION CENTER
3100 Airport Rd.
Boca Raton
(561) 347-1888
www.boomersparks.com**
Wanna be a hero to your kids? Then pack 'em in the car and bring 'em to Boomers! The hardest thing about going to Boomers is deciding what to do. When you walk in, you'll see more electronic and video games than you've ever seen in your life. Much to your surprise, you'll probably find yourself playing one of them before long—having a motorcycle race against your child, navigating through a maze, driving in the Indy 500, or perhaps dueling to the death with a villain.

You can play miniature golf on one of the coolest courses you've ever seen, with grizzly greens, gnarly nines, wild water, and wacky windmills. You can rev up a high-performance go-kart (real, not virtual) and speed out onto a real track. Have you ever enjoyed bumper cars in an amusement park or carnival? How about bumper cars on the *water?* It's somewhat akin to a demolition derby on water—with the added benefit of being able to shoot your water cannon at whoever's unfortunate enough to come within your sights.

You might also to try some mini-bowling at "Highway 66 Lanes" or enter the very dark, very exciting world of laser tag in a dark maze where everyone is "it" and you'd better tag them with your gun before they tag you. If you're up to it after all this activity, try the Rock Wall or sit and relax while your younger kids cavort in Kids' Playland.

**COCONUT COVE WATER PARK &
RECREATION CENTER
11200 Park Access Rd.
Boca Raton
(561) 274-1140
www.pbcgov.com/parks/aquatics/
waterparks/coconutcove**
Coconut Cove Recreation Center is a great place for families, because there's just so much to do here. It's a great place for birthday parties and family reunions. And there are some nice special events here, such as an Annual Daddy Daughter Dance, and the Annual Spring Eggsplashtacular.

But most kids love to come here for the waterpark. They can ride a tube down a lazy river, making friends along the way. They can take a trip—more likely, 40 or 50 trips—down the bright-yellow, partially-enclosed water slide. They can take a dip in the pool. And while you're watching them, you can relax on a lounge with a good book and a cool drink. The kids can also come to summer camp here and get swimming lessons. Although the Recreation Center is open all year, the waterpark closes for the winter, generally re-opening at the time of Spring Break.

**SOL CHILDREN THEATER TROUPE
3333 North Federal Hwy.
Boca Raton
(561) 447-8829
www.solchildrentheatretroupe.org**
This is a theater company with kids—and for kids. Your kids will enjoy watching their contemporaries pour out their hearts in song and dance on stage. Their attention will be riveted by the classic children's tales being told, such as *Hercules, The Little Prince, Oliver Twist, Through the Looking Glass,* and *The Princess and the Pea.* There are also Improv

Nights for kids. And who knows . . . a star might be born! There are Young Artists' Concerts, as well as talent shows. An afternoon at the Sol Children Theatre Troupe, with your own children, will be an afternoon you won't soon forget.

SUGAR SAND PARK
300 South Military Trail
Boca Raton
(561) 347-3900
www.sugarsandpark.org
Sugar Sand is different than most of the parks mentioned here. For one thing, it's not a county park; it was developed and is run by the City of Boca Raton. And for another, it was purposely created to be different than most other parks. There's less of an emphasis on ball fields and basketball courts here, and more of an emphasis on local culture, interactive learning for children, and a total family experience. It's a 132-acre park with an edge to it. There's actually a performing arts theater here, called the Willow Theatre; and the productions are excellent. There's the Children's Science Explorium, a hands-on facility with an emphasis on interactive activities, and a permanent collection as well as traveling exhibits. At Sugar Sand Park, there's even a Science Playground, with hands-on activities demonstrating various scientific activities all along a three-level wooden structure. There's a water trough and water jets for kids who want to cool off, a magnificent carousel with beautiful lights and real carved horses, a gymnasium for basketball and other sports, two nature trails through scrub pine flatwoods, and tons of special events, including art exhibits, puppet festivals, and Shriek Week at Halloween. Sugar Sand Park has received nine different awards since 2002.

CENTRAL COUNTY

CALYPSO BAY WATERPARK
151 Lamstein Lane
Royal Palm Beach
(561) 790-6160
www.pbcgov.com/parks/aquatics/
waterparks/calypsobay/
When you sit on top of the big slide and look down at the sudden loop it makes at the bottom, you may be tempted to chicken out. But you won't—because your kids are waiting for you at the bottom (and the kids in line behind you are waiting their turn). So you push off, into the unknown, and then—lo and behold—you're back in line again a minute later. After that, you may find yourself swinging from rope to rope as you try and cross the watery playground in the pool. And you'll thoroughly enjoy watching your kids doing their own thing on the playground. That's the great thing about waterparks—they make you remember how much fun you used to have in the water. And they give you a chance to actually spend some time with your kids.

CENTENNIAL FOUNTAIN
Centennial Park
100 Clematis St.
West Palm Beach
In the heart of downtown West Palm is a fountain where people don't necessarily gather to *look* at the fountain but to play in it. This fountain has 105 jets shooting water straight up . . . and then, of course, coming down. You'll see dozens of kids playing in it, getting soaking wet, and having the time of their lives. And they're so happy to be there that their joyful shouting pretty much drowns out the sounds of the fountain. In fact, there are so many kids playing here that there's actually a city employee called a

"fountain guard" who's responsible for making sure that no accidents occur. Nearby are tables under shady oak trees, where you can keep an eye on the kids. Listen to the sounds of your kids playing in the fountain. It'll be the happiest sound you've heard in quite a while.

FUN DEPOT
2003 Tenth Ave. North
Lake Worth
(561) 547-0817
www.fundepot.net

Nothing mysterious about the mission of the Fun Depot. It's a great place for the whole family. There's a long list of great attractions here. The big recent news is the addition of The Mezz, a LAN Gaming Center. The Mezz is for serous gamers, the kind of people who could spend hours up here in this room on the second floor. The LAN Center specializes in multi-player video gaming, and you can buy blocks of time, generally by the hour. If you're looking for a real adrenaline-pumper, try laser tag. You'll find yourself in a 15-minute game of non-stop action (you snooze, you lose), cavorting (often with kids half your age) in a 4,000-square-foot, black-lit, fog-filled, music-pumping maze, full of people who are trying to tag you (electronically, of course) before you tag them.

You can head for the go-kart track, a half-mile oval where the competition is fast and furious. You can test your skill at the batting cages, where a machine will pitch to you at speeds of between 40 and 90 miles an hour. If you'd rather do it a bit more casually, there's also a softball cage. Back inside, try your luck at the arcade, which has a nice mix of new games and old favorites. You can play basketball against Michael Jordan, dodge the bad guys, win the Olympic

high-jump or ski slalom, drive a race car or spaceship, out-swim a shark, and try your luck on a racehorse or slot-machine (tokens, not money!). There's also a playground for the younger set, with a bounce house and an obstacle course.

LION COUNTY SAFARI
2003 Lion Country Safari Rd.
Loxahatchee
(561) 793-1084
www.lioncountrysafari.com

As you head west on Southern Boulevard, the trappings of civilization slowly melt away. Minute by minute, you pass fewer houses, fewer stores, fewer signs. But then you see the entrance for Lion Country Safari, the only drive-through wildlife trail in Florida. Here, *you're* the one in an enclosure (your car) and the animals are the ones who range freely. And they will range freely . . . right up to your car. Don't open the windows, because these visitors will include lions and tigers. When you're that up close and personal, it's hard not to be awed by their magnificence.

Other visitors will wander around your car, and sometimes sit down right in front of it—zebras, ostriches, buffalo, musk oxen, and African gazelles. The hippos and rhinos probably won't; because of their girth, they don't move around too much. But they'll be near the road, and you'll marvel, too, at these prehistoric-looking monsters, who weigh more than the car in which you're sitting.

One of the highlights of any Lion Country Safari visit is the giraffe section. They, too, will wander over—and above—your car, with their surrealistic-looking height and their slow-moving, peculiar gait. They're an extraordinary sight, towering over you and distorting your sense of scale. You'll most likely see babies (who will also tower over your car) with their mothers. There are nearly a thousand animals here and several shows, among them monkey shows and alligator feedings. There's a petting zoo filled with sheep, goats, and pigs, and area with tropical birds of incredible colors. There's a large cafeteria, a nice gift shop, and refreshment stands all over.

PALM BEACH ZOO
1301 Summit Blvd.
West Palm Beach
(561) 547-9453
www.palmbeachzoo.org
You'll see all kinds of fascinating animals here, among them bush dogs, giant anteaters, Patagonian cavies, Jamaican fruit bats, dingos from Australia, llamas from Peru, tigers from Malaysia, naked mole-rats from Africa, and red-bellied lemurs from Madagascar. And you'll see something near and dear to Floridians—a Florida panther, one of a vanishing breed that's endangered by the incredible growth of Florida over the last few decades. And, yes, there are plenty of the better-known animals we've come to associate with good zoos as well.

There's also the Interactive Fountain, with dancing waters and plenty of room for kids to frolic. There's the Harriet W. and George D. Cornell Tropics of the Americas Exhibit, which showcases both the animals and the cultures found in Central and South America. You'll see plants from the rain forest, a real pyramid, and native statues, along with jaguars, Baird's tapirs (with piglike bodies, anteaterlike noses, and lengths of up to eight feet), and capybaras (the largest rodents in the world, up to a science-fiction-like 170 pounds). There's also a magnificent Old-Time carousel with 32 hand-painted animals. And there's the delightful Tropics Café on the shores of Baker Lake.

RAPIDS WATER PARK
6566 N. Military Trail
Riviera Beach
(561) 842-8756
www.rapidswaterpark.com
Water parks are no longer unusual in Florida. But they were when the Rapids was built in 1980. This is the granddaddy of South Florida waterparks, the first, the biggest (25 acres), and the most popular. And people come from all over the county to experience it. There's not just one water slide here—there are 29, from mild to wild. The Wave Pool is more like an ocean pool, the Lazy River really seems like a river (because you don't go past the same spot every minute), and at Criss Crossing you can challenge yourself to make it across the floating ice cubes, tubes, and "alligators." There are four water flumes each with twists, turns, and tricky spots. There are two "thunder" rides: Big Thunder and Black Thunder. Big Thunder is the largest water ride in Florida; you'll toss and turn and swing along the sides of the wall at 20 mph. On Black Thunder you'll be riding a raft on the inside of a pitch-black funnel. Pirates Plunge is not for the faint-hearted, either; you'll twist, turn, and dip down a seven-story run. For smaller children there are several attractions specifically for them.

SCHOOLHOUSE CHILDREN'S MUSEUM AND LEARNING CENTER
129 East Ocean Ave.
Boynton Beach
(561) 742-6780
www.schoolhousemuseum.org
The white-brick building that houses the Schoolhouse Children's Museum really was a schoolhouse built in 1913 and added to the National Register of Historic Places in 1994. In both 2008 and 2009, parents in the

Nickelodeon Parent's Poll voted this the best museum in South Florida.

As soon as you walk in, you'll come upon a 15' replica of the Jupiter Lighthouse. In this museum, you and your kids can step back in time, and see how the town of Boynton Beach and the region of South Florida grew to become what they are today. Get a ticket at the train depot, pick up some luggage, and then take a ride on the Orange Blossom Express. The kids can dress in the period costumes of the conductor or a passenger in the early 1900s. They can ring the bell, shovel coal into the steam engine, or relax in the Library Car. In the farmhouse, they can see how early settlers lived in this area. In Dairy Days, they can visit a farm and milk a cow. At the Pepper Patch Farm, they can fill trays on a conveyor belt with peppers, and then start them on their trip to market. On Old Main Street, they can see what Boynton Beach, Boca Raton, and Delray Beach looked like a hundred years ago.

SOUTH FLORIDA SCIENCE MUSEUM
4801 Dreher Trail North
West Palm Beach
(561) 832-1988
www.sfsm.org

This museum has been packing them in for years due to the quality and the diversity of its exhibits. Hands-on science exhibits will challenge your ideas—and your children's—about science and technology. Interactive exhibits will show you how to create clouds, generate electricity with a bike, create amazing optical illusions, and build and control your own robot!

The permanent exhibits here are renowned in South Florida. In Ancient Egypt: A Celebration of Life, you can view relics as old as 600 B.C., along with a replica of a mummy. In Space Gallery, you can look at a rock from the moon, picked up by astronauts on the Apollo 14 mission. Recollections is a dazzling projection instrument that will let you and your kids create time-delayed images of yourselves. In McGinty Aquariums you can come up-close-and-personal with sharks, eels, and a living coral reef. The Solar Express outside features model trains run by solar power and controlled by you. In the natural history area, you'll meet Suzie, an ice-age mastodon actually found in Palm Beach County. Here, natural history takes on a life of its own as you see authentic and reproduction skeletons of whales, sharks, and dinosaurs.

For many visitors to the South Florida Science Museum, however, the Marvin Dekelboum Planetarium is the highlight. This theater offers 360-degree, full-domed presentations, with unbelievable graphics and photography that are enhanced by laser effects.

YESTERYEAR VILLAGE
South Florida Fairgrounds
9067 Southern Blvd.
West Palm Beach
(561) 790-5227
www.southfloridafair.com/yesteryear village.asp

On the 10 acres at Yesteryear Village, the way it was is the way it is. You're transported to a different time—a time when anyone who lived in South Florida was, for all practical purposes, a "pioneer." A time when if the heat didn't make you sick, the mosquitoes would. A time when you had to get your water from a well, and if it didn't rain, you didn't get water. At the village, children can learn about these days in a living history park, with buildings and artifacts dating from the 1850s to the 1950s. The buildings are authentic down to the last inch, and they include an old schoolhouse, a farm, a blacksmith shop, a general store, and several houses. The park is also home to the only Big Band museum in the United States, called The Sally Bennett Big Band Hall of Fame Museum. The park offers a self-guided tour, or you can take the group tour, which is 2.5 hours. When you walk inside these old buildings, you'll be surrounded by the furniture, books, accessories, crafts, appliances, and furnishings of this long-ago era. This is a great place to bring a picnic lunch. And if you've forgotten anything, you can pick it up at the fascinating General Store.

i Another item that belongs in the don't-leave-your-hotel-without-it category—a hat. It's a good idea to take one with you wherever you go, or to just leave one in the trunk while you're here. Unless you're from a warm climate yourself, it may seem like it's hard to find shade here . . . and, in the summer, it is. That sun can seem relentless. With a hat on, and a visor in front of your head, you *can* find some shade. And it won't seem quite as hot outside. (And if you're shiny-pated on top, this advice goes double for you—even in the winter. Many a bald tourists have burned their scalp because they didn't feel the need to wear a hat in winter.)

NORTH COUNTY

A LATTE FUN INDOOR PLAYGROUND & CAFÉ
9820 Alternate A1A, Suite 206
Palm Beach Gardens
(561) 627-1782
www.alattefun.com

What do you get when you combine a 4,000 square foot play area for kids with a cozy coffeehouse for adults? You get A Latte Fun and a lot of fun. This unique idea has caught on in North County, because it's a place where parents can get some down time—with other adults—and still provide a safe, imaginative play-environment for their children. The play area has an inflatable slide, foam pit, trampoline (on ground-level), tree house, imagination area, and a separate fun space for infants and crawlers. There's all the climbing, sliding, riding, swinging, jumping, and pretending that a kid could ever want. Trained playground supervisors welcome the children and direct them in interactive, creative play. For parents, there's an eclectic cafe with comfortable sofas, tables, and chairs, and free Wi-Fi. And for all ages, there's breakfast, lunch, and healthy snacks. A Latte Fun also offers occasional Night Out opportunities to parents, where they can drop the kids off and enjoy a night out. There are also special events for the kids, with crafts and dancing.

BUSCH WILDLIFE SANCTUARY
2500 Jupiter Park Dr.
Jupiter
(561) 575-3399
www.buschwildlife.com
The Busch Wildlife Sanctuary is a non profit, educational-based care facility for injured animals, and a place where wildlife and people can come together. The original facility here was called the Wildlife Rehabilitation and Environmental Education Center, established in 1983. A decade later, the Peter W. Busch Family Foundation joined forces with the center, and the result was the Busch Wildlife Sanctuary. Today, this sanctuary provides medical and rehabilitative care

to thousands of wild animals each year, under the direction of a staff veterinarian. The ultimate goal is to return the animals to their natural habitats.

The Busch Wildlife Sanctuary offers community outreach programs to over 50,000 people every year, with live-animal presentations and lectures. These sessions offer one-on-one contacts between people and wild animals. It's a rare learning experience. The organization's objective was to create a unique refuge that combines a community nature center with a wildlife hospital. You can also follow beautiful nature trails through pine flatwoods, oak hammocks, and cypress wetlands. Along the way, you'll see wildlife habitats exhibiting a variety of native animals, from bald eagles to Florida panthers. Indoors, you and the kids will enjoy a hands-on discovery center where they can explore nature through a variety of interactive displays.

LOGGERHEAD MARINE LIFE CENTER
14200 US 1
Juno Beach
(561) 627-8280
www.marinelife.org

Sitting adjacent to one of the busiest sea turtle nesting grounds in the world, Loggerhead Marine Life Center is a hospital for sea turtles. Your children can get to see these huge, magical creatures up close and gain a real understanding of the fragile sea-life and eco-system on which Florida is based. The hospital houses sick and injured sea turtles who are cared for by hospital staff. Among the species here are loggerhead, green, hawksbill, and Kemp's Ridley sea turtles. If the kids have questions, volunteer "patient interpreters" and docents are on hand to answer them.

My Palm Beach County

"I spend half the year in New York and half in Florida . . . and I have to say that Palm Beach County has everything New York does—museums, wonderful parks, good restaurants, and a lot of nice retirement communities with great amenities. I walk to the gym at 6 a.m. every morning to work out, including in the winter And I sure couldn't do that in New York. There are a lot of colleges here, and they all offer courses that retired people can take, or sit in on. And the weather, of course. Back in New York this winter, they've had three massive snowstorms in a row; my children tell me it's horrible up there. Here, on the other hand, the sun shines every day. And we make a big deal out of it when the temperature gets below sixty!"

—Mildred Sigadel,
retiree, Boca Raton

Several exhibits give insight into the fascinating world of giant turtles. Rehabilitation and Research shows the process by which a patient is admitted to the hospital, and the ways in which researchers gather information on sea turtles. The Archelon exhibit features the replica skeleton of an ancient sea turtle that lived 65 million years ago, suspended from the ceiling. At Beach Ecology and Shells you'll have an interactive experience and learn how sand is made and which animals "wear" shells. For the younger kids, there's a soft-sand outdoor play area, complete with turtles, manta rays, and seastars. Admission is free; donations accepted.

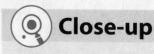 **Close-up**

The Miracle of the Nesting Turtles

If you want your children to see a miracle of nature, take them to Loggerhead Marinelife Center in Juno Beach. At the center, they'll take you and the kids—shhh, no noise—out to the darkened beach at night to see the miracle of turtle-nesting. Many sea turtles come ashore at night or during early morning to lay their eggs. And many others are on the beach at night nesting. The nighttime walks start at 8:45 p.m. and generally take a few hours. Don't bother bringing a flashlight or a camera with a flash-bulb. They're not permitted because they can scare the mother away from her nest, and they can disorient new hatchlings, who might head for the lights rather than the ocean. The Marinelife Center has scouts out looking for the best places to bring visitors. Contrary to some popular belief, there's absolutely no relationship between nesting and the tides or the phases of the moon.

Visitors are advised to wear dark-colored clothing and to bring bug spray and footwear that's appropriate for walking on the beach. Also bring a bit of patience with you as well . . . it may take a while before the center's personnel find a nest. But it's worth it! Call (561) 627-8280, or go to www.marinelife.org.

PLAYMOBIL FUN PARK
8031 North Military Trail
Palm Beach Gardens
(561) 691-9880
www.playmobil.com

As you drive up, it looks sort of like a cross between a medieval castle and Candyland. The castle is white with red stripes on the side and a red roof. There are coats-of-arms over the doorway. This is a wonderland of creative play settings, shapes, and colors. Kids are encouraged to touch everything, to experiment, and to play actively with the toys as long as they want. All play areas are divided according to special Playmobil themes. They can explore a castle, play house, decorate a dollhouse or firehouse, build a farm or racetrack, and interact with friendly cartoon characters. Even the walls are bursting with color and murals. There are plenty of opportunities for parent-child interaction, and the rooms are filled with the brilliantly colored toys of the Playmobil company.

PERFORMING ARTS

Only a few decades ago, South Florida had a reputation as something of a cultural wasteland. These days, however, you won't be able to find enough free time to fit in all the cultural and performing arts attractions. There are vibrant theater companies, all kinds of music groups and companies, dance, and singing performances ranging from country to opera. There are performance venues ranging from the casual and comfortable to the stately and the elegant, from small and little-known to world-class. And the artists who perform in them are not only local; noted performers from all over the world appear regularly in Palm Beach County.

PERFORMING ARTS VENUES

Palm Beach County residents appreciate the arts. Many of them, if not most, moved here some years back from places up north where the arts were a regular part of their lives. Through their hard work and their hard-earned financial contributions, they've made sure that Palm Beach County now has arts venues that rival any in the country. From state-of-the-art facilities hosting internationally renowned luminaries to cozy little theaters hosting home-grown talent, you'll find yourself experiencing many of these places firsthand.

In Palm Beach County, arts venues don't have to be inside. Because our weather is so great, there are plenty of opportunities to enjoy concerts and other performances outside, in the fresh air.

South County

**CAROLE AND BARRY KAYE
 PERFORMING ARTS AUDITORIUM**
Florida Atlantic University
777 Glades Rd.
Boca Raton
(800) 564-9539
www.fau.edu/kayeauditorium
The Carole and Barry Kaye Performing Arts Auditorium is a 2,400-seat venue located on the main campus of Florida Atlantic University. Although it opened in 1982, this is still considered one of the most acoustically sound performing arts venues in South Florida. The auditorium is actually the South Palm Beach County home of a number of acclaimed regional orchestras, in addition to a variety of other types of performances,

ranging from Broadway stars to well-known comedians to internationally acclaimed concerts.

The diversity of the performances that takes place here is nothing short of astounding. Recent performances have included the Gold Coast Opera doing the *Barber of Seville;* the Moscow Festival Ballet with *Coppelia;* the Klezmer Company Orchestra doing *Judeo-Jazzistico;* and the Palm Beach Pops with *A Tribute to the Music of Andrew Lloyd Webber & Les Miserables.* Notable performers such as Frankie Avalon and Linda Eder have also appeared here.

CREST THEATRE
Old School Square Cultural Arts Center
51 N. Swinton Ave.
Delray Beach
(561) 243-7922, ext. 1
www.oldschool.org/crest.asp
The Crest Theatre, which has become a genuine cultural magnet for South County, is a blast from the past. It's housed in the restored 1925 Delray High School building and was dedicated in 1993 as a performing arts center. The theater is actually the original high school auditorium. It was re-designed as an intimate, 323-seat facility combining the original high school color (blue) with warm burgundy and gold accents, along with state-of-the-art lighting, sound, and multi-media capabilities. Surrounding the theater are nine beautifully restored classrooms, now hosting meetings, workshops, receptions, and art classes.

During the Season, The Main Stage Series offers professional theater, music, and dance, along with national touring shows and unique variety shows. The Broadway Cabaret Series (Jan–Apr) brings in some of the hottest performers on Broadway for memorable performances and tête-à-tête with the audiences. The Lecture Series (Jan–Apr) features notable speakers from many fields all around the country, who might speak on anything from foreign policy to the state of the arts in America.

The Crest is one cultural gift that keeps giving, because it also serves as a venue for other organizations, schools, and community groups to present their own productions and meetings. There's also space for cast parties and other get-togethers. The Ocean Breeze Room is located in the Crest Theater building, and is used for ceremonies, receptions, and meetings up to a hundred people. Additionally, The Frances Bourque Library, Lettie McNeill Music Room, and more classrooms are located here.

SCHMIDT FAMILY CENTRE FOR THE ARTS
Count de Hoernle Amphitheater
Mizner Park
590 Plaza Real
Boca Raton
(561) 961-2098
www.centre4artsboca.com/index.php
The Count de Hoernle Amphitheater is a state-of-the-art outdoor amphitheater, colonnade, and concert green that accommodates up to 4,200 people. During the course of a year, Palm Beach County residents will enjoy music, dance, theater, film, and other fine arts, outside in the fresh air. And the range of shows is very wide, from classical to kiddies, from jazz to hip-hop, from country-western to rock, and from pop to Latin.

The Schmidt Family Centre for the Arts puts on Boca's annual Festival of the Arts, a celebration of music and literature that attracts world-class musicians and authors. The Festival gives students the opportunity to attend lectures, master-classes, and open rehearsals with these artists. And the Festival was a hit from its very first year, when it attracted artists such as Itzhak Perlman, Arturo Sandoval, and Pulitzer prize-winning author Edward Albee. Live Nation Events, the world's largest concert promoter, also does rock, pop, and jazz events here, with stars such as Kelly Clarkson, Melissa Etheridge, Fergie, and Earth, Wind and Fire. The City of Boca Raton also gets into the act when it hosts free events such as the Summer Music Series and Cinema in the Park, along with special holiday events.

SHOWTIME DANCE AND PERFORMING ARTS THEATRE
503 Southwest Mizner Blvd.
Boca Raton
(561) 394-2626
www.showtimeboca.com
Showtime Dance and Performing Arts Theatre is a fully equipped, state-of-the-art facility for music and theater, with seating for 100 people. This facility is actually a performing arts school, with five studios for dance, acting, music, and vocal training. There are good acting programs for ages four through adult, including classes in improvisation, character development, movement, scene building, storytelling, puppetry, creative writing, stage song and dance, and more. Past performances by Showtime students have included *Pocahontas, High School Musical, Into the Woods, Mulan, Seussical,* and *Cinderella.* Dance classes are offered for students as young as three, in tap, jazz, pre-ballet, ballet, and hip hop. In addition, Showtime also offers instruction in piano/keyboard, guitar, drums, and voice for ages five and older.

STUDIO ONE THEATRE
Florida Atlantic University
777 Glades Rd.
Boca Raton
(561) 297-3810
www.fau.edu/theatre
Theater and dance—and sharing them with the community—have been integral parts of Florida Atlantic University since its inception. Students, in fact, are encouraged to become involved in the performing arts from their first day on campus. Recent performances have included *Art,* a play about the complexity of human relationships; an exquisite drama called *Talking Pictures,* by Horton Foote; a drama called *Marisol,* by internationally acclaimed playwright Jose Rivera; and performances by the FAU Dance Theatre Ensemble.

SUNSET COVE AMPHITHEATER
12551 Glades Rd.
Boca Raton
(561) 488-8069
www.pbcgov.com/parks/amphitheaters/sunsetcove
This amphitheater is located in South County Regional Park, in west Boca Raton. And it sits in a beautiful setting, with spectacular lakeside views and tropical landscaping. The Sunset Cove Amphitheater serves South Palm Beach County with a variety of productions, including concerts, theater, and other performing arts attractions, out in the sunshine. Recent shows have included acts such as Yes, the famed English group that's been around for several decades; and The American Kennel Club All-Breed Conformation Show, presented by the Boca Raton Dog Club.

Central County

ALEXANDER W. DREYFOOS JR.
SCHOOL OF THE ARTS
501 South Sapodilla Ave.
West Palm Beach
(561) 802-6000
www.awdsoa.org/home/indexhome
.html

The Alexander W. Dreyfoos School of the Arts was founded in 1989 with the intention of creating the premier arts high school in Palm Beach County, the nation's 11th-largest school district. The school's location in downtown West Palm Beach places it in the heart of Palm Beach County's cultural landscape. Just across Iris Street is the Raymond F. Kravis Center for the Performing Arts, and within a few blocks are the Norton Museum of Art, the Armory Art Center, Palm Beach Dramaworks, the Cuillo Center for the Arts, and the Ann Norton Sculpture Garden. Performances at the auditorium here have included *Crazy For You, The Last Night of Ballyhoo*, Chamber Strings Concert, Music Department Pops Concerts, Shakespearean Madrigal Dinner, and Klavier Piano Concert

CRUZAN AMPHITHEATRE
601-7 Sansbury's Way
West Palm Beach
(561) 795-8883
www.livenation.com/venue/
cruzan-amphitheatre-tickets

Cruzan Amphitheatre is a 19,000-seat open-air music venue to the west of West Palm Beach. Owned by the South Florida Fairgrounds, Cruzan is a modern amphitheater that has hosted many of the most famous musical acts in the world over the past two decades.

Performances run rain or shine, and there are no refunds because of inclement weather. So come prepared with a poncho or rain gear. (Umbrellas are not permitted because they block the view of other patrons.) But don't worry about rain. The great majority of performances take place on clear, cool nights. The nearly 20,000 people who are spread out in front of you or behind you couldn't care less if it's cloudy out because they're too wrapped up in the music.

Since opening, the venue has gone through numerous name changes. Its original name was actually the Sony Blockbuster Coral Sky Amphitheater, because the seats face into the west, toward often-spectacular sunsets. As sponsors came and went, it became the Mars Music Amphitheatre, then the Sound Advice Amphitheatre, and in 2008, the venue was renamed yet again, following a new sponsorship agreement with Cruzan Rum. Over the past decade, performers such as The Spice Girls and Brittany Spears have appeared here. Recent acts at the Cruzan include Rascal Flatts, the Dave Matthews Band, Vans Warped Tour, and Tim McGraw.

CUILLO CENTER FOR THE ARTS
201 Clematis St.
West Palm Beach
(561) 835-9226
www.cuillocenter.com

This is a modern, state-of-the-art facility, situated in the heart of the rejuvenated Clematis Street District, and also close to City Place. The 377-seat Mainstage theatre highlights new dramas and musicals on their way to Broadway, as well as traveling companies from hit shows there. The new Second Story Theatre is a great location for cabaret-style concerts, and the Cuillo has become a major player in the Palm Beach County arts scene.

The philosophy here is to host a wide variety of events for a wide variety of audiences. Comedy, drama, musicals, traditional and experimental bands in all types of genres, and dance, both classic and modern, are performed here. Among recent performances have been shows such as *Mod 27,* an improvised comedy theater production; a one-man show called *Back to Babylon,* in which the performer reminisces about his hometown; Marijah and the Reggae All-Stars; a well-known blues band called Blues Dragon; and a pop/rock band called Hollywood LoveScene.

The Cuillo believes in serving the artistic needs of local performers, as well, by giving them an opportunity to step up to the mic. For example, *Build A Band* events give local musicians the opportunity to showcase their talent, and to meet (and perform with) other local musicians. Every Thurs night is *Cuillo Uncorked,* hosted by Platinum-Award-winner Cooper Getschal, who warms up the crowd with his own band, and is then followed by both nationally known bands and good local ones such as Vanilla Monk.

Then there's *Downtown at the Cuillo,* a performing arts series for television developed in a collective effort between The Cuillo Centre For the Arts, The Education Network, and The Palm Beach County School District. The program hosts world-class performers in a variety of musical genres. In addition, there's a segment called *Play with the Pros,* in which local teenagers rehearse and perform with seasoned veterans. The show is shot live-to-tape using five cameras on the Cuillo Centre's main stage. And it's shown, of course, on the Education Network.

DOLLY HAND CULTURAL ARTS CENTER
Palm Beach State College
Belle Glade campus
(561) 993-1160
www.palmbeachstate.edu/x1792.xml

Near the shores of Lake Okeechobee, in a working-class town in the area called "The Muck," is a theater with lighted fountains in front, and, often, world-class entertainers inside. The Dolly Hand Center sponsors a Professional Guest Artists Series, which has featured Benise, who does for Spanish guitar what Josh Grobin does for opera and what Yanni does for New Age, and who takes his act (and his colorful troupe) all over the world. The Golden Dragon Acrobats, a world-renowned company from China, have also performed here, with their impossible gymnastics and their flaming hoops. The Soweto Gospel Choir has brought the touching, poignant chords of African gospel here. And the New York Gilbert & Sullivan Players have also performed here, doing their *I've Got a Little Twist.* The Dolly Hand Center also has a Family Fun Series, with children's theater, dance, and motivational performers. And the Grand Hall often hosts exhibits by local artists.

DUNCAN THEATRE AT PALM BEACH STATE COLLEGE
4200 South Congress Ave.
Lake Worth
(561) 868-3309
www.pbcc.edu/duncan.xml

This 720-seat theater was founded in 1960, and later re-named for the legendary literature instructor Watson B. Duncan III. Located on the main campus of Palm Beach State College, it's renowned for presenting national and international modern dance companies; jazz, blues and folk musicians; and traditional chamber music ensembles. In an effort to better serve the community, the theater has now expanded its offerings to families, with its successful Weekend Family Fun Series. These programs present music and theater for children and families; and they're educating a new generation to the beauty of the performing arts. Past events here include Stellaluna, Jesse Cook, Richard Alston Dance, Classic Album LIVE: The Beatles (The White Album), and Complexions Contemporary Ballet

HARRIETT HIMMEL THEATER FOR CULTURAL & PERFORMING ARTS
City Place
700 South Rosemary Ave.
West Palm Beach
(561) 835 1408
www.cityplace.com/info/harriet Himmel_info.cfm

When you first lay eyes on the Harriet Himmel Theatre, it looks like an old church. And that's exactly what it is. Once home to the First United Methodist Church of West Palm Beach, this 11,000-square-foot cultural arts center is now a busy venue for the performing arts, as well as receptions, exhibitions, fashion shows, seminars, and community meetings. And its restoration provided the basic architectural model for the rest of City Place.

This stunning structure is actually one of the finest examples of Spanish Colonial Revival architecture in America today. It offers a wide variety of cultural programming, including music, dance and theater. And it has an interesting history. The 1914 cornerstone, taken from the original church, was laid on May 2, 1926, and the church officially opened to the public on Christmas Eve less than eight months later. The

interior is architecturally significant because of features like the original cypress ceilings, a tiered mezzanine, and large divided windows overlooking the main floor. There haven't been many major alterations made to the building. Over the years, many of the ground-floor windows were covered with stucco. During the 1950s, the tower room was rebuilt, and a memorial wall commemorating World War II veterans was installed. In 1967, an elevator was added. And that's pretty much been it.

The church housed victims of the 1928 hurricane for nearly 11 months, until all of the people who lost their homes were able to rebuild. When the stock-market crashed the following year, the building had to be deeded back to the bondholders in New Orleans. When the bondholders couldn't sell it, they offered the congregation the option of raising $25,000 to take it over. Church members sold everything—including wedding rings—to make the payment. In 1990, the stained glass windows, organ, sanctuary floor, and original cornerstone were moved to a new church that had been built. But renovations did not begin on the church until 1998.

Now it's a proud urban showpiece and such a magnificent building that you may not be able to resist the temptation to go in. Among the artists who have performed here are The Future of Jazz Orchestra, Palm Beach Dramaworks, and jazz singer Nancy Kelly.

MEYER AMPHITHEATRE
105 Evernia St.
West Palm Beach
www.westpalmbeach.com

The Meyer Amphitheater is a band shell located in downtown West Palm, with seating for 5,000 people. It hosts special events throughout the year, including Fourth on

Flagler festivities, Irish Fest, along with many concerts and many different types of music, as well as dance performances. The amphitheater is surrounded by grass, and you can sit there during the performances. It has a rather interesting history. The original building on Lake Worth was Hotel Salt Air, built in 1913. It was eventually sold to developers in the 1950s, who later demolished it and replaced with the Holiday Inn. But eventually the Holiday Inn was demolished, as well. And since its opening in 1996, the Meyer Amphitheatre has become a gathering point for Palm Beach Countians who love to hear their music or watch their dancing with the city behind them, and Lake Worth/Intracoastal Waterway right in front of them.

PALM BEACH ATLANTIC UNIVERSITY THEATER
901 South Flagler Dr.
West Palm Beach
(561) 803-2000
www.pba.edu

The Theatre Department at Palm Beach Atlantic University puts on some very-well-received shows. The musicals are particularly good, and past shows have included *Nunsense, South Pacific,* and *Man of La Mancha.* But good dramas are also here, both classic and new. The department has also done Shakespeare, Chekhov, and Moliere.

RAYMOND F. KRAVIS CENTER FOR THE PERFORMING ARTS
701 Okeechobee Blvd.
West Palm Beach
(561) 832-SHOW
www.kravis.org

When the Raymond F. Kravis Center opened in 1992, it bestowed instant recognition that Palm Beach County was now in the cultural

big leagues. This is truly a performing arts *palace,* elegant and evocative and yet modern and comfortable. The sound and lighting systems are the finest. And there's an unending parade through these doors of the finest actors, dancers, and singers in the world.

Performers here include the highly-regarded Palm Beach Opera and the Palm Beach Pops, along with international acts such as the Russian National Orchestra, Bette Midler, the Joffrey Ballet, *Jersey Boys,* The Acting Company's *Romeo and Juliet,* the Schleswig–Holstein Festival Orchestra, Bill Cosby, the Beach Boys, Chita Rivera, Johnny Mathis, Miami City Ballet, Celtic Woman, Neil Sedaka, and hit shows such as *Les Miserables* and *Cats.* And that's just a sample from the 2009–10 season!

The Kravis Center actually is the site of three venues—the 2,193-seat Alexander W. Dreyfoos Jr. Concert Hall, the 300-seat Rinker Playhouse, and the outdoor Michael and Andrew Gosman Amphitheatre, with a capacity of 1,400. The number of events hosted annually has grown to more than 800, and more than 500,000 people attend them. And a number of regional arts organizations now call the Kravis Center home, among them Miami City Ballet, the Palm Beach Opera, and the Palm Beach Pops.

SOCIETY OF THE FOUR ARTS
2 Four Arts Plaza
Palm Beach
(561) 655-7226
www.fourarts.org

Palm Beach residents of the 1930s had suffered less than just about anyone in America during the Depression. They wanted the cultural amenities they had grown used to up North. And they wanted them *now.* So the Society of the Four Arts was founded in

1936 by a group of prominent residents, to meet these demands. The four arts which constitute the Society's mission are music, drama, literature, and art.

Every season from Nov through Apr, The Four Arts presents notable speakers, concerts, films, educational programs, and art exhibitions to the public. The Esther B. O'Keeffe Gallery Building houses both an art gallery and a 700-seat auditorium. The gallery runs exhibitions throughout the season, and the Walter S. Gubelmann auditorium features concerts, lectures, and films. The original Four Arts building now houses The Gioconda and Joseph King Library, which contains over 65,000 books, periodicals, videotapes, and DVDs. Here, children can borrow books, use the computers, and enjoy special programs free of charge. Art exhibitions for the younger set are displayed in the Mary Alice Fortin Children's Art Gallery throughout the year. And free story time programs for pre-school children are held most Mon, Tues, and Thurs.

The Philip Hulitar Sculpture Garden is an elegant park, with beautiful landscaping, sculptures, and fountains. Benches and chairs provide great spots for reading, or just sitting and enjoying the silence. The Four Arts Gardens, owned by The Society and maintained by The Garden Club of Palm Beach, are demonstration gardens originally designed in 1938 to display the diversity of tropical plants in the South Florida climate.

Recent speakers at Society events have included Senator Chuck Hagel and conductor/pianist Andre Previn. Recent lectures have run the gamut from "Yoga and Pilates" to "The Flowering of the Arts and Culture of France: From Louis XIV and the Court of Versailles to World War I." Recent performers have showcased people such as acclaimed Irish musician Percy French, and the Jupiter String Quartet. And recent theatrical productions have included *Tosca* and *Carmen*.

North County

THE ATLANTIC THEATER
6743 West Indiantown Rd.
Jupiter
(561) 575-4422
http://theatlantictheater.com
The Atlantic Theater is a newly established professional theater, with a somewhat different twist to its mission. Its goal is to bring seldom-produced dramatic and comedic "straight" plays to the stage—plays that are story- and character-driven, that provoke and inspire, and that challenge the actors as well as the audience. The theater is also home to live music of all genres, and focuses on showcasing local singer/songwriters. There's also live comedy, dance performances, children's theater, and art exhibits. The Atlantic Theater's emphasis is clearly on eclectic, and the desire to bring an interesting mix of arts and entertainment to North County. In addition, the theater is also home to The Jove Comedy Experience. Some recent performances have included standup comic Keith Barany, The Irish Comedy Tour, and *Beatlemania*. This 180-seat theater is located in the Atlantic Arts Academy, where classes for students are available in improvisation, dance, music, in addition to other disciplines.

EISSEY CAMPUS THEATRE
Palm Beach State College
11051 Campus Dr.
Palm Beach Gardens
(561) 207-5900
www.palmbeachstate.edu/EisseyCampus Theatre.xml

The 750-seat Edward M. Eissey Campus Theatre is a major cultural hub for northern Palm Beach County, with a wide variety of performing arts companies on stage, diverse educational programs for the community, and family entertainment through its popular Arts in the Gardens guest artist series. Besides being a performance space, The Eissey Campus Theatre serves as a theater training facility for Palm Beach State College students, as well as the local community.

The variety of the acts that appear here is demonstrated by a few of the Eissey Theatre's recent events. The Moscow Festival Ballet performed *Coppelia* here. The Florida Classical Ballet Theatre did *For Such a Time as This: The Story of Queen Esther*. The New Gardens Band, from Palm Beach Gardens, performed *Classics for Concert*. And Bob Lappin and the Palm Beach Pops presented *A Tribute to the Music of Andrew Lloyd Webber and Les Miserables*.

MALTZ JUPITER THEATRE
1001 East Indiantown Rd.
Jupiter
(561) 575-2223
www.jupitertheatre.org
In only seven years, the Maltz Jupiter Theatre has become one of Florida's preeminent professional theaters. Its three goals are performance, production and education, through collaboration with local and national artists. MJT has already received multiple Carbonell Awards, South Florida's highest honor for artistic excellence—and it's increased its subscription base to more than 7,100. The theater recently built world-class facilities in support of its Conservatory of Performing Arts, which serves hundreds of students in after-school, weekend, and summer programs. After receiving a prestigious John

D. and Catherine T. MacArthur Fund grant, MJT developed the Musical Academy for the New York Musical Theatre Festival, where it won the Daego International Musical Festival Production Award. In addition, under this program, the theater also commissioned the world premiere of *Fanny Brice: The Real Funny Girl*.

The Maltz Jupiter Theatre has a capacity of 554. And it hosts innovative programs such as Talk Backs, moderated by artistic director Andrew Kato. These are interactive question-and-answer sessions that take place immediately after a play's performance, and they offer audiences a behind-the-scenes look into the process of creating live theater. And some of the people with whom you'll be talking will be the actors, directors, choreographers, and creative teams.

In addition, a new program called Emerging Artists in Musical Theatre Playwriting Series will nurture the creation of new musical theater at the Maltz Jupiter Theatre. Past performances, as demonstrated by the rapidly rising subscription base, have been very warmly received, among them *Noises Off, Barnum, Beehive, Evita, The Boyfriend*, and *Man of La Mancha*.

SEABREEZE AMPHITHEATER
Carlin Park
750 South A1A
Jupiter
(561) 966-7099
www.pbcgov.com/parks/amphitheaters/seabreeze/
Seabreeze Amphitheater is a sea-side venue adding another entertainment dimension to an already diverse park. Bring a lawn chair or blanket, picnic basket, and even your dog (on a leash). This is a great venue for good local bands. Past performers have included J. P.

Soars and the Red Hots, The Big Band Hall of Fame Orchestra, Strictly Business, The Blunts, and Crossroads. In addition, there's also a popular event called Shakespeare in the Park.

PERFORMING ARTS COMPANIES

The main proof of a growing arts area, though, has always been in the number and vitality of its local organizations, and in the talents of their performers. And, if that's the case, what was once a cultural desert is now a blooming orchid.

South County

BOCA BALLET THEATRE
7630 N.W. Sixth Ave.
Boca Raton
(561) 995-0709
www.bocaballet.org
Established in 1991, the Boca Ballet Theatre is today the 6th-largest dance company in Florida, and considered one of the top civic companies in the United States. During this time, the School of Boca Ballet Theatre has educated more than 5,000 young people. It now holds classes for more than 500 people every week—about a fifth of whom are adults. Every year, the company performs 13 times in four different programs, at Florida Atlantic University and at the amphitheater at Mizner Park. The Boca Ballet Theatre focuses on the classics, and recent productions have included *The Nutcracker*, George Balanchine's *Serenade* (set to the music of Tchaikovsky), and *Giselle*.

BOCA RATON SYMPHONIA
2285 Potomac Rd.
Boca Raton
(561) 376-3848
www.bocasymphonia.org

My Palm Beach County

"I've always found Palm Beach County to be a fascinating place. If you head west, you'll find some of the poorer communities in the country, while to the east are some of the wealthiest. As a former TV reporter here, I've had an opportunity to experience both walks of life. In the (western) Glades communities I've met incredibly talented people who possess an amazing zeal for life, but who, many times, are not given the chance to thrive.

"Conversely, the island of Palm Beach is home to some of the most affluent people in the world. The annual galas are over the top, the atmosphere as if it was pulled from the pages of *The Great Gatsby*.

"To me Palm Beach County is home, and—believe it or not—there's nothing better then returning from a trip and feeling that first wave of humidity. I love it! One of my favorite spots here is Jupiter—the restaurants, the people, and, of course, spring training baseball. It's a laid-back lifestyle in much of the county, one I would not change. One of the obvious reasons I love this county, too, is because it's where I met my wife! We've shared in so much love here, and so many spots bring back great memories."

—Corey Saban, President,
CS Media Works, West Palm Beach
(www.CSMediaworks.com)

Rising on the ashes of the Florida Philharmonic, which closed in 2003, the Boca Raton Symphonia has become a first-class small orchestra, and a major contributor to the South County cultural scene. Its first season concluded in 2004 with a concert at Mizner Park and 4,000 people attended. Since then, it's been onward and upward. The Symphonia now has the stature to be able to bring in well-known soloists to feature in its concerts, such as violinist Erno Kallai. The classics are the company's forte, and they play the music of composers such as Mendelsohn, Schumann, and Mozart. The Symphonia recently introduced the Family Classical Concert Series, on Saturday afternoons, so that parents and their children can enjoy beautiful music together. All concerts take place at the Roberts Theater at Andrews Hall, Center for the Performing Arts, Saint Andrew's School, 3900 Jog Rd., Boca Raton.

CALDWELL THEATRE COMPANY
7901 North Federal Hwy.
Boca Raton
(561) 241-7432
www.caldwelltheatre.com
For 35 years, the Caldwell Theatre Company has been a symbol of quality on the Palm Beach County stage. Anyone who's anyone in the South Florida acting community has been on stage here (or has wanted to be on stage here). And now, they've recently moved into a new home, so the quality of the theater experience here is even higher.

The company sometimes stages new productions of old stories, some of which are not typical theater productions, such as Hemingway's classic *The Old Man and the Sea*. It also produces newer plays such as *Distracted*, a drama about a nine-year-old boy afflicted with ADD, by playwright Lisa Loomer. The Caldwell has always believed in breaking new ground—and that means bringing performances that are not actually "plays" to the stage. For example, the 2010 season saw performers such as Nancy Dononval, a Midwest storyteller who spins stranger-than-fiction stories that'll keep you riveted; two-time Grammy winner Bill Harley, who uses song and story to spin hilarious pictures; and Heather Forest, who uses a unique minstrel style of singing and storytelling to enchant her audiences. The theater has also hosted its share of accomplished national and international actors, as well, among them Charles Nelson Reilly and Len Cariou.

Caldwell Theatre Company entertains more than 50,000 people annually with a variety of classics, revivals, small musicals, and original plays. The company also sponsors a Play Reading Series to introduce new works, and a Professional Adult Storytelling Series.

CREST THEATRE BROADWAY CABARET SERIES
Crest Theatre
Old School Square
51 North Swinton Ave.
Delray Beach
(561) 243-7922
www.oldschool.org
Here, in this magnificently restored school from the early 1900s you can see excellent cabaret performances that you'll remember for a long time. It's called The Broadway Cabaret Series, that during the 2010 season, featured Will and Anthony Nunziata, identical twins who have performed with the Boston Pops and the Cleveland Pops. Or you might have seen a true American icon— the amazing bundle of energy known as

Chita Rivera, Broadway's most accomplished singer/dancer/ actress, and a recipient of The President's Award. You might have seen Christine Andreas, star of stage and screen, and a multiple Tony Award nominee and winner of the prestigious Theatre Award. There was also Christine Ebersole, who's won Tonys for her performances in *Grey Gardens* and *42nd Street*. Adam Pascal, nominated for an Emmy for his touching performance on Broadway in *Rent,* played the same role in the movie.

Housed in the restored 1925 Delray High School building, the Crest Theatre was originally the high school auditorium. Before its opening in 1993, it was re-designed as a charming, 323-seat, state-of-the-art facility combining the original high school color (blue) with warm burgundy and gold accents. It's now a truly intimate entertainment experience, particularly in a format such as cabaret. The Broadway Cabaret Series runs from Jan to Apr.

DELRAY BEACH PLAYHOUSE
950 Northwest Ninth St.
Delray Beach
(561) 272-1281 (ext. 4)
www.delraybeachplayhouse.com
The Delray Beach Playhouse is in a park setting, overlooking scenic Lake Ida. It's one of the best places for talented local performers to hone their skills in actual productions. The playhouse was founded 60 years ago, when a half-dozen would-be actors held a performance in a church parish hall. Later on, they moved to the old Civic Center, on the site of the present City Library. Now the Playhouse has its own building, a modern theater that seats 238 people. The Theater's policy has always been to hire experienced professionals with the skills to teach talented

young performers. As a result, it's one of the most successful community theaters in the country.

The people who perform here are not professionals. They're a diverse cross-section of local people, among them doctors, lawyers, businessmen, students, carpenters, and writers, of widely varying ages, who got their roles in open auditions for the parts. Lighting and sound effects, set- construction, and costuming are all handled by volunteers. Nonetheless, you'll find yourself standing and applauding as the curtain goes down. Recent performances have included shows such as *Fallen Angels,* a comedy by Noel Coward, and *The Prisoner of Second Avenue* by Neil Simon.

Central County

FLORIDA STAGE
Plaza del Mar
262 South Ocean Blvd.
Manalapan
(561) 585-3433
www.floridastage.org
Florida Stage was originally called the Learning Stage when it was founded in 1985 by award-winning actor/director Louis Tyrell. Today it's a leading producer of contemporary works by both established and emerging playwrights. The company's first home was the Duncan Theatre Second Stage, at Palm Beach State College. In 1991, the company moved to a new 250-seat space in nearby Manalapan, and became Pope Theatre Company. In September of 1997, to begin its second decade, the company took its new name, Florida Stage. It has carved an exciting niche for itself, and it's now recognized as the Southeast's largest theater dedicated to producing exclusively new and developing work. The company has staged

the world premiers of more than 30 plays, including works by renowned playwrights such as William Mastrosimone, Deborah Zoe Laufer, and Nilo Cruz. Florida Stage is consistently nominated for Carbonell Awards, the highest theater honors in South Florida.

The 250-seat, three-quarter thrust auditorium is designed to maximize the quality of the sound and the sightlines. Innovative productions over the past year included *Two Jews Walk Into a War*, a funny, poignant play based on a true story about the last two Jews left in Afghanistan; a world premiere of *The Storytelling Ability of a Boy*, a dark comedy about an English teacher who gets too involved in the lives of two of her students; and *Sins of the Mother*, about the tragic truths that bind the families of an old fishing town together, and the secret that threatens to tear them apart.

An afternoon or evening at Florida Stage promises to be provocative, intriguing, and thought-provoking. And you'll be one of the first to see a play that you may very well hear about on larger stages a few months down the line.

PALM BEACH DRAMAWORKS
322 Banyan Blvd.
West Palm Beach
(561) 514-4042
www.palmbeachdramaworks.org
Palm Beach Dramaworks is a professional, not-for-profit company that goes for "provocative" and "timeless" plays. It's only 11 years old. But in that brief time, it's established a reputation for its hard-hitting productions of shows that have long proven their value to American audiences. Over the years it's shown some of the most powerful plays in theater history to Palm Beach County audiences, such as *American Buffalo*,

A Doll's House, The Gin Game, A Moon for the Misbegotten, The Subject Was Roses, Agnes of God, and *Betrayal*. And so many more, like *That Championship Season, Educating Rita*, and *Who's Afraid of Virginia Wolff?* Palm Beach Dramaworks has also gained a reputation for excellent acting and directing, with many of its people having moved on to larger companies. If you love the American Theatre, be sure to see at least one play here.

PALM BEACH LIGHT OPERA COMPANY
2100 South Ocean Blvd., #308S
Palm Beach
(561) 283-2400
www.pblightopera.com
The Palm Beach Light Opera Company is a recently formed theater company based in Palm Beach and dedicated to the preservation and performance of classic operettas. It's a volunteer organization, and it gives talented singers and musicians in South Florida the opportunity to perform in these productions. The Palm Beach Light Opera Company's premiere production, *The Chocolate Soldier*, was performed in January 2009. One of the shows staged in the most recent season was *Naughty Marietta*, by Victor Herbert.

PALM BEACH OPERA
415 South Olive Ave.
West Palm Beach
(561) 833-7888
www.pbopera.org
Palm Beach Opera is one of the old-timers on the Palm Beach County cultural scene; it's been around since 1961. This company has one main goal—to produce quality opera at an international standard of excellence. And anyone who's seen one of their productions will tell you that they succeed very handsomely at this goal. Its performances

take place at the showpiece of Palm Beach County culture, the Kravis Center for the Performing Arts in West Palm Beach.

The people who perform in these productions are world-class talents. The Palm Beach Opera often brings renowned guest artists in from all over the United States as well as abroad; many have performed at all the world's major opera houses. The Palm Beach Opera Chorus consists of 50 talented local singers, and the Palm Beach Opera Orchestra includes musicians who have worked with major professional orchestras around the world. Here, you'll see the classic favorites that have enchanted operagoers for centuries—*Othello*, *Don Giovanni*, and *Carmen*.

Each year, the company sponsors the Palm Beach Opera Vocal Competition, introducing audiences to outstanding new talent. This competition, open to anyone in North America, was established in 1969. And many of its winners have gone on to achieve international recognition. Palm Beach Opera also has a Young Artist Program for emerging professional opera singers. This endows emerging talent with a five-month residency here, allowing them to polish up their performance skills while learning from the professionals. Young Artists are also featured in the company's One Opera in One Hour Series, which gives the public a taste of opera in a non-traditional setting, at the Harriett Himmel Theater at City Place.

PALM BEACH POPS
500 South Australian Ave., Suite 100
West Palm Beach
(561) 832-7677
www.palmbeachpops.org
The house lights dim and the spotlight comes on, as Maestro Bob Lappin, one of South Florida's cultural icons, takes his place on stage. He taps his baton, and the Palm Beach Pops is off on another upbeat, contagious romp through the Great American Songbook. From Gershwin to Goodman, Tin Pan Alley to Broadway, and Judy Garland to Frank Sinatra, the Palm Beach Pops takes you on a musical journey through the songs of your life and the songs of American history.

Founded in 1991 by Lappin, The Palm Beach Pops didn't take long to distinguish itself as a world-class pops orchestra. Its first three concerts drew a total of 6,000. Soon after, James Taylor invited The Palm Beach Pops to appear with him in concert at the Kravis Center. The following year, the Pops received national recognition when it was invited to perform at Lincoln Center in New York City—a first for a Florida orchestra. Since then, the orchestra and its reputation have continued to grow, expanding the number of patrons and concerts each season. Currently, Bob Lappin and The Palm Beach Pops perform 36 concerts at the Kravis Center, Florida Atlantic University Performing Arts Center in Boca Raton, and Eissey Campus Theatre at the Palm Beach State College campus in Palm Beach Gardens.

In 2006 the orchestra recorded its first commercial CD, *Yours is My Heart Alone*, which garnered both public and critical acclaim. And selections from this compilation of beautiful love songs have been featured on XM radio's *Frank Place*, Dick Robinson's *American Standards by the Sea*, the Dick Carr program, and other syndicated radio programs.

Over the years, Bob Lappin and The Palm Beach Pops orchestra have performed with guest artists such as Doc Severinsen, Mel Tormé, Hal Linden, Lena Horne, Maureen McGovern, Ricky Skaggs and Kentucky

Thunder, The Mills Brothers, The Count Basie Orchestra, Cleo Laine and John Dankworth, Judy Collins, jazz legends Bucky Pizzarelli and John Pizzarelli.

North County

FLORIDA CLASSICAL BALLET THEATRE AT THE ESTER CENTER
10357 Ironwood Rd.
Palm Beach Gardens
(561) 630-8235
www.fcbt.org
Florida Classical Ballet Theatre is a not-for-profit company committed to the goal of preserving classical ballet and enriching the local community through the ethereal beauty of this art. Its 2010 calendar reflected its stated goals, including performances such as *For Such a Time as This: The Story of Esther, Giselle, A Midsummer Nights Dream and other Dances,* and *The Nutcracker.* Artistic director Colleen Smith has been applauded for the quality of her productions, and she works with a couple of talented artists-in-residence.

The company recently went on its first overseas trip, to Budapest, Hungary, and won plaudits for its eight performances. They performed *The Story of Queen Esther* and *Grace* in two prisons, a coffeehouse, a restored old cinema, and even a subway station. Florida Classical Ballet Theatre has both a Senior Ensemble and a Junior Ensemble.

ART GALLERIES

People who visit here for the first time are always pleasantly surprised at the number of art galleries in Palm Beach County—and at the quality of their displays. But, when you think about it, it makes a lot of sense. South Florida still is "new"; there wasn't much here a hundred years ago, in contrast to most of the rest of America. And, in many ways, there's still something of an entrepreneurial, pioneer spirit here, in the arts as well as in other fields. And south Florida's artists are producing world-class work in a wide variety of fields.

There's also another good reason for the width and depth of the art galleries you can find here. Most folks in South Florida are from somewhere else (those places where there *was* a lot there a hundred years ago). Many come from urban areas with great arts amenities. And, when they got down here, they demanded the same. And they got it—in all the artistic and performance fields.

In Palm Beach County, you can see the great Impressionists, cubism, surrealism, abstractionism, Southwestern, Caribbean, old masters, new masters, and amazing works in more media than you can count, among them glass, ceramics, woods, fibers, sand, composite, marble, granite, soapstone, onyx, metals, wax, papier-mâché, seaweed, coral, rock, and on and on. You can see glass that's almost like looking through a kaleidoscope; you can see imaginative creations made with natural materials; you can see talented newcomers, and world-famous masters.

SOUTH COUNTY

ADDISON GALLERY
345 West Plaza Real
Boca Raton
(561) 338-9007
www.addisongallery.com
This is a long-time, very prestigious Boca space that specializes in representing the finest in contemporary realism, Impressionism and abstract art.

AVALON GALLERY
425 E. Atlantic Ave.
Delray Beach
(561) 272-9155
www.avalononatlantic.com/about.htm

Here, you'll find an extensive collection of the best American art and crafts, in a beautiful space that invites art-lovers to really indulge their passions.

FORMS GALLERY
415 East Atlantic Ave.
Delray Beach
(561) 274-3676
www.formsgallery.com
If you like Southwest art, visit Forms. But be prepared for some very unusual "forms" of Southwest art. There are certainly some traditional touches here, such as painted

gourds, turquoise jewelry, peace pipes, kiva ladders, and ceremonial items. But most of the art is more avant-garde Southwestern, bringing a modern touch to a classic art form.

ELAINE BAKER GALLERY
608 Banyan Trail
Boca Raton
(561) 241-3050
www.elainebakergallery.com
Elaine Baker has been a force in the South County art scene for many years. This gallery specializes in displaying quality paintings, sculpture, and major works on paper.

GRIFFIN GALLERY
608 Banyan Trail
Boca Raton
(561) 994-0811
www.griffingallery.net
This is an unusual gallery in an area that always seems to be racing toward the future. There are more than 500 authentic artifacts here, including tools and pottery, reflecting the civilizations of the ancient world.

KEN MCPHERRIN INTERNATIONAL
   GALLERY
4851 North Dixie Hwy.
Boca Raton
(561) 417-9122
www.kevinmcpherrin.com/about.htm
The gallery represents the work of 14 artists from nine countries. These particular artists work in very different forms, media, and styles, and each piece is unique. The styles range from European transitional pieces to cutting-edge abstracts to photo-realistic figurines.

PAVO REAL GALLERY
6000 Glades Rd.
Boca Raton
(561) 392-5521
www.pavoreal.com
Boca has many unique galleries, representing a wide variety of art forms and subject matter. But this is one of the most unique. Established in 1976, Pavo Real Gallery is a vivid celebration of the animal form—both realistic and surrealistic—in sculpture and jewelry.

SALVATORE PRINCIPE
200 N.E. Second Ave., Store #106
Delray Beach
(561) 278-1557
www.salvatoreprincipe.com
Salvatore Principe's creates distinctive and whimsical works on canvas in his Signature Heart's Collection.

SPOTTED ON 2ND GALLERY
200 N.E. Second Ave.
CityWalk Building, #102
Delray Beach
(561) 272-2220
www.spottedon2nd.com
This is a colorful craft arts gallery highlighting American crafts and American craftspeople. It carries the work of over a hundred talented American artists in a variety of media. The selection includes jewelry, ceramics, glass, metal, wood, and original and limited-edition prints.

SUNDOOK FINE ART GALLERIES
8903 W. Glades Rd., Suite K-2
Boca Raton
(561) 852-0017
www.sundook.com

Sundook Galleries has been a West Boca fixture for many years, for both the quantity and the quality of its art. Here you'll find original paintings, limited-editions, bronze and acrylic sculptures, all from the highly acclaimed artists around the world. They also do framing.

CENTRAL COUNTY

CLAY GLASS METAL STONE COOPERATIVE GALLERY
605 Lake Ave.
Lake Worth
www.clayglassmetalstone.com
The Flamingo Clay Studio is a not-for-profit collective of clay, glass, metal, and stone artists. It is a gallery as well as a workspace, and, if you're lucky, you'll see some of the artists at work here. And you'll see some very unusual shapes, forms, and angles.

EATON FINE ART
435 Gardenia St.
West Palm Beach
(561) 833-4766
http://eatonart.net
This gallery specializes in 19th-century, 20th-century, and contemporary American and European fine art, including paintings, sculpture, photographs, drawings, prints, mixed media works, installations, video, and film.

GALLERY VIA VENETO
250 Worth Ave.
Palm Beach
(561) 835-1399
www.princemonyo.com
This is a special place, a special gallery, on a special street. Galleries on Worth Avenue must have distinctive collections or else they won't be galleries on Worth Avenue for long. The specialties in this one are bronze sculptures and paintings.

GASIUNASEN GALLERY
415 Hibiscus Ave.
Palm Beach
(561) 820-8920
www.gasiunasengallery.com/html/home.asp
The gallery offers artworks from some of the most famous artists in history, among them Pablo Picasso, Marc Chagall, and Henri Matisse. Gasiunasen Gallery is also one of the few galleries in Palm Beach that carries the works of Fernando Botero, the popular Latin American artist known for his whimsical rotund figures.

HOLDEN LUNTZ GALLERY
256 Worth Ave.
Palm Beach
(561) 805-9550
www.holdenluntz.com
The art of photography is the specialty here. Holden Luntz Gallery exhibits a broad range of vintage and contemporary American and European photographers, all of whom have left a definitive stamp on the development of this medium.

LIMAN STUDIOS—PALM BEACH
139 North County Rd.
Palm Beach
(561) 659-7050
www.limangallery.com
This is art of the current times, and of the future. There are fascinating, multi-faceted, multimedia exhibits that change with the seasons.

MARGOT STEIN GALLERY
512 Lucerne Ave.
Lake Worth
(561) 582-5770
www.margotsteingallery.com

Margot Stein Gallery has a reputation for collecting fine artworks from interesting artists. The gallery features painting, sculpture, and works on paper by major post-War and contemporary artists.

MARY WOERNER FINE ARTS
3700 South Dixie Hwy. #6
West Palm Beach
(561) 832-3233
www.marywoernerfinearts.com
Mary Woerner Fine Arts represents a group of contemporary artists working in a variety of styles. As you roam around this gallery, you'll find some interesting surprises, in media such as paintings, drawings, sculpture, collage, photography, and original graphics.

ROBERT ST. CROIX SCULPTURE STUDIO
1400 Alabama Ave.
West Palm Beach
(561) 832-3933
www.robertstcroix.com/contemporary_sculpture
Robert St. Croix has been creating wonderful bronze sculptures for nearly 40 years, and you can see it all in this studio. Here, you can take what the artist calls a "kaleidoscopic journey" into his world, and into his art.

SUROVEK PRINT GALLERY
Via Parigi
Palm Beach
(561) 655-2665
www.surovekgallery.com
The John H. Surovek gallery specializes in American paintings, drawings, watercolors, and prints of the 19th and 20th centuries, in everything from portraits to landscapes to villages to seaports.

WALLY FINDLAY GALLERIES
165 Worth Ave.
Palm Beach
(561) 655-2090
www.wallyfindlay.com
Wally Findlay Galleries is a fixture on Worth Avenue, and no art buyer or collector worth his salt would even consider not stopping here. It's considered one of the foremost authorities on the French School of Rouen. In addition, while specializing in French Impressionist and Post-Impressionist masters, the gallery also exclusively represents a group of distinguished contemporary artists, both European and American.

NORTH COUNTY

ART GALLERY
Eissey Campus of Palm Beach State College
Palm Beach Gardens
(561) 207-5015
www.pbcc.edu
North Palm Beach County arts lovers have been streaming for years to the Palm Beach Gardens campus of Palm Beach State College. And this gallery is one of the reasons. The art is innovative, multi-faceted, interesting, and unusual.

CLEARVIEW GALLERIES
11345 Legacy Ave.
Palm Beach Gardens
(561) 622-3700
www.clearviewgalleries.com
ClearView Galleries specializes in original paintings, sculpture, and fine-quality giclees (reproductions on canvas) by well-known artists from around the country and around the world.

DUBLIN KAHN ART GALLERY
1201 US 1
North Palm Beach
(561) 630-6862
http://dublinkahnart.com
The gallery features noted artists such as Harry McCormick, Joseph Rensaw, and Gardani. They also have a wide collection of Fine Art etchings, engravings and lithographs of the 20th-century masters, including works by Renoir, Picasso, Chagall, Rembrandt, Miró, Calder, and Dali.

MIRASOL ART & FRAME GALLERY
Mirasol Walk
6231 PGA Blvd.
Palm Beach Gardens
(561) 799-3772
http://mirasolartframe.net
This gallery offers a large selection of original art, including oil paintings, sculpture, fine art glass, and original hand-embellished photo frames from the world's leading artists.

ONESIMMO FINE ART
4530 PGA Blvd., Suite 101
Palm Beach Gardens
(561) 355-8061
www.onessimofineart.com/index.html
This gallery features a wide variety of pieces of choices of genres, ranging from Old and Modern Masters to contemporary artists whose work has won renown and whose value is well-established.

ROSETTA STONE FINE ART GALLERY
1001 Jupiter Park Dr., Suites 121 & 122
Jupiter
(561) 743-3340
www.rosettastonefineart.com
The owner of Rosetta Stone is internationally known artist J. B. Berkow, who has carefully selected high-caliber works from emerging and mid-career artists from all over the world for her North County gallery. Whether your taste is classical or contemporary, whether you prefer painting or sculpture, you'll find something here that you like, that says who you are, and that inspires you.

WENTWORTH GALLERIES
3101 PGA Blvd.
Palm Beach Gardens
(561) 624-0656
www.wentworthgallery.com
Wentworth is known for the width and breath of its collections, and the choices that affords the people who roam its colorful aisles. The gallery carries some of the most collected artists in the world, such as Peter Max, Alexandra Nechita, Paul Stanley, Charles Fazzino, David Schluss, and Grace Slick (yes, that Grace Slick, of Jefferson Airplane fame, and, in her "second life," an accomplished artist), as well as Masters like Chagall, Picasso, Pissaro, Matisse, Renoir, and Miro. Wentworth travels far and wide to find talented new artists whose works are sold exclusively through them.

RECREATION

In an area that fronts the Atlantic Ocean on one side and the Everglades on the other—and is sunny all year long—you'd expect to find an incredible array of recreational opportunities. And you'd be right. In Palm Beach County, you'll find world-famous sailing, fishing, and golf, of course. But you'll also find other delightful diversions, and you can do them on sandy beach coves and on horizon-piercing wetlands, in the waves of the Atlantic or the calm of the Intracoastal, on the mainland or on islands, and on land or in the air. The climate plays a role in the recreational choices and the participatory activities, but not as much as you think. You can still run or play golf or go biking during the summer; just make sure you do it early in the morning.

BIKING

Bike Paths:

- **Caloosa Park,** Boynton Beach, (561) 736-2812; www.co.palm-beach.fl.us/parks/locations/caloosa.htm
- **Dyer Park,** 7301 Haverhill Rd. N, West Palm Beach; (561) 966-6600; www.pbc gov.com
- **Glades Pioneer Park,** Belle Glade, (561) 924-2728; www.pbcgov.com
- **John Prince Park,** Lake Worth, (561) 582-7992; www.pbcgov.com

Mountain Biking:

- **Dyer Park**—4.7-mile, single-track perimeter trail; 2.4-mile, single-track trail on the Hill. The Hill trail is built upon the face of a previous landfill, which has been converted into a natural setting and then transformed into a winding, climbing/descending single-track trail—the only location in South Florida with appreciable climbs and descents.

- **Okeeheelee Park**—The trail head is located on the east side of Pinehurst Drive, south of Forest Hill Boulevard; 3.2-mile, single-track trail for intermediate riders with beginner bypasses.

BOATING

Boat Rentals:

- **Okeeheelee Park Rentals,** West Palm Beach, canoe, kayak, and paddleboat rentals; (561) 582-7992; www.pbcgov .com
- **Riverbend Park Rentals,** Jupiter, (561) 746-7053, www.pbcgov.com

Boat Charters

- **Black Dog Fishing Charters,** Jupiter; (561) 744-5700; www.blackdogfishing .com
- **Deep Sea Drift Fishing Charters,** West Palm Beach; (561) 628-6302; www.west palmbeach.com/activities/charter.php

- **Final Pursuit Charters,** West Palm Beach; (561) 352-6314; www.finalpursuit charters.com
- **Fish Addict Charters,** Boca Raton; (561) 212-8928
- **Natural Sportfishing Charters,** Palm Beach; (561) 379-7306; http://palm-beach-fishing-charters.com

BOWLING

- **AMF Boynton Beach Lanes,** 1190 W. Boynton Beach Blvd., Boynton Beach; (561) 734-1500
- **Greenacres Bowl Inc.,** 6126 Lake Worth Rd., Greenacres; (561) 968-0100
- **Jupiter Lanes,** 350 Maplewood Dr., Jupiter; (561) 743-9200
- **Palm Beach Strike Zone,** 6591 S. Military Trail, Lake Worth; (561) 968-7000
- **Strike Zone of Boca,** 21046 Commercial Trail, Boca Raton; (561) 368- 2177
- **Verdes Tropicana Bowling Lanes,** 1801 Belvedere Rd., West Palm Beach; (561) 683-5424

CAMPING

- **John Prince Park Campground,** (561) 582-7992; www.co.palm-beach.fl.us/ parks/camping/johnprincepark/
- **Peanut Island Campground,** (561) 845-4445; www.co.palm-beach.fl.us/parks/ peanutisland/campground.htm

CANOEING/KAYAKING

Canoe Rentals (and information about where to go canoeing):

- **Adventure Times Kayaks,** 521 Northlake Blvd., North Palm Beach; (561) 881-7218; www.kayakkayak.com

- **Canoe Outfitters of Florida,** 9060 West Indiantown Rd., Jupiter; (561) 746-7053; www.canoeskayaksflorida.com
- **Jupiter Outdoor Center,** 1000 Coastal A1A, Jupiter; (561) 747-0063; www.jupiter outdoorcenter.com
- **Visit Palm Beach,** 110 Tenth St., Lake Park; (561) 881-9757; www.visitpalm beach.com

Kayak Rentals (and information about where to go kayaking):

- **Adventure Times Kayaks,** 521 Northlake Blvd., North Palm Beach; (561) 881-7218; www.kayakkayak.com
- **Canoe Outfitters of Florida—Canoe-ing and kayaking on the Loxahatchee River;** (561) 746-7053; www.canoes kayaksflorida.com

DIVING/SNORKELING

- **Force-e Scuba Diving and Snorkel-ing,** Riviera Beach; (561) 845-2333; www .force-e.com/stores/palm_beach_scuba_ center.shtml
- **Narcosis Dive Charters,** Riviera Beach; (561) 630-0606; www.narcosisdive charters.com
- **Peanut Island Snorkeling Tour,** Keylypso of the Palm Beaches; (561) 718-2723; www.westpalmbeach.com
- **Scuba-Adventures,** Palm Beach; (888) 901-DIVE; www.scuba-adventures.com/ index.php
- **Splashdown Divers,** Boynton Beach; (877) 736-0712; www.splashdowndivers .com
- **Sunstar Aquatic Services,** Boca Raton; (561) 368-9952; www.diveboca.net/ contact.html

FISHING

- **Captain Steve's Fishing Charters,** 200 East 13th St., Riviera Beach; (561) 236-2387; www.fishsteve.com
- **Sea Mist III,** 700 Casa Loma Blvd., Boynton Beach; (561) 732-9974; www.seamist3.com
- **Slim's Marina,** Tory Island Road, Belle Glade; (561) 996-3268; www.fl-camping-review.com

GOLF

Palm Beach County is home of the Professional Golfers Association (PGA), which has several championship courses at its Palm Beach Gardens headquarters. In addition, there are a number of other notable courses scattered throughout the county. At last count, Palm Beach County had more than 140 golf courses. Some of them, of course, are private. For your convenience, we've listed some public courses in the three main areas of the county, as well as country clubs that accept outside players.

South County

BOCA DUNES GOLF & COUNTRY CLUB
1400 Country Club Dr.
Boca Raton
(561) 451-1600
www.bocadunes.com
Eighteen-hole public course designed by Bruce Devlin/Robert von Hagge that opened in 1970. Tee times can be made up to three days in advance. Walking not allowed. Soft spikes only. Lighted driving range, lessons and memberships available. Don Law Golf Improvement Center, (561) 451-1128.

i For golfers—If you hit a ball into the water, do not go in after it! Repeat, do not go in after it. Alligators spend most of their time in water, or seeking out water. And they're not all that particular about the location of the water they choose. Forget about the ball. Forget about any stroke-penalty. It's not worth losing an arm—or worse!

DELRAY BEACH GOLF CLUB
2200 Highland Ave.
Delray Beach
(561) 243-7380
www.jcdsportsgroup.com/delray_beach_golf_club/index.html
Delray Beach Golf Club is a 1923 Donald Ross design located off of Atlantic Avenue just 3 miles west of the historic Downtown Delray Beach area. This jewel is a meticulously manicured championship track, and features 6,907 yards and a par-72. Delray Beach Golf Club is the home of many of the most prestigious special events in the area, including the annual Jameson Classic Pro-Am, and the annual Beth Daniel Clinic. Delray Beach Golf Club is a full service operation, with a driving range, putting area, lesson programs, and full restaurant, bar/lounge, and banquet facilities.

LAKEVIEW GOLF CLUB
1200 Dover Rd.
Delray Beach
(561) 498-3229
www.jcdsportsgroup.com/lakeview/index.html
Lakeview Golf Club is an Executive Golf Course, and is a par-60 spanning 3,006 yards. This 1972 classic is in exceptional condition with phenomenal greens, and is a favorite for beginners, senior golfers, and juniors.

POLO TRACE GOLF CLUB
14379 Hagen Ranch Rd.
Delray Beach
(561) 495-5300
www.polotracegolf.com
Eighteen-hole, semiprivate course, designed by Karl Litten and Joey Sindelar that opened in 1983. Tee Times may be reserved up to one week in advance. Full time club memberships available. Polo Trace Golf Academy lessons available.

SOUTHWINDS GOLF COURSE
19557 Lyons Rd.
Boca Raton
(561) 483-1305
www.jcdsportsgroup.com/southwinds/index.html
Southwinds Golf Course is a beautiful par-70 located just minutes from the Gold Coast beaches of the Atlantic in the heart of Boca Raton.

VILLA DEL RAY GOLF CLUB
6200 Via Delray
Delray
(561) 498-1444
www.villadelraygc.com
Tucked away in west Delray Beach, South Palm Beach County, where golf is at a premium, this 18-hole semiprivate course offers a tremendous value. Designed in 1971, by Frank Batto, this course is set amid Florida wildlife and recognized as one of the finest in the area. During the season, tee times may be reserved up to three days in advance. Please note, the course allows only soft spikes. Villa del Ray also offers a driving range, putting green, full service restaurant, snack bar, and the Good Start Golf School.

Central County

ATLANTIS COUNTRY CLUB
190 Atlantis Blvd.
Atlantis
(561) 965-7700
www.atlantiscountryclub.com
An 18-hole course Robert Simmons designed in 1971. Tee times available five days in advance. Soft spikes only. Driving range, lessons, and memberships available.

BINKS FOREST GOLF CLUB
400 Binks Forest Dr.
Wellington
(561) 333-5731
www.binksforestgc.com
Eighteen-hole, daily-fee course was originally designed by Johnny Miller and Gene Bates in 1989 and redesigned by Gene Bates in 2007. Tee times available seven days in advance. Soft spikes only. Driving range, lessons, and memberships available. Host course for the Gateway Tour and of the Golf Channel Tour.

THE CLUB AT WINSTON TRAILS
6101 Winston Trails Blvd.
Lake Worth
(561) 439-3700
www.winstontrailsgolfclub.com
Eighteen-hole semiprivate course designed by Joe Lee that opened in 1992. Lessons and club memberships available. Practice range, soft spikes only.

CYPRESS CREEK COUNTRY CLUB
9400 Military Trail
Boynton Beach
(561) 732-4202
www.cypresscreekcountryclub.com
Eighteen-hole semiprivate course designed by Robert von Hagge that opened in 1964. Tee times can be reserved up to five days in

advance for the general public. Metal spikes not recommended. Walkers not allowed. Club memberships available.

GRAND LACUNA GOLF CLUB
6400 Lacuna Blvd.
Lake Worth
(561) 433-3006
www.grandlacuna.com/homepage/
start_page.php
An 18-hole public course designed by Joe Lee. Soft spikes only. Driving range, lessons, and memberships available. Fine, full-service restaurant.

LAKE WORTH GOLF CLUB
1 Seventh Ave. N.
Lake Worth
(561) 582-9713
www.lakeworthgolf.com
An 18-hole, par 70 municipal course designed by William Langford and Theodore J. Moreau that opened in 1926. Lessons and club memberships available. Metal spikes allowed. No driving range.

THE LINKS AT BOYNTON BEACH
8020 Jog Rd.
Boynton Beach
(561) 742-6501
www.boynton-beach.org/government/
departments/golf/index.html
An 18-hole and a 9-hole public course designed by Robert von Hagge and Devlin Charles. Soft spikes only. Driving range, lessons, and memberships available for Boynton Beach residents.

THE LINKS AT MADISON GREEN
2001 Crestwood Blvd. N.
Royal Palm Beach
(561) 784-5225
www.madisongreengolf.com

A public course designed by John Sanford with an additional four sets of tees. Driving range and Aqua Range available. Tee times can be reserved online. Individual and group lessons available. Junior Golf Academy also available.

LONE PINE GOLF CLUB
6251 N. Military Trail
West Palm Beach
(561) 842-0480
An 18-hole, par 62 (executive) public course. Soft spikes only. Driving range, lessons, and memberships available.

OKEEHEELEE GOLF COURSE
7715 Forest Hill Blvd.
West Palm Beach
(561) 964-GOLF
http://golfproservices.org/okeeheelee
.htm
A 27-hole public facility, which includes the Eagle, Osprey, and Heron courses. Tee times may be reserved up to four days in advance. Full service golf shop; adult and junior lessons are available.

PALM BEACH GOLF COURSE
2345 S. Ocean Blvd.
Palm Beach
(561) 547-0598
www.golfontheocean.com
An 18-hole, public, par-3 course designed by Dick Wilson that opened in 1960. Tee times are not reserved. Driving range and lessons are available.

PALM BEACH NATIONAL GOLF & COUNTRY CLUB
7500 St. Andrews Rd.
Lake Worth
(561) 965-3381
www.palmbeachnational.com

Eighteen-hole semiprivate course designed by Joe Lee that opened in 1965. Tee times can be reserved up to seven days in advance. Metal spikes not allowed. Club memberships available.

THE VILLAGE GOLF CLUB
122 Country Club Dr.
Royal Palm Beach
(561) 793-1400
www.thevillagegolfclub.com
An 18-hole public course designed by Mark Mahannah that opened in 1968. Driving range and lessons are available.

WELLINGTON GOLF & COUNTRY CLUB
1900 Aero Club Dr.
Wellington
(561) 795-3510
A 36-hole semiprivate course designed by Ted McAnlis and Johnny Miller. Tee times can be reserved up to four days in advance. Players can walk the Lakes Course any time. Soft spikes only. Driving range, lessons, and memberships available.

WESTCHESTER GOLF AND COUNTRY CLUB
12250 Westchester Club Dr.
Boynton Beach
(561) 734-6300
An 18-hole semiprivate course designed by Bruce Devlin/Robert von Hagge that opened in 1989. Tee times can be made up to four days in advance for non-members and up to seven days in advance for members. Soft spikes only. Driving range, lessons, and memberships are available. No walking. Don Law Golf Improvement Center, (561) 451-1128.

WEST PALM BEACH GOLF COURSE
7001 Parker Ave.
West Palm Beach
(561) 582-2019
www.jcdsportsgroup.com/west_palm_beach/index.html
An 18-hole, public, par-3 course designed by Dick Wilson that opened in 1960. Tee times are not reserved. Driving range and lessons are available.

North County

ABACOA GOLF CLUB
105 Barbados Dr.
Jupiter
(561) 622-0036
www.abacoagolfclub.com
An 18-hole public course designed by Joe Lee that opened in 1999. Tee times may be reserved up to 30 days in advance. Soft spikes only. Driving range, lessons, and memberships available.

GOLF CLUB AT JUPITER
1800 Central Blvd.
Jupiter
(561) 747-6262
www.golfclubofjupiter.com
An 18-hole public course designed by Lamar Smith that opened in 1981. Driving range, lessons, and memberships available.

JUPITER DUNES GOLF CLUB
401 N. A1A
Jupiter
(561) 746-6654
www.jupiterdunesgolf.com
An 18-hole par-54 public course designed by Bob Erickson. Soft spikes only. Lessons and memberships available.

NORTH PALM BEACH COUNTRY CLUB
951 US 1
North Palm Beach
(561) 691-3433
www.village-npb.org
An 18-hole semiprivate course designed in 1926. Soft spikes only. Driving range, lessons, and memberships available. Walking allowed for members and North Palm Beach residents only. Tee times available five days in advance, seven days for members.

PALM BEACH GARDENS GOLF CLUB
11401 Northlake Blvd.
Palm Beach Gardens
(561) 626-PUTT (626-7888)
www.pbgfl.com/content/76/138/default
.aspx
An 18-hole public course carved out of the Loxahatchee Natural Preserve. Tee times may be made seven days in advance, 14 days for Palm Beach Gardens residents. Soft spikes only. Driving range, lessons, and memberships available. Walking is allowed after 3 p.m.

GOLF SCHOOLS

BOCA GOLF ACADEMY CLINIC
501 East Camino Real Rd.
Boca Raton
(561) 447-3419
www.bocaresort.com/resort_activities/
dave_pelz_scoring.cfm
The Boca Raton Resort is home to a Dave Pelz Scoring Game School. This unique facility is dedicated to teaching golfers the finer points of chipping, pitching, sand play, putting, all from 100 yards.

THE BREAKERS GOLF ACADEMY
2 South County Rd.
Palm Beach
(561) 659-8474
www.thebreakers.com/golf/academy
The Breakers' professional academy staff offers world-class private golf instruction, school, and clinics all aimed at improving the golf experience. Plus, personal video analysis, on-course instruction, club fitting geared toward corporate golf programs, and Junior Golf Academy.

THE INTERNATIONAL GOLF SCHOOL
The Village Golf Club
122 Country Club Dr.
Royal Palm Beach
(561) 793-1400
http://pavisnet.com/igs
Offers professional "total game" instruction for individuals, couples, and small groups in privately scheduled half-day sessions, with a certified PGA of America instructor/coach. Winter season availability only.

JOHN PRINCE GOLF LEARNING CENTER
4754 South Congress Ave.
Lake Worth
(561) 966-6666
http://pbcgov.com/parks/sports/golf
This is a lighted, 42-station driving range with a practice fairway bunker. Also available are three regulation practice holes and 16,000 square feet of practice greens, featuring top-ranked LPGA and PGA instructors.

PGA NATIONAL GOLF ACADEMY
400 Avenue of the Champions
Palm Beach Gardens
(561) 627-2000
www.pgaresort.com/404.aspx?aspxerror
path=/golf/pga_golf_academy.aspx

Located on-property, the PGA National Golf Academy provides an individualized, results-oriented experience to golfers of all skill levels. The PGA National Golf Academy is a first-of-its-kind golf instruction program featuring the top two instructors in the world, Dave Pelz and David Leadbetter.

GYMNASIUMS

- **Jupiter Fitness Center,** 1200 W. Indiantown Rd., Jupiter; (561) 575-2622; www.jupiterfitness.com
- **Lantana Fitness,** 700 W. Lantana Rd., Lantana; (561) 585-3300; www.lantanafitness.com
- **Peter Blum Family YMCA of Boca Raton,** 6631 Palmetto Circle South, Boca Raton; (561) 395-9622; www.ymcaspbc.org

HORSEBACK RIDING

- **Delray Beach,** (561) 499-6383
- **Free Spirit Riding Academy and Show Stables,** 16028 Rustic Rd., Wellington; (561) 352-3301; www.riding-in-wellington.com/index.html
- **Johnson's Folly Horse Farm,** 14052 Fifty-second Ave. South; www.johnsonsfolly.com
- **Wandering Trails Riding Academy,** 5705 Hood Rd., Palm Beach Gardens; (561) 622-8130; www.wanderingtrails.com

LITTLE LEAGUE

- **Boca Raton Little League,** 1 South Ocean Blvd., Boca Raton; (561) 750-8755; www.hometeamsonline.com

- **Delray Beach American Little League,** Delray Beach; (561) 243-7250; www.mydelraybeach.com
- **East Boynton Beach Little League,** Little League Park, Boynton Beach; (561) 732-6712; www.eastboyntonll.com
- **Jupiter–Tequesta Athletic Association,** P.O. Box 3024, Tequesta; www.jtaa.org/baseball

MARTIAL ARTS

- **Palm Beach Boxing and Mixed Martial Arts,** 1611 N. Military Trail, West Palm Beach; (561) 833-2131; www.palmbeachboxingcenter.com
- **Ultima Fitness,** Xtreme Tae Kwon Do, 12799 West Forest Hill Blvd., Wellington; (561) 795-2823; www.ultimafitness.com
- **XF Martial Arts,** 2875 S. Congress Ave., Delray Beach; (561) 276-1774; www.xfmartialarts.com

RACQUETBALL

- **Sand Pine Park,** 300 Newcastle St. N.E., Boca Raton
- **South County Regional Park,** 11200 Park Access Rd., Boca Raton
- **Powerhouse Gym Aerobics & Racquetball Club,** 6900 Okeechobee Blvd., West Palm Beach; (561) 687-4611; www.powerhousegym.com

ROWING

- **North Palm Beach Rowing,** 13425 Ellison Wilson Rd. Bert Winter's Park, Juno Beach; (561) 309-9966; www.npbrc.com
- **Palm Beach Rowing,** 2957 N. Australian Ave., West Palm Beach; (561) 848-1767; www.palmbeachrowing.org

RUGBY

- **Boca Raton Buccaneers Rugby Club,** (800) 123-4567; www.bocaratonrugby.com.

SAILING

- **Biscayne Lady Yacht Charters,** (800) 910-5119; www.biscaynelady.com/palm-beach/palm-beach-boat-rentals.php
- **Delray Beach Water Sports Rentals,** 400 S. Ocean Blvd., Delray Beach; (561) 279-0008; www.delraybeachwatersports.com
- **Old Port Cove Marina,** 112 Lakeshore Dr., North Palm Beach; (561) 626-1760; www.opch.com

SKATING

- **Atlantis Skateway,** 3100 Jog Rd., Greenacres; (561) 964-4300; www.atlantisskateway.com
- **Palm Beach Skate Zone,** 8125 Lake Worth Rd., Lake Worth; (561) 963-5900; www.pbskatezone.com

SOCCER

- **Royal Palm Beach**—Individual players can register for men's (ages 40 and older) and women's leagues (ages 18 and older) at the Royal Palm Beach Recreation Center, 100 Sweet Bay Lane; (561) 790-5124; www.royalpalmbeach.com. Games are played on Sunday at Katz Fields. The season begins in Feb.

SOFTBALL

- **Boca Raton Softball Association,** (561) 361-8477; www.bocasoftball.com

- **Palm Beach Gardens Youth Athletic Association,** Palm Beach Gardens; (561) 627-9665; www.pbgsoftball.com
- **Palm Beach Senior Softball Association,** pbssa@pbssa.org; www.pbssa.org

SOFTBALL LEAGUES

- **The Gumbo Limbo Adult Women's Slow-Pitch Softball League**—Games are played in central Palm Beach County. Interested players or teams should contact raynboleague@aol.com or (561) 758-8082.
- **The Okeeheelee Senior Softball Association**—Practices are held at 9 a.m. on Tues and Thurs at Okeeheelee Park. The 55-and-older slow-pitch league begins its season Jan. For applications and more information, call Alvin Segal at (561) 478-4534.
- **The Palm Beach County Department of Parks & Recreation** runs men's softball leagues at three county parks—John Prince Park, Okeeheelee Park, and South County Regional Park; pbcparks@co.palm-beach.fl.us.
- **Royal Palm Beach Parks & Recreation**—Adult softball leagues: men's, women's, co-ed; (561) 790-5124.
- **West Boynton Park and Recreation Center**—Adult softball leagues; (561) 355-1125; www.co.palm-beach.fl.us/parks/recreationcenters/westboynton/.

SPORTS ORGANIZATIONS

- **Jupiter-Tequesta Athletic Association,** P.O. Box 3024, Tequesta; www.jtaa.org
- **Palm Beach County Sports Commission,** 1555 Palm Beach Lakes Blvd., Suite 1410, West Palm Beach; (561) 233-3180; www.palmbeachsports.com

- **Palm Beach Gardens Youth Athletic Association,** Palm Beach Gardens; (561) 627-9665; www.pbgyaa.com

SWIMMING

- **Aqua Crest Pool,** 2503 Seacrest Blvd., Delray Beach; (561) 278-7104; www.pbcgov.com/parks/aquatics/pools/aquacrest/index.htm
- **Lake Lytal Park,** 3645 Gun Club Rd., West Palm Beach; (561) 233-1426; www.pbcgov.com/parks/aquatics/pools/lakelytal/index.htm
- **Meadows Park Pool,** 1300 N.W. Eighth St., Boca Raton; (561) 393-7851; www.ci.boca-raton.fl.us/rec/pools/meadows.shtm
- **Peter Blum Family YMCA of Boca Raton,** 6631 Palmetto Circle South, Boca Raton; (561) 395-9622; www.ymcaspbc.org

TENNIS

- **Delray Beach Tennis Center,** 201 West Atlantic Ave., Delray Beach; (561) 243-7360; www.jcdsportsgroup.com/delray_beach_tennis/contact_us.htm
- **Patch Reef Park,** 2000 Yamato Rd., Boca Raton; (561) 997-0881; www.ci.boca-raton.fl.us/rec/parks/patchreef.shtm?7
- **South County Regional Park,** 11200 Park Access Rd., Boca Raton; www.pbcgov.com/parks/locations/south_county_regional.htm
- **Wellington Tennis Center,** 12165 West Forest Hill Blvd., Wellington; (561) 753-2484 ext. 4777; www.ci.wellington.fl.us/html/Departments/ParksRec/Parks_Facilities/tennis_center.html

WAVE RUNNING

- **Blue Water Powerboat Rentals,** 200 East Thirteenth St., Riviera Beach; (561) 840-7470; www.bluewaterboatrental.com
- **Intracoastal Jet Ski Rentals,** 106 N.E. Sixth St., Boynton Beach; (561) 735-0612; www.wavejumpers.com
- **Jupiter Inlet Boat Rentals,** 1095 N. A1A; (561) 741-1212; www.jupiterinletboatrentals.com/jet.htm

WIND SURFING

- **Delray Beach Water Sports Rentals,** 400 S. Ocean Blvd., Delray Beach; (561) 279-0008; www.delraybeachwatersports.com
- **Palm Beach Water Sports,** 3201 Tuxedo Ave., West Palm Beach; (561) 478-7171; www.palmbeachwatersportsflorida.com

YOGA

- **Bikram Yoga Boca Raton,** 21073 Powerline Rd., Boca Raton; (561) 451-8845; www.bikramyogabocaraton.com
- **Bikram's Yoga College of India,** 1815 Parker Ave., West Palm Beach; (561) 366-0072; www.bikramwpb.com
- **YogaSol,** 215 N.E. Twenty-second St., Delray Beach; (561) 272-8699; www.yogasol.com

SPECTATOR SPORTS

You'd expect to find a wide variety of spectator sports in a region (South Florida) with nearly six million people. From professional through college, you'll find your sport—every sport, and great places to watch them—in or near Palm Beach County.

There was a time, however, several decades ago, when the only sports you could watch if you came to Palm Beach County were on the fields or courts of local high schools. Thanks to the explosive growth of the past 30 years, however, that's no longer the case. In fact, now, not only can you enjoy professional teams in every major sport, but you can also enjoy major-college teams in football and basketball, as well. And those high school games to which earlier visitors were restricted? Well, if you're a football fan, you may know that South Florida is considered one of the best spots in the country for high school football and a talent-rich recruiting ground for colleges all over the country. The same is true for high school basketball here. Many of today's major college and professional round-ball stars came from South Florida.

Today, the problem for sports-lovers is somewhat different than the one in earlier years. Today, the problem is that you couldn't possibly see it all, no matter how good you are with a calculator and a calendar.

PROFESSIONAL SPORTS

Baseball

FLORIDA MARLINS
Sun Life Stadium
2269 Dan Marino Blvd.
Miami Gardens
(305) 623-6100 (Sun Life Stadium)
Tickets: (877) MARLINS
www.sunlifestadium.com
www.floridamarlins.com

The Florida Marlins have probably had the most successful first two decades of just about any team in Major League history; they've already won two World Series championships, in 1997 and in 2003. They habitually produce young teams that are always exciting to watch, if not always in the thick of pennant races. The Marlins' big news of late,

actually, is that they're leaving Sun Life Stadium. It's a facility that was built for football, not baseball, and is not necessarily conducive to watching baseball games, or for the smaller crowds attracted by baseball (which, after all, has a 162-game schedule, as opposed to the 16 games of pro football). So "The Fish" are building themselves a new baseball stadium in downtown Miami, a modern showpiece with a partial roof on the land where the legendary Orange Bowl stood for 70 years. That new stadium will be ready for the 2012 season, and Miami fans are already watching it go up with great interest. When it opens, the Marlins will officially become the Miami Marlins, not the Florida Marlins.

In the meantime, it's still a jolly-good show at Sun Life Stadium, which is just off the Florida Turnpike, about 25 miles south of Palm Beach County. The stadium may not be ideal. But the game is still baseball. The Marlins still field exciting young teams. The crack of bat against ball—especially to real baseball fans—still sounds the same. And the hot dogs are still just as good.

JUPITER HAMMERHEADS
Roger Dean Stadium
4751 Main St.
Jupiter
(561) 775-1818
http://jupiter.hammerheads.milb.com

Minor League baseball is alive and well in Palm Beach County, with affiliates of two Major League teams, the hometown Florida Marlins and the St. Louis Cardinals. (And if you're a New York Mets fan, the Mets train just up the road in Port St. Lucie, a very short drive from Palm Beach County.) Minor league games offer everything the Majors do but without the cost and without the traffic. The baseball's good, the beer's cold, the hot dogs are hot, and the fans really get into it. But, lest we forget . . . the Big Guys train here, as well. Both of the parent clubs, the Marlins and Cardinals, hold Spring Training here, and both play their home exhibition games here. So, if you're here in March, you'll get a sneak preview of what to expect from these two teams during the upcoming season.

PALM BEACH CARDINALS
Roger Dean Stadium
4751 Main St.
Jupiter
(561) 775-1818
http://palmbeach.cardinals.milb.com

Minor League Baseball; St. Louis Cardinals affiliate. The St. Louis Cardinals has one of the proudest histories—and possibly the best

fans—in baseball. In fact, Cardinals' baseball is almost like a religion back home by the big arch and the Mississippi River. You can watch the big club train here every spring, and play their home exhibition games here. And you can take a sneak peek at who might be playing under the arch in the near-future. A great family day, for a great family price.

Basketball

MIAMI HEAT
American Airlines Arena
601 Biscayne Blvd.
Miami
(786) 777-1250
www.miamiheat.com

The Miami Heat was born in 1988, and downtown Miami hasn't been the same since. Their presence has helped reinvigorate Miami, a city that now has one of the most impressive skylines in America.

The Heat won the National Basketball Association championship in 2006. When Shaquille O'Neal played for the team for a couple of years—including their championship season—it was virtually impossible to get tickets. However, the team's play has been inconsistent the past few years, and you can generally get seats—and often good seats—if you buy them in advance.

American Airlines Arena is in the heart of downtown Miami and holds 20,000 people. It's about an hour's drive from Boca Raton, approximately 50 miles south. Built in 2000 it is a comfortable place to watch a game, with good sightlines no matter where you're sitting. The arena is right across the street from Bayside, a harborside collection of funky shops and kiosks in a Caribbean-marketplace theme.

There's also a way that you can see the Heat before they actually start the season.

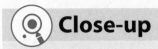

Close-up

Bucky Dent

If you're a fan of either the New York Yankees or the Boston Red Sox, and you're over 40, you remember Bucky Dent. On October 2, 1978, Bucky Dent broke the hearts of the Red Sox Nation. The Yankees and the Red Sox were in a one-game playoff to determine the winner of the American League East Division. In the top of the seventh, Bucky Dent—who had hit only four home runs all year—blasted one out of the ballpark, giving the Yankees the victory. And to this day New Englanders still speak of his name as "Bucky F***ing Dent."

Bucky Dent is still around—here in Palm Beach County. For years, he's been running the well-respected Bucky Dent's Baseball School in Delray Beach. The school is open to anyone, of any age. They'll teach you the fundamentals. They'll put you in a uniform and out on the field with professional coaches. You'll feel your spikes on the soft grass, and you'll hear, once again, that precious sound of childhood, of bat against ball. You'll meet Bucky, of course. And you'll probably meet some of the other ex-ballplayers who stop by from time to time. Who knows . . . if you grew up loving the game, this could be your "Field of Dreams." **Bucky Dent's Baseball School,** 490 Dotterel Rd, Delray Beach, FL 33444; (561) 265-0280; www.buckydent baseballschool.com.

They hold their pre-season training camp at Florida Atlantic University (FAU) in Boca Raton, and some of their practices are open to the public. The pro basketball season starts in Oct and runs into Apr (not including playoffs).

Football

MIAMI DOLPHINS
Sun Life Stadium
2269 Dan Marino Blvd.
Miami Gardens
(305) 623-6100
ds@dolphinstadium.com
www.sunlifestadium.com
www.miamidolphins.com

The Miami Dolphins were the pioneers of the South Florida sports scene and the first professional franchise in the region.

Their first season was 1966, and they were the laughingstock of the National Football League. They didn't stay that way for long, though, winning the Super Bowl in 1972 (when they were undefeated; as of this writing, they're still the only team in history to go through a season undefeated). Then they won the Super Bowl again in 1973. And, in so doing, they captured the hearts of South Florida sports fans forever. The Dolphins are still the dominant professional franchise in the region, even though the Super Bowl Victory in '73 was their last. Almost as soon as one season ends, the fans start talking about prospects for the following season.

Sun Life Stadium holds 77,000, and about 55,000 of those seats go to season ticket holders. However, there are generally a few tickets available as late as the week before the game. It's a nice place to watch a football game—and it's the focus of most of South Florida's attention on Game Days. The stadium is located about 25 miles south of Boca Raton, just off the Florida Turnpike. Traffic, as you might expect, is very dense on game days, so head out early if you've got tickets. And if the Dolphins are not having a particularly good season, you may even be able to walk up to the ticket window and get a ticket the day of the game—but don't count on it. If you do get in, you'll find yourself enveloped in sea of aqua and orange.

If you're in town in late-July and Aug, you can watch the Dolphins practice at their facility in the town of Davie, also about 25 miles south of Boca. The pro football season starts in early Sept and generally runs into the first week of Jan.

Hockey

FLORIDA PANTHERS
BankAtlantic Center
One Panther Parkway
Sunrise
(954) 835-PUCK
www.floridapanthers.com
Where you else can you drive to a major league hockey game with the top down, or the sunroof open? Where else can you take your jacket *off* when you leave the arena at the end of a game, rather than put it on? Although the Florida Panthers came into being in 1993, it still seems like a novelty for many fans—especially those who grew up in the northerly climes—to be able to do these things, and to walk out of the arena into a winter night that's 60 degrees and clear, with swirls of stars overhead, instead of into snow and ice.

The Panthers play in BankAtlantic Center, off the Sawgrass Expressway in the western-Broward County town of Sunrise. It's about a half-hour from southern Palm Beach County, and easily accessible off this wide, smoothly flowing highway. The arena is a modern, airy place with 20,000 seats. As of this writing, the Panthers haven't been in the playoffs for 10 years (even when they've had winning teams). As a result, even though they have a dedicated core of fans, there are generally some tickets available even on the day of the game. And the arena has a very exciting atmosphere, with cowbell-clanging fans who are very vocal in their support of the Cats. The arena is also very family-friendly, with special kids' fun zones and a lot of contests and activities to keep the younger set very involved. There are always a lot of fun things going on here, in fact, for adults, as well, including on-ice musical chairs, trivia contests, free prizes, etc. And the game of hockey itself is fast, intense, and colorful. The puck flies toward the goalie at upwards of 90 miles an hour, the hits are bone-jarring, and the skills of the players as they back-pedal on skates or weave through opposing defenders while still controlling a puck are breath-taking.

COLLEGE SPORTS
Basketball

FLORIDA ATLANTIC UNIVERSITY
  BASKETBALL
FAU Arena
777 Glades Rd.
Boca Raton
Ticket office: (866) FAU-OWLS
www.fausports.com
The Owls basketball teams—both men's and women's—play in modern, comfortable FAU Arena. It's a beautiful place, although a bit unusual in one respect—the most comfortable, padded seats actually in the upper

My Palm Beach County

"I love the beauty of living in Palm Beach County. We've lived in The Sanctuary (an exclusive area of Boca Raton) for over 25 years now. I've been walking the neighborhood about four times per week since we moved in. I love it . . . especially at sunset in the winter, when the sky is sprinkled with incredible colors.

"If you figure out how many times I've walked, it's about 200 times per year . . . and about 5,000 times over the 25 years. It's still beautiful to me, every time. When I walk, I just feel the stress melting away. And I never tire of it."

—Cliff Viner, Owner of the Florida Panthers National Hockey League Club; Founding Principal of AVM, Ltd.; Chairman of the Board for Sunrise Sports & Entertainment (holding company of the Florida Panthers and the arena in which they play)

half of the arena, rather than the lower. (The nice arena, no doubt, contributes to the fact that the Miami Heat holds their pre-season training camp here.) Both the men's and women's teams are generally competitive in the Sunbelt Conference, and the games are exciting. The FAU campus is very easy to get to, just off the Glades Road exit on I-95 (go East) in Boca Raton; it's less than a 45-minute drive from anywhere in Palm Beach County, and tickets are reasonably priced. Several of the county's most popular restaurants are right across the street.

Football

FLORIDA ATLANTIC UNIVERSITY FOOTBALL
Lockhart Stadium
(754) 321-1210
Ticket office: (866) FAU-OWLS
www.fausports.com

Florida Atlantic University started its football program only in 2001. In 2007, it became the first team in history to go to a bowl game in only its seventh season. It won that bowl game. Then it received another invitation to a bowl game in 2008—and won that one, too. The Owls play in old Lockhart Stadium in Fort Lauderdale, with a seating capacity of 20,000, and a 20-mile drive from the campus in Boca Raton. But it looks like things may be changing. The University is on an aggressive fund-raising campaign for an on-campus stadium, and plans have been developed for a 30,000-seat stadium and a surrounding area of shops and restaurants. One of the driving forces behind the new complex is the legendary coach of the Owls, Howard Schnellenberger, who won a national championship as coach of the down-the-road Miami Hurricanes in 1983.

It's not hard to get to Lockhart Stadium, which is just off I-95 in northern Fort Lauderdale. And there's not a bad seat in the house. The Owls play in the Sunbelt Conference, with opponents such as Troy University, Arkansas State, North Texas State, and Louisiana Tech. And the tickets are very reasonably priced.

UNIVERSITY OF MIAMI FOOTBALL
Sun Life Stadium
2269 Dan Marino Blvd.
Miami Gardens
(800) GOCANES
(305) 623-6100
www.hurricanesports.com
www.sunlifestadium.com

The fabled University of Miami Hurricanes left their beloved Orange Bowl for newer pastures in 2007 The old stadium, scene of so many legendary games and championship contests in both college and pro football, was torn down shortly afterward. However, it can't be denied that Sun Life Stadium is a much nicer place to watch a game than the Orange Bowl, which had been built in 1937. This stadium is modern and comfortable, with easy access, clean restrooms, better food, and better seats, and it's much more easily accessible from Palm Beach County than the Orange Bowl was. The Hurricanes transformed the game of college football forever in the 1980s and '90s, winning five national championships in the years between 1983 and 2001—a feat that may never be repeated. They're not quite that dominant any more, although they still produce winning and very exciting teams. The College Game is fun to watch, and the pageantry—with marching bands and cheerleaders and chanting fans and the alma mater songs—is a colorful slice of Americana.

The 'Canes play in the Atlantic Coast Conference, against opponents such as Georgia Tech, Virginia Tech, Boston College, and their in-state rivals, the Florida State Seminoles. Games against the Florida States sell out, as do games against other national powers such as the University of Oklahoma. However, there are generally seats to be had against most of the other teams on the schedule. On a sunny autumn Saturday, there aren't many better places to be than here.

Various Sports

LYNN UNIVERSITY
De Hoernle Sports & Cultural Center
3601 North Military Trail
Boca Raton
(561) 237-7281
www.lynn.edu

Lynn University is a small private university in Boca Raton, with athletic teams that have nevertheless achieved a good reputation in baseball and soccer (both men's and women's). Keep in mind that, in Florida, college baseball seasons start in Feb; there's no need to wait until the warmer weather of Apr.

NORTHWOOD UNIVERSITY
2600 North Military Trail
West Palm Beach
Athletic Department: (800) 458-8325
http://seahawks.gonorthwood.com/dept/

This is a branch of a private university with several campuses across the country. They field men's teams in baseball, basketball, and others. The men's basketball coach is actually a name you'd know if you're a longtime college hoops fan. He's Rollie Massimino who led Villanova University to a National Championship back in the 1980s. There are also women's teams in several sports. Northwood is called the Seahawks.

PALM BEACH ATLANTIC UNIVERSITY
Sports Information Department
901 S. Flagler Dr.
West Palm Beach
(561) 803-2529
http://pbasailfish.com/page.asp?articleID=123

Palm Beach Atlantic is a small private college that fields men's teams in baseball, basketball, soccer, and other sports; and women's teams in basketball and soccer, among others. The teams' nickname is the Sailfish.

PALM BEACH STATE COLLEGE
Main Campus
4200 Congress Ave.
Lake Worth
561-868-3350
www.pbcc.edu/x1788.xml
Palm Beach State College was Palm Beach Community College only a short time ago. But today the Panthers field teams in a variety of sports, among them men's basketball and baseball, and women's volleyball and basketball.

PARKS AND RECREATIONAL FACILITIES

Palm Beach County is blessed with a sun that never stops shining, weather that warms both the body and the soul, and a wide diversity of terrain and topography, ranging from beach dunes to swampy marsh. And it's blessed by the foresight of human beings, as well, who had the initiative to capitalize on this diversity by creating wonderful parks and recreational facilities in which you can build your body, soothe your mind, enjoy a picnic, play with your kids (or your inner-child), and explore a variety of topographical features. Or, just get away from it all.

All together, there are nearly a hundred parks in Palm Beach County, ranging from neighborhood pocket-parks to large, multifaceted ones with a ton of facilities and fields. There's a good chance that, by the time you leave (or even if, like many people, you never leave)—one of them will be "your" park.

LAKE OKEECHOBEE
West of the Palm Beaches

In the language of the Seminole Indians, Lake Okeechobee means "big water." And the name is accurate—it's the second largest freshwater lake wholly within the United States. It covers an enormous land area (730 square miles—approximately 450,000 acres), has an average depth of nine 9 feet, and contains an estimated 1.05 *trillion* gallons of water. It's been described as the "liquid heart" of Florida, because it pumps life-giving water into the complex Everglades ecosystem.

The lake also plays a vital role in the region's economy, ecology, and way of life. It is home to prized bass and speckled perch fisheries that generate close to $30 million in revenue. It's a principal source of drinking water for lakeside towns, and a backup source of drinking water for the six million residents of Florida's lower east coast. Lake Okeechobee also provides irrigation water for the $1.5 billion-per-year agricultural sector. In addition, it's a vital habitat for wading birds, migratory waterfowl, and endangered species (including the Everglade snail kite, wood stork, and Okeechobee gourd).

And it's a recreational wonderland—the largest recreational resource in South Florida, and perhaps the state. It boasts one of the most productive freshwater sport fisheries in North America. It's also an important waterfowl observation and hunting area. And more than six million people visit the 38 recreation areas around the lake each year to boat, picnic, sightsee, camp, swim, hunt, ride airboats, hike, bike, and horseback ride.

Probably the most popular of all these activities is fishing. More than 40 species of fish are found here, including Largemouth Bass, Blue Gill, Black Crappie (known locally as specks), and the famed Okeechobee Catfish. Salt water species like tarpon and snook are also a feature of the Okeechobee waterway, particularly near the W. P. Franklin Lock and the St. Lucie Locks. Florida's very conscientious about protecting its natural resources, particularly in light of ecological strains on the lake, so fishing regulations may apply. Be sure to check them out at: http://myfwc.comhttp://floridaconservation.org/fishingareas.html. Various guide services are available to show visitors the prime fishing and hunting sites. A few are listed here.

- Balon's Pro Guide Service, www.balons proguideservice.com
- Big "O" Guide Service, www.bigofishing .com
- Bud Keefer's Guide Service, www.bud keeferguideservice.com
- Haug Hunter Guide, www.hawghunter .net
- Roland Martin Marina, www.rolandmartin marina.com
- Ron's Guide Service, www.ronsguide service.com
- Walt Reynold's Bass Fishing, www.walt reynolds.com

NATIONAL PARKS

ARTHUR R. MARSHALL LOXAHATCHEE NATIONAL WILDLIFE REFUGE
10216 Lee Rd.
Boynton Beach
(561) 732-3684
www.fws.gov/loxahatchee

Arthur R. Marshall Loxahatchee National Wildlife Refuge is the last northernmost outpost of the Everglades. It sprawls out over 221 square miles of Everglades habitat. And it's home to the American alligator, the critically endangered Everglade snail kite, the turkey vulture, and hundreds of other species of animals and plants. In any given year, as many as 257 species of birds may use the Refuge's diverse wetland habitats.

The Refuge has recently unveiled its newest facility, a state-of-the-art Everglades Exhibition. You'll take a seat and then begin to move, and the seats and floor start to vibrate. You'll feel the breeze blowing from the screen in front of you as your "boat" skims over the water. You're about to experience a virtual Airboat Tour. Other new exhibits include the history of the Refuge, Everglades Attitudes, the Refuge Management Game, an alligator diorama, and night sounds of the Everglades.

This is also an important research facility, one that's constantly searching for ways to preserve the gift that is the Everglades, and ways in which to balance the needs of a growing region with the preservation of the natural ecosystem. Scientific studies on the hydrology, water quality, wildlife management, fire management, and natural resource management are conducted by scientists here. And the information that results from these studies helps the Refuge make better management decisions. When you stand here, in the silence, and look out across an endless horizon of wetlands, small islands called hammocks, stands of mangroves, you realize just how much of a gift the Everglades is.

STATE PARKS

JOHN D. MACARTHUR BEACH STATE PARK AND NATURE CENTER
10900 Jack Nicklaus Dr.
North Palm Beach
Entrance gate: (561) 624-6950
Nature center: (561) 624-6952
www.macarthurbeach.org

This area is not only a recreational treasure, but also a biological one—an area

My Palm Beach County

"A successful team beats with one heart"—Anonymous

"This anonymous quote exemplifies the spirit of our accomplishments at the Marshall Foundation. In particular, the many ways that our team of volunteers has worked together to bridge the divide between children and the outdoors. I firmly believe that more families in Palm Beach County have a new appreciation for our American treasure, the Everglades. I am most proud of the insightful team of volunteers who continue to inspire and educate public about our water source . . . the Everglades. Whatever the occasion, they are there to encourage children and their families to protect our American Treasure. A favorite passage comes to mind from Proverbs 18:15. Intelligent people are always open to new ideas. In fact, they look for them! This is indeed what makes a successful team beat with one heart for the Everglades."

—Nancy Marshall,
President of the
Arthur R. Marshall Foundation

the sea, the sun, and the sand all come together to create a place that's as suited for quiet contemplation as it is for a wide range of recreational activities.

John D. MacArthur Beach State Park is situated on a barrier island, and its 325 acres encompasses a mangrove-fringed estuary, coastal hardwood forests, and close-in reefs. This place has been called an "island in time" because, here, the lush subtropical coastal habitats that once covered southeast Florida still remain. The park has nearly 2 miles of unspoiled beach, touching very clear Atlantic waters. Along the way, you can stroll shady nature trails, join a bird or butterfly walk, or paddle through the estuary and Munyon Island in a kayak The park offers special events throughout the year, among them children's programs, guided snorkeling adventures, recreational skills lessons, MacArthur Under Moonlight concerts, summer day camps, and special holiday celebrations.

There's a nature center with displays and live animals. In addition, there are two picnic pavilions with barbecue grills, a playground, and an amphitheater area that can be rented for special events such as family reunions, birthday parties, and weddings.

JONATHAN DICKINSON STATE PARK
16450 Southeast Federal Hwy.
Hobe Sound
(772) 546-2771
www.floridastateparks.org/
jonathandickinson/default.cfm

Jonathan Dickinson State Park has long been a cherished natural resource for the people of Palm Beach County (it's actually just across the county line in Martin County, however). People here know that, whenever the stresses of modern life get to be

to be protected, enjoyed, and studied. In the 1970s, millionaire John D. MacArthur donated a section of his property for use as a public park. Palm Beach County residents starting flocking to it immediately, and they haven't stopped since. This is truly one of Palm Beach County's special places, where too much, there's always this park with its winding paths through dense forests, the river running through it, the wildlife, and the colors, shapes, and sounds.

Jonathan Dickinson is so diverse that it has 13 natural "communities," among them sand pine scrub, pine flatwoods, mangroves, and river swamps. The Loxahatchee River, Florida's first federally designated Wild and Scenic River, runs through the park. You can travel down it in a canoe, down to the pioneer homestead of the legendary frontiersman known as Trapper Nelson. You can take a guided tour of the 1930s homestead and cabin. You can ride a bike, on paved trails and off-road scrub. Or, you can ride a horse on an equestrian trail, or walk or run on a hiking trail. There's boating, kayaking, and canoeing. You can fish, on the riverbank or from a boat. You can wander through the wonderful exhibits at the Elsa Kimbell Environmental Education and Research Center. Camp at two full-facility campgrounds, or at a youth/group primitive campground. Rent a motorboat., or if you'd like to have someone else do the driving, you can arrange to see the Loxahatchee on a boat tour.

COUNTY PARKS

Instead of noting every park in Palm Beach County, we've noted about 20 of the best. Small pocket parks or neighborhood parks, even though they may be great, are not noted here. Instead, we'll pick out the larger ones that have a variety of offerings, rather than neighborhood parks that only offer a short walking path, etc. We'll focus on parks with boating or recreational offerings, with bike paths, perhaps hiking trails, swimming pools, water parks, and interesting playgrounds.

South County

PATCH REEF PARK
2000 Yamato Rd.
Boca Raton
(561) 367-7035
www.ci.boca-raton.fl.us/rec/parks/
patchreef.shtm

This is one of those parks at which you could easily spend the entire day because its 55 acres are filled with fun. There are baseball, football, soccer, and softball fields, a playground, basketball courts, and eight picnic pavilions, all with charcoal barbecue grills. And the Patch Reef Park Tennis Center has 17 courts, a hitting wall, pro shop, locker rooms, and a concession stand.

SOUTH COUNTY REGIONAL PARK
11200 Park Access Rd.
12551 Glades Rd.
West of Boca Raton
(561) 966-6600
www.pbcgov.com/parks/locations/
south_county_regional.htm

This sizable park has a wide range of activities available. The Sunset Cove Amphitheatre is set amid a lake and tropical foliage, and it's a great place to watch a musical or dance performance. There are 2 miles of trails that can be used for biking or walking. You can romp with your four-legged, furry friend at Canine Cove Dog Park. If you want to exercise without any friends (four-legged or otherwise), you can do so at the eight-station exercise course. You can cast a line at the lake. There are wonders of nature at the Daggerwing Nature Center (see Attractions), with an exhibit hall with live animals and interactive state-of-the-art exhibits, laboratory, lobby, reading area, and an elevated boardwalk (with an observation tower for a larger perspective) which takes you on a relaxing journey through a swamp. Animal life here includes osprey, woodpeckers, butterflies, endangered wood storks, and alligators, and plant-lovers will see a wide variety of bromeliads. The Ruddy Daggerwing butterfly, after which this nature center is named, flutters through the trees. There's a radio-controlled car track in the park, as well. And then, to top it all off, there's the Coconut Cove Waterpark, and you'd better prepare yourself—because it won't be easy to get the kids out of here! There's an interactive water playground, a river ride, and a water slide.

SOUTH INLET PARK
1298 S. Ocean Blvd.
Boca Raton
(561) 966-6600
www.co.palm-beach.fl.us/parks/
locations/southinlet.htm
This park is only 11 acres—but those 11 acres are on the beach. There are picnic areas with grills (so you can combine the aromas of the sea with the aromas of the steaks you're grilling), as well as a playground. And when you're done eating, you can sink your toes into the soft beach sand and take a walk with the surf running up to greet you.

WEST DELRAY REGIONAL PARK
10875 Atlantic Ave.
Delray Beach
(561) 966-6600
www.co.palm-beach.fl.us/parks/
locations/westdelrayregional.htm
The Gold Coast Archery Club operates a target range in this 313-acre park (permit required), and stages its competitions here. There's a primitive camping area (as opposed to an

RV camping area), an equestrian trail, a lake for freshwater fishing, and a non-motorized boat launching ramp. There are radio-control fields for airplanes and helicopters, and also a lake for radio-controlled boats. And if you want to get away from it all, you can, on the walking trail.

Central County

CALOOSA PARK
1300 S.W. Thirty-fifth Ave.
Boynton Beach
(561) 966-6600
www.co.palm-beach.fl.us/parks/
locations/caloosa.htm
This park has 65 acres, including a 3-acre lake with 1,900 feet of frontage, and fishing. And there's along list of amenities, such as baseball fields, basketball courts, a 20-station exercise course, multi-purpose fields, a playground, picnic pavilion, racquetball and handball courts, tennis courts, and even two roller-hockey (which is popular here; we don't get real snow!) rinks.

DYER PARK
7301 Haverhill Rd.
West Palm Beach
(561) 966-6600
www.pbcgov.com/parks/locations/dyer
.htm
Dyer Park is a beautiful space that contains both a walking trail (4 miles) and an equestrian trail (3.5 miles); there are even 7 miles of mountain-biking trails. The list of amenities includes baseball fields, basketball courts, four open fields, picnic areas with grills, a picnic pavilion, two playgrounds, and even a facility for devotees of radio-controlled planes and helicopters.

My Palm Beach County

"I am, of course, partial to West Palm Beach. We have many features that make us special. Almost half of our city is covered by grassy water preserve—20 square miles of our water supply, and natural habitat to thousands of creatures and plants. It's a fringe of the Everglades and one-of-a-kind for any city in the world.

"From a Chamber of Commerce perspective, we have great weather, beautiful natural resources, world-class cultural institutions, governmental and court buildings, commerce, access to major transportation. But what makes us most special is the diversity of our population, all ages, colors, religions, sexual orientation. And we really embrace and cherish this aspect of our city."

—Lois Frankel,
Mayor, West Palm Beach

GREEN CAY NATURE CENTER AND WETLANDS
12800 Hagen Ranch Rd.
Boynton Beach
(561) 966-7000
www.pbcgov.com/parks/nature/green_cay_nature_center/
This is a different kind of park. You won't find any ballfields here or any tennis or basketball courts. Instead, what you'll find is an up-close-and-personal look at the natural beauty and ecosystem that is found in Palm Beach County. This is, in fact, the county's newest nature center, overlooking a hundred acres of wetland, and providing great educational opportunities about this unique habitat. The wetland features 1.5 miles of elevated boardwalk, with interpretive signs about the habitat. And the Nature Center includes a lecture hall, gift shop, and live animals in an extensive exhibit room that highlights the ways in which the wetland affects the lives of every person in Palm Beach County. Bring the kids, or just come to relax by yourself.

JOHN PRINCE MEMORIAL PARK
Three entrances:
2700 Sixth Ave. South
4759 South Congress Ave.
2520 Lake Worth Rd.
Lake Worth
(561) 966-6600
www.co.palm-beach.fl.us/parks/locations/johnprince.htm
This is one of the largest parks in South Florida, with 726 acres, 338 of which are on a lake. The park includes biking and walking paths, a 20-station fitness course, and a number of unique offerings, including fishing, the John Prince Golf Learning Center, four fishing piers jutting out into the lake, a splash park for the kids, picnic pavilions with grills, two areas for the European game of bocce, and a wheelchair exercise course. And, of course, there's the usual assortment of baseball fields, basketball and tennis courts, volleyball courts, etc. As far as parks go, John Prince has it all.

LOXAHATCHEE GROVES PARK
13751 Southern Blvd.
Loxahatchee
(561) 966-6600
www.pbcgov.com/parks/locations/loxahatcheegroves.htm

Loxahatchee Groves is 30 acres of greenery, with thick strands of pine and palm trees. If you're a horseman or woman, there's a beautiful milelong equestrian trail through the woods here. There's a 10-station exercise course, along with ball fields, picnic pavilions, and a playground.

OCEAN INLET PARK
6990 N. Ocean Blvd.
Ocean Ridge
(561) 966-6600
www.co.palm-beach.fl.us/parks/
locations/oceaninlet.htm

There's one very unique feature at this park—frontage on both the ocean and the Intracoastal Waterway. You can pull up into the marina in your boat. You can barbecue a steak in the picnic area. You can go saltwater fishing. Or, if you'd rather let someone else do the fishing, you can eat some fish that someone else has caught at the Taste of Chicago Waterfront Café.

OKEEHEELEE PARK
Two entrances:
7715 Forest Hill Blvd.
7500 Forest Hill Blvd.
West of West Palm Beach
(561) 966-6600
www.co.palm-beach.fl.us/parks/
locations/okeeheelee.htm

This park is huge—1,700 acres. And there are very few activities that you can't find here. There are 8 miles of biking and walking paths. There's a BMX track, where you (well, probably your kids rather than you) can test your biking skills up and down the hills. Three's a boat-launching ramp, and boat slips. There's a dog park called Pooch Pines. The 111-acre, world-class equestrian showplace has a covered arena, an open

riding area, and training rings. The 20-station exercise course is a mile long. There's fishing in a lake, and there's everything you could possibly need here to hone your golf game—three 9-hole golf courses, a chipping area, driving range, practice putting green, pro shop, and snack bar. There's mountain biking, and 2 miles of nature trails. You can rent a canoe, kayak, pedal-boat, or a bike. The Okeeheelee Nature Center has hands-on exhibits, animal encounters, and a nature-related gift shop. You can watch birds of prey, touch a live snake, or prowl for owls during one of the programs for families, youth and adults. The center also has 2.5 miles of trails winding through 90 acres of pine flatwoods and wetlands.

PEANUT ISLAND PARK
6500 Peanut Island Rd.
Riviera Beach
(561) 845-4445
www.pbcgov.com/parks/peanutisland

Peanut Island, off the coast of Riviera Beach, is one of the more unusual parks in Palm Beach County. It was the site of a bomb-shelter constructed when John F. Kennedy was president (1961–63), during the height of the Cold War, and fears about nuclear war between the United States and the-then Soviet Union. It's actually a man-made island, constructed in 1918, and enlarged since then. There are now 80 acres, most of which are used as a spoil-site for dredging of the Intracoastal. The name Peanut was given when the state authorized use of the island as a terminal for shipping peanut oil. Plans for this venture were dropped in 1946, but the name stuck. Today, despite the fact that the interior of the island is used as a spoil-site, the perimeter of the island is used as a park.

The park is a perfect place to test your salt-water fishing skills in the Lake Worth Lagoon. It's pretty much the only place in the Intracoastal Waterway where you can swim; and there's a snorkeling area adjacent. There are boat slips, a camping area with a firepit, picnic areas, a walking path, and an observation tower with incredible views in any direction. There's plenty of wildlife on the island, too, especially birds. Peanut Island is also the site of the Palm Beach Maritime Museum (see Attractions). And keep in mind that there are no bridges to this island; you've got to come across via the Palm Beach Water Taxi or one of the private firms offering the short trip here.

SEMINOLE PALMS PARK
151 Lamstein Lane
Royal Palm Beach
(561) 966-6600
www.co.palm-beach.fl.us/parks/ locations/seminolepalm.htm
Seminole Palms has 70 acres, with baseball and multi-purpose fields, picnic areas, and playgrounds. But your kids will probably head straight for the Calypso Bay Waterpark, with giant slides, an interactive water playground, and a river ride. Call (561) 790-6160 for the water park (www.co.palm-beach.fl .us/parks/aquatics/waterparks/calypsobay/). The water park closes for winter, and opens in late-March.

WEST BOYNTON PARK AND
 RECREATION CENTER
6000 Northtree Blvd.
Lake Worth
(561) 355-1125
www.co.palm-beach.fl.us/parks/ recreationcenters/westboynton

This is a district park with 47 acres that includes a gym, baseball fields, basketball court, 15-station exercise course, picnic pavilions, playground, a skate park (for skateboarders and inline skaters), and a roller hockey rink. There are also some softball programs for adults and children.

North County

BURT REYNOLDS PARK
805 N. US 1
Jupiter
(561) 966-6600
www.co.palm-beach.fl.us/parks/ locations/burtreynolds.htm
This park has 36 acres and boating access to the Intracoastal Waterway, along with 2,000 feet of frontage. You can go fishing in the Intracoastal here. You can play horseshoes, grill a steak at one of the picnic pavilions, and play volleyball, as well. This park is also the site of the Loxahatchee River Center (see Attractions).

CARLIN PARK
400 S. S.R. A1A
Jupiter
(561) 966-6600
www.pbcgov.com/parks/locations/carlin .htm
This 100-acre park is the site of the Seabreeze Amphitheater, a small sea-side venue that hosts a lot of good bands. There's an exercise course with 20 stations, picnic pavilions, baseball field, tennis, and volleyball. Oh, yes, one other little thing—the park is on the ocean, with 3,000 feet of beach frontage. And if you get hungry, head for the Lazy Loggerhead Cafe.

My Palm Beach County

"I've been interested in the natural world ever since I was a child growing up in Alabama. Nothing was more fascinating to me than going into the woods at various times of the year to see the animals and plants that were at home there. I eventually completed a Ph.D. in animal physiology and biochemistry at Iowa State University, and I was a faculty member and administrator at Auburn University before coming to Florida Atlantic University several years ago. In Palm Beach County, I found a world rich in biodiversity, from the alligators of the Everglades to the burrowing owls that live in holes in the ground on FAU's Boca Raton campus. Here, students of all ages can find nature's classroom right outside their front door."

—John F. Pritchett, Ph.D.,
Former Interim President, Florida
Atlantic University, Boca Raton

DUBOIS PARK
19075 DuBois Rd.
Jupiter
(561) 966-6600
www.pbcgov.com/parks/locations/
dubois.htm
Dubois Park has a very scenic setting—it's on a lagoon off the Jupiter Inlet (and you can swim in the lagoon). It has picnic areas with grills, and a playground. And it has a definite charm because the serenity of the setting has a very calming effect. In addition, this park is also the setting for the DuBois Pioneer Home, which is listed on the National Register of Historical Places (561-747-6639), as well as an old Indian mound.

JUNO BEACH PARK
14775 S. R. A1A
Juno Beach
(561) 966-6600
www.co.palm-beach.fl.us/parks/
locations/junobeach.htm
This park, too, is on the beach, and has a 1,000-foot-long pier for fishing, with a bait shop and snack bar on it. There are also picnic tables. From Mar through Oct, this is a turtle-nesting area, where turtles come to lay their eggs. Since they come at night, the park closes a half-hour before sunset.

JUPITER BEACH PARK
1375 Jupiter Beach Rd.
Jupiter
(561) 966-6600
www.pbcgov.com/parks/locations/
jupiterbeach.htm
There's 1,700 feet of beach frontage in this 46-acre park, along with a picnic area with grills, and a sand volleyball court. But the real stars here are the views of the water—and the water itself, where you can wash away all your cares in the soothing surf.

JUPITER FARMS PARK
16655 Jupiter Farms Rd.
Jupiter
(561) 966-6600
www.co.palm-beach.fl.us/parks/
locations/jupiterfarms.htm
This park boasts a pretty equestrian area that's available for public use, along with baseball and softball fields, a multi-purpose field, and a playground. There are 52 acres on which to roam.

LOGGERHEAD PARK
14200 US 1
Juno Beach
(561) 966-6600
www.co.palm-beach.fl.us/parks/
locations/loggerhead.htm

This is a beautiful spot, with beach dunes and sea oats and the ocean. The park has a nature trail that wanders among those beach dunes, and if you stoke up an appetite while walking it, you can throw a couple of steaks on the barbie in the picnic areas. The kids will enjoy the playground. This is also the site of the Loggerhead Marinelife Center, where you can view all types and sizes of turtles—including red ones! This is a turtle-nesting area, and it's a wonderful sight to see the staff at the center care for injured turtles.

ANNUAL EVENTS AND FESTIVALS

Once upon a time, Florida—and Palm Beach County—had pretty much nothing going on in the Low Season in terms of special events and festivals. Things have changed a bit, though, and now there are a few selected events going on in the spring and summer. But, basically, summer is our hibernation period. Autumn is when this area really comes alive. When the rest of the country is gathering its acorns and getting ready for several months of its own hibernation, Palm Beach County is bursting out all over. We have festivals dedicated to the glory of just about any worldly object you can think of, with one-of-a-kind events full of sound, color, and fun. If you can sing it, paint it, sculpt it, photograph it, write it, cook it, create it, hear it, craft it, buy it, sell it, play it, carve it, trade it, weave it, build it, eat it, or drink it, you can be sure that there's a festival or three celebrating it.

There are too many art and music festivals, in particular, to count, along with other special events virtually every weekend from early October through April. In fact, perhaps the only hard part associated with this is deciding which event to attend on any selected weekend. The outdoor events are particularly wonderful. They afford you the chance to wander around at your own pace, warmed by very pleasant (not hot) sun, caressed by the soft ocean breezes, and enjoying the fresh, humid-free air.

And "The Season," here, ends not with a whimper, but with a bang. In May comes one of the biggest of all Palm Beach County festivals—SunFest.

JANUARY

ART PALM BEACH
Palm Beach County Convention Center
Okeechobee Road
West Palm Beach
(239) 949-5411
www.artpalmbeach.com
The floors of the Convention Center are transformed into a mazelike wonderland of paintings and fine art at this mid to late Jan show. Paintings of all media and all types—such as surrealist, modern, classic, impressionist, photo-realist, abstract, southwestern, and far beyond—are displayed on tall, stark white structures that serve to make the colors really jump out at you. Also here are lifelike wax figures; glass sculptures of people, animals, and faces; stand-alone abstract structures of metal, stone, glass, or wood; huge displays of papier-mâché or ceramic figures; three-dimensional, multi-media wall art; modern art using wood or straw; glass collages such as a city skyline; "primitive" art; mirror art; photography, both artistic and realistic; and ceramic ornaments and pottery. Admission is charged.

BLUFFS SQUARE SIDEWALK ARTS & CRAFT SHOW
Bluffs Square, 4060 US 1
Jupiter
(772) 336-0606
www.craftlister.com
This is a fairly new show, but one that's growing in prominence year by year. At first local artists comprised the majority of exhibitors. Now, however, good artists are coming from around the state and from other states as well. The art is imaginative, and the artists only too happy to speak with you about their work. Held in late Jan; free.

BOCA FEST
The Shops at Boca Center
Military Trail, Boca Raton
(954) 472-3755
www.artfestival.com
This free festival in early Jan is special because it takes place at the magnificent Shops at Boca Center, a sweet spot that's filled with several of the best restaurants in town, as well as several chocolatiers, ice-cream shops, coffee shops, and a very-cool Harley-Davidson store that'll bring out the biker in you. There's also an interior plaza that's a nice place to relax and watch all the people lugging around their newfound treasures. In addition, the quality of the work and the artists is always very high here. You'll see a hundred things that'll catch your eye. More than 150 artists from all over the country converge here, and they work in such media as paint, photography, glass, metal, sand, jewelry, wood, and clay. Each booth seems to have something different and eye-catching, and the artists are happy to take time to discuss their work. Their stories are fascinating, ranging from the I-was-born-to-be-an-artist to the I-left-everything-I-knew-just-so-I-could-follow-my-passion-for-art. While you're here, take the time to peruse the shops.

BOCA RATON FINE ART SHOW
Royal Palm Place
(248) 684-2613
www.hotworks.org
This is a juried fine arts and craft show, spread out amidst the distinctive shops and restaurants of Royal Palm Place in downtown Boca. This free show in early to mid January is widely known for the imaginative works on display, and for the caliber of artists it attracts. You'll find beautifully painted clay figurines. Turquoise jewelry and jewelry made from gleaming precious stones. Glass-blown bowls swirled with colors you've never seen before. Batik paintings. Metal objects that are utilitarian and striking in their simplicity. Hand-made dolls, as well as old-time butchers, laborers, soldiers, priests, rabbis, fishermen, doctors, angels, golfers, dancers, and anything else that one can make. Wax human beings that are so lifelike you'll be tempted to say hello. And wood that's carved or bent into shapes and angles you wouldn't believe.

CITY PLACE ART FESTIVAL
City Place, South Rosemary Ave.
Downtown West Palm Beach
(561) 366-1000
www.cityplace.com
At this late January free festival, you can wander through the paintings, photography, jewelry, crafts, glass-art, wood-art, ceramics, and multi-media artworks in West Palm's vibrant downtown plaza, perhaps while eating some fudge, ice cream, or gelato. It's a beautiful winter day, and the sun reflects off the surrounding high-rise office and apartment buildings.

FOTOFUSION
Palm Beach Photographic Centre
415 Clematis St.
West Palm Beach
(561) 276-9797
www.fotofusion.org
This is an international festival of photography and digital imagery, which promoters refer to as "Where creativity and technology fuse." The photographs here are traditional and boundary-pushing at the same time because they rely on the same light, shadows, shade, and subjects used by photographers for 150 years, while incorporating new visual tricks and thinking into the process. The images are striking, and you find yourself staring at them, eventually moving on to another piece, and then coming back to the first one. The digital images are incredible journeys through colors, angles, and textures, and the artist's own mind. There are portfolio reviews by experts, seminars and panel discussions, hands-on computer labs, multimedia presentations, book signings and gallery walks. And Fuse and Schmooze parties nightly. For art without boundaries, get to this show. The show runs for five days in mid to late Jan; admission is charged.

OSHOGATSU (JAPANESE NEW YEAR)
Morikami Museum and Japanese Gardens
4000 Morikami Park Rd.
Delray Beach
(561) 495-0233
www.morikami.org
In early to mid Jan, the serene grounds of the Morikami Museum and Japanese Gardens turn into a giant Japanese New Year's celebration, with festivities just about everywhere you look. Oshogatsu is the most important holiday of the year in Japan, and

a time when people look to the new year for physical and spiritual renewal. The Japanese people make a conscious effort, in the weeks before the new year, to clear away their debts and financial obligations, in order to start the new year with a clean slate.

Before Oshogatsu arrives, many Japanese gather at important shrines and temples, where they greet the stroke of midnight with exclamations of *Akemashite omedeto gozaimasu!* (Happy New Year!). Those who are celebrating in their homes toast the new year with a ceremonial drink called otoso, a sweet sake, while eating a traditional stew dish called ozoni. The festivities at the Morikami will be the same ones enjoyed in Japan. There will be pounding of the rice, and then the making of rice cakes. Calligraphers will express New Year's greetings with a flowing, artistic beauty and sweet thoughts. You can visit with a fortune teller, watch performances by the Lion Dancer to the accompaniment of taiko drumming, and watch the beautiful tea ceremonies. The kids can play Japanese games, try their hands at traditional crafts, and enjoy an occasional lift in the bounce house. Admission is charged.

PALM BEACH WINTER ANTIQUES SHOW
Crowne Plaza Hotel
1601 Belvedere Rd.
West Palm Beach
(561) 483-4047
www.zitawatersbell.com
More than 50 prestigious dealers from the United States, Canada, and Europe make this a first-class show and a wonderful place to find precious treasures. Held in mid to late Jan, this show has been around for more than 30 years, with an emphasis on fine antiques and period furniture. Because of the

diversity and the quality of the items shown here, this is a great buyer's show. There's a strict vetting process for the vendors and the items they're looking to sell, and the show won't accept any items newer than mid-20th century. Each year's show has a special theme. The show brings in speakers to give presentations about purchasing fine antiques, as well as subjects relating to international or period furniture and furnishings. In addition, there are often exhibits on loan from private collections, such as rare photographs, letters, and railroad items from the longtime historian of the Florida East Coast Railroad. Admission is charged.

SOUTH FLORIDA FAIR
Southern Boulevard
West Palm Beach
(561) 793-0333
www.southfloridafair.com
This is the Big One, folks. The biggest, longest, most colorful, most exciting, and most well-attended county/regional fair between Miami and Jacksonville. It's a midway lined with rides, attractions, crafts, and great food. It's cable-car rides and whirling tea cups, upside-down pirate ships, roller coasters, fortune-tellers, horses and cows and camels, cotton candy and corn dogs, Polish sausages, and the Biggest Pig (Horse, Chicken, etc.) in the country. It's 17 days of non-stop fun and thrills, as farmers and horsemen come in from the western communities, young families come in from the suburbs, and Native Americans come from the reservations to partake of the fun. You can ride a cable-car from one end of the midway to the other—over thousands of people walking right under you.

There's every type of ethnic food—Florida/Caribbean, conch fritters from the Bahamas, jerk chicken from Jamaica, souvlaki from Greece, giant turkey legs, pizza, candy apples, hot dogs and hamburgers, and just about every other food you can think of. There are name entertainers, and a 4-H agricultural center with prize cows, chickens, sheep, and rabbits. There are fish-bobbing and ring-tossing contests, strongest-man contests, fortune-tellers, and palm reading. There's a haunted house and antique fire trucks for the kids. It's all in the great American tradition of the good, old-fashioned country fair. Beginning in mid to late Jan; admission is charged.

FEBRUARY

A LA CARTE IN THE PARK
Meyer Amphitheatre
104 Datura St.
Downtown West Palm Beach
(561) 822-1515
http://events.pbpulse.com
Timed for the Sat right before Valentine's Day, this is a romantic holiday present that anyone would love. What's not to like? There's great food and drink, top-notch performers, and it's all in the heart of downtown West Palm. Some of the top gourmet chefs in Palm Beach County will offer up the special dishes that have made them local celebrities, along with fine wines, cocktails, and craft beers. The music on stage is great, too, and you've likely heard of some of the people performing it. Admission is charged.

AMERICAN INTERNATIONAL FINE ART FAIR
Palm Beach County Convention Center
650 Okeechobee Blvd.
West Palm Beach
(239) 949-5411
www.aifaf.com

Since its founding in 1997, the American International Fine Arts Fair has occupied a prominent place in the pantheon of world-class art events. There are no hot dogs or nachos here, and no T-shirts or tank-tops; this is no street festival. Some of the most discriminating (and wealthy) collectors in the world wander among the hundreds of exhibits, viewing everything from modern sculpture to Old Masters paintings. Single items here have sold for over $100 million!

Well-dressed, whispering people move comfortably and knowledgeably among works by some of the most famous artists of all time, discussing both the intrinsic artistic value and the intrinsic financial value. You will never see a greater number of magnificent antiques in one place at one time. In addition, this fair has been said to have the world's finest collection of haute and period jewelry. It is the only American fair rated five stars by *The Art Newspaper*, and many collectors see this as the finest art, antique, and jewelry show in the country. You'll find exquisite stained glass; Victorian furniture; Impressionist paintings (by the *real* Impressionists); marble busts; jewelry from royal families; whole roomfuls of hand-carved, hand-painted, gilded Italian or French furniture; gold statuary; Grandfather clocks from colonial times; ornate candelabras and chandeliers from European palaces; antique china and vases; and much more. Many of us won't earn as much money in a year as some of the attendees will spend in one afternoon.

Held for five to six days in early Feb; admission charges for one-day passes and multi-day passes.

ARTIGRAS FINE ART FESTIVAL
Abacoa Town Center
Jupiter
(561) 748-3946
www.artigras.org

ArtisGras's beginning was humble. In a small country club in 1986 there were 150 artists who exhibited and 2,500 people who attended. Since then, this free, mid-Feb festival has grown in both size and stature. ArtiGras is now ranked as one of the top 20 events by the Southeastern Tourism Society, and as one of the top 50 festivals in the country by *Sunshine Artist* magazine. There are now over 300 artists at this juried show. At the Artist Demonstration Stage, you can learn how the artists create their art. At the Beer Garden, you can cool off with a brew. A pick-up area means you don't have to cart your purchase around; you can bring your car to the volunteers, and they'll load your art into it. The Homegrown Art area allows you to see the work of—and meet—up-and-coming local artists. An ArtiKids area allows the younger set to create their own art out of recycled materials, and there's a Youth Art Competition Gallery and a Tiny Treasures Children's Art Boutique. There's music, too, with bands playing jazz, blues, Caribbean, flamenco, Cajun, and pop. Also a fashion show, and plenty of food.

BIG CYPRESS SHOOTOUT
Billie Swamp Safari
Big Cypress Seminole Reservation
Florida Everglades, Clewiston
(800) GO-SAFARI
www.when.com

The Big Cypress Shootout is a reenactment of a battle between the Seminoles and the U.S. Army in the Second Seminole War (1835–42). The occasion honors the Seminoles' struggles to remain in their homeland, and the sacrifices they made in that effort. The weapons and the uniforms from both sides are authentic, as are the tactics used. Along with the "hostilities," there'll be music, Seminole food, Seminole and pioneer artisans, tomahawk throws, authentic Seminole and soldier camps, and more-modern pursuits such as venomous snake shows and alligator-wrestling. One other thing is authentic, as well—you're on an Indian reservation and surrounded by the magnificent isolation of the Everglades, the endless "River of Grass" that flows out into the horizon. Held in late Feb.

BLUEGRASS MUSIC JAM
John D. MacArthur Beach State Park
10900 Jack Nicklaus Dr.
North Palm Beach
(561) 624-6952

Get out your overalls, your old plaid shirts, your straw hat, and wrap that ole bandana around your neck 'cause we're goin' fiddle-pickin', friend. Get out the banjo, the guitar, and the harmonica, 'cause we're gonna be stompin' our feet and clappin' our hands till the sun goes down. Darned if it don't bring me back to my old Kentucky home! The music's great (and you'll see it for yourself—it really is hard to stay in your seat once they get to jammin'). Bluegrass is one of the relatively few authentic American art forms. It's played very well here. The food's good. And it doesn't hurt that the whole thing takes place in a scenic park right at the beach. Held in mid to late Feb; admission fee per car.

BOCA RATON MUSEUM OF ART JURIED ART FESTIVAL
Mizner Park
(561) 392-2500
www.bocamuseum.org

This is one of the big ones, for a couple of reasons. One is that the Boca Raton Museum of Art is the finest art museum in South County, and it has a diverse collection of treasures that will please even the snobbiest Big-City art-lover. Accordingly, some of the best artists from around the country want to be in shows put on by the Boca Museum; especially this one, which is sponsored by local TV stations, major companies, large civic and arts organizations, and the National Endowment for the Arts. The second reason is that the museum—and this art show—are located in Mizner Park, Boca's beautiful downtown urban core. It's filled with unusual shops, as well as green spaces and fountains where you can sit and watch the people-parade. Palm Beach County's art festivals take care not only of your artistic tastes, but also your sensory ones; booths at the fair cater to every conceivable taste for foods that can be fried, grilled, or roasted outside. Even when you're done wandering the artists' aisles, you'll want to wander Mizner Park, for the treasures you'll find in the exclusive shops and restaurants. Held in early Feb; free.

BUCKLER'S CRAFTS FAIR
South Florida Fairgrounds
9067 Southern Blvd.
West Palm Beach
(386) 860-0092
www.bucklercraftfair.com

Buckler's attracts award-winning craftspeople from all over the country, showing off their country crafts, folk art, primitive, Victorian, Southwestern, furniture, crafted wood, toys, dolls and doll houses, hand-carved and hand-painted wooden schoolhouses and fire stations, clothing, accessories, blankets and other woven items, quilts, and custom jewelry. But these aren't the only works of art here. Try the varieties of homemade fudge, peanut brittle, or old-time candy. Held in late Feb, mid May, late Aug, late Oct, and mid Dec. Admission is charged.

CHOCOLATE DECADENCE
The Shops at Boca Center
5050 Town Center Circle
Boca Raton
(561) 620-4772; ext. 2
www.bocachocolate.com
Here, amid the fashionable shops and bistros at Boca Center, an event that draws chocoholics from all over South Florida takes place. Whether you come because you're an aficionado of the sweet, rich, taste of excellent chocolate, or just because you've been reading lately about the health benefits of chocolate (riiiight!), this evening is a Chocolate in Wonderland fantasy. Held in early Feb, Chocolate Decadence draws approximately 1,500 people to taste and enjoy not only all things chocolate, but all things indulgent, including food, wine, jewelry, and shopping. You'll be sampling the finest chocolate from South Florida's best restaurants, chocolatiers, manufacturers, caterers and more. Great food and wine, music, and entertainment add to the ambience—and the pleasure. Admission is charged.

DELRAY BEACH CHILI COOK-OFF
At the GreenMarket in the Park
Downtown Delray Beach
(561) 276-7511
www.delraycra.org
Once a year, on a Sat in mid to late Feb, Palm Beach County's chieftains of chili get the chance to strut their stuff, and to see who's the best chili cook of all. Here, the weapons of choice are large pots, and ladles. The event takes place right at the GreenMarket in downtown Delray. Come hungry because the chili's great. And you'd be amazed at the different types of chili cuisine, among them traditional, New Age, and vegetarian. You'll taste chili concoctions at all levels of "heat". You'll taste it with all types of accompanying food chopped up in the chili. You'll taste it with all kinds of spices and peppers, from the sublime to the scorched-throat variety. Both samplers and a panel of judges get to vote on who the Big Chili Honcho in town really is—there's a Peoples' Choice Award and a Judges' Choice Award. Trophies—and bragging rights for the next year—are handed out. Free.

DELRAY BEACH CRAFT FESTIVAL
Pineapple Grove
Downtown Delray Beach
(954) 472-3755
www.artfestival.com
Some of America's top craftspeople display their works at this one. And why not? There aren't many better places to be in late Feb than in downtown Delray, where you're surrounded by one-of-a-kind shops, bistros, and galleries, and very close to the beach. You'll find an incredible diversity of crafts at this fair—carved, hammered, soldered, fused, cooked, painted, strung, woven, or otherwise assembled—ranging from $5 to a few thousand. There's everything from handmade jewelry to ceramics and wall hangings, handmade oven mitts, and ceramic prongs to pull out hot oven shelves. In addition, there are also natural cosmetics and toiletries, candles made of soy, and food and produce items at the green market. The Pineapple Grove area is a special neighborhood of good restaurants and bistros, just off Atlantic Avenue, Delray's Old-Times downtown boulevard. Held in late Feb; free.

DELRAY BEACH GARLIC FESTIVAL
Atlantic Avenue
Downtown Delray Beach
(561) 279-0907
www.dbgarlicfest.com

A garlic festival? In Delray Beach, Florida? Nobody plants "the stinking rose" here. Nobody grows it. Nobody exports it. Nobody imports it. Well, the founders of this event must have known something—because their crazy little idea has since grown into one of the largest festivals in South Florida. And its allure has extended way beyond garlic lovers.

This mid-Feb event is now a big happening, and tens of thousands of people flock to be part of it each year. There are now many other foods besides garlic on display, as well as cooking and kitchen utensils, handicrafts, and housewares. Half-a-dozen bands—both local and national—play over the weekend, from reggae to rock. There's great finger-lickin' food all over the place. There's Garlic University, an interactive play and educational area for kids. At Gourmet Alley you can sample the festival's signature dish—flaming shrimp scampi (with garlic, of course)—in addition to garlic crab cakes, garlic bruschetta, garlic pizza, garlic Argentine barbecue with garlic black beans and rice, garlic portobello sandwiches, and many other dishes. You can roam through the International Wine Garden, wet your whistle at the Garlic Oasis Bar, and watch the Smokin' Hot & Spicy Fire Fighter Barbecue Competition and the Garlic Chef Competition. Admission is charged.

PALM BEACH JEWELRY, ART, AND ANTIQUE SHOW
Palm Beach County Convention Center
650 Okeechobee Blvd.
West Palm Beach
(561) 822-5440
www.palmbeachshow.com

More than 200 prestigious fine-art dealers display their wares at this show, and thousands of collectors and aficionados come to see them. The art is rare and often spellbinding—oils and watercolors by important American and European painters in the 1800s; antiques of glass or silver from Europe, and of jade from the Orient; beer jugs from 17th-century Eastern Europe; silver pitchers from colonial America; old weathervanes and bells from England; 19th-century still-lifes; 19th-century game boards; Tiffany lamps; glazed and painted bowls and vases; and hundreds of other items of similar artistic value. Held in mid Feb; admission is charged.

PALM BEACH MARINE FLEA MARKET & SEAFOOD FESTIVAL
Palm Beach Kennel Club
1111 N. Congress Ave.
West Palm Beach
(954) 205-7813
www.flnauticalfleamarket.com

This is a huge festival in late Feb, with more than 400 marine and nautical vendor booths, new and used boats, live music, and plenty of great food. If it can be transported here (and transported away from here), vendors are selling it new, used, close-out, or liquidation—boats, fishing rods, reels, lures and lines, antique collectibles and maps, teak furniture, tournament gear, nautical art, crafts and jewelry, marine artifacts, boating apparel, taxidermy and fish reproductions, diving equipment, marine accessories parts, and even floating docks. Bands rotate on and off the stage all weekend long. And the food? Lobster, crab, clams, oysters, mussels, scallops, and all kinds of fresh fish that you can eat for dinner tonight. Admission is charged.

STREET PAINTING FESTIVAL
Lake and Lucerne Avenues
Downtown Lake Worth
561) 582-4401
www.streetpaintingfestivalinc.org/
This is not your idea of a classic art festival. There are no booths and no judges. But there's a lot of fun. More than 400 street artists take to downtown Lake Worth with their buckets and their brushes. Their canvas is the pavement and the buildings. As they transform downtown into an outdoor urban-art museum, their scenes bursting with color and with passion. Chipped, dirty old streets seem to come alive, with artwork ranging from fantastic to whimsical to gritty-realistic. There's also music and a children's play area. Held in mid to late Feb; free.

MARCH

ARMORY ART CENTER FESTIVAL
Armory Art Center
1700 Parker Ave.
West Palm Beach
(561) 832-1776
www.callsforart.com
The Armory Art Center was one of the first concrete steps in the revitalization of the West Palm Beach downtown core. Its name comes from the fact that it was actually a National Guard armory, which fell into disrepair after the Guard left for other quarters. A bunch of civic leaders got together to raise some money to re-purpose the old building. Then some local artists and friends of the arts got together to help rehabilitate the structure, and eventually filled it with imaginative art from many types of media. It's now not only a showcase for local artists, but also for national and international ones. And it hosts a wonderful festival each spring in late Mar. This show is juried, and no commercial,

manufactured, imported, mass-produced, or purchase-for-resale items are accepted. (In other words, it had better be original.) You'll see a lot that you like here, and perhaps some items that you won't like.

ART ON PARK FESTIVAL
Park Avenue
Downtown Lake Park
(561) 881-3338
www.artonpark.org
This free, late-Mar festival debuted in 2010, and its organizers—who chose Burt Reynolds as their first Honorary Jury Chair—have high hopes for the future. There are some good artists here, who express themselves through ceramics, jewelry, photography, painting, sculpture, and a variety of other means of self-expression. This festival is an important part of the downtown Arts District in Lake Worth, with the aim of getting local residents more involved.

BOCA BACCHANAL
Various locations
Boca Raton
(561) 395-6766
www.bocabacchanal.com
Some of the best gourmet-food producers and vintners in the world come to Boca for this event. Held in mid Mar, this three-day weekend of true elegance and wonderful new taste sensations requires advance-purchase tickets.

On Fri night, dinners take place at magnificent private homes in the Boca area, with white-glove service and samples of many different foods and wines. The conversation is convivial, the ambience is warm, and you're all there because you have a love of distinctive food and wine. On Sat evening at Boca Raton Resort & Club (501 East Camino

Real) there are presentations by numerous producers, chefs, and winemakers, and you'll leave the event a much more knowledgeable person than when you walked in. You'll get to sample the foods, of course. And there's also a silent auction. On Sun things are a bit more informal with an outdoor festival at the Center for the Arts in Mizner Park in downtown Boca Raton. There will be nearly 150 wines for tasting, along with the specialties of some of the area's best restaurants. If you go to one wine or food event this year—and you've got the financial wherewithal to go to this one—do it.

DELRAY BEACH ST. PATRICK'S DAY PARADE
Atlantic Avenue between Gleason Street and Swinton Avenue
Delray Beach
(561) 279-0907
www.festivalmanagementgroup.com
After 44 years, this parade is certainly a Delray tradition, and it's one of the largest St. Patrick's Day parades in Florida. According to legend, the parade had very modest origins. Maury Power was having a drink in a bar with some of his friends in Delray on St. Patrick's Day in 1967, and was lamenting the fact that the town had no parade to commemorate the occasion. Egged on by his friends—and a wee bit of Irish whiskey—he decided to stage a parade himself. He disappeared for a few minutes. When he returned to the bar, his friends were startled to see him in a top hat, and holding a shillelagh. He calmly walked out onto Atlantic Avenue, and began walking down the middle of the street. And the rest, as they say, is history. Since then, hundreds of thousands of people have followed his example. And the party doesn't stop when the parade does. People gather in Old School Square afterward to enjoy the food, the entertainment, and the atmosphere. Erin go bragh! Free.

EASTER BONNET DOG PARADE
Swinton Avenue and Northeast Second Avenue
Downtown Delray Beach
(561) 276-7511
www.delraycra.org
The participants in this parade are dogs wearing Easter bonnets. There are some Delray wags who call this the fashion event of the year. Certainly the participants—bulldogs, poodles, Ihasa apsos, Pekingese, and dachshunds, among others—would agree. They're enthusiastic walkers coaxed along by an occasional doggie biscuit or piece of dried beef jerky. And they're definitely fashion-forward; they even have "the walk" down. At the conclusion of the parade, at Old School Square, the judges will hand out the following awards: Most Original, Best Traditional, Funniest, Most Tropical, Most Frou-Frou, Tiniest Teacup, and the highlight of the affair, the Owner-Doggie Look-A-Like award. Held around Easter time in Mar or Apr; free.

FESTIVAL OF THE ARTS BOCA
Various locations
Downtown Boca Raton
(866) 571-ARTS
www.festivaloftheartsboca.org
There are people in Boca Raton who wait all year for this 10–11-day event in early Mar, hosted by the Centre for the Arts at Mizner Park, and featuring world-class art, music, literature, film, food, and wine. Most festival activities take place in or around the Count de Hoernle Amphitheatre, at the north end of this upscale shopping, dining, and residential complex. Daily concerts feature

famous performers of classical, Latin, jazz, and opera music. Leading orchestras from around the world come here to play. Famous writers lecture about their latest books or the craft of writing. Among the luminaries who have appeared here are musicians Yefim Bronfman, Itzhak Perlman, and Arturo Sandoval; playwright Edward Albee; writer Anna Quindlen; and the Russian National Orchestra. The food and wine component of the Festival of the Arts is called the Boca Bacchanal; there will be Vintner Dinners in private homes, and The Grand Tasting at the Amphitheatre. This frenzied week-and-a-half is Boca at its best. Various functions have different prices for tickets and/or entrance.

HATSUME SPRING FAIR
Morikami Museum and Japanese Gardens
4000 Morikami Park Rd.
Delray Beach
(561) 495-0233
www.morikami.org
The Hatsume Spring Fair celebrates the first buds of spring and turns a little corner of Delray Beach into Japan for a weekend. This joyful event takes place in mid to late Mar at one of the most beautiful spots in South Florida—the Morikami Museum and Japanese Gardens, which is green and serene, with red wooden footbridges crossing ponds filled with koi, rock gardens, incredibly intricate bonsai trees, small waterfalls flowing down rocks, and native Florida pines and palms. Three stages provide continuous entertainment, including taiko drumming, traditional Japanese folk music, martial arts demonstrations, origami lessons, plant sales, children's activities, and folk-tale telling. There are booths with craftspeople and artisans (and a booth that sells all the great old

Japanese monster movies!), plenty of good Japanese food, and a Kirin Beer Garden. Admission is charged.

IRISH FEST
Flagler Street
Downtown West Palm Beach
(954) 946-1093 or (800) 882-ERIN
www.irishflorida.org
It's that special time of the year on St. Patrick's Day when everybody's Irish. And nobody does it up quite like West Palm Beach. Flagler Street is closed off, and all things Irish have the run of the waterfront on this day. Well-known performers such as The New Wolfe Tones, the Tir Na Greine Dancers, Mac Talla Mor (Gaelic for "great echo"), and Noel Kingston bring the sights and sounds of Ireland to Flagler Street. There'll be some Irish jigging, some high-stepping, and a whole lot of blowing of the pipes. There's a marketplace with authentic gifts from Ireland, as well as artists and craftspeople showing their creations, an international food court, Irish comedians, and storytelling. And what would an Irish celebration be without a pub tent and real Irish food? There's a Keltic Kids Korner for the wee ones, with games, crafts, storytelling, and shows. So wear something green, hoist a glass, and shout out, "Slainte!" Admission charge for adults, children 14 and under get in free.

JUPITER/JUNO BEACH ART FEST BY THE SEA
A1A between Donald Ross Road and Marcinski
Jupiter
(954) 472-3755
www.artfestival.com
This free festival in mid Mar, which began in 1989, has become a harbinger of early spring

for North County residents. It's well-attended by both well-known artists who have been coming here for years, and creative new talents on the scene. You can find sculptures from six inches to life-size; paintings so vivid you'd swear they were photographs (and photographs so artsy you'd swear they were paintings!); one-of-a-kind, handmade jewelry items that no one else in the entire world will be wearing; and ceramics that will not only catch your eye, but enchant it. And it all takes place on A1A, Palm Beach County's Oceanside Road, so you'll be right next to the ocean and the sea breezes.

PALM BEACH FINE CRAFT SHOW
Palm Beach County Convention Center
Okeechobee Road
West Palm Beach
(561) 832-1776
www.craftsamericashows.com
This show brings more than a hundred top artists from around the country to West Palm. You'll have a chance to meet and talk with the artists, and they'll explain their work in media such as ceramics, glass, fiber decorative (and wearable) art, carved-wood, furniture in styles ranging from minimalist to whimsical, shaped metals, and imaginative jewelry. There'll be eye-catching glossy wooden bowls, misshapen human figurines of metal, carved metals and gold on wooden or marble bases, beautiful baskets, and one-of-a-kind jewelry pins and accessories. There's a special private reception the night before the show opens called a vernissage, and classes and lectures during the show. This is a juried show. Artists who display here also have works in prestigious museums and private collections across the country, as well as in the White House Collection of American Craft. Held in early Mar; admission is charged.

PALM BEACH GEM, JEWELRY, AND BEAD
South Florida Fairgrounds
9067 Southern Blvd.
West Palm Beach
(941) 954-0202
www.frankcoxproductions.com
If you can polish it, cut it, or string it, you can probably find it here. The gems are startling in their colors and clarity. The jewelry is a combination of classic looks and funky interpretations of same, hand-cut and shined. And the beads are of every color in the rainbow—and then some; and they're strung together in every conceivable pattern and design. Held in late Mar; admission is charged.

PALM BEACH HOME SHOW
Palm Beach County Convention Center
650 Okeechobee Blvd.
West Palm Beach
(954) 946-6164
www.palmbeachhomeshow.com
If you can put it into a home, use it in a home, or even dream about putting it in a home, it's here. And if it's colonial English, country French, Florida/Caribbean, contemporary Italian, Southwestern, Mexican, Mediterranean, Oriental, contemporary, modern, retro, King George the Fifth, or Louis the XIV, it's here. There are guest speakers who can tell you how to make your home beautiful, tell you how to get the most out of it, tell you what should go where, how to decorate your new home, how to re-decorate your old one, how to get the most from your decorating dollars, how to make your home environmentally friendly, tell you about design trends, give you inside tips on furniture, and even tell you how to sell your house. There are hundreds of specialists in furniture, decorating, landscaping, remodeling, and

exterior design all here to answer your questions. You'll have the opportunity to speak with experts in the fields of kitchen and bathroom design; pools and spas; outdoor living; tile, stone, and surfacing materials; window treatments and accessories; storm protection; and home security systems. You can wander to your heart's content around 150,000 square feet with more than 400 local, national, and international exhibitors. Held in mid Mar; admission is charged.

PALM BEACH INTERNATIONAL BOAT SHOW

On the waterfront along Flagler Street
Downtown West Palm Beach
(954) 764-7642 or (800) 940-7642
www.showmanagement.com
Take a county, if you will, that sits right on the Intracoastal Waterway and the ocean, and whose residents just happen to include some of the wealthiest people in the world. Think boats are popular in Palm Beach County? This boat show in late Mar is considered one of the top 10 in the country. Hundreds of boats—nearly $400 million dollars worth of them—are lined up at the docks and available for inspection (and, of course, in many cases, purchase). You'll see craft from many different countries, but not every one of them is necessarily a floating palace. Indeed, the collection actually has some 8-foot inflatables and dinghies. Then it goes through the ranks, starting with personal watercraft, bow riders, powerboats, fishing boats, speedboats, center-consoles, and finally ending at the Superyacht category—some of them 150 feet long. There's also a schedule of activities, including fishing clinics for the kids, and Xtreme Sport Fishing seminars for non-kids. Admission is charged.

REGGAE FEST

Bryant Park, on the Intracoastal Waterway
Lake Worth
Late-March
(561) 582-4401
www.lwchamber.com
In late Mar at Bryant Park you can picnic on the shores of the Intracoastal while grooving to some genuine roots-rock-reggae, as well as other music from the Caribbean. You'll sway with the plaintive, lilting rhythms of reggae from Jamaica, or calypso from Trinidad, or steel drums from the Bahamas. You can sample Caribbean foods like jerk chicken (a Jamaican specialty), conch fritters, spicy conch salad, turtle soup, or peas 'n rice. You can watch the brilliantly costumed stilt-walkers, purchase Caribbean handicrafts, or buy Bob Marley memorabilia.

ROYAL PALM ART & MUSIC FESTIVAL

Royal Palm Beach Boulevard at Southern
Boulevard
Royal Palm Beach
(561) 790-6200
www.palmswest.com
This festival enjoyed a successful debut in 2010. There's something for everyone here: a juried art show, street painting, street performers, music, cook-offs, and a beer garden. And the kids won't be bored, either, with a bounce house and carnival rides. There's also a Kids Edible Art Kitchen, where the kids are the artists who get to eat their art, rather than display it! All art and crafts are original; they can't be imported, manufactured, or mass-produced. Held in late Mar; free.

SAVOR THE AVENUE

Old School Square
Delray Beach
(561) 279-1380
www.eventful.com

At Savor the Avenue, you can be a guest at the longest dining table in Florida (and probably anywhere else, for that matter). In late Mar, 15 or so of Delray's finest restaurants fill that table with a breathtaking variety of foods, colors, textures, and aromas. You'll be sitting down with strangers, but by the end of the evening they'll be friends. This is an event for foodies, who love the experience of discovering new cuisines, new wines, and new restaurants. In the past, participating restaurants have included notable Delray eateries like Vic & Angelo's, City Oyster, and La Cigale. You'll choose from price-fixed menus ranging from the mid-thirties up to a hundred or so. The event kicks off with a cocktail party at 5:30 p.m. and a Grand Toast at 6:30 p.m.. And it's all for a very worthwhile cause—the Big Heart Brigade, a local organization that helps people in need. Ticket purchase required for admission.

APRIL

CIRCLE ON THE SQUARE
Old School Square
Downtown Delray Beach
(561) 243-7922
www.oldschool.org
If you're a foodie (or a wine-y), you won't want to miss this event in mid Apr. More than 20 well-known purveyors of fine foods and wines set up shop in historic Old School Square, and you can sample their products before buying them. In addition, a number of local restaurants also participate, so you'll be able to try out the food from that restaurant you've been thinking about trying. The local chefs who cook it will be there to talk with you about their work. And this is a great place to learn about new vintages and new trends in the world of fine wines. A great time, and a great food-and-wine education. Admission is charged.

THE DELRAY AFFAIR
Atlantic Avenue
Downtown Delray Beach
(561) 278-0424
www.delrayaffair.com
When it comes to art festivals in Palm Beach Count, this is the Big One. Held in early to mid Apr and free, it's the most popular arts and crafts street festival in the county. And when you stand at one end of the fair, on Atlantic Avenue, and look down the street at the mass of humanity filling your eye until it seems like it nearly hits the ocean, you'll see. The year 2010 was the 48th year of the Delray Affair. Well-known artists and craftspeople from all over the country—more than 600 of them—come to exhibit their work—pottery, sculpture, jewelry, crafts, photography, watercolors, oils, acrylics, natural wood, stained glass, tin, copper, brass, mixed-media . . . it's all here, used (and fused) in amazingly creative ways. And it doesn't matter if you come with no intention to buy, because it's certain you'll leave with something.

There are rides and games for the kids. The food here is lip-smackin' good (and a nutritionist's nightmare!)—conch fritters, Greek gyros, Polish and Italian sausages, fried bread, churros (fried dough, twisted and then coated with powdered sugar), sub sandwiches, hot dogs, cheese fries, nachos, hamburgers, pizza, ears of corn, legs of turkey, sweet nuts, ice cream, arrepas (a local Cuban specialty, with ground meat or cheese tucked inside and baked with dough), fried chicken, wings, etc. The Delray Affair is another one of those festivals at which you can make a day of it, because you're walking amidst the shops and sidewalk cafes of Atlantic Avenue, and you're just a couple of minutes from the beach. There's a free park-and-ride service.

PALM BEACH INTERNATIONAL FILM FESTIVAL
Various locations
Palm Beach County
(561) 362-0003
www.pbifilmfest.org

In a relatively short time, the Palm Beach International Film Festival has grown to become a world-class cultural event, with innovative new films from all over the world, visiting stars, and seminars and speakers. It's been called one of the top 25 independent film festivals in the world. Since its opening in 1989, the festival has showcased thousands of award-winning films, and hosted filmmakers, actors, industry professionals, and media from around the globe. There are generally more than a hundred new films shown here every year, with provocative themes and superb acting. More than 25,000 film fanatics come to see them every year. In all, PBIFF has hosted more than 160 world premieres and more than 1,200 films, from nearly 60 countries. Visitors have included, among many others, Academy Award® Winners Adrien Brody, Anthony Hopkins, Tommy Lee Jones, Faye Dunaway, Dennis Hopper, Louise Fletcher and Michael Caine, as well as other actors such as Salma Hayek, Edward Norton, Sylvester Stallone, Woody Harrelson, Roger Moore, Faye Wray, and Samuel L. Jackson. If you live for the love of film, this is one occasion you can't miss. Held in late Apr; admission is charged.

SUNFEST
Flagler Street on the waterfront
Downtown West Palm Beach
(800) SUNFEST (786-3378)
www.sunfest.com

This, quite simply, is the biggest event in Palm Beach County history, and one of the largest outdoor festivals in America. Founded in 1982, SunFest is Florida's largest waterfront music and art festival. Held annually in late Apr/ early May in downtown West Palm Beach, it attracts more than 300,000 visitors. Organizers call it "Where Music Meets the Waterfront" and that's probably the best way to describe these four to five days (and nights!). There's rock, reggae, hip hop, oldies, country, Latin, rap, Caribbean, folk, bluegrass, and jazz non-stop in the daytime and in the night. Performers have included James Taylor, Randy Bachman (Bachman-Turner Overdrive and The Guess Who), UB40, Spyro Gyra, Matisyahu, Sheryl Crow, Jimmy Buffett, Fergie, John Legend, George Clinton, Little River Band, and the Black Crowes. Captain Morgan's Floating Oasis— three barges—will tie up at the docks, and they'll offer the finest new concoctions using Captain Morgan's Rum. There's a juried fine arts and crafts show, with nearly 200 accomplished artists and craftspeople. The Youth Park has a wide range of activities and entertainment for the kids. SunFest always ends with a fantastic fireworks show—one of the largest on the East Coast. Admission is charged; children five and under are free.

MAY

DELRAY BEACH CRAFT FESTIVAL
Delray Beach Tennis Center
Atlantic Avenue
Downtown Delray Beach
(954) 472-3755
www.artfestival.com

This free festival has pretty much the same name as a festival in Mar, but it's a totally different festival. It takes place in late May on the grounds of the Delray Beach Tennis Center. This art show features handmade jewelry, as well as ceramics in the form of planters, vases, ceremonial bowls, and kitchenware, both utilitarian and elegant. You'll find paintings in all sorts of media that you never imagined before, such as 3-D acrylics. You'll find artists who can do amazing things with wood, taking a raw material from nature and turning it into a rich-looking masterpiece. You'll also find plants, orchids, and other exotic flora, and homemade soaps and bath items. All items are handmade in the USA.

JULY

THE FOURTH ON FLAGLER
Flagler Street, on the waterfront
Downtown West Palm Beach
www.wpb.org

Over the years, this has become one of Palm Beach County's signature events, and people come in to town from all corners of the county to take part. It's become the biggest Fourth of July celebration in South Florida. The fireworks begin at 9 p.m., and it's always a breath-taking display; but there's much more going on here than just fireworks. There are three stages for entertainment. Name bands play all their hits, and you can dance the night away in a separate area with a DJ. The kid's area has a bounce house, games, toys, and entertainment. The largest American flag you've ever seen is unfurled. In the Firefighter Splash & Dash, local fire departments compete against each other in watery games that are actually designed to test their real-world firefighting skills. There's plenty of food from all over the world, along with American favorites like dogs and burgers and fries. Free.

PALM BEACH CHAMBER MUSIC FESTIVAL
Palm Beach Gardens &
West Palm Beach
(800) 330-6874
www.pbcmf.org

This is a three-week-long festival from early July to early Aug that brings the beautiful sounds of chamber music to a Palm Beach County summer, in three different venues: Helen K. Persson Hall, Palm Beach Atlantic University, West Palm Beach; Eissey Campus Theatre, Palm Beach State College, Palm Beach Gardens; and Crest Theatre, downtown West Palm Beach. Not only is it a welcome addition to a rather-sparse summer cultural schedule in South Florida, but, people who listen to this music for the first time generally like it. The festival's mission is to give Palm Beach County residents the opportunity to enjoy truly good classical music, and to give talented local musicians the opportunity to play it. Lovers of classical music can listen to music by composers such as Beethoven, Dvorak, Ravel, Stravinsky, and Brahms.

AUGUST

BON FESTIVAL
Morikami Museum and Japanese Gardens
4000 Morikami Park Rd.
Delray Beach
(561) 495-0233
www.morikami.org

Obon is an ancient Japanese holiday when families honor their ancestors and thank them for the good life their descendants are living. At the Morikami, the traditional version of Obon isn't celebrated, but the Bon Festival is celebrated with great gusto. On the night of the festival, the grounds reverberate with the strong echoes of taiko drum performances. There's traditional Japanese folk-dancing—with audience participation—and a street fair with games and vendor booths selling crafts. The highlight of the evening comes at sunset, when the lake is transformed into a brilliant sea of lighted lanterns that, in accordance with Japanese custom, guide the departure of the souls of the ancestors who have come for a brief visit among the living. A fireworks display follows. Held in mid Aug; admission is charged.

SEPTEMBER

DELRAY BEACH CRAFT FESTIVAL
Atlantic Avenue
Downtown Delray Beach
(954) 472-3755
www.artfestival.com

This is another one of those Delray Beach craft shows that people here love, this time held in late Sept and still free. You'll be amazed at the diversity of the offerings, and the excellence of the craftsmanship. If you need something for the home or for a gift, there's a good chance you'll find it here.

OCTOBER

DELRAY BEACH CRAFT FESTIVAL
Fourth Avenue and Atlantic Avenue in downtown Delray Beach
(954) 472-3755
www.artfestival.com

This is one of the first art festivals in South Florida, heralding the return of fall and the cooler weather, along with the start of "The Season." Held in early Oct, it attracts creative types from all over the state, displaying their imaginative woodwork, weaving, household and kitchen items, handmade signs, and jewelry.

HISPANICFEST
Bryant Park
Lake Worth
(561) 582-4401
www.lwchamber.com

Palm Beach County's Latin population has increased dramatically in recent years, bringing a new flavor to the area. HispanicFest is Palm Beach County's largest Latin celebration. Timed to occur during Hispanic Heritage Month in mid Oct, it's a colorful and rhythmic whirl of great Latin music, food, dancing, arts, and crafts. Salsa bands and 10- or 12-piece orchestras, as well as talented vocalists, will bring you to your feet before you can count *uno, dos, tres*. There are 10 or 15 local Hispanic dance companies who strut their stuff with colorful costumes and incredible enthusiasm, to the steady beat of conga drums, horns, and the clave—a wooden instrument that generates the persistent beat found in much of Latin music. The food is wonderful here, with specialties such as *arroz con pollo* (chicken with rice), *arrepas* (a Cuban dish in which cheese, sometimes with ground meat, is fried inside a doughy wrap), fried plantains, barbecued pork, and churros (twisted fried dough that's dipped in powdered sugar). HispanicFest attracts well-known performers like Frankie Negro and Oro Solido. At this fair, it's a sure thing that the music is gonna get you. Admission is charged.

NOVEMBER

BREWTOPIA FESTIVAL
Morikami Park & Museum
4000 Morikami Park Rd.
Delray Beach
(561) 368.7164
www.thrillist.com

If you love good beer, if you love to talk about good beers of the world, and if you love to discuss the brewing process, come to the Brewtopia Festival in late Nov. A regular admission ticket gets you into the big tent, where you can enjoy and talk about some one hundred beers from all over the world, generally about 50 of which are microbrews, and 30 Belgian. If you spring for a VIP ticket, you will get in before everyone else and have access to some rare beers, as well as high-alcohol beers that the other attendees can only dream about. And if the names of these high-octane brews are any indication, be prepared for some really animated discussions (among the stiffer ones is Bell's Brewery Hopslam IPA, and there's rare stuff like Lost Abbey, Vintage 120 Minute Dogfish Head IPA, and Pizza Port. Admission is charged.

DELRAY BEACH THANKSGIVING WEEKEND ART FEST
Pineapple Grove
Downtown Delray Beach
(954) 472-3755
www.artfestival.com
Delray Beach has something going on—of one sort or another—pretty much every weekend during the Season. This free festival celebrates the beginning of the holiday season in late Nov. Pineapple Grove is a beautiful neighborhood just off Atlantic Avenue, with interesting clubs, bistros, and galleries. This one attracts good artists from all over the country, who somehow manage to lug their often-weighty pieces here. There are swinging metal horses almost the size of a real horse. There are life-size sculptures of people playing golf, birds flying, fantasy animals, etc. There are wonderful paintings, and a lot of great pottery, from Southwestern to surrealistic. And great food, as well.

HOLIDAY CRAFT FESTIVAL ON THE OCEAN
A1A between Donald Ross Road and Loggerhead Park
Juno Beach
(954) 472-3755
www.artfestival.com
The small seaside community of Juno Beach is host for this event, and you actually can see the beach (A1A runs right beside it). It's a pleasant setting for this mid-Nov crafts event. This is one of those shows that displays the talents of many artists who convert artistic dreams into pieces of everyday usability and value for the kitchen, the bathroom, even the bedroom. Stop in the candle booths; smell the candles while you admire the craftsmanship that went into creating them. Think about luxuriating in one of the hand-milled soaps or organic beauty products. And don't forget to take a good, solid breath of the sea air.

TASTE OF THE PALM BEACHES
PGA Commons
PGA Boulevard
Palm Beach Gardens
(561) 630-8630 or (877) 207-3779
www.tasteofthepalmbeaches.com
In early to mid Nov on one night, you can stroll through the PGA Commons streetscape while sipping fine wine, tasting tidbits of specialty cuisine, talking with award-winning chefs, enjoying bartending contests, browsing through the solid mile of wonderful shops, and stopping in at VIP lounges. Although the chefs are from Palm Beach County, the food is international. Thousands of foodies come from all over the county to enjoy it. Some 50 to 60 restaurants show their stuff, including Thai, Greek, Italian, Mexican, American, Irish, and many more. Sixty or 70 wines are sampled on a dozen tables. In addition, fine vodkas, rums, and other beverages are available for tasting and purchase. The week before the Taste of the Palm Beaches is filled with pre-event parties. This is one of the most anticipated—and fun—events of the season. Admission is charged.

VINTAGE—A SHOW & SALE
Palm Beach County Convention Center
650 Okeechobee Blvd.
West Palm Beach
(561) 483-4047
www.zitawatersbell.com

This show pays homage to the vintage period that started just after World War II, and ended in the mid-1970s. When the war ended, 12 million American servicemen and women came home and helped unleash a burst of creative energy in business, the arts, fashion, design, and popular culture that changed the world forever. Think poodle skirts, Danish-modern, hula hoops, the Twist, automobiles dripping with chrome and fins, glamorous costume jewelry, and real jewelry that Tiffany never could have conceived of in earlier days. There are three separate areas of the show. The first one has high-end designer clothing and jewelry. The second one features very nice items, but not necessarily with designer names. And the third section features the more-affordable items. Guest lecturers discuss the styling and furnishings of the Vintage period, which ranged from the conservative post-war "let's just get back to work" ethic to the halcyon days of the '70s, when we wore bell-bottoms and platform shoes (woman *and* men). Other lecturers discuss how to integrate vintage items into a modern lifestyle. Held in mid to late Nov; admission is charged.

DECEMBER

ART FESTIVAL & CRAFT FAIR
Masters Park
7100 Fairway Dr.
Palm Beach Gardens
www.craftlister.com

A show with an interesting and diverse range of artists, in all the traditional media, and some not so traditional. This free show in mid Dec began only in 2007 and has grown every year since. It's in a pleasant park setting, and the holiday spirit is present everywhere you look.

DELRAY BEACH HOLIDAY ART & CRAFT FAIR
Pineapple Grove
Downtown Delray Beach
(954) 472-3755
www.artfestival.com

It's the merriest week of the year in late Dec, and this is always a good show. It's filled with unusual types of art and crafts. There's plenty of great painting, photography, sculpture, pottery, and jewelry, of course, much of it by artists whose work you may have seen before in the newspapers or on TV. But there's more. Adjacent to the fair is a Crafter's Marketplace, where you can peruse stalls selling hand-crafted toiletries and cosmetics, beautiful and beautiful-smelling candles, and wooden plant holders and kitchen utensils. In addition, there's a large green market filled with colorful produce, unusual plants, and wonderful colors and smells. Free.

DELRAY BEACH NEW YEAR'S WEEKEND CRAFT FESTIVAL
Pineapple Grove in downtown Delray Beach
(954) 472-3755
www.artfestival.com

This free, late-Dec show features crafters only, no artists. If you're looking for that striking, one-of-a-kind gift, this is the place to find it. You'll want to spend the day here and in the surrounding streets of Delray, which are lined with some of the best restaurants, galleries, ice-cream, and coffee shops in South Florida.

PALM BEACH FOOD & WINE FESTIVAL
150 Worth Ave.
Palm Beach
(561) 366-1226
www.palmbeachfoodandwinefestival
.com

This event takes place in early to mid Dec, and it's a great time to be celebrating the variety and quality of Palm Beach County's dining scene. Thirty to 40 of the county's best restaurants get a chance to strut their stuff, each with a tasting station of their own. The most sophisticated eateries in Palm Beach County are generally represented here, but there have also been participants such as Hamburger Heaven and (one of my personal favorites, as far as names go) Grease Burger Bar. Each station is decorated in the motif of the host restaurant (Mexican, French, etc.); and the colorful foods on display make a stunning sight. Many of the chefs are there, filling up those stations with the specialties for which they're noted. As you wander among all the stations just after you enter, trying to get your bearings, you'll realize that you're going to have a heck of a time deciding what you want because it all looks great. Come hungry. And, if you haven't yet bought a ticket online, come early—because the line of hungry foodies gets pretty long.

PALM BEACH HOLIDAY BOAT PARADE
Intracoastal Waterway through North County
www.palmbeachboatparade.com

It's a spectacular sight. A parade of boats as far as the eye can see, including some of Palm Beach County's most elegant floating palaces and some of its coolest waterborne craft, gliding by in an unending procession of multi-hued strings of holiday lights reflecting off the water, and brightening the evening

as they do the season. You'll hear "oooohh" after "ahhhh," as each one passes, each one more spectacularly decorated than the one before it, and each filled with revelers making the most of this very special time. The boats travel 15 miles, from Peanut Island to the Jupiter Lighthouse, through seven North County towns, thrilling the crowds along the waterway—which exceed 100,000 people.

The day will actually kick off with a Family Fun Fair at Kelsey Park in Lake Park with games and entertainment, exhibits from the Marinelife Center, and a live band. One of the best viewing spots for the parade will be at the Riverside Event Plaza and Harborside in Jupiter. There'll be music and entertainment, and there's a rumor going around that Santa often stops there on his way from the North Pole. And just in case the boats didn't shine enough, a great fireworks display will light up the night even brighter.

ONGOING FESTIVALS

ART & JAZZ ON THE AVENUE
Atlantic Avenue
Downtown Delray Beach
www.downtowndelraybeach.com

Art & Jazz on the Avenue is an ongoing festival that begins in autumn and runs through winter and spring. People come out of their homes and cars and onto Atlantic Avenue, which is closed to traffic every Thurs from 6 to 10 p.m. The shops stay open late, the restaurants and clubs are packed, and a festive spirit runs up and down the street. You can listen or dance to bands playing Brazilian Bossa Nova, Dixieland, the Blues, jazz, country, pop, or junior-Frank-Sinatra. And the sidewalks are flooded with all kinds of art, including art you can sit on and art you can wear. Art & Jazz on the Avenue is like starting the weekend early.

ANNUAL EVENTS AND FESTIVALS

CLEMATIS BY NIGHT
Centennial Square, top of Clematis Street
Downtown West Palm Beach
(561) 822-1515
www.clematisbynight.net
For a really cool experience, head for the fountain in Centennial Square on any Thurs night from 6 to 9 p.m. You'll be one of thousands of people heading to the same place. Especially on winter evenings, it'll seem like half of West Palm Beach is here The music's great, with reggae, rock, rhythm and blues, soul, Latin, swing, and very good local bands playing them. And there's more than just music. Stores stay open late, and many display their merchandise right on the sidewalk. There's great food all over the place. Free.

DELRAY BEACH GREEN MARKET IN THE PARK
S.E. Fourth Avenue, off Atlantic Avenue
Downtown Delray Beach
(561) 276-7511
www.delraycra.org
Every Sat during the winter and early spring, from 11 a.m. to 1 p.m., Delray Beach goes green. This is a very popular market just off Atlantic Avenue, the location makes it a destination for people who want to spend the day in downtown Delray. All the fruits and vegetables are locally grown, and the growers are happy to talk with you about their methods and their missions. You'll find plenty of organic produce, wonderful baked goods, gourmet pastas, olive oils, vinegars, hot (and hotter!) sauces, artisanal coffees, fresh Italian cheeses, organic juices, and for the non-vegetarians, barbecue. There's also a good selection of flowers and plants. And there's live music, too. Free.

FIT WINTER EQUESTRIAN FESTIVAL
Palm Beach International Equestrian Center
3401 Equestrian Club Rd.
Wellington
(561) 793-5867
www.equestriansport.com
The format for this event is "the Hunters." Picture a fox hunt in England, where, in order to catch the fox, you (and your horse) have to ford rivers, jump fences, gallop hills and meadows, and sometimes jump fences into water. That's what this event is all about. This is show-jumping, where artistry counts as much as fences cleared successfully. Horse and rider are judged not only on the proficiency with which they take the obstacle-fences, but also on the style with which they do it. It's a family-friendly atmosphere, with competitions ranging from small children to adult amateurs to Olympic champions.

Held every Wed through Sun, 8 a.m. to late afternoon, from mid Jan to early Apr. General admission is free for most events. There are shops, coffee and wine bars, good food, and recreation areas for the junior set. This is a pleasant way to spend a beautiful South Florida winter day, and to be exposed to something you may not have considered before.

MAIN STREET CRUISE (MONTHLY CLASSIC CAR SHOW)
Abacoa Town Center
1155 Main St.
Jupiter
(561) 627-2799
http://events.pbpulse.com
Are you old enough to remember the Rascals singing *Cruisin?* Are you old enough to remember *American Graffiti?* Cruising is, of course, one of the Great American Dreams.

Remember how cool you felt when you were finally able to take your baby (car, not girl or guy) cruisin' down Main Street? Well, at Abacoa Town Center, it happens every month. This is the largest classic-car show in Palm Beach County.

On the first Sat of every month at precisely 8:30 p.m., some 400 classic cars go on what is probably the world's longest cruise, along Main Street. The show actually starts at 5 p.m. when you can ogle the cars, and get in the mood with a live band that starts playing at 7 p.m.—oldies, naturally. You should see these babies: 1950s Chevys and Chryslers and Fords, spit-and-polished and shiny to the nines, rear shark fins dripping with chrome; SS396 SuperSport logos all gleaming silver; green vintage Mustangs from the first years ('63 and '64) emitting that low, throaty rumble; beautifully preserved classics from the post-World War II years (or jeeps from the World War II years), putting you in the mood to swing, perhaps. Convertibles, hard-tops, coupes, sedans, Woodies, original Volkswagen vans and bugs, station wagons, pickup trucks, early black Fords. The owners are justifiably proud; and if there's one thing a classic-car owner loves almost as much as working on his car, it's talking about it, and showing it to people.

SUNDAY AT THE MEYER
Meyer Amphitheatre
Flagler Drive, West Palm Beach
www.wpb.org

Sunday at the Meyer is a welcome addition to the summer entertainment schedule in West Palm Beach, and people come from all over the county to experience it. This free concert, held select Sundays in summer and early fall, gives you an opportunity to enjoy both the great music and the great views; the Meyer is an outdoor amphitheater sitting right on the waterfront. Sometimes the acts are talented local bands. Other times, they're bands whose names you know; many of them achieved fame during the 1970s or 1980s, such as the funky/soul sounds of the Ohio Players; the soulful vocal harmonies of Firefall, the British group that gave us *Just Remember I love You* in the mid-1970s; the mellow, romantic sounds of Ambrosia, who spun out '70s hits like *You're the Only Woman, Biggest Part of Me,* and *How Much I Feel;* or the Tokens, who sang about the lion who slept at night in the 1960s. All of these groups have appeared at Sunday at the Meyer. Touring groups like the Legends of Doo-Wop (who really are original doo-wop'ers) also make stops at the Meyer. This is a great summer-and-fall vibe.

TASTE OF THE GARDENS GREEN MARKET
Gardens Park
4301 Burns Rd.
Palm Beach Gardens
(561) 630-1100
www.pbgfl.com

Spend a relaxing Sunday morning from late Oct through late Apr tasting Florida's bounty, as you wander through the aisles of produce, plants, flowers, nuts, honey, artisanal cheeses, fresh baked goods, handmade crafts, and prepared food and drink items. The produce is fresh and grown locally. But, just in case the atmosphere gets too relaxing for you, you can wander over to the stage, where there's a live band performing. The vegetables and fruits are a hundred brilliant colors, and the aromas of all the foods are very enticing. It's hard to leave without taking something with you! Free.

SHOPPING

If you can't find it in Palm Beach County, you can't find it anywhere. For one thing, Palm Beach's Worth Avenue may be the most famous shopping street in the world. (And, yes, many of the items for sale on Worth Avenue may be beyond the reach of most people. But it's sure fun to browse!) There are other tony shopping districts and centers, as well. But there are also hundreds of small one-of-a-kind places where you'll be delighted with the discoveries you come upon. From the funky to the fantastic, from bargain to *beaucoup bucks,* from the outlandish to the classic, and from clothing to kitchenware, music, art, home furnishings, souvenirs, and thrift, Palm Beach County has it. There are surprising treats waiting for you.

There is so much great shopping, in fact, that there are actually specific shopping districts in Palm Beach County—in addition to the thousands of individual shops outside these districts, as well as regional malls. The state sales tax in Florida is 6 percent.

SHOPPING DISTRICTS

South County

ATLANTIC AVENUE
Delray Beach
www.downtowndelraybeach.com
A darkened street of derelict businesses (and people) two decades ago, Atlantic was transformed in the 1990s into a fashionable destination-type area, with brick sidewalks, old-fashioned street lamps, and very new-fashioned galleries, restaurants, and clubs. The shops are a funky collection of the cool and the unusual. Some have actually been around since the derelict days, but have survived because of the quality of what they sell, and because local residents didn't want to let them go.

MIZNER PARK
Boca Raton
(561) 362-0606
www.miznerpark.com

Born in the mid-1990s, Mizner Park brought the "downtown" back into Downtown Boca. It's a multifaceted urban center with beautiful shops and restaurants, and upscale high-rise apartment and condos overlooking it all. You'll find very unusual men's and women's clothing boutiques such as Bolufe, specialty shops such as Spice and Tea Exchange, interesting bar/eateries such as The Dubliner Irish Pub, jewelers such as Van Cleef & Arpels, cultural options like The Centre for the Arts at Mizner Park, entertainment options including a cinema, and dining possibilities such as Ruth's Chris Steak House and a Boca landmark called Max's Grille.

ROYAL PALM PLACE
Boca Raton
(561) 392-8920
www.royalpalmplace.com

Royal Palm Place was Boca's original downtown upscale shopping and dining center, which has undergone a renovation in recent years that has restored it to its original glory. It was referred to for many years as "The Pink Plaza," for the Addison Mizner-type tropical-pink color that it still wears. There are many one-of-a-kind boutiques, salons, and services here, among them the Yaacov Heller Gallery, with an artist who has crafted custom jewelry for a Who's Who of the international set; the ultra-chic Gianni's Hair Salo; and Exor Galleries, a treasure-trove of distinctive art works. And there are some wonderful international eateries here, many of which offer outside dining.

i In Delray Beach, Atlantic Avenue gets most of the publicity. And it deserves it. But, when you're there, don't forget to explore the colorful neighborhood known as the Pineapple Grove Arts District. It's on Second Avenue, right off Atlantic and it's filled with surprises. Spend an hour or two wandering the aisles of Murder on the Beach Mystery Book Store. Ogle some art at Joanne Coia Gallery. Pick up a one-of-a-kind item at Museo. Enjoy a tortilla at Monterey Grill & Cantina. Improve your photography skills at the Palm Beach Photographic Center. Sample some Pad Thai at the House of Siam. Or just relax and watch the world go by at the Dolce Amor Café. But—whatever you do in Pineapple Grove—make sure you walk. Because this neighborhood was *made* for walking.

THE SHOPS AT BOCA CENTER
Boca Raton
(561) 361-9804
www.bocacenter.com

This is a place of quiet elegance, a place that doesn't have to shout out loud how wonderful it is because its customers do it. It's a collection of fine specialty and apparel shops, jewelry and one-of-a-kind gift shops, gourmet food and chocolate shops, and some of the coolest restaurants in town. It's an outdoor plaza; all shops have front doors opening to the outside. You can pick up a special wine or gourmet food at Joseph's Classic Market, while you're savoring something from Hoffman's Chocolates. Or, you may want to pick out a suit from Guy LaFerrera or Jos. A. Bank, and then enhance the day by treating yourself to one of Morton's the Steakhouse's thickest, juiciest cuts of beef. Perhaps you'll want to pamper yourself at Spalano Salon and Spa.

TOWN CENTER SHOPS
Boca Raton
(561) 368-6000
www.simon.com

This is where Boca comes to shop for variety and quality. There are nearly 200 upscale shops here, ranging from the tiny Swarovski shop to anchor department stores like Bloomingdale's, Nordstrom, Saks Fifth Avenue, and Macy's. You'll also find excellent specialty shops offering apparel, jewelry, gifts, and housewares, along with household names like Ralph Lauren Polo, American Eagle, and Banana Republic. There are also dozens of kiosks with items you probably haven't thought much about before, but which you just gotta have now. The mall is covered by a "soft" roof which allows sunlight in. It's always filled with discriminating shoppers. And you're bound to see a celebrity or two if you look carefully enough.

My Palm Beach County

"After working in Broward County all day, I love coming home to the peace and quiet of my western Palm Beach County home. Where I live, in west Boynton Beach, it's very quiet. All the developments are fairly new, and beautiful. And people are friendly. And everything you need is close by . . . good restaurants, movies. And the shopping is great. The Boynton Beach Mall is 10 minutes away, and Town Center in Boca is only 20 minutes away. And I'm right near the Florida Turnpike, so I can be pretty much anywhere in the county in a half-hour."

—Marcie Appleman,
Professional Educator

Central County

CITY PLACE
West Palm Beach
(561) 820-0074
www.cityplace.com

City Place was built in the mid-1990s to resemble an Italian town center. But its net effect was to transform downtown West Palm Beach into the glittering urban core it was always meant to be. You'll walk among atmospheric sidewalk cafes, interesting stores like Williams–Sonoma (exclusive kitchen and housewares), Restoration Hardware (with imaginative items for the home), Macy's, Barnes & Noble, an IMAX theater, and swank nightclubs. And, just like the Italian plazas it was meant to resemble, the central plaza here is filled with fine shops (including

a gelato shop, speaking of Italian), street performers, and people strolling with bags of chocolate and taking it all in.

CLEMATIS STREET
West Palm Beach
(561) 833-8873
www.westpalmbeach.com

Clematis Street was the original heart of West Palm Beach. But, like so many other Main Streets in urban America, it fell into disrepair (and disrepute) toward the end of the 20th-century. However, the city's Downtown Development Authority came to the rescue. Today, Clematis Street is better than ever, a gleaming testament to what an urban Main Street should be. It's a 24/7 hot-spot, crowded during the daytime with professionals and businesspeople, and at night with a fashionable crowd eager to try out each new restaurant and nightspot. For shopping there's Bright Idea Design Studio, Uomo Fashion, Green Olive Market Place, Authentic Provence, Eaton Fine Art, Atmosphere, Michael's Jewelers, Richard Plumer Design, and many more.

DOWNTOWN LAKE WORTH
Greater Lake Worth Chamber of Commerce
(561) 582-4401
www.lwchamber.com

Lake Worth, some years back, was in danger of folding into the Palm Beach County woodwork—unloved, un-visited, and un-busy. But that was before some local entrepreneurs got together and decided to convert old buildings with failing businesses into refurbished buildings with exciting new businesses, while still preserving the charm that had made those buildings so notable in earlier days. Now downtown Lake Worth is filled with unusual and interesting shops, galleries, and restaurants. And you'll enjoy a day spent wandering around here, and ducking into those interesting shops. And, most likely, walking out with something special.

WORTH AVENUE
Palm Beach
(561) 659-6909
www.worth-avenue.com

What can you say about Worth Avenue that hasn't already been said? It's one of the two or three most elegant shopping streets in the world, and it's one of the most beautiful streets in the world. It's great fun to go there even if you can't afford to buy anything, because the people-watching (and the celebrity-watching) is so great. This Mediterranean street is flowing with names like H. Stern, Tiffany, Chanel, Cartier, Giorgio Armani, Neiman Marcus, Michael Kors, Maus & Hoffman, Louis Vuitton, Gucci, Ralph Lauren, Saks Fifth Avenue, Salvatore Ferragamo, and Van Cleef & Arpels.

North County

ABACOA TOWN CENTER
Jupiter
(561) 748-8118
www.abacoatowncenter.com

Abacoa is laid out like a Main Street; it's very pedestrian-friendly. And that's a good thing because you'll want to walk into pretty much every doorway. For sports there's Bonanza Sports & Collectibles. For the latest from London and Paris stop in at Style So Chic. Is your dog getting a bit ratty? He/she will walk out of Every Dog Has Its Day ready for a show. Want to pamper yourself? Visit Abby Couture Boutique Salon & Day Spa. Work off the lunch you just finished in one of the great eateries at Xpress Fitness. To puff on a good stogie, go into Angry Moon Cigars.

THE GARDENS MALL
(561) 775-7750
www.thegardensmall.com

Whatever you need, you'll find it at the Gardens Mall. It's the place where North County comes together to shop, dine, and be entertained. This is a beautiful facility, and there's always a lot of special events going on. But the most special event of all may be just walking into the shops. Just a partial list would include Brookstone, Burberry, Lily Pulitzer, Anthropologie, Banana Republic, Louis Vuitton, Brooks Brothers, Tiffany, and Tommy Bahama. Want more? How about Lucky Brand Jeans, Ralph Lauren, Salvatore Ferragamo, White House Black Market, Victoria's Secret, and Johnston & Murphy.

PGA COMMONS
Palm Beach Gardens
(561) 630-8630
www.pgacommons.com

In some ways, PGA Commons is like a park; there are meandering brick paths, outdoor sculptures, and chess and checkers tables. But don't let that fool you. This is one of the sweetest shopping meccas in Palm Beach County. It boasts boutiques and specialty shops such as Bamboo Clothiers and Philip Simmonds Menswear; galleries like Onessimo Fine Art and Studio E; and salon and fitness spots like the Gilded Spa & Salon and Fitness Together. For when you need a break from shopping, there's a Kilwin's here so you can treat yourself to gourmet chocolates or ice cream or both!

ANTIQUES SHOPS

ANTIQUE MALL AT SIMS CREEK
1695 Indiantown Rd.
Jupiter
(561) 747-6785
www.simscreekantiques.com

One of the specialties here is ladies' hats, and the Antique Mall has many unusual ones. You can find them with purple feathers on top, with silk flowers, tons of fur, tiny metal cylinders, and in pillbox-style a la Jackie Kennedy. You can also find stunning quilts. For the child still inside you there are rare comic books in mint or near-mint condition. It might be Walt Disney's *Uncle Scrooge* from June 1956, *Archie* comics from December 1958, or *Detective Comics* from March 1959.

BLACKAMOOR ANTIQUES
3611A South Dixie Hwy.
West Palm Beach
(561) 721-1340
www.blackamoor.com
Blackamoor has an extensive collection of interesting antiques, ranging from 18th-century French bedroom furniture to jade sculptures and statuettes from the Ming Dynasty period. There are smaller English pieces, elegant in their simplicity. You may stumble upon flabbergasting finds—a 52"-high ceramic horse from the Ming Dynasty from approximately 200 B.C. Or perhaps Chinese ancestral portraits or Taoist art. Or that early 20th-century desk that you just have to have.

BRUCE KODNER GALLERIES
24 South Dixie Hwy.
Lake Worth
(561) 585-9999
www.brucekodner.com
Kodner Galleries is an 18,000-square-foot showroom in which you'll find a wide variety of art and antiques. These third-generation auctioneers specialize in old oil paintings and Oriental rugs, Tiffany and original items by Rene Lalique, and items by Royal Copenhagen, Lladro, Royal Doulton, and Hummel.

They also have a good selection of American and European flatware, tea sets, and fine dining items.

D AND G ANTIQUES
3234 South Dixie Hwy.
West Palm Beach
(561) 835-0461
www.dandgantiques.com
Located in the Antique Row area of South Dixie Highway, D and G has a good selection of antiques, furniture, and collectibles, ranging from the 18th century to the middle of the 20th. There's interesting mirror art and glassware, and a large collection of chandeliers and hanging lamps. Also in evidence here are plenty of dining sets and vases.

DELRAY BEACH ANTIQUE AND CONSIGNMENT MALL
1350 N. Federal Hwy.
Delray Beach
(561) 274-8000
www.delraybeachantiquemall.com
This store has over 16,000 square feet of antiques, mid-century furniture, consignment furniture, and collectibles. You'll find lamps, tables, chairs, rugs, sofas, armoires, dressers, desks, vases, and chandeliers, from British-Victorian to Oriental to contemporary.

ELITE ESTATE BUYERS, INC.
Quantum Town Center
1034 Gateway Blvd., Suite 106
Boynton Beach
Palm Beach (561) 301-9421
Boca Raton (561) 998-4332
www.eliteestatebuyers.com
This company carries (and purchases from estates) so many items that it would probably be easier to list what they don't sell. The owners are third-generation antiques

dealers, with over a hundred years of auctioneering experience between them. They focus on art, collectibles, jewelry, diamonds, gold, platinum, silver, coins, and currency. And if you can't get to them, they'll come to you; they'll actually stage an antiques road show in your home, development, or office.

KOFSKI ANTIQUES
315 South County Rd.
Palm Beach
(561) 585-1976
www.kofski.com
Established in 1939, Kofski claims to be Palm Beach's oldest antiques store. As you browse through here, you'll come upon some very unusual items. One example might be a Mottahedeh Cat, from the Rockefeller Collection. Another might be some sterling silver nut dishes from Europe, with intricate carving, or a set of 18th-century French cups and saucers, exquisitely hand-painted. Walk down a different aisle, and you may come upon a hand-painted figurine of two bakers sitting amidst their products, from Victorian England.

MAURICE'S OLDE WORLD
 FURNISHINGS
950 Jupiter Park Dr.
Jupiter
(561) 747-4539
www.mauricesfurniture.com
Maurice's imports furniture from all over the world, and specializes in restoring old pieces to their original beauty and functionality. And they carry some very unusual items, such as a large selection of antique window screens, shutters, window frames, and door panels. They've carried items such as shoemakers' stands, wheelbarrows, iron stoves, wine presses, and umbrella stands. Another specialty is intricately painted hand trunks from Tibet and other countries in Asia.

N. P. TRENT ANTIQUES
3729 South Dixie Hwy.
West Palm Beach
(561) 832-0919
www.nptrentantiques.com
This is another quality gallery located on West Palm's Antique Row. Owners Audrey and Stuart Peckner deal in period English and continental furniture, art, and decorative accessories, focusing on pieces from the 17th to the early 19th centuries. The Peckners say they try to focus on the classic, and on the unusual. Their store has a variety of desks, dining sets, china cabinets, mirrors, and chandeliers. Items that have come through the store in recent months include a pair of Louis XV corner kingwood cabinets from the mid-17th century; English rolling library steps (think *My Fair Lady*) from ca. 1800; an Italian mirror of mahogany and satinwood ca. 1800; and an Italian Neoclassical gilt and painted console from around 1780.

REYES FINE ARTS & ANTIQUES
1045 East Atlantic Ave.
Delray Beach
(561) 330-8399
www.reyesfinearts.com
The owners travel all over the world to find pieces for their store, and you'll see the international flavor as soon as you walk in. They specialize in original decorative arts and antiques, including oil paintings, giclees, chandeliers, porcelain sculptures, ivory and jade carvings, furniture and lighting, and silk and wool rugs. They also have fountains and garden bronzes on display in the courtyard.

TRUE TREASURES ANTIQUES
1201 US 1, Suite 15
North Palm Beach
(561) 625-9569
www.truetreasuresinc.com
Room-size Oriental rugs, dining room sets from 18th-century Britain, a Marquis vase by Waterford Crystal, a country French two-door chest from the 18th century. At True Treasures, you never know quite what you're going to find. And that's why it's so much fun to go there. Another reason is that there's always something you can buy, whether your wallet is fat or thin; items start at five dollars, and run well into the thousands. Want a painting of 17th-century French nobility, need a Tiffany lamp from the 1890s, need a new purse or old one . . . an Italian vintage black suede evening bag? Two other locations include the Annex store in the Home Depot Center at 3936 Northlake Blvd. in Palm Beach Gardens (561-694-2812) and the Boutique outlet at 617 Northlake Blvd. in North Palm Beach (561-844-8001).

WILSON ANTIQUES
3716 South Dixie Hwy.
West Pam Beach
(561) 802-3881
www.wilsonantiques.1stdibs.com
The specialty is 18th- and 19th-century European items . . . hundreds and hundreds of pieces. You might find an 18th-century Venetian console, or an Italian wrought iron table. Maybe a French mirror, an 18th-century French pump, or a sideboard piece (a small dresser) from Tuscany. There is a painted four-panel screen, a French picture frame, Spanish chandeliers, and wrought iron lanterns. And, of course, with any good antiques dealer, the list changes all the time.

BOOKSTORES

BARNES & NOBLE
University Commons
1400 Glades Rd.
Boca Raton
(561) 750-2134

333 North Congress Ave.
Boynton Beach
(561) 374-5570

The Palladium at CityPlace
700 Rosemary Ave Unit #104
West Palm Beach
(561) 514-0811

11380 Legacy Ave.
Palm Beach Gardens
(561) 625-3932
www.bn.com

BOOK EXCHANGE AND COMIC SHOP
807 Northlake Blvd.
North Palm Beach
(561) 863-1555

BOOK RACK
3821 West Woolbright Rd.
Boynton Beach
(561) 734-2767

BOOKS-A-MILLION
1630 South Federal Hwy.
Delray Beach
(561) 243-3395

6370 West Indiantown Rd.
Jupiter
(561) 743-8094
www.booksamillion.com

BOOKSMART
670 Glades Rd.
Suite 180 Boca Raton
(561) 394-6085

4469 S. Congress Ave. Suite 116
Lake Worth
(561) 964-0023

BOOKWISE
399 N.E. Spanish River Blvd.
Boca Raton
(561) 347-6455

BORDERS
9887 Glades Rd.
Boca Raton
(561) 883-5854

10300 West Forest Hill Blvd.
Wellington
(561) 792-4012
www.borders.com

CHANGING TIMES BOOKS & GIFTS
911 Village Blvd., #806
West Palm Beach
(561) 640-0496

CLASSIC BOOK SHOP
310 South County Rd.
Palm Beach
(561) 655-2485
www.classicbookshop.com

CLEMATIS STREET BOOKS & CAFÉ
206 Clematis St.
West Palm Beach
(561) 832-2302

MY BOOK PLACE
124 Bridge Rd.
Jupiter
(561) 747-9597

MURDER ON THE BEACH
273 Pineapple Grove Way
Delray Beach
(561) 279-7790
www.murderonthebeach.com

SHINING THROUGH
426 East Atlantic Ave.
Delray Beach
(561) 276-8559

WALDENBOOKS
600 Glades Rd., Suite 1166
Boca Raton
(561) 394-0193

East Boynton Beach Blvd.
Boynton Beach
(561) 736-5531

10300 West Forest Hill Blvd., #248
Wellington
(561) 792-4012
www.waldenbooks.com

BOUTIQUES/GIFT SHOPS
South County

BOCA FLOWERS
6345 N. Federal Hwy.
Boca Raton
(561) 998-8180 or (800) 480-7445
www.bocaflowers.com
This shop is family-owned and operated.
Whatever the occasion, they'll create a beautiful arrangement that will satisfy both you
and the recipient.

BOCA GIFT BASKETS
940 Clint Moore Rd.
Boca Raton
(561) 994-8495
www.bocagiftbaskets.com
In a State of the Industry survey in 2006, Boca
Gift Baskets was named one of the top 50
basket companies in America. They create
the most beautiful or the most whimsical
baskets—your choice—overflowing with
great treats for the taste buds. You can order
a gourmet basket filled with fine wines,

cheeses, crackers, jams, pretzels, spreads, and other good stuff. You can order one of just wine and cheese, or a fruit basket with pretty much every color of the rainbow represented. On the whimsical side order a Spongebob Squarepants basket overflowing with junk food.

CONVERSATION PIECES
187 N.E. Second Ave. (Pineapple Grove Way)
Delray Beach
(561) 274-6915 or (888) 274-6917
www.econversationpieces.com
Located in the colorful Pineapple Grove Arts District of Delray Beach—right off Atlantic Avenue—this shop carries an eclectic range of fine handcrafted gifts and accessories for the home. Everything is hand-crafted by talented artists from all over the world, and many items are one-of-a-kind, or limited-edition. They specialize in unique jewelry, housewares, personalized gifts, seasonal decorations, handbags and scarves, items for the office, and Judaica. And, of course, special gifts for special occasions, such as Valentine's Day.

EDIBLE ARRANGEMENTS
Mission Bay Plaza
20437 State Rd. 7
Boca Raton
(561) 470-1414
www.ediblearrangements.com
The problem with baskets from Edible Arrangements is that you might finish them off before you are able to give them to someone. They're filled to the brim with fresh fruit, much of which is covered with chocolate, or enhanced with marshmallows or other good stuff. The Slam Dunk Delight is a fruit basket that's actually in the colors and shape of a basketball.

EXCEPTIONAL FLOWERS & GIFTS
2800 North Federal Hwy.
Boca Raton
(561) 353-4720
www.exceptionalflowersgifts.net
You can't miss when you remember a friend or loved one with a beautiful bouquet of fresh, colorful flowers. On the other hand, you can't miss, either, when you remember a friend or loved one with a Sweets in Bloom Celebration Chocolate Candy Cake! Send it locally, or send it anywhere across the country. It'll get there when you want it to. And the recipient will enjoy every sniff . . . or every taste!

HAND'S OFFICE AND ART SUPPLY
325 East Atlantic Ave.
Delray Beach
(561) 276-4194
Delray Beach has certainly changed over the years. Just in the past two decades, Atlantic Avenue has transformed from a blighted, empty street into a downtown destination, filled with trendy shops and boutiques. Yet, in all these years and through all these changes, there's one thing that hasn't changed—Hand's stationers. The store is still owned by the family that founded it some 70 years ago. And it's still filled with one of the widest varieties of art supplies—and eclectic gifts for the home and office—of any store in the area. If you're in the market for paints or canvases or an old-time rollback desk, this is the place to find it.

MARIA HAMILTON DESIGNS
P.O. Box 812241
Boca Raton, FL 33481
(561) 400-5383
www.mariahamiltondesigns.com

Maria Hamilton creates beautiful custom jewelry (rings, bracelets, and necklaces) that's influenced by her Venezuelan roots, and her innovative mixing of colors, textures, and materials. She uses silver, gold, leather, crystals, shells, and semiprecious stones, mixing and matching to create unique combinations, such as a necklace of black leather, pearls, and silver. In addition, she also reinvents vintage jewelry, giving it a fresher, shinier look. Hamilton works by appointment only.

SECOND TIME AROUND WOMEN'S CONSIGNMENT BOUTIQUE
10 S.E. Fourth Ave.
Delray Beach
(561) 278-0493

You know that wonderful vintage-type dress that you've always wanted, but never been able to find in a store? Well, you should try looking here. All of the clothing is in excellent condition (some of it never worn), and the designs range from new to vintage. Whatever the fashion or style, from Roaring Twenties to psychedelic '60s, garish 70s to formal-elegant and contemporary-casual, there's a good chance you can find it at Second Time Around. You'll have a great time just looking around and probably end up finding something you like.

SMART DECO
1501 Northwest Boca Raton Blvd.
Boca Raton
(561) 620-0287
www.smart-deco.com

Smart Deco calls itself a Lifestyle Boutique. Here, you can find a wide variety of products for the home, ranging from the traditional to the sleek and contemporary, from selected European and American designers. The specialty is coffee—coffee beans, coffeemakers, espresso makers, cappuccino makers, along with other items such as specialty teas. There's also a wide selection of floor lamps, tables, chairs, and chests, as well as home accessories and just about anything you can think of for the kitchen.

Central County

ANGELIQUE'S FLOWERS & GIFTS
6311 South Dixie Hwy.
West Palm Beach
(561) 577-7288
www.angflowers.com

What could be better than a beautiful bouquet of fragrant flowers? Well, perhaps the same bouquet with a teddy bear, or a bottle of champagne, or champagne and Godiva chocolates . . . and no flowers. Or, perhaps all of the above. At Angelique's Flowers & Gifts, there are so many of each (flowers and gifts) that you can mix and match to your heart's content. On their Web site, there's even a page where you can create your own arrangement.

BLOSSOM SHOP FLORIST & GIFTS
402 East Ocean Ave.
Boynton Beach
(561) 732-3722
www.blossonshoppeflorist.com

This shop is family-owned and operated. They can create a wide variety of floral and culinary gifts for you. And they can create these gifts with a special motif to match any occasion, any holiday, or any season. Included in their line-up are silk arrangements, dried flowers, special gifts, foods, and wines. There are also selections of greeting cards, candles, and various plants.

BOUTIQUE GIORGIO ARMANI PALM BEACH
243 Worth Ave.
Palm Beach
(561) 655-1641
www.giorgioarmani.com

What do you get for the person who has everything? Something from one of the greatest designer boutiques in the world. Clothing, accessories, wallets and purses, watches, suits for men and women, pants, shirts, belts, cufflinks and small jewelry items, shoes, items for personal use, items for the home . . . and, of course, some of the most distinctive fragrances you'll ever have the fortune to smell. But that leads to another question: Why does the person for whom you get this gift have to be someone else? Why shouldn't it be you?

BROOKSTONE
The Mall at Wellington Green
10300 West Forest Hill Blvd., #166
Wellington
(561) 793-6205
www.brookstone.com

If you've ever been inside a Brookstone, you know what to expect—the unexpected. And the most modern and functional designs in appliances, clothing, furniture, housewares, and recreation. The coolest electronic video games and music players; the funkiest design in chairs and lounges; ergonomic beds, sofas, and chairs; and easy chairs with massagers for your neck, back, and even legs. There are back supports that help you stand straighter, and pillows that help you relax easier. State-of-the-art elliptical machines, stair-steppers, and exercise bikes. And surprising new things coming in almost daily.

CARTIER
301 Worth Ave.
Palm Beach
(561) 655-1550
www.cartier.com

When you say Cartier, you really don't have to say much more. Whether you're looking for something special for a friend or for yourself, this shop is filled with special things. This is the home of one of the world's greatest lines of fragrances, of course, originally created by Coco Chanel and now carried on by her corporate heirs. But there's much more here, as well—makeup, skincare items, watches, ready-to-wear apparel, sunglasses, jewelry, handbags, shoes, costume jewelry, scarves, ties. And, of course, the satisfaction of buying something that says Cartier on it.

CHANGING TIMES BOOKS & GIFTS
The Village Commons
911 Village Blvd., Suite 806
West Palm Beach
(561) 640-0496
www.changingtimesgifts.com

Since 1990, Changing Times has been a relaxing center of knowledge and personal growth, providing the tools to live a more "conscious" life. The focus here is on New Thought and spirituality, in ways that can help people achieve their goals in life. Toward that end, the shop has an interesting collection of gifts and books, along with classes, and readings with professional psychics. Even just roaming around the shop, you'll feel a sense of peacefulness come over you, and perhaps, even a sense of clarity. If you know someone who's spiritual, you can find the perfect gift here.

EDIBLE ARRANGEMENTS
13873 Wellington Trace
Wellington
(561) 422-3232
www.ediblearrangements.com
Colorful fruit, sweet chocolate, and an occasional teddy bear thrown in. A combination like that can brighten the most miserable day. Edible Arrangements has arrangements of fruit, candy, and small gift items.

EDISON QUIJADA'S FLOWERS & GIFTS
4120 Tenth Ave.
Lake Worth
(561) 856-7121
www.quijadaflowers.com
No matter the special (or sad) occasion, no matter the season, no matter the age or gender of the person receiving it, Edison Quijada has the perfect gift. Flowers, of course, in arrangements that will please both your nose and your eyes. But also food, gift baskets, small gift items, and other items that can brighten anyone's day. And they'll even deliver it to you.

GODIVA BOUTIQUE
Wellington Green
10300 W. Forest Hill Blvd.
Wellington
(561) 792-5899
You only have to say the word—Godiva—and you'll get a picture in your mind, of smooth, hand-dipped chocolate, of a quality that rivals any in the world, arrayed along a counter and filled with different types of cream, nuts, or just more smooth chocolate.

GREEN ACRES FLORIST
7155 Lake Worth Rd.
Lake Worth
(561) 966-4417
www.greenacresflorist.com

Need a little pick-me-up? Here's a taste of spring and a special gift for someone who's having a hard time or a joyous time. They have a wide variety of arrangements of flowers and tropical plants. Green Acres Florist can help you pick out the arrangement that's right for your special friend.

TROPICAL FRUIT SHOP
261 Royal Poinciana Way
Palm Beach
(561) 832-3449
www.tropicalfruitshop.com
In South Florida, any business more than 20 or 30 years old is considered old. This business, however, has been around since 1915. It was the first to ship fruit out of the state. And the fact that it's still in business nearly a hundred years later says something about the dedication to serving their customers, and the loyalty of those customers. Most of the fruit is grown locally, a bit to the north in Indian River County, and it's juicy and delicious. Tropical Fruit Shop can create a basket for every occasion, from corporate meeting to romantic anniversary. And it's not just fruit. They can add jams, crackers, cookies, spices, and candies.

TUESDAY MORNING
The Village Shoppes on 441
10209 Southern Blvd., Suite 230
Royal Palm Beach
(561) 792-7608
www.tuesdaymorning.com
At Tuesday Morning, new deliveries arrive—you guessed it—every Tues morning. At this store, you'll find a treasure trove of things for your home and for your life. You'll find things for the bedroom and the bathroom. You'll find a variety of beautiful crystal, decorative home accents, gourmet foods, lawn and

garden accents, toys, and much more. You'll see names like Martex, Limoges, Murano, Wedgwood, Samsonite, Royal Doulton, Lego, Madame Alexander, and Steinbach. And the best thing about Tuesday Morning is that you'll see them for much less than you would at any other store.

YANKEE CANDLE COMPANY
Boynton Beach Mall
801 North Congress Ave.
Boynton Beach
(561) 752-9554
www.yankeecandle.com

If you're like most people, it's hard to walk by Yankee Candle Company without noticing the colors, and, especially, the aromas. And once you notice those aromas, it's hard not to walk in. Before your eyes will be the most diverse collection of candles you've ever seen. In this store, almost every candle tells a story, and candles have a calming quality, of course.

North County

THE AMERICAN GOURMET
Village Square
257 US 1
Tequesta
(561) 744-1660
www.the-american-gourmet.com

The American Gourmet is actually a restaurant. But it's also a retail store, with wonderful baked goods and gift baskets. Everything is baked fresh on the premises, including aromatic (and very tasty) pies, cakes, pastries, and muffins. Cakes are custom-made; you can even get one with flowers on it. The gift baskets are great; the breakfast gift basket, for example, has smoked salmon, fresh fruit, scones, and tea or coffee. The presentation of the gift baskets are so attractive.

ANNA FLOWERS
450 S. Old Dixie Hwy. Unit 6
Jupiter
(561) 746-1288
www.annaflowersjupiter.com

Do you know how to help flowers last longer? Do you know how to keep them looking fresh and crisp? Do you know about seasonal varieties? And how's your plant knowledge these days? Family-owned and operated, this shop has a wonderful selection of fresh flowers, and they also take the time to answer questions such as these, and to help you pick out the flowers and the arrangement that's right for you.

CUSHMAN FRUIT COMPANY
204 US 1
North Palm Beach
(561) 848-6686
www.honeybell.com

When Ed Cushman opened a small fruit store in West Palm Beach in 1945, he probably had no idea his little store—now this store in North Palm Beach as well as the original in West Palm—would still be around 65 years later. And that it would still be operated by his family. The Cushman family still picks the best crops, and still picks the choicest fruit. And—just like all those years ago—people who visit Palm Beach County are still contacting the Cushmans, and still asking for some of that delicious fruit to be shipped back to them up North.

CUSTOM SWIMWEAR
1237 East Blue Heron Blvd.
Singer Island
(561) 845-7848
www.customizedswimsuit.com

At Custom Swimwear, you don't have to fit into a bathing suit. They'll make one from scratch that fits you perfectly. They've been in business for 20 years, and they have a reputation for stylish swimsuits that fit perfectly. Not only that, you can bring them your old suit that doesn't fit quite right or that has something missing or broken—and they'll fix it. No one-size-fits-all philosophy at this shop. You'll walk out with a bathing suit that fits your body, and fits your style.

ELEGANT LADY CONSIGNMENT BOUTIQUE
11575 US 1
North Palm Beach
(561) 842-0107
Need a sundress for summer or a formal gown for a big affair? Need a Saturday night dress for a big date or a night out with friends? Elegant Lady has something more vintage, in a dress or a hat, something sexy, and something more conservative. There are smart clothes for the office And really unique items.

FLORAL GARDENS & GIFTS
7100 Fairway Dr.
Palm Beach Gardens
(561) 622-5740
www.floralgardensandgifts.com
If you want a beautiful flower or plant arrangement, but you're not sure what you want it to look like, come in to Floral Gardens & Gifts. They'll take the time to go over all the options with you, and you'll learn something in the process. Of course, they also have the little gifts and add-ons that can make a flower arrangement extra special.

JUPITER HOBBIES & CRAFTS
Sims Creek Plaza
1695 West Indiantown Rd.
Jupiter
(561) 744-3800
www.jupiterhobbies.com

This shop is not only a kid's wonderland, it's a wonderland for the kid in all of us. If you can think of a hobby, you'll find it here. There are remote-control cars, planes, helicopters, and boats, plus rockets, science kits, kites, puzzles, and trains. All types of arts and crafts kits, painting supplies, drawing supplies and colored pencils, and ceramics are here. This shop is nirvana for model-builders—plastic models, wood models, and models from renowned manufacturer Revell. The only problem with planning to stop here is that you won't want to leave.

KILWIN'S CHOCOLATES & ICE CREAM
PGA Commons
4580 PGA Blvd., Suite 101
Palm Beach Gardens
(561) 296-6226
www.kilwins.com
If you want to give a gift that shows you care, how about chocolate? At Kilwin's, you'll be enveloped in a world of chocolate, created in incredible shapes, filled with incredible creams and fruits, hand-dipped, and baked into sweet fudge, right before your eyes. Chocolate is chopped into tiny bits and stuffed into cookies that melt in your mouth, and wrapped in brilliant colors and in whimsical containers. Kilwin's is considered by many to be the best confectionary/ice-cream store in South Florida.

LJA DESIGNS
Lauren J. Alexander
13909 Deer Creek Dr.
Palm Beach Gardens
www.ljadesignsinc.com
Lauren Alexander creates unique custom jewelry from sterling silver, gold, and semiprecious stones. Her designs have been featured in *Playboy, Elle,* and *Seventeen,* and have been

sold in high-end stores such as Neiman Marcus. She specializes in necklaces, bracelets, and earrings, often enhancing them with stones such as garnet, blue topaz, and amethyst. When you sit down with Lauren Alexander and work out a design, you'll know that, when you walk out with it, no one else in the world will be wearing the same piece.

SWAROVSKI BOUTIQUE
The Gardens of the Palm Beaches
PGA Blvd.
Palm Beach Gardens
(561) 799-9880
www.swarovski.com

Swarovski Boutique is a crystal wonderland of reflections and whimsical forms, ranging from one-inch high to a foot or two. Every shelf has distinctive forms and shapes, both adorable and incredibly intricate at the same time, and throwing off subtle yet vivid shades of blues, lavenders, reds, and greens. Swarovski has always stood for original pieces and quality workmanship. It might be a tiny piano, or frog, or butterfly. Or it might be beautiful wine glasses, or crystal jewelry boxes. But something is going to reflect so brightly that it's going to catch your eye, and you won't be able to leave without it.

THINGS REMEMBERED
The Gardens
3101 PGA Blvd.
Palm Beach Gardens
(561) 776-8263
www.thingsremembered.com

Know a guy who would enjoy having a pair of engraved cuff links, or a pocket watch on a chain? Know a lady who might love having a sterling heart necklace or key chain? What about a gift for a graduate, a beautiful writing instrument, perhaps? At Things Remembered, there are all sorts of imaginative gifts in gold, silver, and glass, and you can get them all engraved on-site. They have fancy photo albums, beautiful jewelry boxes, and special mementoes for special occasions.

WILSON'S JEWELERS
11941 US 1 North
North Palm Beach
(561) 775-2022
www.wilsonsjewelers.net

The first hint you get that Wilson's is different is when you drive up. The business is housed in a magnificent Art Deco building of light pink, with columns on the bottom and 1920-ish glass-block windows on top. Once you get inside, you're surrounded by distinctive hand-crafted treasures in diamonds, gold, silver, and semiprecious stones. They have a wonderful collection of pretty much any type of jewelry you might want.

CHILDREN'S CLOTHING

ABERCROMBIE & FITCH
Town Center at Boca Raton
6000 Glades Rd., Space #1211a
Boca Raton
(561) 368-2247

Wellington Green
10300 West Forest Hill Blvd, Suite 186
Wellington
(561) 333-4031

The Gardens of the Palm Beaches
3101 PGA Blvd.
Palm Beach Gardens
(561) 775-9410

A PINK PRINCESS
1120 S. Federal Hwy.
Boynton Beach
(561) 733-3123

BABY GAP
401 Town Center Rd.
Boca Raton
(561) 391-2224

CONSIGN-A-KIDS
660 Linton Blvd.
Delray Beach
(561) 276-9798

THE CHILDREN'S PLACE
Boynton Beach Mall
801 N. Congress Ave.
Boynton Beach
(561) 742-9106

KID'S KLOSET OF JUPITER
651 W. Indiantown Rd. #L
Jupiter
(561) 743-7716

TJ MAXX
2430 PGA Blvd.
Palm Beach Gardens
(561) 625-4117

COLLECTIBLES

People have been visiting Palm Beach County—and leaving things behind—since the 1700s. And they have also been bringing things here from their home towns, or buying interesting things once they got here. Some of them, no doubt, were interesting only to the buyer. But, lo and behold, as the years—and the centuries—have passed, some of these items are now pretty valuable, both in terms of monetary value and emotional value. In Palm Beach County, you'll run into both types of items—those that have appreciated in monetary value over the years, and those you just have to have.

South County

FIELD OF DREAMS
Boca Town Center
6000 Glades Rd., #1017
Boca Raton
(561) 395-6288
www.fieldofdreams.com
This is a place where sports buffs can congregate and debate for hours, and it's got an exceptional collection of memorabilia. There are signed shirts by football stars such as Peyton Manning and Drew Brees, autographed baseballs from the days when the Los Angeles Dodgers were still the Brooklyn Dodgers (pre-1956), a basketball autographed by Ernie DiGregorio of the late (but not so great) Buffalo Braves, and an autographed photos from another team no longer in existence, the old Hartford Whalers of the National Hockey League. The treasures never run out here. And neither does the great conversation.

GIFT SHOP AT THE BOCA RATON MUSEUM OF ART
Mizner Park
501 Plaza Real
Boca Raton
(561) 392-2500
www.bocamuseum.org
The Boca Raton Museum of Art has more than 4,000 masterworks of art in its collection, and that doesn't include the ones in the gift shop. You can find classic statuettes here; hand-made, signed glass paperweights created by noted artist Robert Held; glass with brilliant colors inside; Greek vases; souvenir umbrellas; soapstone and rock sculptures; and wooden dolls. The gift shop is the type of place in which you could easily spend an hour browsing.

SPORTS IMMORTALS
6830 N. Federal Hwy.
Boca Raton
(561) 997-2575
www.sportsimmortals.com

This may be the perfect place to find a unique gift for the man in your life. But be careful. If you come here with him, you may not get him out for a while. This is a museum and gift shop, and the gifts are all one-of-a-kind. You can get him a helmet worn by a racing legend like A. J. Foyt or Mario Andretti. If baseball's his passion, you can get him a program from the 1919 World Series. If he lives for football season, you can get him a jersey won by Bart Starr, the immortal Green Bay Packers quarterback. If he's a golfer, you can get him a club used by Arnold Palmer or Jack Nicklaus. How about a hockey stick used by Wayne Gretzky, the greatest scorer who ever lived? For a sports buff, a trip to this place is a must.

WILLIAM YOUNGERMAN, INC.
Bank of America Building
150 East Palmetto Park Rd., Suite 101
Boca Raton
(561) 368-7707
www.goldcoinsdealer.com

William Youngerman has an astounding collection of coins, stamps, bullion, ancient money, currency from many nations, trading cards, jewelry, art, and antiques. And well he should—because he's been collecting these things for more than 40 years. He's got a four-cent stamp with a Native American pursuing a buffalo on horseback. He's got a Babe Ruth baseball card. He's got a British coin from 1619. He's got gold coins from Austria, a coin from ancient Rome, and many other treasures. If you love collectibles, you should at least stop by; it's worth it just to see the collection that's taken a lifetime to gather.

Central County

A. B. LEVY RARE ANTIQUES AND FINE ART
211 Worth Ave.
Palm Beach
(561) 835-9139
www.ablevypb.com

This shop has the country's largest selection of in-stock René Lalique glass, and a superb collection of original art glass by Galle, Daum, and Tiffany—including an impressive assortment of Tiffany lamps. If 19th-century antiques are your passion, you can find a wide selection of furniture, candelabras, clocks, vases, and many other works of art from this period. Should your tastes run to fine art, there are works by La Belle Epoque painters and sculptors. For collectors of fine silver, there's an impressive 19th- and 20th-century selection.

BETTERIDGE AT GREENLEAF & CROSBY
236 Worth Ave.
Palm Beach
(561) 655-5850
www.betteridge.com

This shop has been here since hardly anyone else was here—1891, to be exact. And, since Palm Beachers have the money to buy fine silver and jewelry wherever they want, that record of longevity really says something about Betteridge. You'll see renowned names such as Buccelatti, Nicholas Varney, and Lotus Arts de Vivre here, on magnificent watches, earrings, rings, bracelets, brooches, and cuff links, among other items.

CV DESIGNS
6152 Terra Rosa Circle
Boynton Beach
(561) 317-5812
www.cvdesignsfl.com

Cristina Vollstedt is a multi-faceted artist, specializing in hand-crafted gourds, gifts, special orders, and custom wall murals. The gourd is related to the squash, and, when dried, is durable and woodlike. Native Americans have used them for centuries, as bowls, spoons, planters, birdhouses, pipes, and baby cribs. The gourds painted by Vollstedt are exceptionally beautiful. Her wall murals range from kids' to Oriental. And she also carves and paints wonderful wooden candlestick holders.

CYNTHIA'S COUNTRY STORE BEARS
The Mall at Wellington Green
12794 West Forest Hill Blvd., Suite 8A
Wellington
(561) 793-0554
www.cynthiascountrystore.com
This shop stocks bears by Steiff, as well as bears and other crafts by well-known artists R. John Wright and Deb Canham. There are bears everywhere you look here, of all different sizes, all different colors, and all different materials. Two of the more popular animals are Alexandra, the Butterfly Bear; and Gloria, the Springtime Bunny. And pink pigs in five different sizes, each one more cuddly than the last. You may also see The Happy Couple, two newlywed bears by Lladro, and, of course, porcelain bears by that famous company. Whatever your bear or other animal is made out of, though, you can be sure it's the highest quality workmanship.

ORLEY SHABAHANG
240 South County Rd.
Palm Beach
(561) 655-3371
www.shabahangcarpets.com

You will never see a collection of authentic Persian rugs and carpets more impressive than the one at Orley Shabahang. Their carpets run the gamut from contemporary to traditional to antique, and from fine wool that's colored with vegetable and natural dyes to smooth silk. Each carpet, as you'll be told, tells a story, of the region from which it comes, of the lives of the people of that region, and of the weaver. And if you take one home, don't worry about walking on your art. Good Oriental rugs actually appreciate with use. The complexity of the designs will amaze you. And so will the quality.

My Palm Beach County

"One thing that I always find remarkable about Palm Beach County is the generosity of its people. As president of the Office Depot Foundation, I have the opportunity to interact with dozens of nonprofit organizations and volunteers. People here are incredibly willing to give their time—and their funds—to causes that they believe are making a difference. We organized a volunteer project last year to assemble care packages for college kids who had aged out of the foster care system. More than a hundred volunteers participated— and they ranged in age from 5 to 87. It was truly inspiring."

—Mary Wong, President of the Office Depot Foundation, Office Depot Corporation, Boca Raton

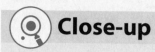 **Close-up**

Take a Walk with Henry Flagler

If you thought Henry Flagler passed away last century, think again.

He's still alive—sort of—in the person of James Ponce, who holds the unofficial title of "Palm Beach's Only Two-legged Historical Landmark." Ponce, complete with top hat, tails, pocket watch, and cane, leads a popular walking tour called "Historical Walking Tours of Wonderful Worth Avenue." And if anyone on Palm Beach can affect Henry Flagler's persona, it's Ponce because his father actually knew Flagler. (His family, however, preceded Flagler to Florida by just a bit; he can trace his Spanish ancestry in Florida back to 1594.) On these once weekly tours, Ponce gives his guests an up-close-and-personal look at the glories (both historical and present-day) of Worth Avenue. He's long been considered the island's unofficial historian. In fact, Ponce is actually the star of a 30-minute documentary on Worth Avenue's history, which actually began back in 1918 with the opening of the posh Everglades Club.

Ponce will take you into the secret spots, the alleys and the "vias", and the courtyards. And he'll turn this island's history into a living, breathing, spellbinding story. Call (561) 659-6909 or visit www.worth-avenue.com.

North County

BONANZA SPORTS & COLLECTIBLES
5500 Military Trail, #22-378
Jupiter
(561) 743-1003
www.bonanzasports.net

Jim and Laura Sage opened Bonanza Sports and Collectibles in January 2007, and they haven't had a dull day since. The reason is that sports collectors keep making their way here, to enjoy one of the top collections in Palm Beach County. Bonanza offers a great selection of autographs from sports heroes of the past, present, and future; but autographs are just the start. There's also a good selection of gifts and collectibles, from trading cards to key-chains to mugs and glassware. You might come upon an 8x10 photo signed by former heavyweight champ Joe Frazier, a football signed by both Dan Marino and Peyton Manning, or an autographed photo of one of the most famous moments in American sports history . . . soccer hero Brandi Chastain celebrating (minus her shirt) her winning goal against China in the Women's World Cup championship of 1999.

BOOK EXCHANGE AND COMIC SHOP
807 Northlake Blvd.
North Palm Beach
(561) 863-1555

This is more of a marketplace than just a mere shop, because you can buy, sell, or trade. Not just comics but also anime (stylized Japanese animation), manga (Japanese comic books), new and back-issue comic books, out-of-print paperbacks and hardcovers, and rare or used audio books and DVDs. If you grew up with adventure novels (like

The Hardy Boys) and classic comics (like *Classics Illustrated* or *Superman*), you're going to love this store.

FARMERS' MARKETS

South Florida is an agricultural horn of plenty. Although the citrus and vegetable industries—which once supported this area—have shrunk drastically over the past 50 years, the area still has a surprising number of growers. And their harvests are on display all over Palm Beach County on winter weekends, filling the green markets with not only wonderful smells, but a hundred vibrant colors. These farmers' markets are a wonderful place to come and sample South Florida's bounty!

ABACOA TOWN CENTER GREEN MARKET
Abacoa Town Center
Main Street & University Blvd.
Jupiter
(561) 756-3600
www.abacoa.com
Held mid-Oct through late-May. Local vendors with organic products and produce, baked goods, crafts, jewelry, and more.

BOCA RATON GREEN MARKET
Royal Palm Plaza
(561) 239-1536
www.localharvest.org/farmers-markets/ M1173
Sat mornings, from Oct through May. The market takes place on South Federal Highway in the southwest parking lot of Royal Palm Plaza, at the intersection of South Federal Highway and South Mizner Boulevard. Parking is conveniently located adjacent to the GreenMarket vendor site.

BOYS FARMERS MARKET
14378 Military Trail
Delray Beach
(561) 496-0810
The Boys is not a weekend green market. It's been here for years, open every day. And South County residents have always streamed here for the freshest, largest, juiciest, and most colorful produce—much of it grown locally. There's even an Asian food section, as well as perhaps the most impressive selection of cheeses you've ever seen.

DELRAY BEACH GREEN MARKET
Delray Beach
(561) 276-7511
www.localharvest.org/farmers-markets/ M1175
Opening on last Sat of Oct, continuing every Sat from 8 a.m. to 1 p.m. through mid-May. In the street on S.E. Fourth Avenue, half block south of Atlantic Avenue

OCEAN AVENUE GREEN MARKET
129 East Ocean Ave.
Boynton Beach
(561) 752-8598
www.localharvest.org/farmers-markets/ M32285
The Green Market is a seasonal event, Oct thru May, tied to the South Florida harvest season. Locally grown, fresh and organic produce is brought in directly from Boynton Beach farmers. Held each Sat morning at the historic Schoolhouse Children's Museum.

OCEANSIDE FARMERS' MARKET
John G's Restaurant
Lake Worth
(561) 547-3100
http://oceansidefarmersmarket.com/ wordpress/?page_id=2

SHOPPING

The Oceanside Farmers Market is located on A1A at John G's restaurant, south of the Four Seasons Palm Beach, east of the Intracoastal Waterway every Sat morning, rain or shine!

PALM BEACH GARDENS GREEN MARKET
Gardens Park
4301 Burns Rd.
Palm Beach Gardens
(561) 630-1100
www.pbgfl.com/content/76/144/default.aspx
Held every Sun morning, late-Oct through late-Apr. The "Taste of the Gardens" is a farmers' market, art, entertainment, and food event, where North County residents can get together and enjoy the locally grown produce and the activities.

VILLAGE FARMERS' MARKET
Southern Palm Crossing Shopping Centre
11001 Southern Blvd.
Royal Palm Beach
(561) 547-3100
http://villagefarmersmarket.org/wordpress
Held at the Costco shopping center parking lot every Sunday morning

WEST PALM BEACH GREENMARKET
Second Street and Narcissus Avenue
Downtown West Palm Beach
(561) 822-1515
www.wpb.org/greenmarket
Every Sat morning, mid-Oct through Apr.

WOOLBRIGHT FARMERS' MARKET
141 West Woolbright Rd.
Boynton Beach
(561) 732-2454
www.woolbrightfarmersmarket.com

This family-owned and operated market specializes in only the freshest local and organically grown fruits and vegetables. Open Tues through Sat.

My Palm Beach County

"I really enjoy living in Palm Beach County, and working here. I love the palm trees, the sunshine, and the beautiful beaches. What I love best, however, is the multi-cultural atmosphere. You can find people from all over the world here."

—Erika Grodzki, Ph.D.,
Associate Professor of Advertising/Public Relations,
Lynn University, Boca Raton

FLEA MARKETS

Palm Beach Countians love to get out and hunt for treasure on weekends (and during the week, too). You never know what you might find—perhaps a bayonet from the Civil War, or a kitchen utensil from the 1930s, or that 45-rpm record you've been searching for ever since you fell in love with it as a teenager. Perhaps it's Florida fashions, or discounted (but brand-new) watches or jewelry, old antique signs, or one-of-a-kind collectibles. But whatever your dream item is—even if you don't know what it is yet—chances are you'll find it at a Palm Beach County flea market!

BEACH SWAP SHOP
1301 Old Dixie Hwy.
Riviera Beach, FL 33404
(561) 844-5836

Started in 1965, this outdoor market sells mostly used and new merchandise and fresh produce, and all kinds of goodies. There is a nice snack bar with restrooms on the premises.

CARNIVAL FLEA MARKET
5283 West Atlantic Ave.
Delray Beach
(561) 404-5794
http://carnivalfleamarket.reachlocal.net
This is a 35,000-square-foot air-conditioned building, with more than 180 booths filled with all-new merchandise at discount prices. Besides the shopping, there's a full deli, bakery, and garden market with fresh produce. And they brag that they have the best ice cream and frozen yogurt in town.

DELRAY SWAP SHOP & FLEA MARKET
2001 North Federal Hwy
Delray Beach
(561) 276-4012
This swap shop has been around for a while. And if you can't find what you want here, you probably can't find it at all.

DR. FLEA'S INTERNATIONAL FLEA MARKET
1200 South Congress Ave.
West Palm Beach
(561) 965-1500
www.drfleas.com
This was Palm Beach County's first flea market and probably the one with the best name. Still going strong after all these years. From silk plants to cowboy boots to Chinese tea sets to hand-crafted candles.

FORTY FIFTH STREET FLEA MARKET
1701 Forty-fifth St.
West Palm Beach
(561) 863-6424
This is a popular place, particularly for the jewelry and custom-made shirts and T-shirts.

LAKE WORTH HIGH SCHOOL FLEA MARKET
1701 Lake Worth Rd.
Lake Worth
(561) 439-1539
Since the mid-80s, this market has contributed more than one million dollars to student scholarships. Every weekend, the school parking lot is chock-full of dealers selling books, antiques, collectibles, produce, new and used merchandise, rugs, luggage, garage sale goodies, and discount groceries.

SUNSHINE FLEA MARKET
1941 South Military Trail
West Palm Beach
(561) 963-1434
A good place to find unusual items.

UPTOWN-DOWNTOWN FLEA MARKET
5700 Okeechobee Blvd.
Palm Beach
(561) 684-5700
An outlet mall and largest flea market in the county, all under one roof, which features more than 350 merchants, an international food court, a full-service beauty salon, and many other services.

MEN'S CLOTHING

AMERICAN SOUL
11701 Lake Victoria Gardens Ave., Suite 3108
Palm Beach Gardens
(561) 624-4300

A/X ARMANI EXCHANGE
200 Rosemary Ave.
West Palm Beach
(561) 366-1000

BROOKS BROTHERS
3101 PGA Blvd., #J209
(561) 625-0832

GUY LA FERRERA
5050 Town Center Circle, Suite 227
Boca Raton
(561) 620-0011

JOSEPH A BANK CLOTHIERS
5050 Town Center Circle
Boca Raton
(561) 367-1140

LACOSTE
206 Worth Ave.
Palm Beach
(561) 655-5666

**MEN'S WEARHOUSE CLOTHING &
TUXEDO RENTAL**
11295 Legacy Ave., Suite 110
Palm Beach Gardens
(561) 691-1661

PAC SUN
801 N. Congress Ave., #623
Boynton Beach
(561) 736-4604

TOWN CENTER AT BOCA RATON
6000 Glades Rd.
Boca Raton
(561) 361-9640

WOMEN'S CLOTHING

ANN TAYLOR LOFT
Mizner Park
449 Plaza Real
Boca Raton
(561) 362-9440

3101 PGA Blvd., #A117
Palm Beach Gardens
(561) 691-9599

AQUA BEACHWEAR
267 South Ocean Blvd.
Manalapan
(561) 585-8211

BANANA REPUBLIC
10300 West Forest Hill Blvd., #272
Wellington
(561) 793-4685

DOTS FASHIONS
4368 Okeechobee Blvd., #53A
West Palm Beach
(561) 242-0101

SNAPPY TURTLE OF KENNEBUNKPORT
1100 E. Atlantic Ave.
Delray Beach
(561) 276-8088

LUCKY BRAND DUNGAREES
6000 Glades Rd., #1210
Boca Raton
(561) 361-6429

STYLES SO CHIC
1200 Town Center Dr., #119
Jupiter
(561) 776-2442

VICTORIA'S SECRET
3101 PGA Blvd.
Palm Beach Gardens
(561) 626-5451

DAY TRIPS AND WEEKEND GETAWAYS

One of the best things about Palm Beach County is that you're within a few hours of most places in Florida, as well as most places in the Caribbean. True, Florida does have the biggest tourist attractions in the world—within a few hours of Palm Beach County—but it's also got so much more than just the major theme parks. In fact, you'd probably be very delighted to learn just how close you are, when you're in the county, to so many incredible things to do and see. So let's start exploring!

DAY TRIPS

The drive-times given below originate from West Palm Beach (and they don't take into account rush-hour, accidents, etc. . . .).

The Bahamas

Yes, this is listed under Day Trips because that's exactly how close you are. You can take a boat from West Palm Beach and be in Bimini, the closest Bahamian island, in a little more than an hour; and be back in time for dinner. Or, you can fly, and be there in a half-hour. Bimini is a small island full of brightly painted little houses, friendly people, and great seafood (try the conch chowder, fritters, and salad!). Freeport, with its luxury hotels and grand casinos, is also close by. (Visit www.bahamas.com.)

Downtown Stuart

Stuart is a town in Martin County, just north of Palm Beach County about a 40-minute drive from West Palm Beach. Stuart restored its downtown area back in the 1990s, and it's now a really pleasant place to walk around.

There are cute little shops and restaurants, and a restored old theater that hosts plays and other performing arts productions. And you'll get a kick out of "Confusion Corner," a traffic circle that Charles Kuralt once profiled in his famous *On the Road* series back in the 1970s and 80s. As soon as you drive up to it, you'll know how it got its name! Stuart also boasts the House of Refuge, an old wooden structure on Hutchinson Island that used to serve as a shelter for any shipwrecked sailors who were able to make it to shore. It's now a museum. (Visit www.martincountyfla.com.)

Everglades National Park

The best way to get into the park is to drive down to Miami, then head west on Tamiami Trail, about a two-hour drive from West Palm. Here you'll find the entrance to a portion of the park known as Shark Valley. There are no sharks here, for sure, and no valley. But there are hundreds and hundreds of square miles of America's only tropical jungle, along with alligators, all kinds of snakes (both poisonous and not), red-shouldered hawks, purple gallinules, and hundreds of other species that you can't see anywhere else in the world. Shark Valley has an 8-mile biking/hiking path if you're the adventurous type. And the entrance to the national park is right at the site of the Miccosukee Indian reservation. The Miccosukee are a branch of the Seminole nation that never actually signed a peace treaty with the United States. Here, you can roam around their village on guided tours, watch craftspeople still creating the traditional crafts (such as the most colorful dresses you ever saw), see the *chickees* (huts of thatched straw), take an airboat ride, watch alligator wrestling, and learn about the history of this matriarchal society. (Visit www.nps.gov/ever/index.htm.)

Fort Lauderdale

About 40 minutes from West Palm Beach along I-95, Fort Lauderdale has become a sizable city in recent years, and it offers a vibrant nightlife, cultural attractions, and great shopping spots. Take a walk along Riverwalk, which winds through downtown along the New River, bringing you past many symbols of both the old Lauderdale (cabin of the first settler) and the new (Broward County Center for the Performing Arts). Visit the Museum of Science and Discovery, especially if you've got kids; it's one of the best of its kind in the country. Stroll through the restored old buildings of the Himmarshee Historic District. Take a ride on the Water Taxi. Wander the shops, sidewalk cafes, galleries, and music clubs of beautiful Las Olas Boulevard, a European thoroughfare that hops into the wee hours. And don't forget to visit one of the most famous beaches in the world. (Visit www.sunny.org.)

Jensen Beach

This is a quaint little community about 45 minutes north of West Palm Beach, in Martin County. The compact downtown area has colorful, funky wooden shops and restaurants, and is a fun place to walk around. You can also access the beaches of Hutchinson Island from here, along a beautiful causeway over the Intracoastal that's filled with fishermen cleaning their catches . . . and pelicans waiting for the scraps. On Hutchinson Island, besides the great beaches, it's also very interesting to visit the nuclear power plant of Florida Power & Light Company, with an interactive museum. (Visit www.martincountyfla.com.)

Miami

About 70 minutes south of West Palm Beach, Miami has one of the most impressive skylines in America; it's truly a stunning city. For a good look at this city, take the MetroMover monorail around downtown and through the financial district. Sample some great Cuban food in one of the unassuming but great restaurants in Little Havana, centered around Southwest Eighth Street (Calle Ocho). A must-visit is the Bayside Marketplace, a Caribbean-themed collection of open-air shops, cafes, and bistros, along with some of the funkiest kiosks you've ever seen, right on the harbor. If it's basketball season, catch a Miami Heat game across the street in American Airlines Arena. Cross Biscayne Bay to mingle with the International Set in the cafes and galleries of Ocean Drive, in famous South Beach. Or take a ride to the upscale island of Key Biscayne, right in Biscayne Bay, with an incredible view of this futuristic city on the water as you drive. Family attractions in Miami include Parrot Jungle Island and the Seaquarium. (Visit www.miamiandbeaches.com.)

Seminole Indian Reservations

There's one reservation in Hollywood, about 50 minutes south of West Palm Beach, and another one in the Everglades, in an area called Big Cypress, about two hours away. The one in Hollywood is certainly interesting (and there's a Hard Rock Hotel & Casino there). But for a more realistic look at the way the Native Americans lived, head out west on I-75 (in Broward County) toward the Big Cypress Reservation in the Everglades. In this isolated little community, you can see how the people lived then, and how they live today. You can sample Indian foods such as frybread or spicy frog legs. You can wander through the fascinating museum, or take an airboat ride on the *River of Grass*. And you can even spend the night in a *chickee* on stilts (alligators, you know). (Visit www.semtribe.com/TourismAndEnterprises/BigCypress/.)

WEEKEND GETAWAYS

If you'd like to get away for more than a day, Palm Beach County is close to a variety of interesting—and often, exotic—destinations. Within a few hours' drive or boat ride—and less than that in a plane—is a stunning variety of cities, natural wonders, foreign cultures, people, arts and crafts, and entertainment. If you're looking for a place to just kick off your shoes—or just get sand in them—you'll find it close to Palm Beach County. And if you're looking for a place to get gussied up for an elegant night on the town at a famous club, restaurant, resort, or casino, you'll find it close to Palm Beach County. From the foreign to the domestic, from the familiar to the exotic, it's all just a few hours away.

My Palm Beach County

"Natural wonders like the Loxahatchee River, Lake Okeechobee, and Everglades National Park provide wonderful day-trip destinations. Plus, Palm Beach International Airport, the Tri-Rail, and Amtrak station are also within a five-minute drive which can take us anywhere in South Florida—or the world! We also have great city and county leaders, many of whom we know on a first-name basis. Now that retirement is on the horizon, we're looking for a place to buy a second summer home, but it's going to be hard to find any place as great as West Palm Beach. I don't think life gets any better than this!"

—Margie Yansura,
Public Relations Consultant,
West Palm Beach

The Bahamas

Nassau, the capital of the Bahamas, is less than an hour away by plane. This is a colorful old colonial town with surprises down every street. Bay Street is lined with international shops. The side streets have rustic-looking (or just plain old!) restaurants with surprisingly good food, with Bahamian specialties such as turtle soup or steak, cracked conch, and peas 'n rice. At the straw market, you'll see hundreds of women busily creating their one-of-a-kind hats, baskets, and gift items. And Nassau's just across the bridge from Paradise Island, where the resorts are world-class, the dining is gourmet, and the casinos are exciting. (Paradise Island is not the original name of this island, however. It's actually Hog Island. But the Bahamian government changed it when they decided to develop the island as a tourism resort. Wonder why!) (Visit www.bahamas.com.)

Tampa

Cross the state to Tampa—about four hours—and you'll see a different side of Florida. The West (Gulf) Coast of the state is significantly different than the eastern (Atlantic) coast, in lifestyles, in outlook, in where most residents came from (the Midwest as well as the East), and, of course, what they see when they look at a sunset or a sunrise. Tampa has a lot to see and do. There's Busch Gardens with great rides, slides, and roller coasters, and tons to see and do. There's the in-town, colorful section called Ybor City. This was the original home of the Cuban community that first came to Florida in the late-1800s. It's now an authentically restored neighborhood with colorful restaurants and shops and craftspeople—including some who still make real hand-rolled cigars. Nearby to Tampa are the beachside communities of St. Petersburg and Clearwater. (Visit www.visittampabay.com.)

Cape Canaveral

This is the home of Kennedy Space Center about 2.5 hours north of West Palm. Here, you can see the real Space Shuttle. You can roam wonderful museum exhibits, with hands-on interactive displays. You can see space shows, and the launching pads. You can stand in awe at the memorials to those astronauts who did not return from their trips. And, if you're lucky, you can even meet an astronaut or two. (Visit www.kennedy spacecenter.com.)

The Florida Keys & Key West

The first of the string of pearls known as the Florida Keys, strung out into the ocean just south of Miami, is Key Largo, about two hours south of West Palm Beach. It's another 3–4 hours to Key West. On the way, you'll be driving over the ocean, passing isolated little keys every so often, or a larger key with a town, such as Marathon. On your right will be the Gulf of Mexico, and on your left the Atlantic. All of the keys are great; the inhabited ones often have colorful fishing camps and old restaurants that serve much better food (especially seafood) than you might think by looking at their exteriors. The resort of Hawk's Cay on Marathon is truly magnificent, restored from the time when Franklin D. Roosevelt used to stay here. And at the end of the line is Key West, the funkiest, coolest, weirdest, wackiest, most colorful town in America, with the shops and restaurants of Duval Street, a thriving literary and arts community, old gingerbread and Victorian homes, and bed-and-breakfasts lining leafy streets. There are the houses of such people as Ernest Hemingway, John Jay Audubon, and Tennessee Williams, as well as President Harry Truman's complex. Be sure to visit the Mallory Docks at sunset; it's a real "event." Not only will you see the most beautiful sunset you've ever seen, but you'll share it with hundreds of people, among them stilt-walkers, fire-eaters, jugglers, and snake charmers. (Visit www.fla-keys.com.)

Mount Dora

There's really not a mountain here (or anywhere else in Florida, for that matter). But there is a beautiful old town from the late-1800s, with most of its original buildings still standing and a wood-plank sidewalk in some areas. Many of the graceful old Victorians of the early days have been turned into beautiful bed-and-breakfasts, with period furnishings and down comforters and breakfasts to die for. This town is known as one of the best places in America to find interesting old antiques shops, and they have a number of big antiques shows here annually. As you wander around, you'll find atmospheric bookstores and music shops with creaky wooden floors and lace curtains, as well as offbeat restaurants and clothing shops. The town sits on Lake Dora, a huge lake offering a ton of sailing and recreational opportunities. Sitting astride it is the Lakeside Inn, an inn from the 1800s in a Victorian/colonial style, where you can relax in a wooden rocker out on the deck overlooking the lake, and enjoy gourmet food inside. And the drive around the lake is a pretty one. (Visit www.visitflorida.com/Mount_Dora.)

Naples/Marco Island

Naples is a beautiful small town on the southwest coast of Florida (about 2.5 hours from West Palm Beach), with a magnificent downtown filled with unique shops, restaurants, and galleries. The pace here is slower than on the eastern coast, but there's still a lot to see and do. Walk along Fifth Street and Third Street, elegant boulevards where every doorway holds something interesting. For excellent downtown lodging, stay at the elegant Inn on Fifth. And for a multi-faceted beachfront experience, stay at the famed Napes Beach Hotel & Golf Club. You'll enjoy wandering through the one-of-a-kind shops in the woody Tin City marketplace, right on the water. For an unusual gastronomic experience on the water, take one of the charter boats or regular harbor cruises put on by Sip N Sail; they lay out a buffet of gourmet treats and special wines for you to try, as you cruise at sunset (or other times) past islands inhabited only by eagles. And Marco Island has a variety of good beachside hotels and restaurants. (Visit www.paradisecoast.com.)

Ocala National Forest

About three hours from West Palm is another world, pretty much the only place in the United States where you can find both bears and alligators. The Ocala National Forest is an ecological wonderland, of dense forest, marshland, beach sand, small hills, and lakes. Here you'll find Wekiwa Springs State Park, where you can paddle along rivers so primeval that you almost feel as if you're the only one who's ever traveled them. There are also hot springs at Wekiwa, said to have restorative powers by some, and hiking paths through the woods. And—nearby Ocala being horse country—you can also see it all from the top of a horse. Wekiwa State Park and the Ocala National Forest are the way Florida was for time immemorial. (Visit www.fs.fed.us/r8/florida/ocala/ and www.floridastateparks.org/wekiwasprings/.)

Orlando

Where do you start when describing a place like Orlando (about 2.5 hours from West Palm Beach)? Of course, it's the largest tourist attraction in the world. And the faces you'll see at the various parks of Disney World, Universal, and SeaWorld come here from every country on earth. If you have kids, the looks of excitement and anticipation that you'll see on their faces will be ones you'll remember the rest of your life. In addition to the world-renowned parks like these, there are also smaller theme- and water parks that offer great fun. There are some 4,000 restaurants in the area, with every conceivable type of cuisine. There's downtown Orlando, right on Lake Eola, with interesting museums and old Victorian homes. There's sophisticated dining and shopping at places such as Disney Boardwalk, Downtown Disney, and Universal/Islands of Adventure. And there are some 90,000 hotel rooms for you to choose from. (Visit www.orlandoinfo.com.)

Sanibel Island/Captiva Island

About 3.5 hours from West Palm Beach, in the Fort Myers area of the west coast of Florida, are two precious little islands. Sanibel Island is a place of cute little shops and restaurants, bicycle paths, and reasonably priced hotels ideally located both for exploring the town and exploring the beaches. It's the kind of place where everyone says Hello . . . and they really mean it. There are also a lot of interesting crafts shops and studios. Captiva Island, on the other hand, has no town and just a few atmospheric motels or lodges. What it does have, however, is peace and quiet, forests, beautiful beaches with little coves where you can watch the spectacular west coast sunsets, and funky beach houses. And it also has the Bubble Room Restaurant, a multi-colored, ramshackle old shack filled floor-to-ceiling with Americana, including photos of old Hollywood stars like Frank Sinatra and Lana Turner, cowboy articles, handicrafts from the early 1900s, old songs playing in the background, and an actual choo-choo train that circles around the room overhead as you eat. And the food's incredible, as well, real American comfort food, served by young ladies and men in "Bubble Room" scout uniforms. This is an outrageous place—fun for the whole family. (Visit www.sanibel-captiva.org.)

St. Augustine/Amelia Island

About four hours drive north of West Palm Beach is the historic town of St. Augustine, the first permanent town in America settled by Europeans. Here, you can see well-preserved old forts and cannons, in a town over which have flown seven flags. The town is constructed in old-style buildings, some in Tudor-style, others in the Spanish–Mediterranean of the people who first explored this area. The intrepid Ponce de Leon never did find the Fountain of Youth, but he founded a town that's still with us today. Not far away is Amelia Island, with the restored Victorian town of Fernandina Beach, where a horse-and-buggy with a driver will take you all over town, and tell you the stories of conquerors and the conquered, of Civil War, of winners and losers, traitors and patriots, pirates and privateers, and swashbucklers and scoundrels. (Visit www.staugustine.com and www .ameliaisland.com.)

Appendix

LIVING HERE

In this section we feature specific information for residents or those planning to relocate here. Topics include real estate, education, and much more.

LIVING HERE

REAL ESTATE

The real estate market in South Florida, like just about every other real estate market in the country, has had to pass through some very stormy weather in recent years. But now, some of the clouds are starting to part, and a little bit of sun is even shining through in some spots. Of course, how you view the housing crash depends on where you're watching it from. If you're a seller, things are still tight, if getting better. If you're a buyer, though, the bargains are still there. And one thing above all remains the same in the South Florida housing market—people will always want to live here.

If you want to see a housing market that was truly ripped to shreds by the housing meltdown and the recession in 2008–10, look no father than South Florida. This area, by many standards, was the hardest-hit in the entire country. It could almost be labeled "A Tale of Two Markets."

In November of 2005, the average home in Palm Beach County was worth $421,500—the highest ever. In the summer of 2006, Realtors will tell you, they routinely had offers the first day a home went on the market . . . and, quite often, bidding wars for the home, sending the price straight up. Often, a home was sold to the first person who took a look at it—because that person knew that someone else would want the house immediately if they didn't. And they didn't want to take a chance on losing it. There were regular

tales of people making offers sight-unseen. And if you called the second week a nice house was on the market, you were too late. Sellers were walking away with fortunes—even from fairly modest homes. At that time, homes in upscale developments west of Boynton Beach were selling for $800,000 and were snatched up as soon as they went on the market. As a result, price pressures were heading north.

Cut ahead two years. Those same houses were on the market for $400,000, and some of them are *still* on the market. In South Florida, when the roof fell in on the housing market, it fell all the way to the basement. Townhomes in nice neighborhoods in West Boca that had been worth $400,000 in 2006 were on the market for $190,000 in 2008—and still not selling.

What does all of this mean for you? Well, very good things, if you're in the market for a home. As of this writing, most experts believed that the market had not yet quite hit bottom, but that the bottom would come toward the end of 2010, and then stay there for a little while. Which means that you could be the beneficiary. You could pay $400,000 for that Boynton Beach home that originally sold for $800,000. You could pay $190,000 for that West Boca town house that was valued at $400,000 in the summer of '06.

"Because of the low prices, demand is really starting to pick up," said Paul Owers, senior writer for the *South Florida Sun-Sentinel,* who covers real estate. "For example, GL

Builders opened a new development west of Delray Beach with estate homes. And the demand was such that people camped out overnight to get a crack at buying one."

Owers says that Wellington is a high-demand area (with prices that are still low), because of the good schools and the nice lifestyle there. Royal Palm Beach, Wellington's neighbor city, will also be in demand. Boca Raton was devastated by the crash, but people will always want to live there because . . . it's Boca Raton. The areas to the west of Delray Beach have always been in high demand, but, again, prices even there are still low. Also, there are beautiful condos and apartment buildings in downtown West Palm Beach that have a lot of empty units now, but will fill up over the next few years, because of the location.

Owers predicts that now through the end of 2011 will be a great time to buy in Palm Beach County, because the number of houses on the market will remain high and the prices low. Which, of course, not only gives you the opportunity for a lower price, but also a wider selection.

It's a complicated process, of course, and you'll need a good Realtor to walk you through it. But you can start by deciding your priorities as far as lifestyle; location; distance from the beach; urban, suburban, or rural; convenience; cultural amenities; shopping; etc. It's a long list, obviously. But you can go through it with a pretty good level of confidence that you're going to find a house that makes you happy. And you're going to find it at a price that makes you happy, as well.

Here are two contacts that may be able to help:

REALTORS ASSOCIATION OF THE PALM BEACHES
1926 Tenth Ave. North, Suite 410
Lake Worth
(561) 585.4544
www.rapb.com

i Palm Beach County has the state's highest per capital annual income, $55,311, compared with the statewide average of $36,720.

PALM BEACH COUNTY BOARD OF REALTORS
50 Cocoanut Row, Suite 119
Palm Beach
(561) 659-3810
www.businessfinance.com/palm-beach-board-of-realtors.htm
In addition, the Chamber of Commerce in the town(s) you're considering will also be able to help, with information on neighborhoods, businesses, schools, etc.

RETIRING HERE

This is a great place to retire. Warm weather all year long. You can sit at your TV and have a good smirk when you watch what's going on in the rest of the country during winter! Or even better, you can phone your friends up north and complain about the slow group ahead of you on the golf course this morning! We have eternal sunshine, plenty of other retirees, plenty of living areas and developments that are geared to retirees, great golf, the beach and the ocean, a vibrant cultural scene, wonderful shopping, an efficient retiree infrastructure of governmental and private agencies, great medical care, and award-winning hospitals. If you like to travel, the ability to be pretty much anywhere in the world within 12 hours. No

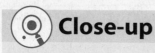

Close-up

"The Donald" in Palm Beach

Even though it's just on your left as you drive north on A1A into storied Palm Beach, you'll probably drive right past it. There's no sign at the entrance (because, if you need a sign to tell you that you've arrived, you haven't *really* arrived). True, it is a magnificent entrance; but many homes on this island have magnificent entrances. But this one is actually no longer a home. And not every mansion on Palm Beach is owned by Donald Trump.

It's called Mar-A-Lago (Spanish for "from sea to lake"). And, oh, if these walls could talk!

If these walls could talk, they'd tell you that this place—126 rooms on twenty acres—has had a lifetime of elegance, renowned guests, kings and queens, and fascinating goings-on. It's so majestic that it took three years to built, from 1924 to 1927. The couple that built it were Marjorie Merriweather Post, heir to the Post Cereals fortune (and mother of actress Dina Merrill), and her husband, financier Edward F. Hutton (E.F. Hutton).

Mrs. Post was an avid philanthropist, and she threw lavish fund-raisers here for the International Red Cross and the American Red Cross, filling the public and guest rooms with kings and queens, princes and princesses, dukes a duchesses, and the royalty of international entertainers, celebrities, and dignitaries. She died in 1973. In 1985, Donald Trump acquired the 20-acre property. He immediately renovated it. And when the estate emerged from the renovation, it had 58 bedrooms, 33 bathrooms, 12 fireplaces, a 29-foot marble table in the dining room, 6 tennis courts, a waterfront pool, and—just in case—3 bomb shelters.

Trump actually lived in the home for 10 years. In 1995, he turned it into the Mar-A-Lago Club . . . and, as you might have guessed, this club is the last word in elegance. Guests can sup on world-class culinary creations, while away the hours playing bridge, luxuriate in the spa, bang the tennis ball around, play croquet, go down to the private beach club, hob-nob with the other rich-and-famous at wine-tastings and dinners, enjoy private performances by internationally known entertainers, or play a round at the nearby Trump International Golf Club.

There's no public knowledge, really, about the cost of joining Mar-A-Lago. But if you have to ask . . .

state income tax, if you still want to work. No capital gains or estate taxes. Lower prices—especially in housing—than you had if you come from the Northeast. And, oh . . . did we mention the warm weather and eternal sunshine?

The following are some resources for retirees.

AREA AGENCY ON AGING OF PALM BEACH/TREASURE COAST, INC.
West Palm Beach Office
4400 North Congress Ave.
West Palm Beach
(561) 684-5885
www.myanswersonaging.org

One of the best ways to find out more is by contacting the Area Agency on Aging of Palm Beach. It's basically an aging resource center and private nonprofit organization dedicated to serving the needs of seniors and their caregivers in Palm Beach County and the counties to the north. Their Web site is a treasure-trove of information on retiring to this area, and on all the resources and organizations available to you. Business hours are Mon– through Fri, 8 a.m. to 5 p.m.

They also have an **Aging Resource Center Elder Helpline:** (561) 214-8600 or (866) 684-5885, TTY: (866) 768-4550.

PALM BEACH COUNTY PARTNERSHIP FOR AGING
(561) 375-6645
www.partnershipforagingpbc.org

Another agency that can be very helpful is the Palm Beach County Partnership for Aging. They, too, have a lot of resources. This agency is a not-for-profit local organization that focuses its energies on enhancing the life of older persons, their families, and their communities through advocacy, information sharing, and education. Members include professionals in the aging network from both the private and public sector, individuals interested in aging issues, geriatric care managers, elder law attorneys, acute and long term health care professionals, university personnel and many others. Open Mon to Fri, 8 a.m. to 5 p.m.

Where to Live

Where you live is up to your decisions about such things as your lifestyle, health, and desire to work. There are a lot of questions that you'll have to ask yourself:

- How important is it for me to be near large malls, and good shopping?
- How important is peace and quiet?
- What do I want to spend?
- Do I want golf courses, walking paths, and jogging trails nearby?
- Do I want to be close to cultural amenities, the airport, parks and recreational amenities?
- East or West? If I'm a beach person, I probably won't be happy in the western communities like Wellington, Royal Palm Beach, Loxahatchee, or The Acreage. And if I'm more of a country person who likes to be surrounded by greenery, I probably wouldn't be comfortable in a beachside community such as Lantana or Jupiter.
- North or South? Do I want to be close to the Miami–Fort Lauderdale areas? Then Palm Beach Gardens is not the place for me. Do I want a slower, more-mellow pace? Then I probably won't be comfortable in Boca.
- Do I want to live near built-up urban areas, such as downtown West Palm Beach or Boca Raton? Suburban communities like Boynton Beach or Palm Beach Gardens? Or quiet small towns like Tequesta or Juno Beach?
- Do I want to live in a retiree community, or surrounded by people in an all-ages development?
- If I choose a senior community, how important are the amenities—pool, tennis, health club, clubhouse, dining room, etc.?
- Is it more important to have a good time with my money, or to leave it for the kids? This will definitely affect where I choose to live.

This is just a short list of important questions to ask, of course, there are many, many more. But it's a good place to start.

My Palm Beach County

"To me, Palm Beach County is a county of contrasts. On one side, you have the wealthiest of the wealthy residing in beachside mansions. On the other side, you have the poorest of the poor, living in squalor in impoverished towns that arose from the canefields. At the south and the north ends, you'll find an abundance of highly educated professionals working as software engineers or financial gurus living in gated communities. In the middle is where you'll find working class folks who drive trucks or build houses, living in town houses or rented apartments. Throughout the county, you'll discover a mix of races and cultures. On any given day you can hear Creole, Spanish, Portuguese, or Italian being spoken. This is where you can sit by the ocean and enjoy an arrepa or Cuban sandwich, a crepe or cannoli. From lettuce farms to luxury homes, from cattle ranches to office towers, Palm Beach County is a place where you can expect the unexpected, and find convention in the unconventional."

—Rich Pollack, President,
Pollack Communications,
Delray Beach

There are as many choices as to where to live in Palm Beach County as there are different types of people. Popular among retirees are such entities as golf retirement communities and 55-plus communities. Continuing Care Retirement Communities (CCRCs) are life-care communities with large campuses that include separate housing sections for those who live very independently, assisted living facilities that offer more support, and nursing homes for those needing skilled nursing care.

The range of senior housing developments that are popular with seniors is enormous. For example, you can find lower-cost apartments at the senior communities of Century Village, in west Boca Raton and West Palm Beach, with one- and two-bedroom apartments generally going for between $40,000 and $65,000. On the other hand, local builder GL builds developments such as Valencia Reserve, a 55+ community west of Boynton Beach, where prices range from $250,000 to $500,000. Then there are senior-heavy communities such as St. Andrew's in Boca Raton, where you can live among retired titans of industry and commerce, but you may have to pay more than a million dollars for the privilege. Boca West, in Boca Raton, is another community with a substantial senior population; it's an expansive community with two golf courses, great amenities, and prices ranging from moderate condos and townhomes to luxurious single-family residences.

West of Boynton Beach is expected to remain popular with retirees, as is west Delray, the areas to the west of West Palm Beach, and, in addition, the Greenacres area west of Lake Worth. A number of "active" communities for seniors are being built in these areas.

If you look carefully—and if you ask the right questions—you'll find your own little piece of Paradise in the tropics.

EDUCATION

The Florida school system is—there's no other way to say it—not ranked very high among the 50 states. However, Palm Beach County schools are fairly good. And Boca Raton schools are among the finest in the state. In addition, the county has a thriving higher-education scene, with a number of good—and growing—colleges and universities.

The Public School District of Palm Beach County (www.palmbeachschools.org) is the only urban school system to earn an "A" rating by the Florida Department of Education for five consecutive years. With 186 schools, and approximately 170,000 students, it's the 11th-largest school district in the nation. There are approximately 90 private schools in Palm Beach County. For a complete list, visit www.southflorida.com.

Colleges and Universities

BARRY UNIVERSITY
1501 Corporate Dr., #230
Boynton Beach
(561) 364-8220
www.barry.edu
Branch campus (main campus in Miami).

BETHUNE–COOKMAN
1900 North Australian Ave.
West Palm Beach
(561) 832-1202
www.bethune.cookman.edu
Branch campus of historically African-American college in Daytona Beach.

FLORIDA ATLANTIC UNIVERSITY
777 Glades Rd.
Boca Raton
(561) 297-3000
www.fau.edu

My Palm Beach County

"When I first moved to south Palm Beach County, Glades Road was two lanes under the Turnpike, Mission Bay was a large field where cows grazed, and Town Center was preparing for its grand opening. The beaches were beautiful, IBM and Pratt & Whitney were booming, and Florida Atlantic University was a small commuter-school whose yearly enrollment increases were a source of great pride. Over the years, growth filled pastures and the economy, creating new wealth to join old wealth that together built the prizes we enjoy and in some cases almost take for granted, from the Morikami Park to the Kravis Center. And while IBM and Pratt are but a shell of their old selves, bio-tech giant Scripps has arrived—and spurred fellow research giant Max Planck to locate here.

"Personally, I raised my three children in our public schools yet have relished the opportunity to enjoy a rich Jewish life that is so unique to south Palm Beach County. On Saturdays I enjoy walking to my synagogue, where I have gotten to know its members who double as my neighbors. This is truly a blessing in a world where people can barely keep up with their immediate family, and often choose to communicate by text message."

—Steve Nichol, founder and owner of Jack Russell Communications, a public relations firm in Boca Raton

Fast-growing university, with more than 25,000 students, significant academic and athletic programs; part of state university system; has branch campus in Jupiter, in North County.

LYNN UNIVERSITY
3601 North Military Trail
Boca Raton
(561) 237-7000
www.lynn.edu
Private university that's growing and gaining recognition.

NORTHWOOD UNIVERSITY
2600 North Military Trail
West Palm Beach
(561) 478-5500
www.northwood.edu
Business and management university with branches in Florida, Michigan, and Texas.

PALM BEACH ATLANTIC UNIVERSITY
901 South Flagler Dr.
West Palm Beach
(561) 803-2000
www.pba.edu
Liberal arts university with a Christian focus.

PALM BEACH STATE COLLEGE
4200 Congress Ave.
Lake Worth
(561) 967-7222
www.palmbeachstate.edu
Recently converted to four-year school from a community college.

LOCAL MEDIA

As is the case all over the country, the media scene in South Florida—particularly the "print" media scene—has been in a state

---

My Palm Beach County

"Because I'm an editor at the *Palm Beach Daily News,* I read a lot of articles about philanthropy here on the island. Yes, I admire the people who make great efforts to organize fundraising events for charities—I suspect it's a nearly thankless job. And of course the causes all are worthy and deserve support. But what I do find a little disappointing is that it seems the majority of the benefits on the island are for groups whose mission is something other than poverty or hunger or homelessness. I do not begrudge arts groups, medical groups, universities, etc., their Palm Beach benefits, but I'd also like to see more visible activity in fund-raising for our local poor, homeless, and hungry—and then maybe our international poor, homeless, and hungry. It does seem as though the last couple years, more of this type of group are fund-raising on the island—and I hope they do well."

—Carol Carnevale, Editor,
Palm Beach Daily News
("The Shiny Sheet")

---

of flux the past few years. However, despite the seemingly mad rush to online media, most people in Palm Beach County still read print material at some point during the day. (And most of us also read the online editions of the media listed here.) Palm Beach County has become one of the most exciting places to visit, and to live, in the country. And both its residents and its visitors (many of whom turn into potential future residents) will be reading its major media for a long time. Between the daily newspapers, the weeklies and community papers, the monthly magazines, and the television stations, you can be kept up-to-date on virtually everything that goes on—or that will go on—in the county.

Daily Newspapers

PALM BEACH DAILY NEWS
(800) 488-8627
www.palmbeachdailynews.com

PALM BEACH POST
(561) 820-4663
www.pbpost.com

SOUTH FLORIDA SUN-SENTINEL
Delray Beach Office
(561) 243-6600
www.sun-sentinel.com

Weekly Newspapers

FORUM PUBLISHING GROUP
www.sun-sentinel.com/news/broward/
cities
Weekly newspapers in Boca Raton, West Boca, Delray Beach, Boynton Beach, Wellington, Royal Palm Beach.

PALMS WEST PRESS
(the Western Communities)
www.palmswestpress.com

TOWN CRIER
Wellington
(561) 793-7606
www.thecrier.com

TV Stations

WXEL—PUBLIC BROADCASTING
(561) 737-800
www.wxel.org

Page 2 Live

If you want to know what's going on in Palm Beach County, read Jose Lambiet's column—Page 2 Live—in the *Palm Beach Post*. But don't expect to read about what's going on in terms of events. What you can expect, however, is an incredible look at the sometimes-seamy underbelly of Palm Beach County. All the gossip; all the celebrity sightings; all the inside dope on government corruption (and there's been plenty of it in Palm Beach County!); all the society who's-saying-what-about-who and who's-doing-what-to-who; all the whispered conversations in the halls of power that the whisperers thought nobody heard; all the who's-been-seen-with-who; all the wacky things that make Palm Beach County Palm Beach County. It's been said that Lambiet has spies all over the place. Many of the county's elite, in fact, turn to Lambiet's page before they read the rest of the paper in the morning—because they want to make sure they're not in it (and that their enemies are!).

WPTV—WEST PALM BEACH (NBC AFFILIATE)
(561) 655-5455
www.wptv.com

WPBF—WEST PALM BEACH (ABC)
(561) 694-2525
www.wpbf.com

WPEC—WEST PALM BEACH (CBS)
(561) 881-0705
www.cbs12.com

FOX-TV
(561) 845-2929
www.wflx.com

Magazines

BOCA RATON MAGAZINE
(561) 997-8683
www.bocamag.com

BOCA RATON OBSERVER
(561) 982-8960
www.bocaratonobserver.com

PALM BEACH ILLUSTRATED
(561) 659-0210
www.palmbeachillustrated.com

WELLINGTON THE MAGAZINE
(561) 793-7606
www.wellingtonthemagazine.com

INDEX

INDEX

Regional Travel at Its Best

gpp travel

To order call 800-243-0495 or visit www.GlobePequot.com

INSIDERS' GUIDE®

The acclaimed travel series that has sold more than 2 million copies!

Discover: Your Travel Destination.
Your Home. Your Home-to-Be.

Albuquerque

Anchorage & Southcentral Alaska

Atlanta

Austin

Baltimore

Baton Rouge

Boulder & Rocky Mountain National Park

Branson & the Ozark Mountains

California's Wine Country

Cape Cod & the Islands

Charleston

Charlotte

Chicago

Cincinnati

Civil War Sites in the Eastern Theater

Civil War Sites in the South

Colorado's Mountains

Dallas & Fort Worth

Denver

El Paso

Florida Keys & Key West

Gettysburg

Glacier National Park

Great Smoky Mountains

Greater Fort Lauderdale

Greater Tampa Bay Area

Hampton Roads

Houston

Hudson River Valley

Indianapolis

Jacksonville

Kansas City

Long Island

Louisville

Madison

Maine Coast

Memphis

Myrtle Beach & the Grand Strand

Nashville

New Orleans

New York City

North Carolina's Mountains

North Carolina's Outer Banks

North Carolina's Piedmont Triad

Oklahoma City

Orange County, CA

Oregon Coast

Palm Beach County

Palm Springs

Philadelphia & Pennsylvania Dutch Country

Phoenix

Portland, Maine

Portland, Oregon

Raleigh, Durham & Chapel Hill

Richmond, VA

Reno and Lake Tahoe

St. Louis

San Antonio

Santa Fe

Savannah & Hilton Head

Seattle

Shreveport

South Dakota's Black Hills Badlands

Southwest Florida

Tucson

Tulsa

Twin Cities

Washington, D.C.

Williamsburg & Virginia's Historic Triangle

Yellowstone & Grand Teton

Yosemite

To order call 800-243-0495
or visit www.Insiders.com

R.C.L.
MARS 2012
G